THE TEMPTATION OF HOMO EUROPAEUS

To the memory of my parents
Ana-Catalina and Andrei Neumann

Victor NEUMANN

THE **TEMPTATION** OF **HOMO EUROPAEUS**

An Intellectual History of Central and Southeastern Europe

Translated by
Dana MIU and Neil TITMAN

Edited, revised and updated

SCALA

CONTENTS

MAPS

PREFACE

Why do we need a new edition of *The Temptation of Homo Europaeus: An Intellectual History of Central and Southeastern Europe*? First and foremost, because it is a topical book whose subject deserves to be better known in universities, administrative-political environments and by the European audience at large. Rooted in primary research, it offers new information, interpretations and analysis of certain so-called peripheral regions. Insisting on the importance of 'cultural corridors' that facilitated the circulation of people, books and ideas between Western and Eastern Europe during the long and difficult transition from medieval to modern, the book demonstrates the role of both temporality and geography in the understanding of history. The current edition retains the structure of its predecessors but introduces new illustrations and includes maps in several chapters, showing the numerous cultural encounters that occurred across Europe from around 1500 to 1800. The Afterword is also new, a concluding chapter that boldly conceptualizes the transition from medieval to modern and represents the outcome of years of research and hypotheses that form the foundation of this book.

Why is such an approach important? First, in order to obtain thorough, objective knowledge benefiting the whole European continent. Second, because Central and Southeastern Europe have a fascinating history, their regions having been ruled by three empires – Ottoman, Tsarist and Hapsburg – with administrations situated in different historical periods and at varying levels of development. Third, during the period between 1500 and 1800 the aforementioned region of Europe was characterized by pluralism and not specificity, by multi- and interculturality and not ethnicity, by an ecumenical and cosmopolitan spirit, and not monolingualism and religious fundamentalism. During the same period, the area excelled in creativity in many fields, including theology, philosophy, historiography, literature and geography, all resulting from East–West and North–South cultural confluences.

The documentary evidence provided in *The Temptation of Homo Europaeus* is accompanied by theoretical evaluations and analyses of the periods of change, religious practices and cultural phenomena. I examine the schools, intellectuals and individual works that led to the emancipation of people, the discovery and acknowledgement of multi- and intercultural communities and the understanding of Europe as a whole. Describing the peculiarities of a certain area – in this case, Central and Southeastern Europe – enables us to observe cultural and civilizational similarities across the continent. The distinctions between East and West, centre and periphery become less relevant as soon as we understand that the diverse historical legacies of the Renaissance, Humanist and Enlightenment periods led to the genesis of a shared cultural code in Europe.

Thirty years of study in archives, museums, libraries and other institutions, examining secular and religious texts, furnished me with a wealth of information which I have analyzed historically, sociologically and philosophically. I have assessed the results of this research in the context of the current state of Central and Southeastern European civilization. Thus, I have avoided judgements and hypotheses that cannot be verified after the passage of the intervening two or three hundred years, instead trying to show, if only in part, what has remained constant in these societies. At times my conclusions paint a picture of suffocation, at others of hope.

Scholars in Central and Southeastern Europe, writing in Latin, Greek, Slavic, German, Hungarian and Romanian, often shared the ideals of Western intellectuals. They were all united by an attachment to the notion of Europe. The intellectual pursuits of Nicolaus Olahus, Johannes Honter, Dimitrie Cantemir, Theophilos Corydalleus, Dositej Obradović, Samuel von Brukenthal and Ignác Batthyány, and many others, resonated widely. I have described their activities and evaluated their aspirations regarding the unity of Europe. Though little known to Western historiography, these figures produced seminal works of history, philology and jurisprudence, and established scientific institutions, printing presses, libraries, academic foundations and museums. Although they were among the first intellectuals in the region to be concerned with the structure of society and its institutions, they overcame numerous obstacles and successfully travelled through Europe's 'cultural corridors', fostering connections between the East and West.

How do we explain the delayed development of the region? From the nineteenth century, intellectuals in Central and Southeastern Europe were enticed by new political ideologies, and their relations with Western Europe assumed a different tone from previous periods. They substituted the historical and political realities of their environments with ethno-cultural myths. *Völkischekultur / Volknation / Volksgeist* – the identity concepts of the German idealist philosophers of the nineteenth century – were assumed and adapted by the intellectuals of the region. Through such influences, legacies were erased or distorted, while the multiple cultural code of previous centuries was forgotten. A large number of writers, historians, professors and priests became ideologists, devoting much of their energy to the origins, faith or language of one or another community. They opposed linguistic and cultural diversity, marginalizing or neglecting the creative output of the so-called 'foreigners within'. The nation states of Central and Southeastern Europe in the nineteenth and twentieth centuries were established later than their Western counterparts, and their main criterion was allegiance to the ethno-culture of the majority. Their administrative structures differed from those of their Western models, whose political and judiciary institutions were the result of 'glorious revolutions'. This is one of the reasons why extreme ideologies, inter-community wars and totalitarian regimes (fascist and communist) found favour in the region. Indeed, the twists and turns of intellectual and political life in Central and Southeastern Europe need to be reconsidered: on the one hand, we must understand the prevailing similarities across Europe in the pre-modern age, while, on the other, we should seek to place the ruptures between Eastern and Western Europe that occurred during the past two centuries within the wider context of continental history.

Homo Europaeus has shown us the way, though we should be mindful that only a minority benefited from his revelations – an elite that has understood only recently that sacrifices are required to assume leadership of a world ripped apart by the pettiness of obscure and irresponsible politicians interested only in the prerogatives of power. He does not deserve to be ignored by the West simply because for five decades he was denied civilization, the means of existence, travel and a consumer society.

This new edition of *The Temptation of Homo Europaeus* is the result of an outstanding collaboration between myself and Dr Neil Titman of Scala Arts & Heritage Publishers in London. I offer my deep gratitude for Scala's keen interest in this type of interdisciplinary studies, and for supporting a book whose purpose is to enrich Western historiography through the inclusion of intellectual creations and contributions from Central and Southeastern Europe.

Victor Neumann
Timișoara, 10 March 2020

I

THE TEMPTATION OF HOMO EUROPAEUS? MEANING AND MOTIVATION

When you will think me completely dead,
I will tremble in your hands again.
Behold, I leave you my soul [book], man [world].
When your whole being will vibrate,
it is I, reader, who vibrates in you.

Miguel de Unamuno

ONE OF THE MOST COMPLEX PERIODS in human history is the transition from the medieval to the modern epoch that European historiography would later designate as the Renaissance. Its importance in understanding human becoming was grasped by the great historians of ideas, philosophy and culture in general. It is not by chance that their studies have been directed towards a detailed knowledge of this age, its socio-economic and political metamorphoses, and especially of its courses of thought, revealing a general picture and, as much as possible, a true one, regarding the origins of the new world – a world reborn of the old, ancient one, rediscovering itself, bringing out spiritual and mental states heretofore partially obscured by medieval dogmas.

The general evolution of humanity has felt the mark of this historical period, its duration in many respects not limited to the often-mentioned Italian *Quattrocento*. We state this knowing well that the humanists' thinking, their minds' efforts and creations of genius in the realm of literature and art were beneficial, then and for ever after, to intellectuals throughout Europe, and that if the West absorbed this wealth of ideas even as they appeared, the central and eastern portion of the continent embraced them, then reproduced them in its own form, a century or two later. This certainly cannot be ignored when studying the echoes of the Renaissance in space and time. As a consequence, whether we are talking about Western, Central or Eastern Europe, culture becomes permanent and widespread, starting with those years of medieval decline, the continent sharing a wealth of concepts, philosophical theories and religious dogmas, many of them surviving up to the present. Thus, between the Renaissance and the Enlightenment we may establish many links which today, due to historical perspective, no longer appear as pure fantasy. And if we direct our research towards Eastern Europe the close links between the two eras are so visible that we are often led to think about long periods, where Olahus and Cantemir, Plethon and Corydalleus can be discussed together.

It is true that communication across the ages is felt much more strongly in the West, where we could use as a model the dialogue between Galileo and Leibniz. We also speak about how close the two eras are, since in the south and east of the continent, although a beautiful Byzantine tradition persisted – a stimulating mix of Greek, Slavic and Roman culture – and even though there are direct connections with the regions that participated in the Renaissance, we are still in a 'Europe without Renaissance'. Under no circumstances, then, will we propose an oversimplified synchronism. But we will show that the ways of life and thought circulated by Westerners in the fourteenth to sixteenth centuries find a brilliant echo among Easterners, and that, especially during the Reformation, the hour of change had also struck for these civilizations. After 1550, a turning point for Romanian culture – as historian Răzvan Theodorescu convincingly demonstrates – the interior of this Balkan-Oriental world begins to move and the creative individual's experience leaves its mark. Gradually, a humanism gains ground, a humanism which will become dominant in intellectual circles in the seventeenth century, a humanism in communication with the Enlightenment of the ensuing century.

The present state of historiography, and its role in the universe of humanistic sciences in charting the main points of human encounters and affinities, compels me to begin my research keeping in mind the great problems confronting the peoples of the world today.

My starting point was the idea that we need communication, that the world cannot be understood without a permanent dialogue, without discovering the universal values of that which is national, without openly declaring the essence of the human spirit, without the discovery and assertion of ideologies, options and dominant political minorities, and finally, of those *formae mentis* which exist within communities. Therefore, I intended to reconstruct the way in which Homo Europaeus was created following his genesis by deciphering the memorable crises of conscience during the transition from the medieval to the modern era. Being familiar with more historical periods plays a definite role, of course, when we wish to explain the essential meaning and the duration of Homo Europaeus' temptation. What we are talking about here is the genesis of the new European Man, indeed of the history of the modern world's ideas, the framework in which Homo Europaeus came into existence through his transcontinental horizon. This concept includes two traditional designations of space, East and West. In our historical approach our starting point was Leo Frobenius' point of view, namely that 'European East and West are not only inexplicable when they are separated from the terrestrial space which generated them, but sterile as well, as long as the other has not sown upon it the mechanist paideuma that has reached the stage of a ripe seed.'[1] The well-known philosopher and historian of culture elaborated the idea of culture's dependence on space, as well as the idea of its organic structure, thus presenting the intellect with intelligible images which metaphysics could not directly apply to conscience. Without evoking the souls of peoples in this way, it is difficult to form a complex image of the endless trails beaten across the entire continent by the man of spirit who was to guide the thoughts of the many at such historical crossroads. It is true that by giving this interpretation to Central-Eastern Man's belonging to Europe, we have before us a very difficult subject, demanding a wealth of information, a detailed knowledge of the domains of cultural life, requiring a command of the characteristic working methods of the historian, the philosopher, the sociologist and the philologist, and, not least, the capacity to synthesize data and facts found in documents and books, as well as those resulting from personal experience; all of these offering the opportunity to discover the workings of human personality, to reveal the most enduring convergences of those ideas and concepts which became the basis of human existence. But now I ask myself, as Fernand Braudel did in 1946, whether today we can have humanism without an ambitious history, conscious of its themes and of its immense powers. Can we surpass fragmentations, subjective appreciations, partiality, and understand the world's movement in its globality without a history of communication and spiritual dialogue? Communion at not only a continental but also intercontinental level can only result by bridging the gap through understanding. I think that this method pertains to the 'Europeanization of historical images' I have previously discussed.

So far I have intended only to clarify things (taking into account a few of the most spectacular and useful contributions of the history of culture), offering a sketch that is theoretical and not merely an account of the main intellectual movements of European Man in the period between Renaissance and Enlightenment, when profound mutations occurred in communities. I considered that I should start by coming closer and showing through examples the direct relationship between the two eras, as well as their possible correspondence (in the case of the East) between the crisis of conscience produced by Renaissance humanism and that with which the Enlightenment began. My principal aim was to suggest a general picture, an introduction to the atmosphere of the period, which was to leave its mark on history with one of the greatest and most continuous struggles at all levels. The entire approach is not and cannot be exhaustive, the subject being extremely vast, and some of the points of view I have expressed, especially the general framework at the beginning, are not meant to be definitive. But formulating these points of view has been a great help in the perception and synthesis of the multiple tendencies of the motion of ideas, of the spiritual movements that dominated the eighteenth century. I wanted to concentrate on the latter period in order to reveal the essential aspects of human metamorphosis, and to clarify the great dialogue between Eastern and Western Europe, which together reveal a reality that, along with the delays often mentioned in historiographic retrospectives, can be felt in the great efforts made to establish a continental balance, at least at the spiritual level. These endeavours did not always succeed, but were fundamental steps in returning Central-Eastern culture to Europe's common table.

In speaking of Homo Europaeus' cultural temptation, I have considered the European continent as a single spiritual organism involving the participation of East and West, of both the Balkan Greek Orthodox and Western worlds and the two halves of the Roman Empire, alongside the contribution of the North, which the empire never succeeded in mastering and later became the territory of the Reformation.

The European Man of the new era's beginning, with his language, customs, impulses and deeds, the warmth of his soul, with his great joys and sufferings, and finally, with the power of his mind, a generator of ideas, are a few of the most important aspects which the present study attempts to elucidate. It hopes to go beyond the image, often used by historians, of a continent made up of many – too many – cultural nuclei. We should acknowledge that great books have been written that attempt to grasp the true dimensions of European spiritual life, but unfortunately many subscribe to the view that Europe ends with Vienna, the area beyond the Austrian capital being marginal, if not actually outside the old continent, or just a region of transition between the West and the great Orient. In order to refute this view one must proceed without prejudice and leave aside exclusivist hypotheses and theories with no place in scientific history. There can be no doubt that the Central-Southeastern zone has countless connections with the East, and oriental religious and political doctrines extended their tentacles into the region, leaving marks one way or another on its personality; we cannot ignore the cultural exchange with Judeo-Christian or other spiritual natures caused by direct communication with Asia, which reveal a world that possessed an unusual power of reception – and, therefore, of a continuously transforming community, permanently on the move. But alongside these influences are those from the West, which disseminated (even to the southernmost point of Europe) its thinking, schools, books, teachers, political-judicial system, and finally, its great concepts, which are a basis of cultural life, without which so many of humanity's accomplishments would not have materialized. So when we speak of Central and Southeastern Europe, we are dealing with an area that benefits from one of the most interesting convergences on the continent, and not only that – by revealing both dialogues, the way they really were, we are recovering the profound truths of a civilization. This explains the title of my work, The Temptation of Homo Europaeus: for the Central and Eastern region the new European Man was always, after Boccaccio in Italy, Rabelais in France and Shakespeare in England, a symbol of civilization, of spiritual heights. The region therefore imitated him, was tempted to come nearer to him, to identify with him. Greek, Russian, Romanian, Serbian, Bulgarian, Hungarian, Polish, Croatian and Slovak representatives of culture provide compelling examples of this phenomenon, and we will see this clearly when presenting their institutions and societies, and the books and ideas they circulated, proving the vitality of human communities less favoured by the general movement of history.

In order to introduce the subject of the first chapters, in which I intend to reveal some basic aspects of the mutations produced in the period of transition from medieval to modern times, and to explain the main causes of the great crises of consciences in Central and Eastern Europe, I will give a brief historiographical overview of this problem, illustrating the assertion of the new world's ideas in the Renaissance and post-Renaissance periods. In the main this historical presentation focuses only on classic works whose construction and scientific orientation were and still are exemplary. It is necessarily a short retrospective, since most major studies of the history of ideas focus only on Western Europe, while I and some of my colleagues also analyze the spiritual dimensions of the Central and Eastern parts of the continent – to date, a subject undertaken only in part, in otherwise unremarkable works.

A brilliant example of richly documented research – conveying a global perspective, with convincingly detailed description of the movement and spiritual assertion of the whole – is the extremely erudite work, full of reflection on the destiny of humanism in the Middle Ages, of Ernst Robert Curtius. It is probably our best aid to understanding the literature, and European culture in its totality, of that period. I refer to his famous book *Europäische Literatur und Lateinisches Mittelalter*, in which he stresses that such a study can only be historical. But not in the way of literary history:

> A narrative and enumerative history only offers a repertory of knowledge of facts, leaving the material in its accidental form. But the function of the historical view is to decipher and gain insight. It should elaborate analytical methods, that is to say methods to 'dissolve' the material, just like chemical reactants, and to reveal its structure. Adherent points of view can only be reached by a comparative investigation of literatures, in other words empirically. Only a literary science using historical and philological means can accomplish this.[2]

We are indebted to this same man of culture for offering us the most complex and complete retrospective of medieval Latin literature, projecting a new image of European spirituality, revealing at the same time the uninterrupted link between Antiquity, medieval and modern times. Curtius extends the concept of the 'Europeanization of historical image' to literature, something necessary for our times. Taking into consideration the course of events he witnessed, he wrote that 'the Europeanization of the historical picture has become a political necessity today, and not for Germany alone'. He agrees that European cultural organisms must be seen and analyzed as one, while by reconsideration of the great intellectual systems, we emphasize that the specific movements of different spiritualities are subordinate to a general movement.[3] It is exactly what, in Frobenius' conception of cultural zones, is defined as the *paideuma*, a super-individual soul of peoples. Such a study carries considerable weight among the philological and historical research of the past decades, suggesting one of the most rewarding means of reconstructing the path taken by human thought at the crossroads of time.

The idea of a modern Homo Europaeus, at least for the West, appears in Lucien Febvre's *Le Problème de l'incroyance au XVIᵉ siècle. La religion de Rabelais*,[4] which follows, step by step, the spiritual adventure of humanity in the sixteenth century, understanding and describing one religious phenomenon that had widespread consequences for the history of European societies – namely, the fever of propaganda, conversion and proselytism that came upon Ignacio de Loyola and his first companions, a fever that was to push Francis Xavier towards the Indies and lead to an increasing number of men of action obsessed by splendid dreams of a unified Christian world, of the incorporation of peoples into a renewed Christianity. Febvre was interested in the attitude of medieval man on the eve of the modern age: a man whose soul and mind was for the most part immersed in Christianity from birth, but who, step by step, freed his spirit of the old dogmas, throwing off the common yoke of religion professed automatically and uncritically by almost all his contemporaries. We find this idea again, though expressed and understood differently, in Johan Huizinga's *The Decline of the Middle Ages*. We should mention, though, that Febvre clears the way for a total investigation, for the history of concepts, a path which his disciple Fernand Braudel was to follow. Febvre writes:

> The lack of faith shown in the sixteenth century, part of which was real, is not comparable to ours, and this is because

Rabelais will never be the head of a linear list culminating in the 'free thinkers' of the twentieth century; these form a compact group differing little among themselves in spirit, in their scientific experience and their particular arguments.[5]

For this well-known French historian, Rabelais was a free spirit of his time, a man of robust intelligence and vigorous sense, free of the prevailing prejudices around him. Between his spiritual freedom and ours the difference is not of degree but of nature – there is nothing in common except a disposition of the spirit, a certain temperament, a certain behaviour. We should also note that, in Febvre's formulation, the generation which was making the transition from medieval to modern era could not lead a serious fight against the Christian religion. Its negations could only have been opinions, or ways of thinking and of feeling – the paradoxes that no one from the outside could see to support or to pronounce in a real and substantial manner, not in science, nor in the philosophy of his time.[6]

As we also saw in Curtius' case, this point of view offers invaluable new interpretive possibilities, enabling us to discover the true collective mentality of Europe. At the same time, I also benefited from the opinions of the American Francis A. Schaeffer's ambitious extra-scientific retrospective entitled *How Should We Then Live? The Rise and Decline of Western Thought and Culture.* Coming from outside historiography and philosophy, but drawing on the arguments of Homo Religiosus – revealing his beliefs and the subjectivity of his point of view – he tries to include in his analysis the ideas and tendencies of European Man, not only in the Middle Ages but throughout his whole existence; he is interested in the type of religious thinking that gave rise to the forms taken by European culture. We should not ignore his contribution – as we were initially tempted to do, possibly out of prejudice – and in particular the way in which he manages to assess the results of the psycho-social metamorphoses that took place at the dawn of the new age. I do want to assert though, that in essence my judgement differs (even when discussing the ethical behaviour of humanity) from all concepts derived exclusively from religion and overplaying its role. In my view, religion negates the conscience of all except Homo Europaeus, whose survival is and will continue to be due to the universality of the spirit that brought him into being. One can still believe in Homo Europaeus: more important than any rite or religion is the belief in a morality of individuals which, in all ages and everywhere, illuminated the way for the many.

One of the most difficult problems for the history of historiography concerns the crisis of conscience that occurs when the leap is made from one system of thought to another – or, to be more precise, from one era to another. The historian Paul Hazard made a highly original contribution to this subject in *La Crise de la conscience européenne 1680–1715*, a work he very ably continued in his study of Enlightenment thinking, *La Pensée européenne au XVIIIᵉ siècle. De Montesquieu à Lessing*. The author minutely tracks the most important modification in the life of humanity, in the evolution of civilization, in the development of ideas that decisively influenced the destiny of humanity from then up to the present day. Hazard evokes a living image of this pageant, revealing before our eyes the sequence of mutations in conscience provoked by philosophical writers and Biblical exegetes, as well as the discourses of certain men of science who, to an extent, anticipated the storms of the eighteenth century. Starting with the history of France, and acknowledging those of Italy and Spain, at times his studies encompass the Central European zone as a whole, for example in his account of the Counter-Reformation. The approach is excellent as it brings out the grave problems of the consciences of those times, showing the many questions facing the individual during the seventeenth and eighteenth centuries, and discussing the role of religious and historical writings in manoeuvering public opinion according to personal or wider political interests. His perspective is, of course, that of a Western historian, and is valid for Western Europe. In the East, as I will stress, the crisis of conscience begins later, its development being slower, but with nonetheless spectacular mutations (if we are only to consider religious doctrines, literature and historiography) that will show clearly the unitary dimensions of European culture, as well as the specifics of the region – which, although making slow progress, also maintains a dialogue with the West during its period of great crisis. Thus, starting with Hazard and keeping him in mind constantly, I will turn the looking glass to see the course of the development of consciences from East to West.

Tracing the long history of European ideas, Bernard Voyenne, a professor of contemporary European journalism, shares with us some of the higher ideas behind the notion of continental life. From his ambitious work *Histoire de l'idée européenne* I retained his account of the historical process whereby conscience is reflected in the principles and aims of the community – in the will of the people who formed that community, a will that is by turns obscure or far-seeing, tenacious or fragile, free or necessary. Analyzing Europe's spiritual adventure, Voyenne shows how its unity came about, formed by different political doctrines, each in its own manner. Europe's spirit is the fruit of mysterious encounters – of countless convergences, we could say – but also of unpredictable happenings and bloody conflicts. And I agree with Voyenne's view that there exists a soul of Europe, where we will always find the source of its force: 'All the rest is appearance and costume. The idea only exists when incarnated in a reality that transcends it and that it cannot live without.'[7] The author's interest lies in the perspective resulting from the succession of facts, by their very arrangement. He was drawn to find an explanation for the confusion of life around him, in order to identify the slow and uncertain birth of Europe, the steps by which it evolved day by day. One of Voyenne's most compellingly accurate conclusions is that a civilization has a consciousness of its own distinct life, that is to say, of a culture: therefore, when we speak of Europe, we are speaking of the civilized world. A mature understanding of the Renaissance and Reformation as an age dominated by movements nationalist in their effects, 'but fundamental in their essence'[8] leads us to believe that Voyenne's analysis is valuable, and not just from a *Geistesgeschichte* standpoint.

Of course, the plausibility of his revelations is dependent on the great research that has been conducted in the fields of social, economic, political and cultural history – for example, the research of the Annales School and, in particular, the work of Fernand Braudel. This historian's studies are a real lesson for European historiography – without them we would not be able to reconstruct the forever intersecting planes of history, the pedestrian circulation of humanity, its infrastructure. *The Mediterranean and the Mediterranean World in the Age of Philip II*[9] offers a sweeping vision of one of the greatest European communities – the Mediterranean. It is based on a wealth of data and solid facts interpreted through archival documents, medieval and modern texts, historical literature, geography, geology, sociology, statistics and so on, which together allow the author to rethink European history as a whole through the perspective of the Mediterranean and its world. Braudel's approach demonstrates how everything moves around and through the Mediterranean and is dependent on it – its climate and geography, the richness of its different zones, its people who have been formed in and through the mentality imposed by this character. It is a thoroughly convincing account that offers a new perspective for the study of Southern Europe and beyond. We understand the events, but also the differences between one region and another; we come in contact with the civilization of the three peninsulas – Iberian, Italian and Balkan – whose destinies are united with those of the interior sea. Through the Mediterranean, Braudel rediscovers European culture and the character and economic interests of an entire continent; his writing takes us into the most intimate components of economic and commercial societies, revealing to us the multiple strategies of change facilitated by that same sea.[10] Europe cannot be separated from the Mediterranean, whether we are talking about the Centre, the East or the North: the sea is a creator of characters, leading us to the history of the cities that watch over it, to Valencia, Marseille, Genoa, Venice, Ragusa, to its gulfs and straits, true bridges between territories, to the islands of Sardinia, Corsica, Sicily, Corfu, Crete, the Balearics and many others, each separately and all together denoting life, a world in motion, sometimes stable, sometimes stormy, but a world that has endured a millennium and beyond and whose traits reveal the profoundness of the European communion. Consequently Europe cannot be understood without reference to the Mediterranean, since without it an essential part of the community's substance would be lost – neither politics, economics, culture or religion can be analyzed without this determining factor of the Euro-Afro-Asiatic civilizations. Putting aside the political events of the fifteenth to sixteenth centuries, Braudel rightly observes that differences of an economic and cultural nature between the West and East of Europe are no barrier to the movement of entities and ideas from one side to the other, nor do they confound that unity which I will also investigate in this book, exposing a few of the spiritual dimensions that contributed to its continuation throughout the ages. Braudel believes that the West has always needed the East and vice versa, first as a market for its goods, for commercial circulation, for its economic life in general, and second for technical innovations, for ideas, for culture.[11] I will take many of Braudel's conclusions into account, especially since a number of the phenomena related to the transition period from the Middle Ages to the Modern Era are key subjects of his research – I will give them due consideration in my examination of human destiny across Europe. Braudel, the leader of this new French school of history, this 'builder of empires', as one of his foremost disciples,

Emmanuel Le Roy Ladurie, called him,[12] brought to its conclusion the opus of his mentor, Lucien Febvre, by explaining the nature of mentalities, an innovation further developed in the works of Robert Mandrou, Jean Delumeau, Pierre Chaunu, Jacques Le Goff, Georges Duby, Alphonse Dupront, Michel Vovelle and others. Together with Braudel, the historian Paul Zumthor completes this picture of everyday Western life, presenting the golden age of Holland, the history of the decades that separate the two great crises of conscience of Western Europe. *Daily Life in Rembrandt's Holland*[13] reveals the Dutch way of life, including religion, education, sentimental life, banquets, sports and public holidays, visual arts, music and literature, industry, agriculture and commerce. It enables us to acquire a detailed knowledge of the conditions in which a number of economic and spiritual contacts with Central-Southeastern Europe took place.

Of the earlier contributions to the subject, I will discuss those of Jacob Burckhardt, José Ortega y Gasset, Johan Huizinga and Petre P. Negulescu. Burckhardt's *Die Kultur der Renaissance in Italien*[14] was a turning point because of the meaning the Swiss historian gave to the word Renaissance, venturing beyond the limited definition of the term. As such the book remains a milestone today. Burckhardt presents the history of an era, making a necessary clarification of the period from 1400 to 1600 in Europe, showing not so much the immensity of raw facts as the reality hidden behind them, carefully tracing ideas and at the same time proposing a new way of interpreting well-known events. The historian, whose conclusions are irrefutable, to a point, shows for the first time in world historiography the course taken by the great spirits at the end of the Middle Ages, trying to reveal their significance for society. His book is a history of ideas that paved the way for the modern age, a history comprising the great signs of decadence, but also the main signs of the birth of a new world.

Burckhardt's point of view dominated Renaissance research for a long time, gradually becoming traditional. Without intending to exclude it – and not blatantly moving the focus of European Renaissance studies away from Italy and France, as Johan Nordström did – I think that new approaches offer a better understanding of the forms of life and thought, placing the Renaissance along a path of natural continuity, of natural transition. And in history, as Huizinga assures us, 'Death and birth are always associated. The old forms of culture die at the same time and on the same ground where the new find nourishment to flower.' Burckhardt negates the vast Middle

Ages, a bridge of understanding, reception and transformation of universal values that preserved both ancient Roman civilization and late Antique Latinity.

Meditating upon the past and the historian's condition, Ortega y Gasset left us a number of important lessons on history and how it should be understood. For the Spanish scholar, history was a fertile source of philosophical thought; in his studies he tried to understand the reasons for the limitations of its practitioners, to discover mistakes, large or small, in their works, suggesting a new way of appreciating known events. Published as En torno a Galileo,[15] his interpretations concern the general problems of history or what he called historiology. He presented the historical origin of life and the concept of 'generation' as an instrument for understanding the structure of permanent change in man and the world he lives in. The author of the 'lessons' set out to establish with 'maximum rigour' the vital situation of the generations between 1550 and 1650 that formed the basis of modern thought.[16] In fact, Ortega y Gasset sets out to do much more than this – to prove that every science of reality, be it corporeal or spiritual, is a construction and not a simple reflection of facts, that history as a science must adopt a new direction, different from positivism, namely to accept to construct. The homage to Galileo and, implicitly, to his age is not accidental: in the brilliant explanation he offers of his personality, Galileo is a summit between two eras, he is a 'divide', a modern man entering a modern world. What may lead us to this view? Galileo was convinced that God wrote the universe in mathematical characters: 'No human research can call itself true science if it does not pass through mathematical demonstrations,' mused the Italian humanist. The mobile and horizontal planes he conceived were strict mathematical figures. We remain interested in the sciences Galileo studied, mechanics and local movements, which are nothing more than modern physics, because his work raised and continues to raise many questions through the implications it had, and still has, for our entire existential system. The dialogue with him, from person to person, was and still is useful. By taking an interest in him, we are implicitly taking interest in ourselves: Galileo is a model for understanding how our being came to be – as such he is a milestone in the evolution of humanity, perhaps even more than Descartes. Discussing the sympathy for him felt by his contemporaries, Ortega y Gasset considers that we are well disposed towards Galileo because he is situated in a firm setting, in which he is set to play a great part in a future that takes a very precise form: it is the beginning of the Modern Era, of the system of ideas, developments and momentum that dominated and enriched the world from Galileo's day up to our times. Our interest in Galileo is not, therefore, as altruistic and generous as we might have initially imagined. Galileo's shadow remains at the heart of contemporary civilization, a civilization characterized above all by the exactitude of the natural and technical sciences. For this reason Galileo is a part of our lives, and not just any part – he plays the mysterious role of an initiator.[17]

Another important book for the history of ideas in modern society is Petre P. Negulescu's *The Philosophy of the Renaissance*, which encapsulates Romania's contribution to the study of this question. A systematic study of cultural life, it explains the peaks of awakening, the genesis of the new thinking that came to dominate Europe beginning in the fourteenth and fifteenth centuries. The philosopher's approach interests us for its rethinking of an era, with its people and institutions, its societies, religions and methods of socio-political government. Negulescu brings to our attention the genesis of the Renaissance of cultural and intellectual forms deriving from classical Antiquity, with its representatives, stressing the role of religion as both cult and culture. A critical view, no doubt, from which he concludes, on the one hand, that the Church was a radiant point

> around which gathered, slowly and with difficulty, the elements of a new political and social organization's forms; on the other hand, opposing the so-called spiritual products of paganism and of teachings considered heretical led to a narrowing which is one of the main causes of medieval culture's exclusivism and inferiority.[18]

Negulescu's book unflinchingly narrates the decline of the medieval West and the Byzantine East, revealing to us the potential for intellectual development among Europeans, illustrating the contribution of both Westerners and Easterners to the new direction in which humanity evolved. Negulescu shares Burckhardt's opinion that the Renaissance was a reaction to the Middle Ages and does not presuppose a complete rupture of all relations between these two great historical periods. Setting aside the philosopher's somewhat categorical point of view, it is useful, for the purposes of our study, to stress that the birth of modern culture would not have been possible without the medieval bearers of the spirit of Antiquity, without the texts, monasteries and monks working in medieval Latin whose efforts, although at times weak and isolated, created a humanist current, the French being the best example of this, as the Swede Johan Nordström asserts. Indeed, ever since the contributions made by Huizinga and Curtius we no longer see in human history the old arbitrary parameters that failed to provide an accurate picture of the course of history. In fact, the Renaissance cannot be understood without considering its genesis in the quintessence of preceding historical times. The benefit of Negulescu's work is that it brings us the knowledge that Renaissance ideas take us closer to the fundamental chapters in the birth of the modern world, in which the Platonic Academy of Florence – and notably the figure of Georgios Gemistos Plethon, as well as Spinoza's predecessor Leon Abravanel – reveals the European cultural dialogue between Hellenistic philosophy, spearheaded by Constantinople, and Italy's *Quattrocento*, as symbols of the same Christianity.

Johan Huizinga's research represents genuine progress in knowledge, 'a complete anatomy' of the fourteenth and fifteenth centuries, 'seen even in its capillaries', as Edgar Papu says, as his historical thought comes to a qualified reconsideration of the dominant ideas of medieval decline. *Herfsttij der middeleeuwen*,[19] even if limited to a relatively narrow geographical area, France and the Netherlands, offered new perspectives from a conceptual and methodological point of view, which were subsequently developed in some of Huizinga's aforementioned research. In order to define a culture and its spiritual aspect, the Dutch scholar used old texts to study the various forms in which thought manifests itself, discovering everyday human life, love's conventional forms, and military and political ideals. He succeeded in creating a lively picture of the times (subject to a detailed reconstruction), which may be compared to the poetry of Dutch painting from Rembrandt and Vermeer onwards. Huizinga was especially drawn to the relationship between Renaissance humanism and the medieval spirit, a more complicated connection than we are tempted to imagine. On a personal note, I appreciated his reflections when I myself came to set Renaissance civilization and medieval civilization alongside one another, the flexibility of Huizinga's judgements guiding my interest towards a deeper, more intimate understanding of the basic atmosphere, of the medieval spirit's characteristics in its final stage. As Huizinga states:

To us, those who see these two cultures as two distinct entities, it seems that receptiveness to Antiquity and repudiation of
the entire outdated medieval way of thinking must have been a
revelation. As if minds tired of allegory and flamboyancy had
suddenly realized: no, not this one but the other... As if classicism's golden harmony had radiated before men's eyes as a
salvation, as if men had rushed into Antiquity's arms with the
exaltation of one who has found his deliverance. But this is not
so. In the garden of medieval thought, among the old luxuri-
ant plants, classicism slowly grew. Initially it was only a formal
element of fantasy. Only later did it become a new and great
awakening, and the spirit and forms of expansion we are used to
considering as the old, medieval ones even then did not die out.[20]

And since I intend to present a Homo Europaeus coming from
Central and Southeastern Europe, it would be useful if I made special
mention of some of the books that convey a modern vision of these
areas, which will help us later on to understand the infinite durability
of that singular Homo Universalis. A great number of historians have
attempted to grasp as objectively as possible the spiritual contributions
made by these regions, aware of the limitations of focusing solely
on the West in any attempt to draw a global picture. The example of
Nicolae Iorga springs to mind when trying to discover and understand
the mentalities and great convergences in the Balkan region. His
studies enable us to plunge into the Byzantine past, to gain access to
the genesis and meaning of the Byzantine Empire, as we follow step
by step the continuous dialogue between East and West. His work also
facilitates our conception of Europe's spiritual map, transmitted by
ancient Rome, which embodies, as the scholar says, 'the ideal unity of
invisible authority'. It is not by chance that I embraced Nicolae Iorga's
lectures presented in *Histoire de la vie Byzantine: Empire et civilization d'après
les sources*, in *Essai de synthèse de l'histoire de l'humanité*, in *Byzance après
Byzance: Continuation de l'histoire de la vie byzantine* or in *Generalities Regarding
Historical Studies*.[21] According to these, any part of history can and must,
in fact, be interpreted as 'a development of unitary human history, its
various domains being one with the dominant unity that corresponds
to the rules of organic life...' Iorga demonstrates the role played and
exceptional position occupied by the Byzantine world in the history of
Europe, giving indisputable evidence in favour of the type of civilization
that the Byzantine organism created, insisting on its continuity

far beyond the century of Constantinople's fall to the Turks. The Hellenistic intellectual legacy, Roman law, as well as Greek Orthodox religion and art in Southeastern Europe gave the historian ample material for documentation and reflection on the 'long durations' created by Byzantium. Iorga sought to reveal the essence of the empire's life, using the sources he consulted to observe the spiritual unity within the empire, as well as the intensity of its communication with the West. He leads us to the heart of memorable cultural events, illustrating not only Western Renaissance influences on the Byzantine world, but also the latter's attempts to respond – a movement in which teachers, publishers, commentators of texts, philologists and philosophers were involved as representatives of an ideal that goes beyond the famous Cretan Theotokópoulos, who would become Toledo's El Greco. As Iorga says:

> They are refugees of Byzantine Koblenz mostly settled in Italy, and their writing, often inspired by the idea of retaliation, which was impossible to realize, influenced many of the most distinguished and most noble spirits of Western Europe, until the beginning of the sixteenth century when the influence was the fancy of all adventurers.[22]

The Byzantine idea spread among the many peoples of Southeastern Europe through the figure who was to become the patron of Greek Orthodox life in the Balkans, the Patriarch of Constantinople. It was destined to survive, though, and I intend to show new evidence of this, through all those historians, orators and archaic poets, painters and architects, politicians or creators of ideology who carried with them to the East or West the signs of Hellenic-Byzantine Renaissance.

To the ideas I have only touched on here, let us add the system of thought Iorga applied in *Essai de synthèse de l'histoire de l'humanité* and *Generalities Regarding Historical Studies*, a system from which we retain, more than anything else, the absolute necessity of forming a judgement, always keeping in mind the guiding lines that traverse the development of humanity as a whole. His considerations ultimately teach us the links between human deeds and thoughts in all places, at all times. This convergence of multiple cultures enables us to construct a unified conception of human historiology.

Victor Papacostea's studies, collected in the volume entitled *Civilizație românească și civilizație balcanică*,[23] gave credence to the idea of a characteristic Southeast European history, an idea previously expressed not only by Iorga, but also by Constantin Jiricek, B. P. Haşdeu, Franz Miklosich, Bartholomew Kopitar and Jovan Cvijić. Papacostea contributed, with rigour and method, and with flexible thinking, to the discovery of some of the most beautiful and enduring cultural relationships in the Southeast, albeit they began with connections between the civilization of the lower Danube and the Slavic spiritual world, or those originating in Greek-Romanian or Albanian-Romanian exchanges. This gave rise to a new and useful revelation of the Southeast's unifying elements, forces that contribute to the perception of Europe as a complex unit: the Thracian-Illyric foundation, Macedonian Empire, Hellenistic civilization, Roman Empire, Byzantine Empire, Greek Orthodoxy, Slavs, Ottoman Empire, Islamic civilization, Romanesque Balkans, post-Byzantine Hellenism, and the new Orthodoxy. Constant contact between the East and the West of Europe resulted in a great exchange of scientific and artistic learning, and this is where the great natural disposition of the old continent's spirit originated. Admittedly, this is very demanding scholarship, including detailed analyses of the Romanian principalities at the end of the seventeenth century and the beginning of the eighteenth, comprehensive investigations of the role of the reigns of Şerban Cantacuzino (1678–88), Constantin Brâncoveanu (1688–1714), Duca Vodă (1665–66; 1668–72; 1678–84), Constantin (1685–93), and Dimitrie Cantemir (1710–11), and conclusions about the politics of equilibrium of these leaders who had to protect their interests in Constantinople as well as in Moscow, Vienna and elsewhere.

Naturally, one cannot ignore research on the history of culture – for example, the origins of higher education in Wallachia, the foundation of Greek and Latin language schools, or schools of Slavonic culture. Papacostea is aware of the need to go beyond 'complexes', understanding that a global vision of Romanian cultural life means connecting all phenomena specific to the system of values in the region and to those that are universal. In addition to this innovation, important steps were made in the development of Balkanology, giving a substantial and certain scientific standing to Balkan studies. This great scientific work made it easier for me to identify the forms taken by the crisis of conscience in Southeastern Europe.

Radovan Samardžić's applied studies refer to a period of about four centuries (fifteenth to the nineteenth) and are important for understanding the socio-political and cultural structures, and changes of mentality in Balkan societies. They are centred around the research of the life and work of a few principal figures of the Serbo-Croatian and Slovenian Enlightenment, revealing the process that formed the national consciousness of the South Slav peoples, describing the original and less-known urban civilization of Southeastern Europe, and the discovery of the commercial system of the Jews, and the economic potential brought by them from the Iberian Peninsula to the Balkan Peninsula, especially the Danube area. 'Les idées du siècle des lumières et l'éveil national des peuples yougoslaves', *The Balkan Urban Culture (15th–19th Centuries)* and 'The Jews of Dubrovnik in the Trade of the 16th and 17th Centuries'[24] are only a few of the titles from a vast bibliography including many more subjects than those mentioned. They are related to the documentary historical work written in the first half of the twentieth century by Jovan Radonić, Dimitrije Ruvarac, Mita Kostić, and more recently by A. Gavrilović, N. Radojčić, N. Gavrilović, R. Flora, S. Mihaijlović and many others. Samardžić is one of those historians of the Southeast who are not indifferent to the methods used in research and the theorizing of the phenomena being studied. Other brilliant examples include his compatriots Bojidar Knejević and Gavo Manolović, the latter known not only as a theoretician, but also as a Byzantinologist and Egyptologist. Radovan Samardžić frequently approached subjects related to schools, historical theories and concepts, believing that his interest in the political and psychological history of the Middle Ages and Modern Era could be sustained by such investigations. This made possible working hypotheses regarding the process by which nations were formed in Southeastern Europe, revealing some important elements on the map of historiographic movement, of the evolution of ideas and political tendencies, and facts pertaining to culture and civilization. The work of this scholar, at a European level, helps us place Eastern society accurately within a universal context.

I gained a better understanding of certain phenomena in Bulgarian history from Ilia Konev and Veselin Traikov, vastly experienced authorities with a knowledge not only of their own culture, but also neighbouring ones.[25] The comparative picture of Southeastern European cultures on the eve of the Modern Era proposed by Konev seems a promising one, reminding me of an excellent zonal characterization of Southeastern European Romanticism made by Paul Cornea.[26] In Konev's opinion, the Southeast adapted to European currents of thought, assimilating them while giving them a local expression. In the age of the Enlightenment, this process ran in tandem with the rest of Europe, spanning every decade of the eighteenth century. The essential results appear in the second half of the century, when 'the historical conscience of the Balkan peoples forms and definitely establishes itself as a factor of their social, political, ideological and cultural progress'. Konev makes significant observations regarding the role of the Transylvanian School in the context of the Southeast – more precisely, in the field of historiography. Alongside the most important writings of the area's representatives, to which they are intimately bound, the books of the great Romanian scholars 'testify to a common process, having typical traits, which occur at the same time, and have a definite national patriotic mission, highly humanistic and enlightening'.[27]

Some of Veselin Traikov's comments, namely referring to currents of ideas that circulated in the region and preliminary concepts behind modern ideological developments, were useful for my study. For instance, noticing the numerous tendencies within the ideas of the Balkan peoples, Traikov reveals Western influences and, in particular, the means by which European ideas were transmitted by Greek merchants, via the roads connecting Northern Russia, Poland, the Romanian provinces and the southern part of the continent, through close contact by Slovenes and Croats with the political and cultural thinking of Central and Western Europe. On the other hand, the author maintains balance in his discourse by giving due attention to connections with the East, including Islam, through the crucial position occupied by the Greek Orthodox Church not only as a religious institution, but also a political one for the Christian population under Turkish domination.[28] Along with the role played by the Greeks in the circulation of ideas in the Southeast, there should have been an acknowledgement of the role of Judaic and Armenian factors in bringing peoples closer and contributing to their mutual knowledge, in creating a civilization with a unified outlook. In one of the early chapters of this book I will show what Judaism meant in Central and Southeastern Europe.

A major step in the development of specialist literature on the subject is represented by the works that include the characteristics of neo-Greek cultural history, research on literary history and comparative literature by Constantin T. Dimaras, Albis Anghelon, Leandros Vranoussis, Panagiotis Pistas and others. I have relied mainly on Dimaras' synthesis *Histoire de la littérature néo-hellénique*,[29] which established the main directions of the development of the modern spirit, recognizing common Southeastern European elements, identifying the phenomena of active reception, and competently discussing scientific and literary results in Europe of the Enlightenment.

Since the present study will include the spiritual evolution of Central Europe, especially the Central-Eastern zone, where Transylvania, Banat, Croatia, Slovenia, Slovakia and Hungary occupied the main mediating position between the continent's East and West, I will mention some of the books responsible for changing the direction of historiography, and of cultural history in general. In his most important book, *Művelődés a XVIII-ik századi Magyarországon*,[30] Domokos Kosáry proposes a *sui generis* image of the Central-Eastern region, his research dealing equally with history, sociology, visual arts, music, literary history, and cultural and ideological currents. The Hungarian historian grasps the European political and economic life of the seventeenth and eighteenth centuries well, is close to the method used by the historians of the Annales School but has also learned lessons from the new developments in French historiography. This enables him to discover the system of relations, class structure and modes of life of the Enlightenment, and especially its spiritual expressions. Using scientific, objective material wherever he could find it, in the historical literature of Hungary, Austria, Croatia, Slovenia, Serbia, Romania and Slovakia, and drawing on his own documentary and purely academic studies – in the process abandoning his previous interpretations and rethinking historical material – Kosáry provides a wealth of information on the region: its education system, press, libraries, societies of Freemasons, personalities and tendencies, political, economic and cultural institutions. Thus he demonstrates, using concrete evidence and not only theory, that the civilization of this region was in no way excluded from circulation of ideas and values across Europe as a whole.[31] Another valuable reference work of Hungarian historiography is the collection of studies, documents and bibliographies *Typographia Universitatis Hungaricae Budae*, edited by Péter Király, to which Romanian historians also contributed. The information obtained here, and what I acquired directly from archives and collections of old books in various Budapest institutions, led to my writing on the definition of lines and points of convergence in Central-Southeastern European culture and civilization.[32]

A method similar to that of Kosáry is employed by David Prodan in his well-known work *Supplex Libellus Valachorum*. A historian with a vast range of expertise, a scientist familiar not only with history and all its associated disciplines, but also literature, philosophy, art, and sociology, Prodan provides an example in his book of how all the angles on a historical problem should be viewed, how to interpret documents correctly, beginning with the major ones and ending with the minor ones. Examining acts, correspondence, memoirs, and various other sorts of information, Prodan reconstructs the society of two, three and four hundred years ago, elucidating its most characteristic features. This is real history, the history of details, based on archival documents, a history which brings out a great deal of data, facts, events and, especially, people – the masses and the personalities who lead and shape them. His work brings to light some essential events in the past of the Romanian people, revealing the deep meanings of socio-economic and political and intellectual movements in Transylvania. His comparative interpretations allow Romanian problems to be correctly integrated into the context of Central and Eastern European history. The description of movements preceding the region's awakening – that is, the period of continuity from the Renaissance through the Enlightenment to Romanticism – is full of invaluable ideas that are essential to any serious student of Transylvanian history. Prodan's *Supplex Libellus Valachorum*[33] offers interesting and useful answers (in the context of our studies) to questions such as: what circumstances and forces brought about spiritual awakening? Where did the wish for the assertion and recognition of national identity come from? To what extent did the small nations of Central and Eastern Europe attempt to reach the same political and cultural level as Homo Europaeus?

I should acknowledge from the outset that without the writings of the scholars I have mentioned in this chapter and many others to whom I will refer later, the centuries of medieval and modern history I am examining would have been immeasurably obscure, and it would have been impossible to define the meaning and duration of the temptation of European Man. I have applied research covering specialized subjects, especially when it served my purposes, stressing one aspect or another of Homo Europaeus' complex world: a world that is part of the history of our civilization itself and which requires analysis from different angles. This is why I deem it necessary to emphasize that in the present synthesis I attempt to create a picture that should itself be refreshed and enriched by new scientific discoveries, from the points of view of both the historiographer and the historian of culture. I will return to this picture and modify it whenever it seems necessary.

Therefore, let us see things from the point of view of the Central and Southeastern European, without excluding the objective, universally valid and long-accepted judgement of Westerners. Let us try to define European Man by identifying his inner workings, the structures forming the area of *Mitteleuropa* as seen and described in its various forms by Fritz Valjavec[34] or, more recently, by David Prodan, Domokos Kosáry and M. V. Friedman, as well as works on the Southeast by Nicolae Iorga and Victor Papacostea or, in our times, by Charles and Barbara Jelavich[35] or Emil Condurachi and Răzvan Theodorescu in the report made at the XVth International Congress of Historical Sciences (Bucharest, 1980).[36] Unlike the interpretative studies and essays to date, my work will briefly describe the genesis of the century of Enlightenment during the period marking the end of the Middle Ages, and then will follow the crisis of conscience in Central and Southeastern Europe, attempting to complete and – why not? – surpass, where possible, the view suggested by the French historian Paul Hazard. I have chosen this subject knowing that for these peoples and their countries, Europe is not just a geographical phenomenon, but also a spiritual one from which they do not wish to be, and indeed cannot be, isolated. The Central-Eastern zone has been a civilization in itself for a long time, a world with its own particular scientific traits, of course, as any other, but also open to influences from all directions for a millennium. As such, let us ascertain both the meaning and duration of the temptation of Homo Europaeus, at the European level, but with particular reference to the Central-Southeastern region immediately after the thirteenth century, which saw an impasse – of a political nature at the very least – followed by the temporary breaking up of Byzantium and birth of a Greek Orthodox patriotism that formed basis for the 'great ethnic idea' ('*Megali Idea*') later embodied by the modern Enlightenment.[37]

I am entirely conscious of the importance of partial studies, and results derived from the direct investigation of literary, historiographic, philosophical and religious texts, and archival documents, as well as from the contemplation of great art monuments. I will therefore try not to generalize continuously and attempt to deduce the overall European character of this region – rather, I will assess the general picture through reputable bibliographical sources reflecting on historical periods across the medieval and modern eras. I would like to go beyond the outdated division of academic disciplines characteristic of medieval and modern universities, a separation criticized by Curtius but unchanged even today. This analytical method will enable me to gather the necessary material and obtain a comprehensive view of the subject.

Attentive and detailed examination of the history of cultural relations in Central and Southeastern European societies, and their subsequent inclusion into the overall European picture, can achieve more than just the progress of historical knowledge – it can also provide useful clarification and awareness. From this starting point, and with the intention of overcoming any 'complex' or existing bias they might possess, historians – along with philosophers, sociologists, and philologists – have felt that it is their duty to offer a clear picture of humanity in its various stages of existence. This statement is justified because until recently we have been accustomed to see the past as a perfectly or almost perfectly linear, often through particular phenomena only tenuously connected to universal ideas. However, the personality of a nation, of a culture, of an area of civilization, along with the questions and answers of man, can be correctly and profoundly understood only by constantly using analogies, parallels, and convergences sustained by modern research. This is exactly what I hope to have achieved by the end of this journey into the genesis of modern Central and Southeast European thinking.

II

THE TRANSITION FROM MEDIEVAL TO MODERN ERA: ECHOES OF THE RENAISSANCE IN EAST-CENTRAL EUROPE AND THE BALKAN PENINSULA

Science is actually an interpretation of facts. By themselves they do not reveal reality; on the contrary, they hide it from us. They face us, that is to say, with a problem of reality. If there were no problems, there would be no enigma, there would be nothing hidden that has to be discovered, revealed. The word by which the Greeks designated truth was alétheia, which means revealing, the raising of the veil that hides and covers something.

José Ortega y Gasset

MEDIEVAL MAN WAS QUICK to glimpse the first signs of the new world to come. Which does not mean that the transition from the Middle Ages to the Modern Era came about suddenly, under pressure from political, economic or ecclesiastical events. Changes do not occur abruptly from one decade to another, they are not sensational; in the centuries before 1500 human society was characterized by the medieval spirit that bore the impression of 'bizarre and overloaded forms'. These images were initially faint, then became sharper in the Italian *Quattrocento*, appearing in more forms of life and thought: in religious belief and passions, in party rivalries, in disputes between well-known noble families, in the feelings of fear and uncertainty engendered by the political systems created by the Church and Monarchy. For example, the Great Western Schism between Avignon and Rome, which began in 1378, was otherwise devoid of any dogmatic basis but quickly became a problem of belonging to one party or another, 'an acute and violent question'[1], as Huizinga calls it, evolving into an antagonism between believers and unbelievers.

In medieval times, man was considered as the member of a family, of a union, of a political and religious community, outside of which he did not think, did not work, did not act. His individuality blended into the personality of the collective. He lived through the dogma that guided his mind and soul, he saw everything through the eyes of the Church to which he belonged, and he saw what was happening around him only as his family permitted. Petre P. Negulescu noted the linear thought and feelings of this mass of people, who awakened only on the eve of the Renaissance, when historical conditions allowed, and went on to replace one way of life with another, asserting a new condition of the spirit expressed in a new way, even though they still belonged to the same Church as before. At this point medieval man begins to consider himself 'as an entity, as an individual in the etymological sense of the word, to discover that he also has rights, not just duties, and to desire more than anything else the freedom to be himself, to think and work through himself'.[2] The crisis of the modern age was to bring about a series of revelations, the first rays of light in a world still strongly dominated by Church and dogma. Even if these ideas came exclusively from the souls and minds of writers – members of the family of scholars slowly leaving the labyrinth of the holy medieval libraries, where their guides had been the ancient philosophers and men of letters – or in the creative works of painters, sculptors or musicians, they energized humanity, paving the way for a time in which culture was to bloom. But the relationship between humanism and the medieval spirit is not as simple as we might sometimes suppose. Let us remember the existing situation, and all the forms in which it manifested itself, during the Renaissance and Reformation – the idea of freedom of conscience setting in motion the fight for political freedom, as socio-economic and especially religious events were shaking the great despotic empires. This enables us to understand how it was possible in the sixteenth and seventeenth centuries that part of mankind passed through two grave, prolonged crises. Spain during the reign of Philip II is one of the best examples for Western Europe, clearly proving, beyond the economic contrasts of this region, the intense conflict of dogmas between Protestants and Catholics, and later between two opposing conceptions, two consciences. The autocratic and centralist monarchy of Spain, abetted by the monstrous Inquisition, created a climate of conflict that extended beyond the

Iberian Peninsula, into France, the Netherlands, Southern Germany and Central Europe.[3]

The differences we tend to construct between one geographical region and another seem exaggerated, to say the least, when we attempt to account for the genesis of the Enlightenment. In terms of the moment when the great changes in culture and civilization which formed the basis of the new world took place, and the ways in which modern society expressed itself, there are, no doubt, obvious differences. There are also differences of scale and form in the key events. Despite this, what seems essential to me is that human communities, no matter where they were located, tended towards a new type of conversation, with extraordinary reflexes in the forms they adopted, which were distinctly superior to previous norms. Medieval particularities continued to coexist with the tone life took on during the Renaissance and Reformation. We need to understand the phenomenon of transition as it played out across the entire continent, even if its tones differed from one region to another; in the Central-Eastern region Homo Europaeus awakened slowly, but this long coexistence of light and shadow gave rise to profound and valid meditations.

Whether consciously or not, the world was now straddling two ages – medieval and modern. The first stage in the genesis of Europe as a spiritual organism was determined by East–West relations, with the pre-eminence of Byzantine ideas, the commitment to *imperium Romanum*, a belief system that prolonged the Greek-Roman-Oriental influence and the medieval system of vassals and sovereignties. The second period was influenced by South–North relations, in which, broadly speaking, the civilizing light of the Mediterranean penetrated the metaphysical fog of the North.

The decline of the Middle Ages triggered a war of religious confessions. This leads us to look more closely at the life of the Church and its congregations behind the scenes, at the episcopal schools and universities, but especially at the professors and students who comprised the educational system, with their personalities and doctrines. Beginning with the thirteenth century, we will notice the diversity of spiritual activity, when thinkers showed contradicting tendencies that served either science, or religious ideals exclusively.

Albert the Great (1193–1280) and Thomas Aquinas (1225–74) attempted to bring these divergent tendencies closer together in their activities at the University of Paris. As promoters of Aristotelianism, they facilitated the adoption of peripateticism by theologians (wanting to put it to religious use), provoking a revolution in the history of Western thought; in the Southeast this revolution will be kindled by the no less famous Georgios Gemistos Plethon, the champion of Neo-Platonic philosophy. Considered to be 'a second Augustine' of Catholicism, Aquinas, canonized fifty years after his death, was a towering personality among medieval scholastics whose writing was dominated by the rationalism which was to create endless possibilities for Renaissance humanism to express itself. His major work, *Summa Theologica*, has been rightly compared with 'the glorious architecture of contemporary gothic cathedrals, especially because of the systematical exposure, structured in parts, chapters, questions, articles and rhythmic successions of arguments, counter-arguments, objections and conclusions'[4] – it is a memorable synthesis based on the harmony between belief and rationality. Aquinas seeks and discovers new ways of reasoning, his studies revealing deep knowledge of ancient philosophy and theology, an acute historical sense, and tendency towards progress and innovation not only in philosophy, but in the science of his times as well. Thomas Aquinas' philosophy is Aristotelian – a rethinking of Aristotle's philosophy, in fact, combined with other influences from Greek theological thought, from Greek commentaries on Aristotle, as well as from Judaic philosophy – Moses ben Maimon (Maimonides) specifically – to form a coherent whole. Catholic Europe, for all its opposition, would later profit greatly from the authority of Thomistic doctrine (as it also would from Occamism or Scotism) – causing Western philosophy to modify its thinking, while in the nineteenth century Pope Leo XII would declare Thomism the official philosophy of the Church. During nine years of research in one of the most famous libraries of the times – Monte Cassino, where the Benedictines had preserved the most valuable creations of humanism – Aquinas analyzed the relationship between philosophy and theology. He argues for an organic union between the two, maintaining that reason and dogma cannot contradict each other, just as reason and intellect cannot denote different powers; both of their acts need to be considered. For Aquinas, human knowledge means obtaining the intelligible truth by means of contracts existing between people, while reason refers to the capacity of understanding. He makes the following distinction:

> This is why the angels, who possess perfectly, according to their nature, the intelligible truth, are not permitted to step

from one to another, finding the truth of things directly and dispensing with reason, as Dionysius says in *De div. nom.*, VII. 2. On the contrary, human beings come to know the intelligible truth by stepping from one to another, as said in the same work, which is why they are called rational beings. It is then obvious that to rationalize is to understanding, as to move is to standing still or to obtain is to having: of which the first term is something perfect, and the other imperfect.[5]

Aquinas anticipates modern human thought in his notion of morality, which he conceives as a journey of the rational creature towards the Creator. His ethics, considered to be one of the most important of the Middle Ages, 'particularly meant to create a Christian ethic, showing not only man's actions, but, more importantly, the role of his will and freedom as a fundamental condition of moral action'.[6]

Preserved in such thinking, first through Aristotelianism, and later, on the eve of the Renaissance, through Platonism, Hellenism was to enrich conceptions about man, nature, laws, religion and politics at the end of the Middle Ages, and was to shape the new world's great ideas; along with reflections of Judaic origin, it would form the basis of modern European spirituality. Here we may note that the relationship with Judaism is especially evident in the case of Moses ben Maimon, Latinized as Maimonides (1135–1204), the best-known and most influential Jewish thinker of the Middle Ages, predecessor of Benedict Baruch Spinoza, as well as of Moses Mendelssohn. His philosophical writings bear the title *Dalalat al-Ha'irin* (*The Guide for the Perplexed*) and exerted a dominant influence on Mosaism – attempting to rationalize its dogmas – on Judaic philosophical currents, and on medieval scholastics.[7] His concept goes beyond sterile dogmatism, which he utterly rejects. Maimonides was a visionary who, discovering the essential causes for the backward state of his contemporary society, reasons, with good measure and rationality, for a true comprehension of humanity and divinity and the relationship between them; he fervently supports man's freedom to know and to behave ethically. The great evils that men inflict on one another, he says, are caused by the dispositions, passions, opinions and multiple beliefs resulting from privations that originate in ignorance:

Just as the blind man has no one to guide his way, hits and hurts himself, and hurts others endlessly, because of his want of sight, so in the adversities between men, each one, in his ignorance, inflicts on himself and others harms that weigh heavily on individual human beings. If they could master science, which is for human beings what sight is for eyes, they would not be allowed to harm themselves and others; because the recognition of truth will cause enmity and hate to cease and stops men from hurting one another, as the prophet said: the wolf shall stay with the lamb and the leopard shall sleep with the goat; the cow and the bear shall go to pasture together and the suckling shall play, etc. (Isaiah, XI.6–8).[8]

The unifying characteristics of the medieval and modern minds were brilliantly represented on the one hand by Nicolaus Cusanus in the West, and on the other by Georgios Gemistos Plethon in the East. The latter established the most important contacts between East and West, between the Byzantine-Orthodox and Roman-Catholic worlds, ample contacts that brought about the long-awaited interaction of the old culture of the Greeks with the modern Italian world. An important part in this process was played by the Council of Ferrara, while Florence (the Council for the Union of the Churches, 1437–42) was the historical framework for the movement of ideas. Cusanus, considered one of the most enlightened men of the Church, played an extraordinary role by creating one of the first great spiritual communions with Byzantium and its learned men. Convinced of the necessity of a 'conciliary doctrine', he introduced a constitutional system into the life of the Church. In De concordantia catholica he supports constitutionalism in ecclesiastical life, his arguments influenced by contemporary conditions and the views of his professors. We should remember that William of Ockham, Marsilius of Padua and Dietrich of Nieheim preceded him in declaring the possibility of Church reform through an ecumenical council.[9] Cusanus saw the superiority of the council over the Holy See:

> The Church is the community of believers that form it. It is not the physical juxtaposition of people, but the spiritual tie that binds them into a unique group, into a community of ideas and feelings that keep them together. They are all brothers unto Christ. Their community is thus their spiritual unity with the Saviour, which is at the same time a union among themselves into a 'sweet harmony', a harmony that is in 'Catholic unity'.[10]

P. P. Negulescu considers that Cusanus' scientific rather than philosophical works display the characteristics linking medieval and modern times. In these works[11] Cusanus attempted to address problems relating to particular categories of natural phenomena – as is customary in the natural sciences – with the aim of contributing to the development of certain subject areas through his methodological recommendations. The content of Cusanus' work is a mixture of old and new – sometimes confusingly so. Without being a man of science in today's sense of the word, he cleared the way for Copernicus and his followers. Through his idea of an infinite universe, for example, his influence reaches much further to modern times, up to Leibniz and Schelling.

In the genesis of Renaissance philosophy, no less important was the direct contribution of Byzantine reformer Georgios Gemistos Plethon. Widely referred to as the original driving force of the Platonic Academy in Florence, he did more than any other scholar to set Europeans on the path towards ancient Greek culture and great ancient philosophy in general. One of the foremost Byzantine intellectuals, Gemistos was influential among Florentine humanists in persuading Cosimo de' Medici to found the Academy. Playing an important role in the life of the Renaissance, it principally propagated the ideas of Neo-Platonists.[12] Gemistos' book, edited in 1858 by Charles Alexandre, is a treatise of which only fragments have been preserved; it focuses on the 'state laws and institutions, beliefs and efforts through which men can hope to reach the best and most beautiful life – or the happiest one, if possible'.[13] The Byzantine scholar's most important contribution was to encourage meditation on Plato's philosophy, shifting the interest of the future Homo Europaeus from Aristotle to Plato. Let us then examine the internal motivation for Renaissance humanism's interest in 'Platonic conversation'. The debate between Cardinal Giuliano Cesarini and Georgios Gemistos at the Council of Florence went beyond the merely religious and moved into philosophical territory, a dialogue that effectively gave birth to Renaissance Platonism. Its first representative was Marsilio Ficino. The ideas derived from Plato's philosophy are expressed in Marsilio's discourses, such as *De laudibus philosophiae*, *Declarationes platonicae ad Cristophorum Laudinum*, and in *Institutionum ad platonicam disciplinam libri quattuor*, and seen in letters to his friends. Ficino studied Plato systematically, and gathered a group of admirers of the ancient philosopher's work including philologists, philosophers and politicians, all interested in the study, understanding and translation of the Platonic dialogues – Amerigo

Benci, Migliore Cresci, Ottone Niccolini, Benedetto Accolti, Pietro Fortini and Cristoforo Laudino. But as we have mentioned, beyond this we are interested in seeing where this emphasis on Plato's philosophy originated, knowing well that during medieval and modern history his work was interpreted in various ways, some of these having nothing in common with his thinking. In *Theologia platonica*, Ficino admits his interest in an ideal type of man more than in an ideal state, which is true to the system of Plato's philosophy and a remarkable statement for the decline of the Middle Ages. Plato – philosopher Constantin Noica warns us – treated the Idea

> the way he understood it, and not the way Aristotle and his cohort of imitators did – and it is exactly because he knew how to combine reality and Idea that he remains even now at the heart of culture. For what else is culture than the marriage of reality and law, in the knowledge of nature as well as in that of man? For simple political constitutions, whose list, interminable even then, Aristotle wanted to produce, Antiquity would not have preserved Plato's work in its entirety, as none of its creators did. It preserved it for the meaning of the Idea, whether seen or just guessed.[14]

Marsilio Ficino was centrally concerned with the Idea, attempting either to 'make' religion philosophical, in *De Christiana religione*, or to 'make' philosophy religious, in *Theologia platonica*. His main goal was to convince the human mind, which does not easily yield to the authority of divine law, to let itself be convinced by the reasoning with which Plato's philosophy sustains religion, so that those who separate philosophy and belief may be persuaded that their 'straying' is at least as bad as that of the ones who 'throw out, for the sake of knowledge, its own fruits'.[15] This is one of the means by which Renaissance thinking separates itself from the medieval Church. The speculations on soul and freedom, the dialogues on love and human spirit, God and eternal life, most often follow the example of illustrious forebears. Ficino is influenced by the reasoning of many philosophers of religion, by religious traditions in their rational forms, his meditations leading to a rationalized religion. His philosophy is essentially a theology, as Ernst Cassirer notes, proving a continuity from scholasticism and the thinking of the Italian *Quattrocento*.[16] By approaching his contemporaries, Nicolaus Cusanus and Georgios Gemistos Plethon, and by bridging the gap with Leon Abravanel and Spinoza beyond the Renaissance, his opus represents a milestone in the history of the birth of modern ideas.

Renaissance humanism becomes dominant in the West in the fourteenth to sixteenth centuries, arriving later in Central-Southeastern Europe. It would dictate, at both ends of Europe, the ways of life of the future, and bring, as Huizinga says, 'a wind of change, when a wonderful idea becomes ripe: that all the splendour of the old goals, which had reflected the world for such a long time, could be regained'.[17] And through spiritual dialogue between East and West, between Byzantine Orthodoxy and Roman Catholicism, Antiquity was slowly brought back to the forefront of history, and its discovery revealed an important part of the culture of ancient civilizations, specifically those of the Greeks and Romans. Antiquity lent force to the new ideals, offering a model of culture based upon reason – the great idea that was now elevated above beliefs, traditions and the Church, in opposition to the principle of authority and processes that go against mankind's natural evolution. The ancient spirit can be found at the heart of Renaissance thought – it was its ultimate source of universal enlightenment. The atmosphere initially inspired by the 'amazing' studies emanating from the so-called Florentine Platonic Academy raised European Man's intellect, motivating him to construct a new temple of wisdom. In this context, the considerations of some important representatives seem justified: 'The golden age' – writes Italian Marsilio Ficino – 'brought once more to light the liberal arts which had been completely obscured before: grammar, eloquence, painting, sculpture, music. And all this in Florence.' 'Blessed will we be,' exclaims Philip Melanchthon, 'if, with God's grace, true studies (classical ones) will be born again.' Even more categorical is Nicolas Bourbon's statement: 'Until now we had lived as blind men. In our minds we had nothing but complicated syllogisms, all sorts of sophisms, dull stupidities, empty words, conceitedness and foolishness. After these monsters were brought down, and in such wonderful ways, truth descended upon Earth again.'[18] A correct assessment of this phenomenon will, of course, enable us to explain certain categorical statements made in their enthusiasm by those who had become the most famous followers of the ancient philosophers. What remains important is that discussion of Christian and Judaic symbols recommenced,[19] as did that of Platonic and Aristotelian ideas, and of the problems facing history and philosophy, all of which had a miraculous effect on society, and echoed throughout Europe. The reawakening through the Renaissance of humanism was no less important in the West than in the East. Initiatives were no less important in the Southeastern area than in the West. The leap towards the modern age was facilitated by different ideas and tendencies. It is no accident that we can associate with this ample movement the name of Georgios Gemistos Plethon and those of Georgios Scholarios (also known as Gennadios, Patriarch of Constantinople), Theodor Gaza (of Thessaloniki, the scholar who translated into Latin Aristotle's writings on natural philosophy), Bessarion (Archbishop of Nicaea, who became cardinal after the Council of Florence), Georgios Trapezuntios (professor of Greek language and literature in Venice, then professor of rhetoric and philosophy at the University of Rome) and with many others who, coming from Eastern Europe, not only cultivated Greek philosophy, as keepers of this great treasure, but created an enthusiastic admiration, and an emulation that previously did not exist. It is no less true that Marsilio Ficino's activity was echoed by that of Westerners Pico della Mirandola, Johann Reuchlin, Agrippa von Nettesheim, Theophrastus Paracelsus, Hieronymus Cardanus and Leon Abravanel. The work of each of them has undisputable merits in the history of European culture, their theories creating an atmosphere in which metaphysics, logics, ethics, theology, physics and mathematics would widely develop. In the Renaissance tradition they were the seekers of good and bad, of truth, but also of divine wisdom. They heralded the coming of Erasmus, the great citizen of the world, the European humanist whose thinking is tied to the dawn of modern times, and in whose work we can first identify a developing universality of spirit. Erasmus helps us, as no one else, to understand the changing times, to grasp the workings of society, to sense the tone of the period and, not least, the ideas hiding behind the many facts. In the same way, but much later, Johann Sebastian Bach was to bring through his music not just a new artistic conception, but also a different psychological essence, namely the humanization of the divine, thus defining an era that treated existence from a human point of view. In this stage of transition, Erasmus belongs to Europe and Europe to Erasmus, the vast adventure of his soul and his mind affording us the first example of an entirely new Homo Europaeus. He considered himself to be a citizen of the world, a citizen of Europe, an ideal that the most brilliant representatives of the Enlightenment, in their time, would apply and support. What humanists and their rightful followers considered as Europe did not correspond at all with the old Carolingian sense of the term (present for many centuries during the Middle Ages). From Erasmus to Leibniz and on to Rousseau, the picture emerged of a Europe formed from nation states, a modern structure in which states were united in an imperial conception. As one of Erasmus' interpreters observed:

> In his view of a European policy, Erasmus thinks not of European nations, nor of nation states. In a way, he accepts the idea of an empire led by Charles V... Naturally in this great, unified Europe, which Erasmus was to proclaim, the role of the sword is insignificant. Europe was to become a continent of peace and of conciliation, without any belligerent intervention, no matter how justified its aims.[20]

It became an ideal for which generations of humanists were to fight with every means in their possession, a belief that was taken up again and asserted with the same force in the age of the Enlightenment. From the century of Rabelais, through the decades defined by Galileo and up to the great French Revolution, this belief is a constant in the history of human ideas, or rather, in the judgement of the elite circles of the European spirit. But let us not exaggerate: this was not the only view of the world's evolution. There were many other opinions that gave rise to other cultural and ideological currents of thought: during the sixteenth to eighteenth centuries we discover, among phenomena, the handicap created by the Reformation, namely Lutheranism and Calvinism, in continuous dispute with Catholicism whose authority was gravely shaken. There was also the offensive of the Counter-Reformation, begun by the Council of Trent (1545–63), a Jesuit attempt to purify the Church, and a second series of injustices – the Inquisition, the persecution of the Jews (especially Iberian Sephardic Jews), and the wars pursued by kings wishing to impose their influence according to the political interests of the moment or personal ambitions. Finally, there was the Enlightenment, which, on close examination, also offers various tendencies, from the current of thought itself to the so-called Counter-Enlightenment, propagated by the most occult groups of the times. It is not by chance, therefore, that the events of 1789 were to end this desperate state, giving our existence an unexpected turn.

RELIGIOUS CONFRONTATIONS IN EUROPE, 1500–1800

After 1500, many different currents of Christian belief and doctrine spread across Eastern Europe. Lutheran-Calvinist reformism reached the East-Central and Southeastern regions, which in turn participated in the Counter-Reformation. A version of Balkan Orthodoxy defended traditional principles against the Wittenberg Theses and the expansion of Catholic jurisdiction. These religious confrontations not only continued but increased with the religious fragmentation introduced by Luther, Calvin and Zwingli. Faith was stifled by the self-proclaimed Homo Religiosus, who in the name of his God violated rules of human communication and communion.

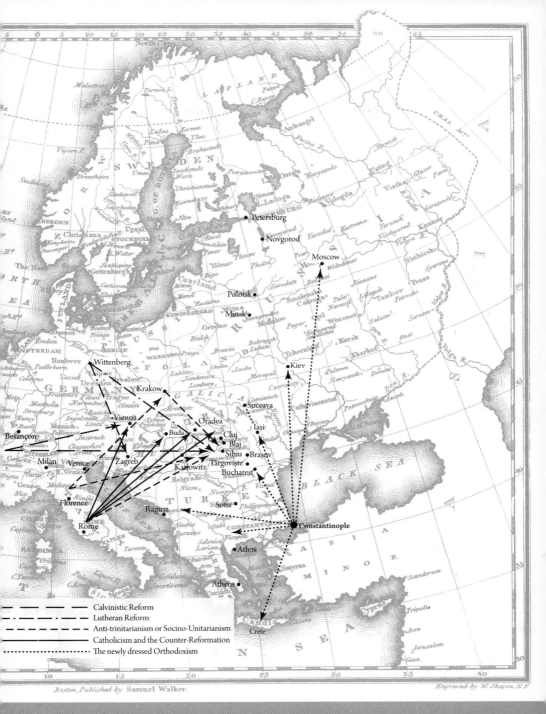

	Calvinistic Reform
	Lutheran Reform
	Anti-trinitarianism or Socino-Unitarianism
	Catholicism and the Counter-Reformation
	The newly dressed Orthodoxism

THE TRANSITION FROM MEDIEVAL TO MODERN ERA: THE ECHOES OF
THE RENAISSANCE IN EAST-CENTRAL EUROPE AND THE BALKAN PENINSULA 53

Let us pause for a moment to comment on the contrary view. The sixteenth century embraced at least as much, if not more so, the idea of Anti-Homo Europaeus. What is the profound meaning of the Reformation? An unequivocal answer would be: a dissension, a definitive rupture with another religion, namely the Catholic Church. Luther was a fighter, a Homo Religiosus completely committed to the imposition of his own doctrine, which he considered to be capable of satisfying the spiritual aspirations of peoples advancing towards a new civilization. He accepted no other form of belief – only his communication with God was real. Roman Catholicism only increased his conviction: its medieval dominance was not merely an era needing radical change, it was characterized by theories devoid of any content, by the false propagation of worship, hostile attitudes towards Byzantine orthodoxy, inconsistencies in doctrine, the interests of a small group placed above those of the majority – mistakes upon mistakes, in other words, culminating in a moral decadence even a simple man would deride. All these failings were, for the moment, to Luther's advantage in the North. Zwingli and Calvin successfully completed Luther's work, following his example, with a few digressions. A continuous feud erupted between the Pope's followers and those of Luther and Calvin. In addition to all this, an extremist current of the Reformation emerged. Unitarianism or Anti-trinitarianism, which was also strongly committed to its form of communication with the divine: negation of the dogma of the Trinity, the divinity of the Holy Spirit, the consubstantiation of the Son and the Father and the pre-existence of Christ in the sacred texts. This tendency was to gain ground in Eastern and Central Europe, with Transylvania and Poland being notable examples. Indeed, the chaos had now doubled, as had the fanatics.

Mankind had reached a crossroads and had only to choose – to tell the good from the bad, the beautiful from the ugly, to approach one Church or another, depending on which he considered would salvage his conscience. The contradictions are obvious. Someone was observing the phenomenon from above, though. Not because he liked to, but because no one had attained this ideal, either before or during this century of brutal changes. Only Homo Europaeus, reasonable and wise, tried to bring his enemies closer, to make them better people, to unite them in feelings and thought. His perception was superior; he saw the unity of belief, of hope, of ideal, of human endeavour in general. The possibility of salvation for his brother in the labyrinth of existence was clear to him. The struggle was often uneven, a utopia facing reality – painful, because the majority not only chose not to support it, but looked upon it as something bizarre, or rejected it with false accusations of paganism. Yet still Homo Europaeus perpetuated and resisted, then as centuries later. His quintessence is body-soul-spirit, the superior form of humanity, beyond arguments, fanaticism, wars, every kind of intolerance, vanity. Erasmus was and still is a bridge between the past and future, even if many avoided his example, or ignored it, stigmatized it, even laughed at it. An entire republic of intellectuals purified itself, accepting the idea of Homo Europaeus. It was their belief and it was utopian, because mankind as a whole did not cleave to it. My argument in these pages stems from this – the temptation of wholeness, without denying the character-istics of human nature, its limits and passions. We should exercise caution, however. It is not through selfishness that we can hope for good or beauty, but by surpassing this condition, in the altruism it is capable of, in the trans-communion of societies, peoples and beliefs. Religions did not understand this phenomenon. The same occurred within secular thought, incapable of accepting it. European Man – universal man – is therefore always in danger, constantly trying to avoid self-destruction. And how else can we imagine Erasmus, other than a mediator between the Pope and Luther? How else can we imagine Galileo, but as a link between old and new, as a peak between two ways of thinking, between two ways of existing, trying to transform, but also to maintain balance in the souls and minds of his contemporaries? Lucien Febvre offers a convincing explanation of their so-called lack of belief, arguing that it is characteristic for the man of letters, the artist, the scholar, living in hostile conditions where the general discontent has led to personal discontent.

In my account of a conscious model of European spiritual unity, namely the ideal form of Renaissance and post-Renaissance thought, I will demonstrate that its origins lie in ancient culture, Latin language and literature having made a great contribution to this reawakening, as its main instrument of communication. Humanists were to struggle with all their might to restore the Latin language and its purity, to save it from scholastic and theological jargon. Latin was the medium of literary expression, so that renewed interest in the language itself gave rise to a period of erudition. With his *De elegantia linguae latinae*, Lorenzo Valla became a brilliant example for Erasmus, in addition to his followers Justus Lipsius, Gerardus Johannes

Vossius, Hugo Grotius and others. Valla was one of those profound thinkers who distinguished himself across the fields of science, literature and philosophy. He inaugurated new methods, devised new concepts and criticized Christian morals in an original way, adopting an Epicurean standpoint, all of which established him as a critic of the beginnings of the Renaissance. We should also remember that the majority of humanists spoke and wrote in Latin, that some rendered their names with Latin or Greek overtones, the examples of Melanchthon of Schwarzerd or Olearius of Oelschlager being the best known. The cult for Antiquity was a bridge for the first great European trans-communion, one which the age of Enlightenment was to assert and even turn to its own benefit.

Since we have mentioned Erasmus, we should state here that his ideas contributed to a new view of life, where the fear gave way to courage and hope. He had repeated contact with the world's spiritual capitals, which he maintained during his extensive travels. It was Erasmus who brought to my attention the consequences of any kind of fanaticism or religious mysticism, and prompted me to review the reasons behind his dialogues with Thomas More and William Mountjoy or his polemics with Ulrich von Hutten and Martin Luther. It made me consider, in a parallel absolutely pertinent to the Central-Eastern region, the profound origins of European thought. All of this reveals the spiritual and mental state of sixteenth-century Europe, and the societies that we see walking in Erasmus' footsteps reveal the essence of an immense crisis traversed by human conscience. In *Laus stultitiae*, Erasmus criticizes everything that authority and the institutional forms that go against rational life stand for, in the form of kings and princes, prelates, monks and popes. Condemning medieval dogmatism, he pleads for freedom of thought, offering a satire of Western feudal society (with its wealth of ambitions) on the brink of destruction, and sees a new world on the horizon. Erasmus writes to More:

> As for my tongue-lashings, my answer is that writers have always had the freedom to describe, unpunished, the humour of everyday life, as long as they do not become passionate. I am amazed by the delicacy of today's ears; they can only bear pompous titles. What's more, we can see many people with such strange ideas about religion, that they would rather admit the greatest blaspheming of Christ than tolerate the slightest

allusion to the pope or the king, especially when their material interest is at stake. Please tell me if he who, without personal attacks against anyone, scolds all of mankind, is making fun of things, or rather is giving advice (to others) and warning them. Under what names would not I then have made fun of myself! Then also, he who forgives no category of men shows that he is not angry with a certain man, but with all vices. If anyone calls out that he has been hit, then he exposes either his conscience or his fear.[21]

It is no accident that we see in Erasmus the predecessor of Rousseau and Voltaire, although these two were alone in applying the innovative ideas of Renaissance humanism, and it was only in the age of the Enlightenment that the possibility of man's and society's perfectibility became dogma.[22]

Although they were unable to change ideal into reality, humanists were encouraged by a dream of happiness – to transform society. It is in their way of thinking that we see the birth of the Enlightenment, the same way as, through their sensibility, we feel the first signs of a European crisis of conscience. By seeing them again, we can perceive the fantastic artistic works of Da Vinci and Michelangelo – I am thinking of how the *Mona Lisa* pleads for harmony, for an ideal, for the exterior and interior type of beauty represented by the statues of David and Moses – and we can follow the ideas conveyed by their achievements and bring ourselves closer to the metamorphoses achieved by the Renaissance. In the same way, Savonarola – 'the monk with a burning soul, the dictator of Florentine moral life', as the historian George Oprescu rightly designated him – signifies anti-humanism, even fanaticism. These considerations will allow us to grasp more readily the character of a society in need of reform. I also believe that the historian or philosopher will uncover the mystery of this world by a sensitive evaluation of the work of Raphael, creator of the High Noon of collective European thinking.

The great reformers accused the Catholic Church and its leaders of sensuality and debauchery, immorality in general – and not without just cause. There are countless examples, which have been enumerated by Johan Huizinga in *The Decline of the Middle Ages*. We should not forget, however, that alongside examples in the West, there are those of Central-Eastern Europe, where territories occupied by Poland, Austria, the Czech Republic, Slovakia,

Hungary, Croatia and Transylvania were all confronted with Luther's ideas as early as the middle of the sixteenth century, while closer to 1600 elements of the Counter-Reformation were strongly felt through its attempts at forcefully reinstating the Catholic spirit. In Vienna, Kaliningrad, Buda, Cluj and Braşov, the forms taken by the Reformation, as well as the Counter-Reformation, decisively prove that this 'zone' is by no means free of major sectarian disputes. What is more, the religious movements of the region show the signs of a crisis that was to appear here in the second half of the seventeenth century. It may be useful to mention that in Poland, Protestantism had serious implications shortly after the Theses of Wittenberg, enriched by Calvin in 1536 – Lutheranism spreading mostly in towns and Calvinism in rural areas. The conflict of opinions on religious subjects swept across the Polish community immediately after the death of Sigismund I the Old (1548), the appeal of the Reformation's representatives being welcomed by the most important writers of the day, among them Mikołaj Rej, who was to translate Rhegius' Lutheran Catechism into Polish.[23] The situation was similar in Hungary and Transylvania, where the Reformation met with favourable conditions and also produced its own creations, such as Anti-trinitarianism, and where one of the great diffusers of the new religion, Francis Davidis, was also an important translator of Biblical texts, along with Gáspár Heltai.[24]

Thereafter, humanist culture rejected clerical and aristocratic isolation, refused the old religious precepts, and renewed itself continuously in towns and through the schools of the Reformation, through art, science and culture, all welcomed by the most prominent minds of the times. On occasions it gave rise to strong protests, causing unrest whenever it assumed a coarse or violent form, with humanists attacking and criticizing religion and the clergy. Still, in some circumstances, the popes, tyrants and princes supported studies in philology, history and philosophy, and they all had some need for literature, or at least an elegant and erudite discourse. The recognition and transformation of Antiquity was possible as mankind experienced a clarification of conscience during the Latin Middle Ages, the period between Theodosius (379–95) and Charlemagne (768–814) being of prime importance for the European tradition. The legacy of the Latin Middle Ages extends to Petrarch and Boccaccio, and the literature of this period exerts an influence – as Curtius astutely observed – 'from without or within the great movements of the beginnings of the Modern Era – Humanism, Renaissance, Reformation, Counter-Reformation'.[25]

This breath of fresh air was characteristic not only of the West: the Netherlands contributed to its circulation across Central and Eastern Europe as well, where the example of Holland, Italy and France held real fascination. Contact with the Germanic West and the Italian Renaissance was especially intense, and contributed to the 'outline of an East European university humanism that is superficial, but brilliant' (R. Theodorescu). This dynamic was facilitated by, for example, the dynastic relations of the Anjou kings and the clear support of Sigismund of Luxembourg (1387–1437), but mostly by Matthias Corvinus (1458–90) in the case of Italy, as well as by commercial exchanges, in which the role of Armenians, Jews and Greeks was indisputable. This was how Florentines managed to reach Poland, Hungary, Transylvania and Banat, and in so doing facilitated the dissemination of ideas and artists forming those 'corridors' of European cultural access. A brilliant example is that of the 'international' Gothic-style altar made by Thomas of Cluj in the fifteenth century at the request of Nicolaus de Sancto Benedicto, lecturer and canon of Győr. Similar examples include the painter Erhardus, to whom is attributed, 'with some reservation', the painting of the Prejmer altar, and the Tyrolean Jacobus Kendlinger, who painted the fresco of the Passions at the bottom of the belfry at the Evangelical church in Dealul Frumos (Sibiu). It is amazing – says one historian of Transylvanian art – to see the stylistic similarity between the altar in Mediaș and that of St Elizabeth's Church in Breslau (1492–1505), discovered and commented on by Fabini.[26] We should also note the presence of Florentine architects in Banat after the Italian Filippo Scolari was named Count of Timiș.

A similar example of how renewal was precipitated through intervention was the centre of humanist learning in Oradea, which represented one of the first and foremost cultural centres of the area: this prestigious capitular school employed a Western model for the training of secretaries and diplomats at the court in Buda. The significance of this school as a European institution is due to the curriculum, based on the *trivium* and *quadrivium* systems, and to the professors whose activities established them as true models – among them was the Greek historian Philip Padocatoras, the Hellenist Pietro Paolo Vergerio, the musician Pierre – a French Templar – the Hungarian scholar G. Számosközi, the Viennese astronomer G. Peuerbach, and many others.[27] The schools of Cluj were no less important, displaying characteristics significant in the context of the emerging modern man of culture. In this regard we should note that the European collegium seminarium was based on the model of those of Bohemia, Poland and Germany.[28] This same impetus of Renaissance and Reformation would lead to the founding, in Transylvania and Hungary, of the famous libraries of Oradea and Buda; in Cluj, the propagation of culture, but also of new sects (the danger of Calvinism) resulted in the Catholics (through the Jesuits) establishing their own university in Transylvania. Common European cultural values were transmitted through the almost 100,000 books circulating here, out of a total of about 150–200 million published in the sixteenth century. Transylvanian intellectuals followed the general cultural direction of Europe during these times, taking the lead of the vast range of spiritual activities emanating from the more advanced regions of the continent. Readers embraced humanism, some of the most popular writers being Erasmus, Cicero, Aristotle, Luther, Thomas Aquinas and St Augustine. This is of obvious significance to anyone assessing the characteristics of Central European intellectual life in the early modern period. According to the chronicle of Számosközi, at the end of the sixteenth century the library of the Jesuit Academy in Cluj kept about 1,000 bound books in its deposits, most of them now lost. An important public library operated in Brașov from 1575, and all across Transylvania many private libraries were founded, belonging to important political and cultural figures: Gheorghe Martinuzzi, Bodog Jozsa, Albert Huet, Michael Weiss, Johannes Baier and Joachim Benkner. In Alba Iulia, the Bathory family received a splendid donation of 1,000 books from the Florentine Michael Brutus. Studying the relations between Transylvanian intellectuals and the European culture of these times, keeping in mind the books that circulated locally and were preserved, historian Ádám Dankanits rightly concludes that the second half of the sixteenth century especially was a time of great receptiveness to new cultural influences.[29]

Central-Eastern as well as Southeastern Europe offers many other examples of intellectual life. Cultural activities at the Prague Imperial Chancellery, the Royal Chancellery in Buda or the University of Pécs all mark the beginnings of humanism in this region (during the fourteenth and fifteenth centuries), but it is during the reign of Matthias Corvinus (1458–90) that it blossoms. Protector of the arts and letters, establishing permanent contacts with Italian towns, with their diplomats and humanists, Matthias quickly understood the importance of the new culture emerging in Italy. Poets, artists and men of science found refuge at his court, and notable humanists such as Antonius Bonfinius and Ioan Vitéz made him famous throughout Europe. Just as renowned, the Corvina Library is the result of this work of centralization of humanist culture in Hungary.[30] We should also mention some of the illustrious names amongst Nicolaus Olahus' contemporaries – foremost among them the Transylvanian Saxon humanist Johannes Honter, whose works, printed in many editions even in the first half of the sixteenth century, were distributed widely in Central Europe. His *Cosmography* (1530) and *Geography of Transylvania* (1532), as well as his *Latin Grammar* (1530) and compendium of *Greek Grammar* (1539) were all held in high regard. His life and work set an example, putting reciprocal knowledge between peoples at the service of education and the dissemination of ideas. This latter point is illustrated by Romanian-Saxon ties in the first years when printing presses came into use. The movement initiated by Honter influenced the development and modernization of the Orthodox Church in Brașov and in Wallachia, by printing the first religious books in Romanian. Honter also contributed to the indispensable dialogue of sciences and arts between this region and the cultural centres of the West and their representatives. This helps explain the composite creation *Odae cum Harmoniis* on Horace's texts, Honter's music being based on ancient prosody. The idea originated in the French Renaissance when the genre's founder, Baif, wrote verses in the same *mesurée à l'antique* for composers Claude le Jeune and J. Mauduit.[31] The passion for music among the citizens of Brașov was confirmed by another original work, that of Valentinus Gref Bakfark ('Orpheus Pannonicus'), one of the great lute players of Europe and the author of several volumes that have become part of universal culture, reflecting the idea of the cultural unity of Europe.[32] We should also mention the important contribution of Christian Schesaeus, whose *Ruinae Pannonicae* had gained renown in intellectual circles not only in Transylvania, but across Central Europe. His narrative poem, which contains significant historiographical material, reveals aspects of the Hungarian, Transylvanian, Moldavian and Wallachian past, from the death of John Zápolya (1540) to the death of John II Sigismund (1571), and is notable for its wealth and exactness of information.[33] The case of Gáspár Heltai is similar: his translations of religious texts represent a significant Renaissance development in the history of the Hungarian language. With his *Five Books of Moses as the First Part of the Bible* and *The New Testament of Jesus Christ*, Gáspár Heltai's efforts join those of Francis Davidis, as well as those of Tinodi Sebestien.[34] Many of their writings are preserved in the great Transylvanian libraries. Despite the practical challenges, some young Transylvanians attended schools of higher learning in the West, in Wittenberg, Tübingen, Krakow, Paris, Rome, Padua, Siena, Leipzig, Vienna and Prague (over 2,496 in the twelfth to sixteenth centuries). Theirs is a true *peregrinatio academica*, demonstrating an enduring desire for knowledge, for mental and spiritual enrichment, a shining example of the continuous temptation of Homo Europaeus.[35] Transylvanian humanists were also great letter writers, examples including the correspondence between poet Iacob Piso (1470–1526) from Mediaș and Erasmus, as well as Olahus,[36] and Deacon Coresi in Târgoviște and Brașov. The act of emancipation represented by the printing of the first Romanian Psalter in 1570 and the Slav Romanian Psalter in 1577, both destined for the Orthodox religion, and the fact that the Romanian language was considered noble enough to be a language of culture, deserve special attention, since we are interested in the state of the receiving culture. The horizon gained by this receiving culture widens when the book is transformed into a bearer of the modern spirit. 'Therefore have I, my brother priests, written unto you these Psalters,' Coresi stated, 'and have thus taken from the Serbian Psalters unto the Romanian language so as to be understood also. So if it please you, my brothers, read it well and give it good thought and you shall see that it is true.' He was convinced that the progress of the people could be brought about through translation, through the development of the Romanian language, through access to old and new religious writings, through wide cultivation of the enlightenment provided by books:

> By the grace of God, I, Deacon Coresi, having seen that almost every language has the word of God in its tongue, only we Romanians have none and Christ said he who reads let him understand and Paul the Apostle too writes that in church better I speak for five minutes to their understanding, so as others to teach, than the darkness of unknown words in other tongues.[37]

Transylvania, Wallachia and Moldavia also proved their receptiveness to Renaissance humanism by entering the Gutenberg fold relatively early. The era of the printing press unfolded decisively across the Romanian territories during the sixteenth century. Târgoviște, Sibiu, Brașov, Cluj, Oradea Mare, Alba Iulia, Abrud, Bucharest, Sebeș,

Orăștie, Iași, Snagov and Suceava were the sites of the first printing presses, producing over 400 printed books in just a few decades of activity.[38] It was also the result of a remarkable upsurge of originality in the art of books, related directly to Byzantine creation or resulting from it. The Slavonic manuscripts of Neamț, written on parchment and paper in the times of the successors of Alexander the Good and during the reign of Stephen the Great, were considered by Nicolae Iorga as some of the most beautiful Byzantine art ever created: 'Front pages of delicate artistry adorn them, and we even find expertly rendered portraits of kings and icons of saints. These represent progress in this domain unknown until the seventeenth century.'[39] The art of Western books also influenced public taste: in Eastern Europe, beautiful books with engravings printed in Italy, France and Germany were in circulation, some of which were bought in the sixteenth and seventeenth centuries and preserved to this day in the great libraries.[40] Similar high standards can be observed in Russia, Greece and throughout the Balkan Peninsula, where the development of the printing press led to a varied production of books printed in Greek, Slavonic and Romanian. It is worth mentioning in passing that Russia in the time of Ivan III maintained permanent ties with the West through the towns of Novgorod and Pskov. These conditions gave rise to an excellent translation of the Bible into Slavonic church language by Archbishop Gennady of Novgorod, and encouraged the activity of two great personalities, Maximus the Greek and Vassian Patrikeev.

Spiritual convergences with Western centres entirely transformed aspects of culture in Poland, Hungary, Croatia and Dalmatia. For example, urban life in Poland looked especially towards the towns of Germany and the Netherlands, embracing basic elements of the educational system, architecture or certain methods and tendencies in the humanist and natural sciences. The aristocratic world of Hungarian and Polish royal and ecclesiastical courts, as well as those of the Balkans and Russia, showed a special interest in Italian architecture and art. As Răzvan Theodorescu writes:

> The morphological and decorative reception of the Italian Renaissance in Central and Eastern Europe in the fifteenth and sixteenth centuries is in itself a very interesting chapter in the cultural history of these parts of the world. The coexistence of Tuscan forms, very pure and 'modern', and of Lombard forms, more decorative and paying greater tribute

to the medieval tradition, in the same monument – which is the above-mentioned Transylvanian chapel in Alba Iulia, at the beginning of the sixteenth century – as well as the local transformation of Italian forms and methods – the case of the Florentine tomb with a niche in Poland or that of the court with arcades in Moravia – all prove the selective and creative spirit of culture in this part of the continent. In this perspective, the best example clearly remains that of Russia, where the northern Italian forms of Milan and Bologna first of all, will lead, before and after 1500 to the building of a Muscovite Kremlin *italico more*, sheltering churches and palaces with forms and exterior details which are tributaries to the Renaissance decorative repertoire, but with specific and traditional structures coming out of the Russian Middle Ages...[41]

Let us expand on at least one of the above-mentioned points. In Central and Central-Eastern Europe there was a direct influence; furthermore, these constructions were all raised under the same Catholicism. In the East, though, influences were adapted to the region's own thinking and forms of religious expression. In order to define this phenomenon, the case of the Roman Catholic Cathedral of Alba Iulia is significant. This example will help us perceive the differences correctly. This place of worship, in architectural and other respects, is synchronous with the West. It combines a mosaic of elements in the Gothic, Renaissance and Baroque styles and a distillation of the medieval-ancient spirit, and as such is both conservative and innovative at the same time. The church welcomes the ideas of Homo Novus, yet without jeopardizing its position. And in order to make us understand that it is protecting itself against all attempts at reform, it constructs, or rather reconstructs, itself. The thick walls of Alba Iulia Cathedral give the sensation of a bastion, a fortified symbol of power with the desire to extend its domination: to impose and to protect the Catholic faith. The stained-glass windows – beautiful artistic representations in myriad colours, genuine stone lacework, all executed with the skill of an artisan and the work of a Benedictine monk – create the impression of battlements, and in some cases even possess the classic form of crenellations, as if they were carved in the walls protecting a fortress. Yet there is a false modesty in all this grandeur: this towering edifice, with apparent openings through arches and arcades, lets in only a paltry amount of sunshine, just enough to ensure that the believer knows his place before the priest – an effective scheme to manipulate conscience. There is meaning to everything you see here, something barely discernible to the eye – a *Deus absconditus*, a blocking of the way, a removal from nature, something outside natural human reality. An apparent opening matched by a definite closing, something cold and foreign to the human soul is emitted by these bastions raised by the Roman Church on the eve of the great crisis. This fear was to be justified by the Reformation, but here it is an intimation, hardly a categorical attitude of rejection or a misunderstanding of that world.

In order to illustrate the echo of the Renaissance, it is worth mentioning that in Balkan towns there was significant cultural activity in the form of printing or copying of Cyrillic books. The restoration of demolished churches and monasteries brought about renewed circulation of ecclesiastical books, with works taken up again by lay copyists (in great numbers) who were to develop a type of literary reproduction promoted by members of the clergy, but also by the prosperous citizens of Balkan towns, especially artisans. At the beginning of the sixteenth century, Bojidar Vuković laid the foundations of a printing house in Venice, which was then continued by his son, Vicenko Vuković. The books printed by Vuković – as we are informed by a Yugoslav researcher who recreated this aspect of cultural life on the basis of the few remaining documentary sources[42] – were sold in the Balkan regions of the Turkish Empire, in Belgrade, Vidin and Nikopolos, often via Ragusan merchants. Around 1550, Prince Radisa Dmitrović founded a printing house in Belgrade, which was run by the Ragusan Traian Gundulović. In 1563, Ștefan Marinović built a printing house in Skadar, as did Kotor nobleman Jerolim Zagulović. At the same time, in Skopje, one of the first bookshops of the Southern Slavic region opened, the property of Kara Trifun, followed by others in Vidin, Belgrade, Târgoviște and Drenopolje.

These facts are proof of a form of resistance to Southeastern European orthodoxy, of the resolute desire for emancipation in the spirit of the Balkan peoples, of the unity of belief and soul which was preserved, through the system of relations constantly maintained by believers. In the immediate vicinity, in Croatia, a region linking Central and Southeastern Europe, the system of European cultural values would be embraced, too, perhaps faster than in the other parts of the Southern Slavic world, most probably due to its direct reception of German Protestantism. During the sixteenth century, a heated conflict of religious beliefs took place there, a compelling example of the Croats' tendency to enter the European limelight in the context of their struggles for freedom, independence and human dignity. In Matija Vlačić Ilirik, Croatia had a personality who became caught up in reformist struggles and whose activities made the major ideas that were to assure the evolution of the region's community known to the West. A professor of Greek at the University of Wittenberg, Vlačić was considered a man of erudition, a scholar, bolstered by references to him by Luther and Melanchthon. History played a significant role in his extensive writings – he focused on conflicts of ideas, which he studied at the highest historical level, tracing the important lines in the development of humanity. Vlačić referred to his country as an ancient fortress facing the West, and the Illyrian language as one of the four important languages of the world. The most important book by Vlačić and indeed of all Southern Slavic Protestantism is *Rasgovoranje megiu papistu i gednim luteran* (*Conversation between a Papist and a Lutheran*), which was published in Tübingen in 1555 under the pseudonym Antun Sejanin.[43]

These are significant moments in Central and Eastern European cultural history, periods which stimulated the circulation of the great works and ideas of the sixteenth century. Undoubtedly, this dialogue between West and East, which first took place from the perspective of Homo Religiosus, generated not only knowledge but also much confusion. In Western Europe, the process reached its climax during this century, while in the East the great crisis, triggered to a large extent by the same religious conflict, did not occur until the second half of the seventeenth century. We should also note, however, that the mechanisms were set in motion (to various degrees of intensity) not only in a political context, but in the sphere of religion and culture – witnessing the assertion of a new European conscience.

Along these lines, the universal idea of Erasmus regarding the destiny of Europe was also embraced by intellectuals from the eastern half of the continent. To cite one of the best examples, Central and Eastern Europe communicated from one end to the other by means of the letters of Nicolaus Olahus and his intellectually fruitful travels across the continent through Brussels, Louvain, Besançon, Madrid, Milan, the Vatican, Vienna, Tirnava, Bratislava and Buda.[44] As early as 1527–38 Olahus acquired the Western world's spirituality and the accomplishments of Homo Europaeus – he read in Latin and Greek, studied the most important works of literature, historiography and ancient philosophy, and expressed Enlightenment in his work. He wrote historical and geographical works, of which *Hungaria* is the most famous. Contact with great scholars instilled in him a complex understanding of the forms of life and thought in the Europe of his times. He cultivated friendships with humanists Hadrianus Amerotius, Levinus Franciscus Craneveldius and, inevitably, the 'peerless' Dutchman Erasmus Desiderius. For Olahus, as for all these famous men of culture, letters were a sure guarantee of the soul, to be kept among their most treasured possessions. But let us allow the Transylvanian humanist to describe relations of this type, this communication from a distance, in his own words:

> The administrator of our community handed me, most learned Levinus, your letter, proof of our recently commenced friendship and of our brotherly love. Your letter appealed very much to me, not only because you ask my trust, as true friends do, something that seems to be in the interest of your order, but also because in it you show me the strong desire you have finally to see our dear Erasmus.

On another occasion, Levinus Ammonius[45] presents us with an identical situation to that of the Romanian scholar, as if not wanting to betray the new belief, the new ideal of culture and moral education that gripped the entire generation of European humanists:

> My heart leapt with joy, on the one hand at the sight of your letter, most brilliant and eminent man, on the other at the long-awaited news it bore from our friend Panagathus, since it is clear that, if nothing goes wrong (which I hope the Lord above will ensure), it will be a matter of only a few days before we see Erasmus. For these tidings I am of course, greatly indebted to you, because you filled me with so much happiness, knowing how much I wish to see him back in his country from exile.[46]

What brought them close together was a certain type of trust, a tone of friendship, a feeling of harmony between souls. Olahus was a prime example of this tendency. It is not by chance that the prince of humanists considered his name to be synonymous with the notion of friendship. In general, Erasmus considered him *optimus et eruditissimus omnium doctorum patronus* (best and most learned patron of all men of letters). He was certainly a great supporter of all men of learning around him, and in this role fostered the production of great literature.

The correspondence between Erasmus and Olahus is proof of a great enthusiasm for culture and learning. Their letters communicate a wealth of information on literature, an immense love of truth, an extraordinary faith in man's capacity for good, in mankind's destiny. They glimpsed a great era of metamorphoses unfolding, in which reason was to become the leading force in society, and they observed how, imperceptibly, through creative dynamism, mankind was renewing itself. I would say – extending Huizinga's statement[47] – that, in the case of Erasmus and Olahus, fantasy is almost always accompanied by sobriety, taking us to the essence of the Renaissance itself. If the aesthetic perfection of Erasmus' work places it alongside that of Rabelais, it is no less true that through his work, in particular his historical works (translations of the Greek and Latin classics), Olahus is an important personality of the times in whom we can see the transition to modern European thinking taking place. He is one of the series of famous humanists whose sound sense, sincere spirit and devotion to the good of mankind determined Erasmus to set his hopes on the fact that out of such men will 'the golden generation of mortals be formed'. As Erasmus wrote:

> I myself was born with an open disposition and I enjoy the friendship of honest men, as it seems you are, as I clearly understood from your letters and from those related by my friend Quirinus,[48] so that there was no more need for your small attentions, which are otherwise very pleasant and to my liking. The features of Olahus have been impressed upon my heart so deeply, that they can no longer be taken out or wiped away; still, it gave me great pleasure to see your repeated solicitude, which, I realize, comes from the fullness of your love. Just as that spoon and fork that you sent me pleased me, thinking, of course, that I shall have my dear Nicolaus Olahus at my table, and that I shall always be able to tell my dear friends: this is my dear Olahus, as long as destiny will deny us the joy of being together.[49]

In light of this, it seems in no way far-fetched to say that relations between Erasmus and the cultural society of Central-Eastern Europe were based on friendship, communication and communion, but also on inner equilibrium and reason, dominant features of humanist societies. This great friendship can be associated with worship of his books, which had been circulated in the East-Central European cultural sphere ever since they had first been printed. This was the case with *Adagiorum*, *Colloquia familiaris*, *Querela pacis*, *Encomium moriae* and many others.

Let us state, at the end of this set of examples – themselves fragments of a vast history – that Hellenism also had an important voice in the birth of the Enlightenment in Central and Eastern Europe, as well as in Southeastern Europe. The Greek intellectual Renaissance was due to the stimulus coming from the West, to the contact established by Greeks with Europe in general. Westerners showed an increasing interest in the traditions of Antiquity, greater curiosity for the sources of knowledge, for the study of the Latin language, for the language and literature of the ancient Greeks. These great treasures were not to be found in the West, however, but in the monasteries and libraries of the Hellenic east, which persuaded the French and Italians to organize expeditions, to create 'missions', as Dimaras calls them in his *History of Neo-Hellenic Literature*. In this context, a Hellenist spirit reawakens 'that will have to rely on the West, to be bound to it organically, or else await its end'. We will come back to Neo-Hellenism when we attempt to identify the extent to which it was implied in European spirituality in the seventeenth and eighteenth centuries, establishing how it was represented in literature, historiography and philosophy when it appeared at the dawn of the age of Enlightenment in Central and Southeastern Europe.

In the eastern region of Europe, due to the overwhelming prestige of Constantinople, the 'Byzantine model' imposed itself in all areas of civilization, contributing to the creation of distinct characteristics of monastic life and art, its own types of institutions, and well-known 'Monastic Republics'. The most renowned of these was Mount Athos, a truly international centre continuing the cenobitical tradition of Constantinople's great cultural focal point, the Monastery of Stoudios. We might recall that Constantinople, which in the sixteenth century had 400 mosques, numerous public gardens, schools and libraries, was compared by Western travellers with Saint-Germain or Orléans. It was a city of wealthy people, its harbour most often used by Western ships, it was the meeting point of Jewish merchants, and its citadel was built in the Frankish style and inhabited by Latin and Greek traders. It would be no exaggeration to liken the world of Constantinople, at least in certain influences, to the European model, thus demonstrating the impact of European civilization on the Islamic world, and the temptation of an opening towards Europe represented by this important commercial, political and spiritual city of the southeastern corner of the continent. It was inevitable that, through the activities of the Greeks and the Jews, this city would forge European aspirations, and maintain economic, financial, commercial and political (and therefore cultural) relations with the West.

The Balkans comprised more levels of civilization, of which the most obvious are the rural and the urban. What is certain is that, in the Middle Ages, the Southeast was a world with a distinct manner of thinking, a special kind of everyday life, with its songs, habits, virtues and vices, in other words, a society that, beginning in the fifteenth century, immediately after the Turkish conquest, came under the influence of Levantine civilization.[50] Central-Eastern Europe also offers brilliant examples of the path taken by its communities in the period of transition to the new historical era. Its medieval-modern civilization can be studied by taking a closer look at the regions of Croatia, Slovenia, Hungary, Banat and Transylvania, as well as the city ports of the Adriatic Sea, where Ragusa was a privileged centre linking Islam and Christianity. Everything points to the originality of this border 'area'. As Fernand Braudel states:

> Its Catholicism is a religion of battle, confronted with the Orthodox world which menaces it from the height of the mountains and with the great Turkish danger. If Dalmatia, despite so many transformations, remains faithful to Venice, as Lamansky noticed so long ago, the explanation is that, beyond Seniority, its fidelity addresses Rome and the Catholic Church. Even a town like Ragusa, so preoccupied with its own interests, situated at once amidst the Ottoman and Orthodox worlds, living, in fact, in the midst of a heretical and unbelieving population, possesses an amazing Catholic fervor. Its religious convictions would be as interesting to study as its economic structures, interests mixing – and why not – with the most spiritual of impulses... Geography, politics, economy, civilization, religion, all contribute to the founding of a homogeneous Adriatic world. And this world overflows the limits of

the sea, penetrates deep inside the Balkan continent up to the essential limit between Latinity and the Greek world.[51]

As I have stated, Croatia, Serbia and Banat may be considered the main points where the Central-Eastern and Southeastern European ways of thinking converge. This region includes elements of *Mitteleuropa*, as well as characteristics of the Balkans, Islam, the Hebrew Orient, Southeastern sentimentality, as well as the Southern temperament of Mediterranean origin and the culture and traditions of the Germanic North. There is the less rigorous and more tolerant Orthodoxy, as well as Catholicism and Protestantism, which in their widespread forms allowed for the extension of Western thought to this part of the continent. In the case of Banat, for example, I have observed its historic destiny as a region of spiritual interpenetration between Romanians, Germans, Serbs, Hungarians, Jews, Slovaks, Turks, Bulgarians and Gypsies, bringing with it a *sui generis* image of the transitional zone between Western and Eastern Europe.

This, then, was a period of extreme complexity, its unprecedented contradictions the result of social, political and religious movements. Educated people, admirers of art and culture existed in ever greater numbers, while, at the same time, the number of religious fanatics, of dissenters, of nihilists, all increased. Thus, the sixteenth century presents us with a cast including Erasmus, More, Olahus, Mountjoy, Henry VIII of England, Francis I of France, Juan Luis Vives and the popes of those times, Luther, Zwingli and Calvin. As Ortega y Gasset says, this century witnessed one of the most formidable generations of all time, but as it asserted itself two currents emerged, led by Erasmus and Luther, announcing a spectacular separation. The contrast was defined most expressively by Nietzsche:

> The Italian Renaissance contained virtually all the positive forces to which modern intellectual civilization owes its existence... The German Reformation came as an energetic protest of backward spirits, insatiable for medieval ideas and that, instead of rejoicing, as it should have, in the signs of its coming apart and of a religious life more and more superficial and external, experienced great discontent. With their energy and their Northern obstination, they flung mankind back, they forced on the Counter-Reformation, meaning a Catholic Christianity of a state of siege. They delayed by two

or three centuries the awakening and reign of sciences. They made for ever impossible the union of ancient thought and modern thought.[52]

Humanism and Reformation were as one at their origins. It was the representatives of the end of the sixteenth century that ushered in the fever for religious conversion and propaganda. The people of those times imposed on themselves devoted respect for the ancient doctrines, even when these only had the value of opinions. Initially, they had lacked a critical attitude, a scientific method, rigour, balance. Inaugurating, after a time, historical and philological criticism, humanism took the path of Biblical exegetes, discovering Homer, Aristotle and Plato in their original texts, later re-establishing the authentic text of the Bible and proving that some of the fundamental dogmas of the Church (the Immaculate Conception, for example) were based on errors of translation. Essential changes took place in thought, in belief, the classifications or analyses of sacred books being the key to an interpretation that the disciples of the Reformation were to use.

I have tried to outline here a few of the defining elements of the period of great transitions, and to take another look at a world, rich in ideas, that brought about the age of the Enlightenment, in a sense paving the way for the continuation of our journey. Reassessing that historical age in terms of the efforts of human intelligence, I have rediscovered how, slowly, a strong crisis of conscience gripped Europe. Seen in terms of a dialogue, but as an indestructible unity, the continent at this early phase of modern life doubtless possessed common elements. As I have said, the means differ, as well as the intensity, duration and the time when they occurred – but these are the only differences. It is the direction in which mankind is going that is of keenest interest, the way it anticipates the future, with greater or lesser clarity, what decisions it makes at crucial moments. I am focusing on this in order to recreate life at the dawn of an existence based on so-called modern principles, and also because at any given moment we stand before convictions that are more or less radical – and we are among the objects of those convictions. I will therefore say, along with Ortega y Gasset, that I will seek to demonstrate how the articulation of convictions transforms our chaotic circumstances into the unity of a world or of the universe.[53] We will come to realize this truth while continuing to analyze the Central-Southeastern region under the manifestation of the great crisis and tempted by Homo Europaeus, the deliverer of modernity.

III

RELIGIOUS REFORM AND THE CRISIS OF CONSCIENCE: FROM THEOPHILOS CORYDALLEUS TO DIMITRIE CANTEMIR

What gives the value of man is not the truth he possesses: it is the sincere effort he makes to approach it. For it is not through the possession, but through the search for truth that the forces bringing us towards perfection increase.

G. E. Lessing

'THE REFORMATION CONTINUES TO REFORM,' said Richard Simon, a contemporary of this time of transition.[1] Even countries that had a single religion over time – such as Italy, France and England – were to experience, once the Reformation began, great differences in both religious and political doctrine. We can better understand the intimate manifestations of this phenomenon by studying the Central, Eastern and Southeastern European world, which possessed great richness and diversity of ideas. Although the region emerged later and asserted itself slowly, its pageantry was just as exciting as the collective Western system of ideas, as has been ably illustrated by the studies of Lucien Febvre, Paul Hazard, Fernand Braudel, Jean Delumeau and others.[2] There is no doubt that common elements can be glimpsed, and that the basic problems of existence and thinking demonstrated by Eastern European society were similar to those experienced in the West – only that they were voiced by other souls and minds, by specific personal experiences and means of expression. It is no accident that the means and indeed the experiences themselves were often different, while the goal remained the same – namely, the changing of the system of values. The intellectual revolution that took place in the decades after 1680 could also be perceived in the East. Here we may speak of a double crisis of conscience for the West, one accompanying the Renaissance and the other originating in the age of Enlightenment, while for Central and Southeastern Europe we can say that in the seventeenth century (and possibly even earlier) the governing intelligentsia had discovered many channels of communication with the world, entering into a dialogue with the humanism of the great Italian and German schools. Likewise in this region, which was relatively isolated, an important crisis of conscience would trigger a significant leap forward in the way of life, of thought, and of social organization.

The history of spiritual life leads us to observe that the aspirations of European Man won over communities east of Vienna. Contact and dialogue between East and West, once they became better known, offered a different picture of European cultural geography, and brought to light the old temptation of Homo Europaeus, who was present not only in the conscience of Westerners, including the Germans and Austrians of Central Europe, but also in the Greeks, Serbo-Croatians, Romanians, Bulgarians, Russians, Slovaks, Czechs, Poles, Hungarians and Slovenes in the East.

In the Southeast the transformations were mostly religious in character, besides the economic and social changes that moved at a slower pace. For the moment, however, let us focus on the time when we can clearly see the influence of mystic literature and the effects of an intense religious life. In the Middle Ages and at the dawn of the Modern Era, the Church wielded power that was at once dynamic and conservative. It exerted this authority over both the elite and the masses, controlling the direction of politics and culture – which themselves operated within the context of the old spiritual background – and thus enlarging its sphere of influence. Elements combined with the Church's authority were of Greco-Latin origin, as exemplified by the didactic works that already circulated (in the fourteenth and fifteenth centuries) throughout the Greek, Bulgarian, Serbian, Russian and Romanian territories. Across the region attempts were made to strengthen old Orthodox tendencies. In this context we encounter Hesychasm, a theological and philosophical doctrine including ad hoc ideas about man and his relationship with the world that perpetuated through successive ages, and left its mark on the collective *forma mentis*. Studying the genesis of the new literature in his country, Constantin T. Dimaras notes that Greek Orthodoxy, closing its eyes to reality, 'had remained with the reasoning of the times when the belief it defended was upheld and imposed by a strong empire'.[3] Mysticism was a clear symptom of the internal upheavals of a society and was not only characteristic of the Balkan world. A culture influenced by such theories will witness corresponding changes in the sciences of education, psychology, law, theology and so on.

Hesychasm (*hesychia* = quiet) was to exert a relatively strong influence, resulting in a series of actions that dominated people's thinking and directed their collective conscience. We can see this in various new emphases introduced by the Church: the development of religious songs; application of a strict system of worship including morning and evening prayers to be said at precise intervals; obligatory participation in the celebration of saints' feast days and long pilgrimages to holy places; fasting periods; erecting churches and monasteries through the efforts of believers; recovery of saints' relics; and finally, the intuitive presentation of Christian teachings and Biblical history. Hesychasm was complemented by numerous 'ascetic' sayings that encouraged a categorical refusal of the thinking of ancient wise men, going so far as to make popular the harmful saying, 'Blessed is the one that kills his willpower, reaching a state of indifference or of apathy.' The works through which the doctrine was disseminated were *The Ladder of Paradise* by John Climacus (whose name means 'of the Ladder'), the 'Hymns' of Ephrem the Syrian, *The Life of Saint John the New of Suceava* and, especially, the books of Gregory Palamas.[4] Through these intermediaries, religious doctrine attempted to promote certain characteristics that would change attitudes, ways of thinking and people's behaviour. One of Palamas' texts, translated and published by D. Stăniloaie,[5] is entitled *Word for those who gain peace through faith. The second to the last. About prayer* (*Cuvânt pentru cei ce se liniștesc cu evalavie. Al doilea din cele din urmă. Despre rugăciune*). The author holds prayer in high regard, yet eliminates anything standing between Man and God. In his view, only in this way can prayer remain composed and undisturbed:

> Those who have not reached this state (of no passion), but aim towards it, must surmount the passion of pleasure (the

sweet passion). But to do this one must kill completely all sinful tendencies of the flesh, which is to secure release from passion, and make one's thought stronger than the evil movements of passion in the world of reason, which is to surmount the passion of pleasure. And if it is so, as it is, while we are ruled by passion we are not able to taste the mind's prayer even by the word on the tip of our tongue, and we shall need to feel with our sense of touch the pain of fasting, of no sleep and other deprivations, if we want to take due care of our prayers.[6]

Palamas is right to a point, by discerning, on the one hand, the limits that stem from passions of the flesh, and on the other hand, the possibility to raise and surpass oneself through the spirit. Asceticism, as advocated in all Hesychastic thinking, plays its role in the entering of a state of communication with the divinity. It is no less true that a long fast (at various points Palamas says, 'Fasting is to a certain extent the essence of prayer', 'The matter of prayer is hunger' and 'Hunger is the quality of prayer') leads to the body's destruction, diminishing willpower and the impossibility of reaching the light. And if I were to risk an explanation, free of any dogma, I would say that fasting is just a means, and hardly a goal, or the essence. Palamas proposes 'release from passion', but in his letters to the monastery of Varlaam, he displays considerable passion himself.

The purpose of my arguments is to understand better the double dimension of human beings, which is why I have tried to see the past as it was, continued in a present that is harder to falsify. Thus, if we consider Hesychastic thought in the context of what occurred in the past and then later in the collective way of thinking, I cannot help but notice some interaction between dogma and society. This interaction existed from the beginning and amplified with the passage of time, creating a way of existing as a *being*, where appearances count more than the essence.

The Christian conception of the world and life was not taken up by laymen in the same way as it was by the clergy: hence it manifested in each in different ways. We can also observe differences within the Church itself, and amongst intellectual believers, for example between conservatives in monastic circles and notable representatives of the Church. The case of Dositheos II, the Orthodox Patriarch of Jerusalem, is one of the best known – a remarkable example of superior understanding of the political and cultural destiny of Eastern and

Southeastern Europe. His interventions in political life in Bucharest, Iași and Moscow were intended not only to maintain ecclesiastic authority or stress its supremacy, but to combat subjection to the State, spread the benefits of the printing press and raise peoples' general cultural level.[7]

The movement of ideas in the sixteenth and seventeenth centuries was by no means limited to religious thinking – it was much richer, often embracing the production of lay history books, textbooks on moral and political education and the science of learning, music texts, even works on medicine, mathematics and astronomy. 'The Teachings of Neagoe Basarab to his son Theodosie' and, later, 'The Teachings of Petru Movilă to his brother Moise, King of Moldavia'[8] are two good examples of a series of writings promoting reason, proving the coexistence of many different forms of expression, all of which had a commanding presence in this part of Europe. It is still religious thinking, but in a rational form where previously formed truths are subject to reasoning because morality is based on a more understanding attitude towards man. The many confluences with the East, with its traditions – and the reception of influences coming from Renaissance and post-Renaissance Italy, the challenging of the intellectual system championed by medieval scholastics or the pre-modern Reformation – create an equilibrium that we will attempt to consider in understanding the essence of spirituality in this part of the world. It is the same point of view we adopted in emphasizing the significance of the Byzantine influence, the role of the Byzantine school, of 'Byzantium after Byzantium' in European cultural life.

Let us examine additional aspects that will allow us correctly to re-evaluate the history of ideas. During the time after the Reformation and Counter-Reformation, in Central-Eastern Europe there were new changes in religious life, including the unification of a part of the Orthodox Church with the Catholic Church that prompted a major crisis. Catholic propaganda generated by the Polish Kingdom was to have direct consequences for Eastern Europe in the last decades of the sixteenth century, putting great strain on Ukraine and Kiev, which were under Polish dominion. In 1596, members of the clergy, aristocracy and Orthodox faithful signed an act of union with Rome at Brest-Litovsk, Poland (present-day Belarus). Despite this, most of the population remained devoted to old beliefs, which led to a severe religious confrontation in the first half of the seventeenth century. These were the years in which Petru Movilă climbed the ladder of the

BYZANTINE AND POST-BYZANTINE TRADITIONS: THE NEO-HELLENIC DIASPORA IN EUROPE (15TH–18TH CENTURIES)

Byzantine culture spread first to Southeastern Europe and then the Eastern Slavic world, followed in the centuries after 1600 by an increased presence in German and Italian aristocratic circles. The Neo-Hellenic diaspora would play a fundamental role in spreading the great spiritual wealth preserved in the Athonite monasteries, the Orthodox Patriarchate and the School of Constantinople.

Church hierarchy, becoming in 1633 'Archbishop and Metropolitan of Kiev, Galicia and of all Russia'. During his leadership the fight of the Orthodox faithful was directed towards regaining freedom of religious beliefs and the right to found new churches, hospitals and printing presses.[9] For his followers, the danger of Catholic expansion in these historical and geographical conditions lay in the rapid modernization of the educational system and adoption of modern Western ideas, resulting in the constant temptation of European cultural values, encouraging the tendency to surmount one's own limits through intellectual effort and integration into the exchange of spiritual ideas taking place across the continent. Movilă's Academy, founded in Kiev, was not an isolated case. It had the character of a university, with a curriculum similar to those of Western institutions of higher learning, and indeed was considered 'the oldest modern Orthodox university', its light radiating over the entire Orthodox region of Eastern Europe. It also served as a sign of, and not an exception to, the consequences of the religious wars.

The first document mentioning 'the Catholic organization of the Wallachians' is dated 1633 and contains the decree of the *Congregation for the Propagation of the Faith* (or *Propaganda Fide*) – this was, in fact, in the written minutes after the decision taken in the Northern Carpathians. The document states:

> The eminent Cardinal Ubaldini reviewed the decree of the *Congregation of Propaganda Fide* regarding the promise made to the Wallachians... promoting the Ukrainian priest Nicephorus to the rank of bishop and delegating him to assist Bishop Simion, old and burdened with infirmity. The Sacred Congregation ordered that the German Nuncio be written to, so that he may discuss this with the Emperor and ask his opinion, especially regarding the fulfilment of Simion's promise and the problems that might arise, as well as the way that they might be solved, so that the goal may be reached.[10]

In Transylvania, the aforementioned union with the Roman Church, which came about at the end of the seventeenth century, triggered a heightening of Romanian national conscience. Vienna, like Rome, considered that unifying the Romanians could play a decisive role on the empire's borders, where Catholicism mingled with Orthodoxy, and it was not by accident that it began a vast propaganda effort to convert the Orthodox masses.[11] This undertaking roughly coincided with the Counter-Reformation, and its agents were the same: the Jesuits. The First Leopoldine Diploma of 1699 proclaiming the union includes not only Romanians but Greeks and Ukrainians from Hungary, Croatia, Slovenia and Transylvania. The act signed by the Orthodox clergy in Transylvania was reissued three times, which explains the difference of opinion over the conditions of acceptance – on the one hand the claims of the Romanians and, on the other, the new state of matters adroitly and successfully imposed by officials. Through the Act of Vienna on 7 April 1701, Bishop Atanasie recognized religious unification and submission to Rome, qualified by certain political clauses.[12] Naturally, union with the Roman Church was in Austrian political interests, and became a useful tool for the Hapsburgs. David Prodan evaluates this crisis of conscience correctly:

> The unification is still uncertain. The masses continue to resist. Confusion reigns. As long as their rites are unchanged, the peasants see no difference between *unified* and *non-unified*; most cannot say to which sect they belong. Their priests contribute, of course, to this disarray, because they do not always admit their beliefs to their followers. Often they are not sure themselves, they waver from one to another, depending on the situation and their interests.[13]

Putting this event into perspective, unification enabled people to assert themselves: their struggles generated crisis but also enlightenment, preparing the way for modern life.

The models offered by Southeast European literature and history in the seventeenth century and at the beginning of the eighteenth enable us to confirm that common traits have their origins in 'the unity of civilization and of historical destiny' and 'hardly in ethnic or linguistic unity'.[14] Historical studies and documents referring to the region's cultural life give sufficient conclusive examples of a dialogue within the Southeastern and Central-Eastern region, as well as between Eastern and Western Europe. Of course, this evidence should not be interpreted schematically, as there are multiple interconnections and these various tendencies have many meanings. What I want to stress, in fact, is the ideas that generated similarities. Relations with Europe (which in the Western sense of the word in the seventeenth century extended to Vienna) and the way that writings, ideologies, political and religious concepts could be accessed, won over the intellectuals of politically inferior peoples. In this way, the cultural life of the Principality of Transylvania witnessed a true blossoming of spirits and embarked on a permanent dialogue with Central and Western Europe. Economic consolidation was closely followed by cultural emancipation, the rule of Gabriel Bethlen and Francis I and II Ráckóczi creating new, modern institutions of European origin. Religion, of course, played a very important role in this new state of affairs. Calvinism, widespread in Transylvania in the seventeenth century, was embraced at the princes' court, directing it towards Central-Western Europe. Most likely, modern ideas circulating in colleges, government and legislation were primarily due to this phenomenon. Let us not forget, however, that Calvinism occasionally provoked dissatisfaction and protests within Orthodoxy, the Romanian clergy adopting a critical attitude when Protestant expansion impinged on the Eastern Church's faithful. After implementing a vast building programme, strengthening the fortresses in Oradea, Alba Iulia, Făgăraş, Deva, Gherla, Odorheiu Secuiesc and Giurgiu, and constructing new castles and princely courts, Bethlen devoted his energy to organizing the education system and founding schools, among them the famous Collegium Academicum, first active in Alba Iulia between 1622 and 1658. The prince ensured that many young people were sent abroad: over one thousand Transylvanians studied in the great universities of Germany, Switzerland, Holland, England, France and Italy during his reign, while professors from German universities were invited to teach at the Collegium Academicum, among them the famous poet Martin Opitz.[15] Bethlen's cultural policy increased the number of learned men whose job was to 'serve the country in many important matters'.[16] The old school of Alba Iulia was expanded and raised to the level of higher German schools, which necessitated the foundation of a proper library. Bethlen himself was a great lover of books – a *liberalissimus litterarum* [most generous supporter of learning] and *litteratorum Maecenas* [patron of men of letters], as Enlightenment scholar Petru Bod calls him[17] – and his collection formed the basis for the Collegium's library, which has been compared with Matthias Corvinus' library in Buda. Partially destroyed in 1658, it rose again in Aiud in 1662, together with the College itself. Historian Zsigmond Jakó is correct when he asserts that the collection's organization and direction met the strict criteria of foreign specialists and created a unique cultural centre, European in content and form.[18] Later, in the context of the Enlightenment in

Transylvania and Central-Eastern Europe more widely, the Reformed college and library of Aiud became an important centre for contact with European spirituality.

Further examples are provided by the achievements of Matei Basarab and Vasile Lupu, voivodes in Wallachia and Moldavia respectively. Under their rule, printers became active for the first time since the end of the sixteenth century. This marks the foundations of humanist culture in the Romanian principalities, a period when historiography and learning flourished, and beautiful secular and Church architecture was built. Matei Basarab founded thirty monasteries, courts and churches, and rebuilt the princely court in Târgoviște.[19] Encouraged by Varlaam, Metropolitan of Moscow, Vasile Lupu founded an Academy in Iași and asked Metropolitan Petru Movilă of Kiev to send learned professors, among them Sofronie Pociațki, former rector of the Kiev Academy, who was appointed Professor of Latin literature and became a clergyman at the Three Hierarchs (Trei Ierarhi) Church. At this time, Moldavia was home to academic activity in Greek, Slavonic and Latin, as well as theology, philosophy, rhetoric, poetics, dialectics, arithmetic, geometry, astronomy, grammar and music. Meanwhile, Metropolitan Varlaam's scholarship led to the creation of the printing press of Three Hierarchs: his *Sermons* contributed to the development of standard Romanian, and his *Answer to the Calvinist Catechism*[20] encouraged Romanian Orthodoxy in Transylvania to resist the spread of Calvinism. This forceful reaction was symptomatic of a religious war that had begun in the West a century earlier, and in the middle and second half of the seventeenth century extended to Eastern Europe, heralding an era of change. The struggle between Reformation and Counter-Reformation provided the catalyst for the initiatives taken by the Romanian rulers: Matei Basarab's programme of reform, for example, was influenced by the Slavonic humanist culture professed by his wife Elena and her brother Udriște Năsturel. As historical sources attest, the Wallachians now lay the foundations of higher learning, such as the celebrated Schola Graeca et Latina of Târgoviște, created with the help of agents of the Counter-Reformation, in addition to the school at Cotnari, founded by Iacob Heraclid (also known as Despot Vodă) in response to the Protestant threat. Both are the expression of a movement against the Ottoman economic system.[21] This was an erudite, philological form of humanism. It offered Greek and Latin, languages much cultivated by the champions of the new current of thought, despite the fact that the principal written language of Southeastern Europe was Slavonic. In the conclusion to his study of Udriște Năsturel's humanism, Virgil Cândea notes as follows:

> Through Slavonic, our culture had come into contact with the Greek and Byzantine writers of late Antiquity. Again through Slavonic, Aristotle and other Greek authors had become known to scholars in our country in the fourteenth to sixteenth centuries. The innovation for which Udriște Năsturel fought was the use of 'pagan' writers in support of Orthodox ethics in search of a new authority.[22]

Personalities such as Năsturel ushered in a cultural rebirth which paved the way for the notable Romanian families of Cantacuzino, Brâncoveanu and Cantemir.

In Russia there was the great civilization of Novgorod, with its churches, monasteries and walls, its age-old Slavic traditions and ethical codes, and its efforts to internalize spiritual life. Although Novgorod was entering its twilight years, its community of humanists – men of culture, artists, politicians and theologians of the highest calibre – continued to exert a powerful influence which was rediscovered in the times of Peter the Great, when the famous city-state handed over to Petersburg and the new Russia. The Novgorod clerical school, with its professors of Slavic, Greek and Latin, played an important role in Eastern Europe. Indeed, Novgorod enjoyed a period of continuity following the great events that had affected the North, and its art, receptive to the Western Renaissance, influenced the artistic destiny of modern Russia.[23]

In the Balkans, while the Bulgarians and Serbs believed in Russia's liberating mission,[24] the extraordinary achievements of the Greeks during the eighteenth century created the conditions for the Enlightenment to reach Southeastern Europe. These activities also prepared the region's communities for a reform that, while it pretended to be a question of dogma, spread ideas of economic and political freedom, and above all an intense cultural life. The Neo-Aristotelianism introduced in the royal Academies of Bucharest and Iași was an early indicator of freedom from inflexible Orthodox dogma. The new way of thinking, considered heretical by the Patriarchate in Constantinople, was applied in Greece and the Romanian principalities by the followers of the well-known philosopher Theophilos Corydalleus.[25] 'The Neo-Aristotelianism of Cesare Cremonini', the historian Victor Papacostea argues, 'prepared the ground for the work of Theophilos Corydalleus, whose courses at the "great school" of Constantinople paved the way for free thinking and especially materialism in European philosophy.'[26] Disciples of the famous Neo-Aristotelian philosopher were warmly welcomed north of the Danube, the royal Academies having helped to bring young intellectuals closer to the great universal culture. The role played by Theophilos Corydalleus in Southeastern Europe, as well as in Russia, was immense: his thinking was known during his lifetime through his philosophical works, which were circulated in manuscript copies, but especially through the aforementioned Academies of Bucharest and Iași, universities of a genuinely European standard. Cleobule Tsourkas, the Greek historian who studied the life and work of Corydalleus, compared the special role of Bucharest and Iași in the Orthodox East to that of Florence and Padua for Western humanism in the fourteenth and fifteenth centuries.[27]

This new and influential current of thought was born in Padua, where Corydalleus had attended the university and the materialist climate of the Greco-Italian thalassocracy had developed. In general, reforms in the Southeast owed much to the University of Padua and Venetian printing presses – the statement that 'Venice was the gate through which the Reformation entered the Balkan Peninsula'[28] was impressed upon his students, the majority of whom were priests, bishops, patriarchs and professors, and indeed Venice enabled the ideas of this last great Aristotelian to be disseminated widely. He does not merely cite Aristotle's work, but classifies and comments on it. His most important studies are *Introduction to Logic*, *Comments on Metaphysics*, *Comments on the Treatise About the Spirit*, *Comments on the Treatise About the Heavens*, *Introductory Course on Aristotle's Physics*, *The Creation and Corruption According to Aristotle* and *Comments and Questions Including all of Aristotle's Work*. His observations tend to be personal and independent. It was principally due to Corydalleus' writings, and currents of thought in the West, that Aristotle's philosophy came to dominate Southeastern Europe: though he is still relatively unknown in the West, his independent approach to religious thinking marked a significant development in the spiritual reconnection of East and West on the eve of the Enlightenment.

Corydalleus is unquestionably a Homo Europaeus, his discourses firmly established among the most important works of his day. Let us take a closer look at the analyses and interpretations he offers in his books. His exegesis represents a rediscovery of the philosophical reasoning and scientific character of Aristotle's work, qualities that Corydalleus considered essential to the needs of secular culture. He had no intention of founding a university to promote the thinking of Plato or any other philosopher, considering that Aristotle's philosophy alone was capable of informing other disciplines and sciences, and thereby forming the basis of a complete system of education.[29] Instead, Corydalleus' aim was to introduce a logical method of presenting Aristotelian thought and enable people to understand its relevance, providing interpretations, definitions, classifications and summaries that would cement Aristotle's status as a philosopher of the first importance:

> Nothing is more beneficial to man's material existence, or more conducive to a joyful life, than the influence of philosophy upon those who participate in intellectual life and strive for the ideal of beauty. Similarly, a logical method duly applied by the scholar is the only means for him to access and appreciate philosophy. For this reason you, who so ardently wish to enter the temple of philosophy, need such a method. It will now be described in introductory outline, as befits your lack of experience and understanding. So that this synopsis may not lack clarity and merit, I have considered it appropriate to communicate ideas through questions and answers.[30]

Corydalleus argues that Aristotle's philosophy expresses the supreme faculty, the intellect, which can be divided into practical and theoretical intellect. He maintains that in the *Metaphysics*, the *practical* philosophy is the work, while the *theoretical* one is the truth behind it, stating that 'according to a first classification, the being, as long as it is cognisant, can be divided in two: material or sensitive and immaterial'.[31] This analysis can be compared to that of other great commentators, but is based on a model rather than being mere imitation. More of an exegesis than an original point of view, the work of Corydalleus is – as Constantin Noica has stated – an indispensable link in a particular stage of European culture. Corydalleus' opinions helped to bring the ancient philosopher back into Greek thought and to forge an independent system of thinking, freeing at least some of the intellectual community from the authority of Church dogmatism.

Corydalleus' work in *Introduction to Logic* and *Comments on Metaphysics* is important from a pedagogical point of view, and indeed all his writings are anchored in the new education system he conceived and to which he was extremely dedicated. It was a reaction to medieval scholastics, following centuries of darkness. His ideas were absorbed by his disciples at the University of Athens (which he founded), the Constantinople Academy and the Greek schools of Cephalonia and Zakynthos, enriching and reforming secular culture, and presenting Aristotelianism as a philosophy that can meet the needs of modern culture. His students – as his most important biographer, the historian Cleobule Tsourkas, informs us – became the intellectuals of a new society spread across a vast territory, from Constantinople to Bucharest and Iaşi. Corydalleus' writings, both those discovered in manuscript copies – in the Library of the Romanian Academy, the Library of Iaşi University and in Constantinople – and his two published works, *Introduction to Logic* and *Comments on Metaphysics*, are an important element in Greece's contribution to the history of ideas, and make a significant contribution to the interpretation of Aristotle's texts.

Corydalleus belongs to an era in which Neo-Hellenism was widely asserted; his impressive, systematic body work completes our picture of higher education in Europe. His teachings mark the starting point of modern thinking in Southeastern Europe, and his fame, even in those times of great crisis, spread far and wide from Athens and Constantinople, beyond the borders of the Turkish Empire, to the Slavic East, Central Europe and even Northern Italy, where some of his writings were published at the beginning of the eighteenth century.

The reawakening of the Southern Balkans was due not only to Corydalleus and the ideas he inspired, but to an impressive number of intellectuals, politicians and writers. Among the Greeks there was Cyril Lucaris, the Patriarch of Constantinople, who stimulated Enlightenment thinking by educating the faithful, founding printing houses and schools, and surrounding himself with the best Hellenic literature of the times. Then there were Corydalleus' students Panagiotis Nikousios, Eugene the Aetolian and Ioannis Caryofillis, whose works enable us to understand society's interests, feelings and ideals. Finally, there was Paisios Ligarides from Chios, a complex and controversial figure because of his contradictory views, but with an impressive grounding in theological and humanist thinking. During the struggles between the Reformation and Counter-Reformation in Eastern Europe Ligarides rose to prominence as the initiator and leader of the Schola Graeca et Latina in Târgoviște and, as an opponent of Corydalleus and his followers, founded the Academia Graeca, bringing back the old school of Plato.[32]

Right up to the beginning of the eighteenth century and the Enlightenment itself, Byzantine culture remained a powerful tradition. Its way of thinking was not dismantled and rejected in Southeastern Europe until much later, which appears to confirm the 'vitality of Byzantine principles', one of the decisive elements being 'the shift in thinking from empire to nation'.[33] This is true, but the 'vitality' was of a conservative nature, which also explains the reserve towards renewal.

A crisis of conscience was now in evidence on both sides of the continent. Homo Europaeus ranged far more widely than many historians have realized, and could be found not only in Oxford, London, Paris, Leiden, Rotterdam, Leipzig and the societies around these spiritual centres, but also in Buda and Pest, Cluj and Aiud, Târgoviște and Iași, Athens and Kiev. Although differences between West and East persisted and could be observed in religion, culture, political life and the mechanisms of daily life, once Central-Eastern Europe entered this phase of crisis there were parallels between the two. Europe was no longer a divided continent, one half of which was known while the other was shrouded in darkness, a phenomenon that continued into the ensuing Enlightenment.[34] The humanist ideal, the new view of the world – of history and the borders and relations between peoples – was expressed by all the great representatives of the Enlightenment,[35] from the masonic societies of Paris and Central Europe to intellectuals in Peter the Great's Russia, whose initial activities sprang from the Theological Academy of the Moldavian scholar Movilă.

Another example in the East was the Moldavian statesman and man of letters Dimitrie Cantemir, whose writings became known across the continent during the first half of the eighteenth century. The universal characteristics of Cantemir's work were recognized throughout Europe, establishing him as an important precursor of Enlightenment historiography. In the context of the great crisis moving across Europe from West to East, the philosopher prince attempted to understand the true sense of history and discover the causes that brought mankind into such a state of turmoil. He was concerned not only with the destiny of the Ottoman Empire but with humanity as a whole. Cantemir regards events from a historical point of view rather than attempting to anticipate the future: abandoning apocalyptic chronology, in the *Description of Moldavia* and *Chronicle of the Antiquity of Romano-Moldavo-Wallachians* he conducts a systematic study of Romanian origins and characteristics. This is even more emphatically the case in his famous *History of the Growth and Decay of the Ottoman Empire*, an acknowledged masterpiece of European historiography. Ample and erudite in its research, replete with valuable comparisons, criticisms and judgements, Cantemir's history represents an exceptional moment in the Eastern European Enlightenment, a famous name and work from the East contributing to the intellectual history of Europe as a whole. Cantemir was a truly modern Homo Europaeus who explained the structures, so little known at that time, of the Turkish Empire that had had such a profound impact on Europe.

Through a series of novel images, Cantemir reveals Ottoman civilization to us, as he does (as we will see later) in *The System of Mohammedan Religion*. His interweaving of religious and secular history familiarizes the reader with various aspects of Turkish customs, the limitations and strengths of specific traditions, social strata, and the political and religious hierarchy. Cantemir is aware that an accurate evaluation of Ottoman civilization requires balance between Mohammedan and Christian perspectives. He is convinced that a chronological history is not possible without continual comparison of dates from both calendars and an even-handed representation of Christian and Muslim descriptions of specific events: only thus can he provide the European reader with an informative account of an ethnic group originating in faraway Asia. His intention is to present a clear and truthful picture that not only will enable the Enlightenment intellectual to gain knowledge of the subject, but will also equip the man of culture to draw his own conclusions on the rise and fall of the Ottomans, and the changes in conscience that took place in Ottoman society at the end of the seventeenth century. As Cantemir states in his Preface:

> Having to present to the public the rise and fall of the Ottoman Empire from its very origins, it is incumbent on us to explain some important historical and genealogical facts on which all too often the great and serious historians of Christianity seem to err considerably. Among these, the most important role should be given to the comparison between the Christian era and the year of the Hegira: we

considered that by following the Mohammedan calculations we could explain this succession better. Secondly, the name and origin of the Turks should be studied. Finally, we will clarify the origin of the Ottoman succession that has for so long been at the head of the Turkish Empire (as it is often called). In this respect, if we were to declare that our views are without blemish or mistake, we would doubtless be accused of breaking the boundaries of human knowledge, and rightly so. For, since we cannot give an entirely perfect and error-free account of events that unfold before our very eyes, only a liar would dare to assert that he will provide all the 'facts', with no deviation from the truth, concerning history that unfolded so many centuries ago, at such a barbarous and uncivilized time (as was the case at the beginning of the Ottoman era). This will become apparent in our work, all the more since we will reveal and try to set right those things said and written inaccurately by many historians who were otherwise of great authority. And we leave it to the discerning reader to decide whether or not we have been more successful.[36]

This sensible and enlightened argumentation gives conclusive proof of the historian's mastery of his materials and the distinctly European spirit of his work, both of which explain the interest in his writing in the West.

The prince's political thinking 'is characteristic for the beginning of that century, which had been born under the sign of pre-Enlightenment rationalism, and was to end under Romantic influences.'[37] The twenty-two years Cantemir spent in Constantinople gave him a mature understanding of the history of the rise and fall of the Turkish Empire, but in particular they allowed him to reflect upon the times in which he lived, and to recognize the importance of a dialogue of ideas and culture between all Europeans. As one of the publishers and commentators of his work states:

Cantemir operates within the limits of formal Greek Orthodoxy, opposing the Catholic Purgatory (as he does in the *Divan*), but does not subscribe to the eschatological ideals of the traditional doctrine. This attitude is not an ostentatious one. Perhaps Cantemir himself did not realize its consequences, simply because he was unacquainted with the writings of

Dionysius the Areopagite, Gregory of Nyssa, Gregory Palamas and the other representatives of Greek Orthodoxy in its radical form.[38]

This is further convincing evidence that Hesychasm had become outdated, and that Southeastern European intellectuals were redirecting their thinking in ways that would have a crucial role in the development of the region's people. Cantemir's writings are anchored in Biblical precepts but contain new ideas: his analyses cover the composition of the soul, the spiritual and the material world, and describe the main characteristics of human behaviour. Ieremia Kakavelas, the Greek scholar who endorsed the publication of Cantemir's book *The Divan, or the Quarrel of the Wise Man with the World, or the Judgement of the Soul with the Body* (one of Cantemir's most widely known works), advises the Moldavian prince 'unto the love of learning and of wisdom', and recommends the authenticity of his spirit to the public: 'Wisdom will crown you, listing you in the book of its great heroes. May you live long, treasure of the Orthodox Church. May you continuously grow in wisdom in your ascent towards God and to the good of your peers. Amen.'[39]

Cantemir's ultimate aim is to enlighten his people: the dialogue of the Wise Man with the World in the *Divan* attempts to identify the meaning of human existence, to put education at the service of man's ideals, to light the way for the many not merely by imposing Biblical precepts, but by philosophical reasoning. Mediating between the two extremes of hedonism and religious asceticism, Cantemir communicates concepts aimed at fostering a love of wisdom. He is not a mere reformer of Greek Orthodox thinking, but successfully overcomes the crisis of conscience within the Greek Orthodox Church. He rejects mysticism and Greek Orthodox traditionalism without breaking with the fundamental Christian concepts that dominated Southeastern Europe at that time. Paying close attention to developments in Western Catholic society, the Romanian scholar understood and aligned himself with the Western rationalist tendency, without denying the originality of the Eastern secular and religious spirit. Cantemir was a key figure in the dialogue between East and West, wishing to contribute, as Theophilos Corydalleus had, to the emancipation of Moldavia through education. Ieremia Kakavelas praises his thinking and his spirituality, his mastery of rhetoric, the beauty he brings to the Moldavian dialect, his great learning and brilliant mind.[40] Written in both Romanian and Greek, the philosophical and ethical basis of the *Divan* appealed to both Romanian and Balkan society at the end of the seventeenth century and the beginning of the eighteenth.

One of Cantemir's most remarkable qualities was his broad understanding of all religions and their forms of expression. An opponent of radicalism, bigotry and superstition, he avoided narrow judgements and proved to be a thoroughly modern thinker. His study of the East instilled in him a newly balanced perspective on society, enabling him to free himself of medieval dogmatism, and thus to evaluate religious or ethnic changes fairly and objectively. 'Let us see right, and praise the good deed, be it of our greatest foe,' wrote Cantemir in *The System of Mohammedan Religion*, where he goes on to say of Turkish scientific learning:

All the great pleasures of human understanding and ingenuity, and the notion we generally refer to as science, are called *ilm* in Arabic. Their grasp of science is demonstrated by the know-ledge of the ancient Greeks, and what they said about it: for the Greeks acknowledged that it was from the Phoenicians and Egyptians (who are peoples of the Arab family and tribes) that they first learnt not only of the sciences, but also of letters.[41]

Cantemir also noted that once the Ottoman Empire had grown in strength, the arts and liberal sciences flourished, and that with the foundation of schools and academies in almost all of its cities – especially Constantinople, Adrianople, Brusa, Cairo, Babylon and Aleppo – Turkish communities blossomed, to the amazement of Western travellers.

Cantemir's overarching re-evaluation raised Southeastern European historiography from mere chronicling to the status of serious study, in which modern method and concepts prevailed and interpretation of the past was based on decisive documents and argu-ments. His work became well known to European intellectuals and his books were circulated from East to West, helping to encourage a deeper sense of a pan-European Homo Europaeus. Cantemir was already the object of high praise across Europe during the Enlightenment, and many articles and commentaries were dedicated to his work, while his *History of the Growth and Decay of the Ottoman Empire* was translated into French, English and German. One indication of his status can be found in the *Bibliothèque Germanique*, which first appeared in Amsterdam in 1720. It hailed him as 'a senior scholar of great merits', a 'member of the Royal Society of Berlin', and described his history of Turkey as 'an excellent work'.[42] In 1743 *Le Journal Universel*, published in The Hague (and later in Amsterdam), gave a brief presentation of *The History of the Growth and Decay of the Ottoman Empire*, which had been published a year earlier in French by Jonquières; in another issue, it speaks of the European reputation of the Romanian scholar.[43]

Interest in Cantemir's writings was also evident in German university centres, expressed in *Göttingische Zeitungen von Gelehrten Sachen* and the work of important philosophers and historians such as Johann Lorenz von Mosheim, Anton Friedrich Busching, Johann Joachim Winckelmann and others.[44] Cantemir, then, made a considerable contribution to the inclusion of the East in European cultural life, firstly because of the subjects he tackled, many of which were of universal interest, and secondly due to the thinking behind his works and the style in which they were presented. Just as Theophilos Corydalleus drew attention to his life and philosophy, and, somewhat earlier, Elias ben Moses Cretensis from the Southern Balkans taught the Italians ancient Greek, so Cantemir added another valuable element to the understanding of the impact of the East, namely Turkish civilization. As a result, Europe was enriched spiritually and its intellectual scope was enlarged.

Constantin Cantacuzino and Nicholas Mavrocordatos were also significant figures in the travel of ideas from the East, both through communication with the West and via the great libraries they founded. They too ensured that the region's spiritual works were connected to Europe more generally.

We are nearing the end of the seventeenth century, when the post-Byzantine Balkans were eager to communicate among themselves, come closer together and recognize their common characteristics at a point when they were becoming more and more distinct, with Central-Southeastern Europe at a turning point. It was in these conditions that two men of letters produced highly influential works and enjoyed a great spiritual convergence, their contact with one another illustrating the intellectual tendencies of the day – the Serb chronicler George Branković and Constantin Cantacuzino mentioned above.

Branković occupies a prominent place in the history of Romanian–Serbian relations and the history of Southeastern European relations in general, being intimately connected to the cultural and political life of Transylvania and Wallachia in the second half of the seventeenth century. This was a time when, spiritually, events were guided by personalities such as Șerban Cantacuzino, Radu Năsturel, Constantin Filipescu, Stoica Ludescu and Constantin Cantacuzino. The connection between the two authors' historical writings becomes clear when we consider Branković's *Chronicles* alongside Cantacuzino's *History of Wallachia*.[45] The friendship between the two scholars began in Cantacuzino's splendid library, hence the sources of their writings were the same. Both the *Lesser Chronicle*, subtitled *The Chronicle of Slovenia, Lower Moesia and Upper Moesia* (edited in Romanian),[46] and *The Great Chronicle* (edited in Slavo-Serbian) demonstrate the results of Branković's systematic studies in Bucharest, 'the author returning to his original intention of expressing his origins in the family of Serbian despots and his kinship with the ruling families of Wallachia, the House of Basarab and the Cantacuzino and Băleanu families.'[47] The Serbian intellectual's master work is the *Great Chronicle*, which recounts a series of events from the history of Wallachia, Moldavia and Transylvania, relating them to Serbian history and especially that of the Branković family.

Constantin Cantacuzino was an important figure in Wallachia at the end of the seventeenth century who invigorated the cultural life of his country, thanks to his Paduan education and large private collection of books. His diverse activities promoted a new, humanist way of thinking. His area of interest, much like that of his compatriot Dimitrie Cantemir, was secular Romanian culture, but his *History of Wallachia* – like the later works of the Transylvanian Enlightenment and the earlier works of the chroniclers Ureche and Costin – also focused on the Roman origin of the Romanian people. He draws attention to his country's old name, the times of Trajan and the Roman settlement in Dacia, and the origin of the word Wallachian (from a Germanic term denoting Romanized Celts and Roman-speaking people generally).[48] *The History of Wallachia* is a highly original book, of interest for historical, political and philosophical reasons. Andrei Pippidi correctly emphasizes the trifold importance of Cantacuzino's thinking: its historical interest lies in its impressive erudition, its political significance resides in the important judgements it makes on the present, and its philosophical value stems from its deep grasp of the Romanian past. These considerations provide the key to Cantacuzino's complex thinking.[49]

In Eastern Europe towards the end of the seventeenth century, the royal courts became increasingly receptive to the reforming influences of the West, and it was in this environment that their chroniclers and writers abandoned outmoded concepts, devoted their lives to reading and writing, perfected their style, and thus became known across the continent. Throughout the region the number of large private libraries grew, and young men of wealthy families either attended the new schools at home or were educated in Western Europe, broadening their horizons. Ideas changed slowly but inexorably, and over time were understood and absorbed by the masses. The slow awakening of conscience in Central-Eastern Europe lasted a century or more, beginning in about 1650, when many contributions to this political and cultural emancipation were in evidence, and peaking during the second half of the eighteenth century. These changes came about through a series of confrontations, and, reflecting the state of the modern world, even these only operated at the highest intellectual level of society.

At this stage society was only partly freed from the control of the feudal state and the Church, and tended to react only insofar as these forces affected daily life. While these everyday factors are not the focus of this study, we cannot ignore the changing nature of economic and social conditions in the second half of the seventeenth century. In this respect we should be mindful of the political reforms of the Cantemir and Mavrocordatos families, petitions against the Turkish dominion and prophesies of the struggles to come. A point of maturity had been reached, and Eastern European consciousness had been galvanized and enriched. Central-Southeastern European Man started to emerge from the shadow of religion: newly aware of his creative capacities, he formed an internal dialogue, embracing a greater freedom of thought and a more independent intellectual outlook. According to some contemporary commentators, the God of the Middle Ages was now *Deus absconditus*, and religion had given way to culture, which now represented the highest values through which European humanity understood and defined itself and with which it identified. A period of change followed, and the diversity of its thinking and its practices came to define the necessary decline of a society, the replacing of one way of life with another, that responded more closely to current collective state of soul and mind. Indeed this crisis ushered in a new stage in the history of human evolution. In the West, the beginning of the new age was characterized by lack of faith,

EAST–WEST CONTACTS ASSOCIATED WITH THE CULTURAL INSTITUTIONS OF THE 17TH–18TH CENTURIES

The great crisis of consciousness that triggered the transformation of medieval organizational structures into modern ones played a key role in the general evolution of humanity in Europe. In Western, Central and Eastern Europe the ideas and religious dogmas of the twilight years of the Middle Ages were perpetuated, and there were easily recognized bridges between the medieval world and that of Renaissance and post-Renaissance Italian art, and the books and ideas disseminated by German-Flemish printing houses, universities and libraries. However, only over a longer period of time can the revelations of Homo Europaeus be fully understood.

- – – – Dissemination of culture
- ·········· Printing and dissemination of books
- ◆ Printing press
- ▮ Libraries
- ▲ Higher and Secondary Educational Institutions

as Lucien Febvre has observed,[50] while Central-Southeastern Europe was focused on spiritual communion with its Western neighbours, being tempted, more than ever, by the now famous enlightenment of Homo Europaeus. At this juncture it is worth reiterating the principle with which we began, namely, the existence of a trans-communion or diachronic communion across Europe, which placed the notion of man above that of nation, yet without diminishing the latter, since it was always woven into the soul of Homo Europaeus. In this vision, the perfectibility of man always required the submission of his ideals to a greater, universal ideal. However, in our hypothesis Homo Europaeus did this not for present or future generations, but for himself, in a timeless vision of the universe.

IV

A DIASPORA THAT CREATES CONVERGENCE? JUDAISM IN CENTRAL AND SOUTHEASTERN EUROPE

The good historian is like the giant from the fairy tale. He knows that whenever he catches the smell of human flesh, there his quarry lies.

Marc Bloch[1]

TO UNDERSTAND MANKIND'S DESTINY we must study man's beliefs, his power to ascend, to surpass others and indeed himself, his aspirations and his temptation to know the Absolute. The destiny of the Jewish people is part of this universal story, perhaps more compellingly so than others, since it survived in exile for two thousand years: it had the opportunity to become universal, yet did not lose its distinct identity. On the contrary, continuity at all levels of life allowed the Jewish people to confirm this identity. Each Jew is a living example of this history – at once an individual and a reflection of the conscience of those around him as a spiritual and mental entity.

The Jewish people represent perhaps the most important aspect of diversity in European civilization. Speakers of another language, often of several other languages, conveyors of other traditions and habits, and, most important, of a foreign religion without idols, for Europe's Christian communities they have symbolized the opposite of their own ways of life. They were a permanent question mark: it is not by chance that intellectuals across Europe have persistently tried to decipher the enduring internal mechanisms of Judaism. In what follows, I have adopted essentially the same method as in the previous chapters, in an attempt to recover the past by going beyond the surface of sources, facts and events.

We remain in Southeastern and Central Europe, whose Jewish diaspora has been studied relatively little, and even then either indirectly or in isolation – a persistent problem since historians generally tend to separate the history of different peoples and ignore the whole in favour of the particular. I prefer to focus on confluence, as the best way to demonstrate the significance of Judaism in the region between Vienna and Constantinople, which enables us to understand its role in merging different peoples. I will adopt a quantitative approach only insofar as data lend credence to the picture I am trying to establish. This is by no means a complete study (which is practically impossible in any case), but I have consulted many important bibliographical sources and documents, some of which had never been used by scholars before.[2] I had the good fortune to discover and then devote long study to these texts, always having in mind the sacred fundamental texts of Judaism, though not at the expense of medieval philosophical-religious thinking or modern and current ideas. What emerges in all of these source documents, through the personal experiences of their authors, is a strong sense of events undergoing a process of reformation, and above all the idea of a civilization that has long existed and will endure – indeed, a civilization that has played an extraordinary role in the emancipation and assertion of Man's personality. This is the reason why the choice of one region or another is only of secondary concern.

Studies of the Middle Ages and the period of transition towards modern times provided me with a great deal of data and facts, which I tried to penetrate in order to perceive the culture and way of thinking of Jews living in the Central-Eastern region. Jews in the Balkan Peninsula represented a distinct group, not only in contrast to their non-Jewish surroundings, but also – to a limited extent and in a strictly cosmetic fashion – to their co-religionists of Western Europe. This requires explanation. Their beliefs remained the same, no matter where they lived. But many specific traits, from clothing to food, from the construction of synagogues to the preservation of traditions, the interior of homes and the language the people spoke, all were present in unusually varied forms, given that these were essentially the same people. Their gestures, expressions and everyday existence displayed a remarkable vibrancy and variety. It is abundantly clear that when I speak of the civilization of European Man, whether in the Balkans, Galicia, Iberia, Britain or the Low Countries, I cannot omit the Judaic civilization which evolved in these regions, since it is present within the others, bringing with it a wealth of colour and both exerting and receiving influence, from beliefs, myths and legends, to the symbols cut into tombstones.

From this point our focus is on a history stretching back into the distant past, yet our approach needs to be simultaneously synchronic and diachronic, ethnographic and pragmatic, because the fifty-seven centuries of this community's existence took place among an extremely diverse and complex array of peoples, cultures and civilizations, institutions and events, and geographical, political and spiritual circumstances. While the community's sacred law is a constant throughout this history, there were also continuous confluences. Simon Dubnov, the author of an important work of Jewish historiography, proves that the history of Judaism is impossible to interpret using a single viewpoint or method, because the results in such cases are always superficial.[3] With this in mind, moving beyond events, names and examples of the communities, I have commented on the ideas that constitute the Jewish spirit, Judaism and its moral basis and practices – these were often influenced by the elite, but also by the traditional Romanian, Hungarian, Greek, Slavic and German cultures.

The history of the Jews should be seen as one of receptivity, but one in which the most important factors are not the explanation, causality and determinism of phenomena, but rather the understanding of a way of life, its power of creation, individuality and pragmatic reality.[4] The presence of Jews in the Balkans and in Pannonia goes back to ancient times, as attested by traces of their cemeteries, synagogues, coins and stone inscriptions discovered in archaeological research in the countries of the former Yugoslavia, Hungary, Romania and Greece. The conditions in which they settled in these regions, as well as the causes, were different: in general, though, they depended on the empires who shared the various spheres of influence in Europe, the Middle East and North Africa. The first contact between Jews and Eastern and Southeastern Europe came about through Roman imperial expansion.

Evidence of this contact is provided by the coins of Simon bar Kokhba discovered at Pojejena, in southern Banat, dated to the second

THE DISPERSION OF JUDAISM IN CENTRAL AND SOUTHEASTERN EUROPE

Jewish civilization has always fluctuated between openness and withdrawal depending on the historical period and the political, social and cultural contexts it encounters. This pendulum effect determined the way in which the movements of the Jewish people established contacts across Europe.

- - → Sephardi Jews
—→ Ashkenazi Jews
▪▪▪ The Ashkenazi Jews' nucleus of formation

century AD when Roman legions that included Jews were settled in the region; the gravestone at Benkovac, on Mount Velebit in Dalmatia, which speaks of a Tiberian Jew and commemorates, in the same century, Aurelius Dionysius; the Jewish grave of Duclea, near Titograd in Montenegro, which is believed to date from the end of the third century AD; the so-called Polyharmos columns discovered at Stobi in Macedonia, among the ruins of a church that was probably built on the foundations of a synagogue, where the names of its Jewish donors are recalled;[5] and Hebrew inscriptions found in ancient Dacian territory[6] or on the Pannonian Plain.[7] These are merely a few and necessarily the most significant examples. What is important is that Judaism has wandered across this region since ancient times, and that this evidence, which shows sudden drastic increases at certain points in time, gives a clear and accurate picture of the direction of events.

The spread of Christianity during the Byzantine Empire naturally brought about changes in the Jewish situation. Christianity, as an official religion, led to a different way of thinking. Although the assertion of an official and different ideology should not necessarily have led to restrictions,[8] this is not the way things were, as has indeed been the case throughout medieval and modern history. Church councils and synods took away the Jews' religious freedom. Sometimes their very means of existence were suppressed. These sanctions led to much harder living conditions, and the situation of Jews in Dalmatia, the regions of the former Yugoslavia and the Southern Balkans, as well as in a number of the important Greek towns, slowly deteriorated and caused successive mass migrations towards the Southern Slavic territories.

In his book A *History of Yugoslav Jews*,[9] Yakir Eventov considers that some Byzantine Jews, speakers of Greek known as Romaniotes, were dispersed across more regions, including those occupied by the Southern Slavs, later uniting with the Sephardic Jews expelled from Spain in 1492, who spoke the Ladino language.[10] They were not protected by the obscurity of the Middle Ages here, either, nor from the excesses of the militants of the Greek Orthodox Church, especially during the centuries of Counter-Reformation zeal. During the Ottoman centuries, particularly when the glory of the empire was declining, the Jews of Serbia and Bosnia enjoyed a brief period of prosperity.[11] The Northern Balkans and neighbouring provinces were home to Ashkenazi communities; to the south were the above-mentioned Romaniotes, the descendants of the old Greek Jews. Family names such as Papo and Romano are the only remaining evidence of the undeniable links between the Sephardic and Romaniote Jews. Mixed communities were formed as a result of Ashkenazi Jews, coming from Central Europe to the Southeast, where a greater religious tolerance accounted for the role of Jews in economic, social and cultural life. These communities were mixed to the extent that the Ashkenazi were admitted into the older Sephardic communities in this region.

A separation then occurred in the eighteenth century, once the Hapsburg domination was established in a few important regions of the Southeast. Documents issued by the Vienna administration, which we will examine in detail later, indicate the distinct lines on which Jewish society was organized according to their rite. Let us give a few more details in order to avoid confusion. Initially, those who had settled in the region of the former Yugoslavia formed a homogenous group, being the descendants of families of merchants coming from Italy (as well as Spain and Portugal), especially from Venice, where they maintained a continuous presence despite the many hostilities they faced. We are looking at the centuries of the Middle Ages, when Ragusa (Dubrovnik) was one of Europe's most vibrant centres of confluence – Ragusa was the gateway into the region for Jews who went on to form the West Balkan communities. Later, a heterogeneous Judaic life emerged as a result of the characteristics of each region – Serbia, Bosnia, Vojvodina, Dalmatia, Croatia and so on – which was also a result of the artificial political frontiers created after the Austro-Turkish Wars.

Internal elements – by which I mean the rite to which the Jews belong – played an undeniable role in this process, and in some cases became essential to the separate development of communities, even within the same citadel or town. However, I will not emphasize this aspect, knowing the hidden relations of Judaism, which break down differences or tensions within its communities at the most significant moments. An admirable unity in its diversity is one of its essential principles. We are only a step away from understanding the characteristic traits of Jewish civilization, but for the moment, we should let history speak.

The controversial problem of the Khazars is also worth examining, if only to exemplify the way Judaism spread over a vast portion of Eastern Europe – between the Volga and the Dnieper rivers, in the region between Crimea and Astrakhan. Converted to Mosaism in the year 740 during the rule of King Bulan, the Khazars are a special case in the history of international Judaism. Despite all the attempts of the Kherson Byzantines to convince them of the superiority of Christianity, despite all the efforts made by the neighbouring Arabs in the name of Islam, the subjects of King Bulan embraced Judaism, creating a state that lasted until the Mongol invasion of Europe. What is certain is that Northeast European Judaism prospered along with the Khazars, at least in the sense that it spread widely, which gave it a greater resistance to incomers or, even more, to other continuous attempts at assimilation in medieval Europe. During the eleventh century, the Khazars encountered Jews who migrated from Bohemia and Germany towards Western Russia. However, the defeat of the Khazars by the Russians in 970, and, in the twelfth century, their being forced out into the region of the new Eastern Slavic state explains why a large number of Jews settled in Poland, where they were received with extraordinary hospitality. Beyond this factual data, we will follow the drama of the wandering Jew.[12] Accompanying him during his adventures through European cities, both where his feet 'could find rest' and where they could not, we will observe what Braudel called 'the ubiquity of Jewish communities'.[13]

At the end of the first millennium and the beginning of the second, many significant events took place in the history of this diaspora: the founding of the community of Serdica (the forerunner of modern-day Sofia), the settling of the first Jewish families in the ports of the Dalmatian coast, the first forms of cultural and administrative organization in Thessaloniki, and the more or less accidental presence of Jews in the region between the Mureş and the Danube, where the first medieval states had already been formed. We obtain this information from the notes of Eustathius of Thessaloniki, Gerard Sagredo of Csanád (Cenad), Benjamin of Tudela and Petachiah of Regensburg.

If we consider only the descriptions of Benjamin of Tudela, it is apparent that even medieval geographical and historical literature brings us close to the unified historical development I have referred to. This is clear from the following fragment from Benjamin of Tudela's Itinerary referring to the Wallachians south of the Danube and their relations with the Jews:

From there, it is a day's journey to Sinon Potamou [probably Sarmia], where about fifty Jews live, headed by Rabbi Solomon and Rabbi Jacob. The town is situated at the foot of the mountains of Wallachia [the Great Wallachia, in Thessaly], where the people called Wallachians live. They are as quick as deer and descend quickly from the mountains to plunder the country of Greece [the Byzantine Empire, at that time under the rule of Manuel I Comnenus]. No one can climb (up to them) and wage war against them, nor can any king keep them under his rule. They do not have Christian beliefs, but give themselves Jewish names [i.e. Biblical names]. Some say they steal from them, but they do not kill them, as they do the Greeks. They belong to no religion...[14]

This picture of Jewish cultural life in Thessaly confirms the continuity of the Byzantine Romaniotes. It is also true that relations with the Wallachians of the South Danube reflects a particular point of view – then, as later, Wallachians were tolerant and often understanding towards Jews. What we have here is above all a human approach, a solidarity that was not at odds with either the infrastructure of society or the intellectual elite. It is important to maintain a clear distinction between this state of affairs and the rule of lay or religious ideology. Provocation always came easily to the powerful – the man of deeds and actions who lacks moral foundation never was and never will be tolerant, his spirit forever in servitude.

Documentary evidence reveals the relations of Jews with Hungarians, Romanians, Bulgarians, Russians, Serbs and Greeks during the early Middle Ages. Relations with the Islamic world also flourished, although this only began once the Southeast was included in the vast Ottoman Empire. Certain papers speak of the expansion of Jews across the entire Balkan Peninsula, in the largest and most prominent cities of Central and East-Central Europe. They mention commercial or marital relationships between Jews and Christians, as well as the often drastic rulings of the royal chancelleries, implementing the policy of forced conversion to Catholicism initiated by Rome. If the risk of being converted was great in the West (especially in Spain, Portugal, Italy and France), in Central and Eastern Europe the Jews protected themselves much more effectively against political and religious impositions.

The geography of the region itself, the routes through the Balkans and towards the west or the east of the peninsula,[15] favoured a retreat from the forces of power. When, in Hungary, the kings Andrew II, Bela II and later Bela XII and Louis I each in turn became intolerant, persecuting even individuals among their own people who embraced

Judaism,[16] Jews moved towards the southern Danube regions, contributing to the formation of the new medieval states of Bulgaria and Serbia. Who lost out from this? One revealing case is the transportation of salt down the Mureş river, which passed from the hands of the Jews, who owned property and warehouses in Transylvania, to the abbey of Bulci, which belonged to the Knights of Malta and the Chapter of Arad, leading to what was, if not a disaster, then at least a noticeable decrease in commerce.[17]

In Venice, on the other hand, two or three hundred years later, exclusion of the Jews was attempted. The Council of Ten was forced to abandon this, with great reluctance, so as to avoid grave consequences for the city's existence. Here, as always, salvation for the Jews, and indeed for the Republic, was owed to economic and commercial considerations: for what else could the monopoly of the grain trade signify, for example? 'Who made the Turks so powerful,' asks Soranzo (who had been a hostage in Constantinople) in his speech before the Council of Ten, 'and where would they have found such skilled artisans to make cannons, bows, cannonballs, swords, and small shields, which allow them to measure up to other peoples, if not among the Jews the King of Spain forced to leave?'[18] Only Louis I's Hungary did not understand the huge potential of the Jewish diaspora. There, as in Edward I's England or Ferdinand VII's Spain, and indeed in many other totalitarian regimes in human history, the necessity for a dialogue with others was not understood.

Judaism, along with Hellenism, was and remains the most influential civilizing force of any people scattered among other peoples. Society does not develop through exceptional acts of medieval legislation such as those issued by Bela IV in 1251; a kingdom flourishes even less.[19] Nothing can develop within itself. The act of Bela IV is worthy of mention for its beauty and its elevating thoughts: Bela had been favourable to Jews by giving them the freedom to trade, to travel freely from one region to another ('Wherever a Jew may pass through our territories, let no one hinder him in any way, nor impede him, nor create any difficulty for him...'), to lead their religious life according to their faith, the synagogues and schools being protected ('If anyone should dare to throw anything at the synagogues [scolas iudaeorum], we require that he should pay the judge of the Jews a mark and a half'). He established rules for the open practice of customs and traditions as well as for the relations between Christians and Jews.[20] It is a special case, rarely seen in medieval Europe.

Later documents referring to Hungary and Transylvania confirm these assertions. The immigration of Jews towards the Southeast was not accidental. In the thirteenth century, the commercial route linking Constantinople to Krakow was in the hands of the Karaites, who dominated the exchanges between Byzantium, Russia and Poland, 'crossing Bulgaria and the Danube countries'.[21] They were joined by Jews coming from Germany and Spain, since the Ottoman Empire offered a safe haven during the fifteenth and sixteenth centuries, displacing the centre of Judaic trade and spiritual life from Western to Eastern Europe (there were 160,000 Jews in Constantinople and Thessaloniki alone). Nothing remained static for the Jewish diaspora, however, and the restrictions and persecution of the reign of Louis I[22] had disappeared by the time of Matthias Corvinus. Things took a completely different turn, because Matthias paid special interest to the Jews of Transylvania and Hungary. This is perhaps unsurprising, as it was an era of humanist horizons – many Renaissance ideas not only reached Buda or, further away, Transylvanian Cluj, but thrived inside schools and libraries, in societies or in privileged associations of scholars, artists, teachers and writers.[23] In these conditions they were granted complete religious freedom and their diplomatic qualities were appreciated: one of the great court dignitaries, Jacobus Maendel, was a Jew.[24] Once more we can observe the phenomenon of permanent movement, where there can be no question of a single direction, but rather a perpetual zigzagging. This allows us to glimpse a fundamental truth – the dependence on time rather than space. Judaism holds this secret, its temporal dimension allowing it to transcend one of the fundamental characteristics of the very infrastructure of history: geography. It is easy to see things in perspective, our faces turned to the future and not to the past.

Whence comes this great freedom if not from a consciousness of mankind's double value, earthly and celestial? This idea guided the Jew towards the verb 'to be' and not 'to have': the wealth of the tradesman, and later that of the banker or of the bourgeois, was a means and not a goal. The Middle Ages and the Modern Age offer many examples of this. The ideals of the Jews lie in books, learning, knowledge. In order to remain scrupulously accurate we will use these sources sparingly. Considerations of profession, meanwhile, are of little value – when we are talking about a Jew, whether a merchant, artisan, intellectual or politician, he is possessed by the curiosity to know because his survival is linked to knowledge of books, to the quantity and variety of

THE PRINCIPAL CENTRES OF THE JUDAIC DIASPORA IN CENTRAL AND SOUTHEASTERN EUROPE

Serbia and Bulgaria, participants in the formation of the Balkan states, saw Jews arrive in large numbers in the years immediately after religious persecutions initiated by Louis the Great of Hungary (1364). This migration was accompanied by another one, represented by the Jews from German principalities, but especially by those from Spain. The accommodation provided by the Ottoman Empire in the sixteenth century (160,000 Jews in Constantinople and Thessaloniki alone) shifted the centre of Jewish economic and spiritual life from Western to Eastern Europe.

accumulated information, to the languages he has mastered. But let us return to concrete history.

Settled in Kavala, Siderokapsa, Gallipoli and Chios, but especially in the most important towns of the Centre and Southeast – Vienna, Buda, Ljubljana, Ragusa (Dubrovnik), Belgrade, Temesvár (Timișoara), Iași, Bucharest, Rusciuk, Sofia, Thessaloniki, Constantinople and Adrianople – in the sixteenth and seventeenth centuries the Jews formed strong communities containing everything that expressed their distinct identity: synagogues and houses of prayer, ritual baths, cemeteries, schools, houses of study or seminaries (in Hebrew, *beit hamidrash*) and their own printing presses. The privileges granted to them by the Turks explain their stability and their economic and financial development.

Spain expelled the Jews, while Turkey welcomed them, only too happy to count on them in their relations with Europe. Under the protection of Suleiman the Magnificent, communities begin a long and continuous cohabitation with the Balkan peoples. Jews gave lustre to the regions in which they worked as merchants, artisans (tailors, weapon-makers, blacksmiths, jewellers, weavers and dyers), doctors, pharmacists, diplomats and writers, and in their turn benefited from the opportunity to carry on their ideals and faith, enriching and creating an enduring diasporan civilization. And the Balkans was the Jews' chosen region. It is also true that an unusual preservation instinct shaped and defined the destiny of the people of Israel, with its strength, its endurance and its anxieties. As always, wherever human contacts exist, there is a 'reciprocity of services rendered'.[25] The Ottoman Empire offered an ample and well-structured political foundation. The sultans enjoyed huge material resources as a result of their conquests, that extended to the north of the Danube.

They did not, however, possess a fundamental knowledge of Europe, of its languages and civilizations – European geography and history, and the thinking and way of life of its peoples were alien to the Turks. They did understand, though, that there were other, more refined means than the scimitar to dominate the territories they had conquered. Intent on optimizing the administration of their vast territories, they were keen to establish ties with Europe, with a world which was in many ways so different from their own. Contact with this other world had to be through an intermediary, a role granted to the Jews because of their culture, their mobility and their skill in creating a system of relations which might have been surprising to the uninitiated, but was entirely plausible to those who approached the Jewish way of thinking, especially the clear-sighted and open-minded communities of Southeastern Europe.

I believe this point of view applies to the whole continent, and I am certainly not jumping to the conclusion that what the Jews achieved in the Southeast was the only or the most important link in the political and commercial relations of the Ottoman Empire. There were other considerations which should not be neglected in the history of the Sublime Porte, for example the Byzantine legacy which connected them to the sea: 'It took them over a century to become adapted to the needs of transportation and then of battles at sea, but they finally succeeded in these endeavours.'[26] We should also give due consideration to the representatives of the Turkish elite, some of whom expressed themselves freely, as in the West, while others separated themselves from religious institutions.

Jewish merchants were present everywhere, prized for their economic organization, their skill in the exchange of goods, and the ideas they circulated. They represented the possibility of material and spiritual communication between the West and East of Europe. The towns of Thessaloniki, Nikopolis and Rusciuk, with their sizeable population of Spanish Jews, influenced economic development, leading to the enhancement of cultural exchanges and the propagation of scientific knowledge. Thessaloniki, a haven for one of the first communities of Turkey, had printing presses, schools and colleges in Hebrew. Over a thousand students attended the city's educational institutions, which suggests the dimensions and role of this community in the Southeast European diaspora.[27] Comparable to Venice from the point of view of Jewish spiritual life, for a long time Thessaloniki was to coordinate the Balkan diaspora, the documents created and preserved by the rabbis of this community describing an uninterrupted dialogue between South and North, East and West. Was this an expression of synthesis? Or the complex reality of a people eager to maintain their identity no matter the place and the historical conditions which they were forced to cross? The Jews never let go of the idea that there was something awaiting them beyond the hardships of their nomadic life – first and foremost, the idea of Eretz Israel. This belief found expression in the medieval Jewish mysticism to which the Judaism of the Balkan Peninsula made a highly original contribution.

From the Thessaloniki documents and other sources we learn what happened to the Sephardi travelling to the north, west and east of the Balkans. In the *Hosen Mispat*, a collection of responses (decisions of the rabbi as president of a council of judges, the Beth-Din) delivered by the great rabbi Samuel de Medina (1505–89), there is mention of the settling of Jews in Bucharest around 1550.[28] This source also mentions a well-established Sephardic community whose members engaged in multiple commercial activities and had ties with many centres to the south of the Danube.

The presence of a Jewish community in Wallachia is confirmed by a paper that documents the case between Arsen, son of Ushen and the Jew Mosko, for 1,000 akce, the price of wool and silk brought from Thessaloniki and which the latter had sold to the former.[29] Another example is the response in 1559 of Rabbi Josef Karo from Nikopolis who, with reference to the killing of a Jew in the village of Dridov, near Bucharest, implicitly speaks of the Sephardi from the Wallachian capital, who had direct relations with the country's ruler and a system of intelligence for the tracking of wrongdoers:

> Since Mr Solomon ibn Benvenist (may he rest in Eden!) sent his brother, Mr Moses Vidal, to collect his dues in Wallachia, where he had among his debtors a non-Jew from the mentioned village as well, who owed him over 10,000 aspres, and since Mr Solomon waited for his brother in vain for a month, and being worried about his safety went to look for him in the said village of Dridov, and upon finding there that non-Jew, who owed him the 10,000 aspres, asked him of his brother, and the non-Jew answered: 'I paid your brother and he left,' and Mr Solomon took the non-Jew and brought him in front of the ruler of Wallachia, and the latter said: 'You have said that Moses Vidal came to your house and that he left after you paid him your debt, if this is so, then where is he now, for we have found him nowhere?' – and he ordered him to go and search for him, because he had admitted that Mr Vidal had been his guest; and, after the passing of over a month, the non-Jew returned and told the ruler that he saw in a dream how Mr Vidal had been thrown in a well in Bucharest; and since there were also present three Jews, Mr Samuel Estrelega, Mr Abraham Salinas and Mr Habib Amato, upon hearing these words they immediately went to the well where Mr

Moses Vidal had been thrown, and there they could see the tracks of the wheels of a cart, from this well to the house of the non-Jew's house in the village of Dridov...[30]

This testimony, one of many that describe the condition of merchants, shows the great solidarity involved in the search for the truth. Some of these acts describing the movements of Jewish merchants were included in the collections of texts I have quoted, and have become first-hand sources for discovering one of the many faces of history.[31]

Information also can be obtained from other collections of documents, laws and orders issued by the royal or imperial courts, from letters, documents from trials, manuscripts on the organization of unions, privileges, forms of oaths taken, and so on. The chronicle of Prince Nicolae Pătrașcu of 1557 mentions the killing of a Jew in the times of Mircea Ciobanul.[32] The report of the imperial agents Ioan Belsius and Marcus Bergkovicz sent from Hârlău on 8 April 1562 to Maximilian of Hapsburg speaks of the tolerant policies of the Prince Despot in Moldavia, a ruler who gave sentences of great fairness and ensured that justice be done to all kinds of peoples who existed there, with their many differing manners and thousands of different faces, as well as their many beliefs: Armenians, Jews, Greeks, Moldavians, Serbians, Transylvanian Saxons, and so on; he pronounced judgement in person in the marketplace of his court.[33] A letter of 1551 from the wife of Transylvanian ruler Ștefan Mailat, addressed to her brother, Tamás Nádasdy, refers to the death of her husband as a prisoner of the Ottomans, and the efforts of the Jew Abraham (as well as the priest Ferencz) to ascertain the details of his disappearance from the dignitaries of the Sublime Porte.[34] An act of 1564, signed by Joachim, Prince Elector of Brandenburg, certifies a debt due to a Jewish creditor, in connection with an older debt of Petru Rareș of Moldavia.[35] A letter of Gheorghe Despot (who claimed to be a relative of Ion Despot),[36] pretender to the throne of Moldavia, addressed to the Signory of Genoa, recommends the messenger conveying it as a Jewish personality of great importance: 'I have chosen as witness the conveyor of this (letter) who is a great Jewish man, a merchant from Lower Wallachia, our country, and who has abandoned all his affairs, his wife and children, in order to look for me, and he has sold many of his goods. And thanks to God's mercy he found me in about a month, in Lombardy...'[37] Then there is the imperial order of Selim II of 1568, addressed to the admiral of the Ottoman fleet, the Turkish judge of Constantinople and the commander of the fortress of Yerni Hissar, specifying that the monopoly of the wine trade with Moldavia was in the hands of the Jew Josef Nassi, Duke of Naxos[38] – this shows the economic power of a Jewish personality, capable not only of intervening in matters with the sultan, as in the case of 'doctor David', but also of being granted free passage from one end of the empire to another, and enjoying the sultan's support and collaboration in the development of commercial relations. Finally, contracts for the transportation of goods (those of 1570, for example),[39] mention the Jews' right to transport goods from Constantinople to Poland, taking them through all the countries of the Balkan Peninsula.

What can be said after having listed all these examples? In the circulation of merchandise across the Levant, the Jews surpassed the Greeks and Armenians. It is probably because of this that they also – as commerce produces such situations – appear in many disputes in the buying and selling of goods. In 1492, Vladislav II of Hungary sent two letters from Buda to the town councils of Sibiu (Hermannstadt) and Braşov (Kronstadt) hoping to calm certain conflicts between Jews and Christians, ordering that justice be done both to Jews in trials with their debtors, and to Christian creditors with Jewish debtors. One of these letters states

> I have found out that some Jews are accustomed to come into this town of ours and present themselves before you with our letters, through which these Jews ask you to judge them and to do them justice with regard to their debtors and those whom they bring to trial, and after justice has been served, to give them complete satisfaction; while, on the contrary, for this reason the creditors of those Jews who do not want to be judged before you have great losses to bear. That is why we wish and, trusting in your faithfulness, order you not to let it happen otherwise – that in everything that is to occur in the future, wherever and whenever you judge and dispense justice accord-ing to our orders and our requests, that they accuse; but in the same way you should judge and do justice to the creditors of these same Jews or to those who bring them to trial...[40]

A similar note is struck by a letter from this king to the ruler of Transylvania in 1499, as well as the petition of Radu the Great, ruler of Wallachia (1495–1508), addressed to the authorities of Kronstadt/

Brașov. Further examples include the answer of 1499 given by Stephan the Great to Alexander, Grand Duke of Lithuania, and the intervention of Ferdinand I of Hapsburg in Augsburg with an order given to the jurors of the city of Cluj (Klausenburg/Kolozsvár).[41] The town council of Lvov appeals for the support of Iaczko Maly, father of the Jew Solomon, after having picked up goods left there. The Knyaz Ilia Konstantynović pledges before the king of Poland to pay customs tax, in the event that it is proven that it has not been paid, for the herds of cattle brought by two Jews from Moldavia. This last example may refer to a practice allowed by Polish-Moldavian economic conventions, and which extended to the eighteenth century, permitting cattle from Poland to be brought to graze in Moldavia without any customs obligations.[42]

As one can clearly observe from the documents I have presented (and indeed from many others), the medieval states and kingdoms of the north and east of Europe, as well as Constantinople, could not do without the activities and initiatives of the Jewish people. This is no exaggeration: we discover that in the imperial capital, in the times of Suleiman the Magnificent and many of his successors, Jews were part of the state machinery, and it was a rare case when a sultan or vizier did not have in their service at least two Jewish bankers. In the sixteenth century, thirty synagogues were built in Constantinople alone.

This number demonstrates the force of the Jewish community, but also the tolerance of the empire at the time. Let us not fool ourselves, however – interests were at play. What is surprising is the intelligence of Turkish diplomacy, which proved amply qualified to approach and conquer a vast amount of European territory. But even in those places where the kingdoms were not willing to make concessions, Jews were admitted as creators of a commercial market in East-Central and Southeastern Europe – to expel them from a territory invariably brought consequences, given their diplomatic and cultural influence. In 1590, in the negotiations between the Sublime Porte and Poland, alongside the Moldavians, an important role was played by two notable Jews.[43]

The reach of the Jewish people went beyond the commercial societies and companies they founded in certain cities: some of them were first-rate political or cultural figures, while the majority were conveyors of spirituality, possessing a knowledge of the Jewish holy texts which was inevitably of interest to European humanists. Juan Miguez, a Portuguese Jew, became a notable personality at the court of Sultan Selim, who raised him to the rank of Duke of Naxos, later known as Don Jose Nassi. He played a role in events in Moldavia, supporting the Prince Despot, but also helped to forge international relations in Eastern Europe.[44] Solomon Ashkenazi, called 'the German' ('Tedeschi'), assisted the ruler of Moldavia in 1591, Aaron the Tyrant, himself a notable character of the Ottoman court, a 'respectable' Jew, 'factotum of the great vizier'.[45]

The scholar doctor Eleazar was summoned from Košice in 1606, to help with the treatment of the well-known Transylvanian prince Stefan Bocskai.[46] In 1622, a report by the envoy of Holland to Constantinople speaks of the diplomatic involvement of the Jews in sustaining a claimant to the throne of Moldavia.[47] This is exactly what happened in sixteenth-century England, where the Jews (after having been expelled in 1290, in the time of Edward I) had returned in various ways, often secretly, and where their spirit was to be felt (in every century since) in economics, as well as in the system of diplomatic relations. What is certain is that England tolerated the presence of Jews and made use of their ability, in the same way as the Turks did in the East – all of which occurred much earlier than their official acceptance in 1664.[48]

Four decades before England's decision, an idea emerged within the intellectual circles of Constantinople: a diploma of privileges for the Jews settling in Transylvania. The idea was inspired by the doctor Abraham Sarsa and brought to life by the chancellery of Prince Gabriel (Gábor) Bethlen in 1623, marking the beginning of modern regulations. It granted Jews the right to settle on the country's territory, religious freedom and the right to observe Judaic customs, the guarantee of exercising their trade and the right to travel without barriers: the prince's express wish was to contribute to the development of Transylvania through the gathering of different confessional communities. Bethlen's words were unequivocal, proving his culture and his adherence to a post-Renaissance humanist ideology of European proportions:

> Having before us the special intervention of the distinguished Abraham Sarsa, a Jewish doctor from Constantinople, I have thought it well to most generously decide the exemptions herewith, appearing below, to all those of the Jewish race who with our merciful consent wish to settle in our country of Transylvania; I have decided [that these exemptions] be meant for them with clemency and generosity and are to be respected by all citizens of our country.[49]

For those familiar with the ruler's intellectual biography, the gesture was not surprising. In fact, in those times there were several important victories of intelligence over medieval barbarism. Bethlen went on to distinguish himself by building bridges with the West: following the tradition of John II Sigismund, he granted greater authority to the intellectual circles of Alba Iulia (Gyulafehérvár).

The Academic College and the Library are irrefutable proof of an atmosphere that seems to have been inspired by the concepts of Erasmus, and illustrated by the document conceived in Cluj (Kolozsvár) in 1623.[50] A few decades later, the Diet of Transylvanian nobles takes up the question of the Jews again, deciding on a binding act: that they could trade freely and also had the right to settle in the fortress of Alba Iulia.[51] Under the rule of Mihai Apafi, they again benefited from the protection of the princely court: 'We order most solemnly that none should ever again dare to insult, to capture, to harm or tax either Jewish inhabitants or foreign Jews, or hinder them in their commerce or permit others to do so, or else they will not be able to avoid my great wrath...'[52]

In the pashalik of Buda, things were much the same. The Turks maintained their interest in Vienna, but in the sixteenth and seventeenth centuries they turned their attention to other cities of Central Europe as well. This not only concerned commerce and diplomacy, but the art of war as well. The pasha himself supported the Jews, and never travelled without some Jews in his retinue. We come across them as permanent inhabitants in Buda, at least at the time of the Ottoman domination. Their number varied in the course of a century (1546–1630) between 100 and 1,000.[53] It is clear that they did well under the Turks, better than the Slavic Christians in the Balkans or the Hungarians in Pannonia. This was true over a long period of history: Elias Canetti, a writer born in Rusciuk, Bulgaria in 1905, describes the continuity of such a state of spirit over all Bulgaria in A Language Saved. The History of a Youth (Die gerettete Zunge. Geschichte einer Jugend). In Hungary, though, towards the end of the seventeenth century, the situation of the Jews deteriorated considerably.

Austro-Turkish conflicts led to massive migrations towards Prague, Berlin, Krakow and Belgrade. The atmosphere in Buda in 1686–1700, with all the sufferings brought by wars, is described in the chronicle of Izsák Schulhof.[54] Its Jewish community survived, however, even in these conditions, largely through its own resourcefulness.

The repeated movements and divergences I have mentioned created many convergences between Ashkenazim and Sephardim, not only in the countries under Turkish domination, but also in some of the regions occupied by the Hapsburgs. Firstly, the Jews enjoyed great privileges in Eastern Europe, as highly valued interpreters: they generally spoke four or five languages, and it was not unusual for them to possess ten or twelve. They thus became mediators of political contacts. 'Those that fled Spain, Germany, Hungary and Bohemia', explains Belon du Mans, 'taught their children the language [of that country], and their children learned the language in which they had to communicate, such as Greek, Slavonic, Turkish, Arab, Armenian or Italian.'[55]

Here is evidence once again of that fascinating universal character, proving how it was possible for the Jews to become good students of the cultures that adopted them or that they met on their journeys. In every Jewish home it was important to know as many languages as possible, because 'knowing them, you could save yourself and many others'. As far as the encounters of Ashkenazim and Sephardim are concerned, things were not as simple as we might sometimes imagine. The laws of the Sephardi were complicated and remained conservative for centuries. They considered themselves different because of their Spanish traditions, and because of the language they spoke, which never changed. Turkish words were rarely used, and even then there were Spanish equivalents.

Their view of life was impenetrable to an outsider. 'Other Jews looked down upon them with naive vanity; there was a word that was always full of contempt and sounded like tedesco, meaning German Jew or Ashkenazi. It would have been inconceivable to marry a tedesca.'[56] And yet, as we shall see, this reserve was not the case everywhere. As we approach the heart of Europe, a civilized sense of geography, a flexibility of thought and action becomes apparent among the Jewish communities. These convergences existed in Belgrade, Ljubljana and Timişoara and had some bearing on the wider survival of the Jews.

As we have seen, large numbers of Jews settled in Moldavia and Wallachia, forming viable communities whose representatives are mentioned in the documents of cities and towns, in a long series of sources revealing the integration of Jews in the history of the Romanian principalities. In those times, Moldavia accommodated the strong organizational structure of Jewish society, which had become the main source of supplies to the ruler and the boyars. In the seventeenth century, once Polish-Moldavian trade flourished, and as a result of the wars started by the Cossacks, their numbers grew. Long before 1700, great synagogues had been built in Iaşi.

Across all of Moldavia and Wallachia, Jewish communities had constructed religious buildings. The privileges guaranteed to Jewish settlers in Moldavia dated from the times of Stephan Tomşa, and made the founding of the first unions of artisans possible.[57] As a result, Jewish science and culture spread all the more. Study of the Kabbalah was of great importance in the spiritual life of the Jews. The Messianic movement gained ground here, too, especially in conditions where discriminatory or assimilating tendencies spread across all of Europe. Around 1650, the reputed Kabbalist Rabbi Solomon Ben Arayo lived in Iaşi, 'one who had been studying the holy books for forty years, thus proving the duration and importance of the local community'. The well-known philosopher and astronomer Rabbi Josef S. del Medigo (1591–1655) also settled here, acquiring, in a decade, 'science and more science'.[58] The local yeshiva was among the most highly esteemed in Eastern Europe. It is not by chance that del Medigo, who later settled in Prague, came to Iaşi straight from Constantinople.

The large number of scholars in the region is mentioned in the writings of medieval visitors to Moldavia, such as the Franciscan missionaries Angelo Petraca da Sonnino and Francesco da San Felice (who passed through this region in 1632–3),[59] or the Swedish preacher Conrad Jacob Hiltebrandt, who spoke of the extraordinary role played by Jews as translators, and of their knowledge of the region's geography, stressing the stability of Jewish settlements in Iaşi and Soroca.[60] Though not as numerous as in Transylvania, Poland or Bohemia, there were Jewish doctors in Moldavia at this point, involved in the social and political-diplomatic life of the times. Rabbis were also well-known personalities of the era, Nathan Hannover and Arie Leib ben Samuel being two other prominent names that complete our picture of the spread of the Judaic spirit across this territory.

As far as Wallachia is concerned (where the first citation of their presence is in Craiova),[61] Paul of Aleppo provides information on Jewish–Romanian relations in 1657, focusing on the dialogues on religious subjects which, it seems, held a special attraction for him.[62] The limits of tolerance were clear. The theological controversies of the first half of the seventeenth century had their say. The judiciary system at the time of Matei Basarab (1632–54) was conceived in a religious spirit discriminatory towards inhabitants whose religion was not Greek Orthodox. *The Guide of the Law* (1652) and other texts on canonical law all imply segregation.[63] Only Christian Jews could hold certain high-ranking positions and were given landed property. Even under these conditions, Sephardic Jews from Turkey continued to settle in Wallachia. Their presence in Bucharest is mentioned in the report of the missionary Urban Cerri.

There was room for Polish Jews, as well, whose existence in the country's capital was first noted in 1550.[64] They traded in all kinds of goods, from cloth to mercury, and undertook every category of work, being anything from butchers to producers of sheep fat or candles. The privileges granted by Constantin Brâncoveanu (1688–1714) are a good example.[65] And they are not the only one. Jewish schools and rabbis were a sign of the interior organization of communities here as well, and prove that education and teaching were prized as they should be. Signs of intolerance appear relatively late. The year of the first pogrom in Bucharest is 1715 (a rabbi's epitaph says he was a 'martyr'), and this can be correlated to the words of del Chiaro's testimony, *demolire la sinagoga degli Ebrei*. In 1726, the first accusation of ritual murder is brought, in Moldavia; the charge was circulated in a notorious hagiographic text called *The Life of Constantine the Great*, based on Western sources, the biography of Pope Sylvester.[66] The truth is that, beyond the intolerance manifested especially under the influence of clerics, Jews occupied important positions at the royal court, in Wallachia, Moldavia and in Transylvania in the times of autonomous princes. One example is the case of Daniel de Fonseca, the doctor of the French ambassador to Constantinople, who had also been the doctor and counsellor of Nicholas Mavrocordatos. The ruler of Wallachia had met him in Constantinople's elite circles, where Latin, French and Italian were spoken and a spirit of religious tolerance reigned, while the sterile dogmatism professed in the Middle Ages which still had strong roots in people's way of thinking was repelled. Bridges seem natural, as soon as both sides promote rational ideas.

These great minds announce the Enlightenment, and their scholarly activities only confirm our suppositions. The concepts of Homo Europaeus penetrated the Southeast, initially through a small group of intellectuals, but in time more and more people drew on these pioneering activities, from the dialogue between East and West. As a protégé of Louis XV, Daniel de Fonseca circulated freely throughout Europe, and was greatly appreciated for his spirit and his erudition; he had affirmed his Jewishness without any reserve, and had done 'long and faithful service' to Christian states and princes.

Jews were needed to sustain the royal court financially, to foster its relations with the Sublime Porte, and in order to support one or another claimant to the throne.[67] We should mention that when commercial activities were forbidden, the only activity open to them was money lending, a practice denounced as 'pitiless', as Alexandru II Mircea specifies in a letter dated 1568. The historian Andrei Pippidi considers that 'the interest is inversely proportional to the region's development',[68] but it is no less true that the practice only appeared as a result of the curbing of Jews' rights. In general, disdain of the Jews' economic and financial activities leads to an exaggeration of their implication in these activities. Things were little different in Venice or Ragusa in the fifteenth and sixteenth centuries. The Venetian state, for example, exerted careful control over these activities, imposing collective taxes on the Jews. In Venice, Bucharest and Alba Iulia, as in any country (and in all restrictive times), there was a dissociation between the existing laws and the pragmatic attitude adopted, which allowed Judaic life to continue.[69]

Let us now turn to Serbia and the shores of the Adriatic to find other common points with Central-Southeastern European society. Dubrovnik's archives mention a relatively large Jewish population even at the beginning of the fourteenth century; during the next few centuries, a strongly organized Jewish community was present here. Like Venice, medieval Ragusa was a meeting point for the two great European ways of thinking, Catholic and Greek Orthodox. Its geographical position on the continent's median line underscores this convergence. Another factor in the composite structure of this fortress city was the spread of Islamic influences to the Dalmatian coast.

As for the Jewish population of Dubrovnik (Ragusa), there was a great influx of Spanish Sephardi after 1492, principally merchants, whose activity led to the town's economic prosperity. Even in the sixteenth century, the Jewish houses and companies of Ragusa were responsible for establishing links between the Balkan Peninsula and the other states of Europe. They wielded great authority in the exchange economy of the times, which peaked during the years of the Austrian–Turkish conflicts, 1593–1606.[70] The Jews in Ragusa were familiar with every type of trading activity in the region between the Mediterranean and the Black Sea, and they realized the surprising economic potential of the Balkan Peninsula, and the exchange system that was professed and asserted itself in the region.

These Jewish settlers came not only from the Iberian Peninsula, but also from the nearer West, from Northern Africa and from the Danube countries. Radovan Samardžić identifies the question as being, on the one hand, of Balkan–Italian–Jewish connections, and on the other, of the ties created, without which the circulation of goods would have been impossible. The Ragusan and Turkish systems were connected to the port of the Adriatic fortress,[71] and the Jews knew well the facilities offered by the geography of the region. But they also made use of the complicated political map, and their strategy can be traced using the excellent information supplied by Yugoslavian and Italian archival documents. Jewish Ragusa enjoyed its triumphs, as did Ancona 'as long as Ancona is still full of life, that is to say until the first years of the seventeenth century'. The two cities were part of a common network.

Movements are often noted in acts of the republican councils.[72] The community of Ragusa became known through its organization (it was led by a consul), its schools and rabbis, and the books written by its scholars and poets, while its Jewish doctors were of international renown. The great Amatus Lusitanus worked here, a doctor and man of culture and great erudition. He wrote a famous work in seven volumes, entitled *Curationum Medicinalium Centuriae Septem*, each volume containing a hundred histories of medical cases. The seventh volume ends with the famous Amatus oath, in which the author declares that he has always been interested in his patients' health more than in personal advantage, and that he has never discriminated a Jew from a Christian or a Muslim.

This same community nurtured the brilliant poet Doctor Isaiah Cohen, also known under numerous pseudonyms – Didacus Pyrrhus, Jakobus Flavius, Jakob Eborensis or Lusitanus. He maintained good relations with the aristocracy and with the town's citizens, with local poets, artists and scientists. His poetry, written in Latin, bears the mark of the Renaissance. His influence in the Southeastern region was considerable. In this same town, works in Hebrew were composed by other writers, such as Aaron Cohen, Shemen Tov and Z'kan Aharon. The activity of Rabbi Aaron Cohen remained important for the Judaic diaspora at the end of the sixteenth century and the first half of the next century. A born orator, a brilliant exegete and writer, Cohen also organized the restoration of the old synagogue in the ghetto, and of the old cemetery.[73] He himself is an example of a Jew's meandering existence in the diaspora. He studied in Italy, at the 'Levantine school' of Venice, and even if science was the guide of his life, Cohen also engaged in commerce, obliged to assume his brother's condition in order to survive. He lived in Sarajevo, Belgrade, Sofia, Ragusa and in Italy. His work, consisting mainly of highly intellectual Biblical commentaries, as well as an ode to God for the salvation of the Jews, was published together with that of his grandfather, and then transmitted across almost all of Europe: Constantinople, Thessaloniki, Rome, Sofia, Ankara, Amsterdam, Italy, Germany, as well as Jerusalem.[74]

A significant number of the Jews of Buda settled in Belgrade after the defeat of the Hungarians in 1526. It was here that, in the next century, the Messianic movement of Sabbatai Zevi was most fervently followed, coming from Smyrna via Thessaloniki. One of the main Jewish communities in Serbian territory was born here. Its development coincided with the arrival of Meir Angel, the first rabbi of Belgrade, and author of several treatises on Judaic law, entitled *Halakha*. The Jews prospered. In 1617, on the initiative of Jehuda Lerma, a yeshiva was opened, later becoming an important centre of Judaic teaching. The great treatise of the prominent *Halakha* specialist Simha Ha Cohen, *Sepher Shemot*, was written here. The contribution of Belgrade Jews to the history of Judaic religious literature in the seventeenth century is significant. Among the most important writers of the Belgrade school is Joseph Almosnino. His work, *Ehud ben Josef*, published by his son Isaac after his death, is the central text for the culture of this community.

The Zohar and the mystic science of the Kabbalah – a form of mysticism organized in the school of Safed whose creator, Rabbi Isaac Luria,[75] was accorded great veneration, accompanied by a yearning for the Messiah, whose arrival was awaited each day – were studied in Ladino, and the spread of these doctrines brought hope to the Jews. The time was ripe, and between 1650 and 1666 the Sabbatarian movement was well received by the oppressed masses, not only in Southeastern Europe, but in Northern Europe, Asia Minor and Africa. The year 1666 was 'apocalyptic' for fanatical Christians, but a Messianic year in the history of Jewish mysticism: 'Through the hopes raised by Sabbatai Zevi, the people's excitement reached such a high level that its author could no longer stand aside and had to join the torrent of events.'[76] He was recognized as the Messiah thanks to his 'disciple', Nathan of Gaza, who organized the movement's theology, assuring its dissemination. News of Sabbatai's arrival enthused the Jewish people.

In fact, this glorification of a 'redeeming apostate' was possible only in conditions of tormented instability (in which one civilization engendered a dialogue with all others), a 'terrible sacrilege' for Judaic thought, a profound and paradoxical mystery. According to historian Mircea Eliade, this was the first serious deviation within medieval Judaism, one that gave birth to religious anarchy. Kabbalah specialist Nehemia Kohen's denunciation of the fake 'Messiah' made the downfall of Sabbatai inevitable. Yet the movement's echoes could not be stopped, and were present in many communities, especially across the Balkan Peninsula. One of Sabbatai Zevi's followers, Nehemya Hayim ben Moshe, was born in Sarajevo around 1650.[77] He himself admitted that his parents came from Sarajevo. Accused by Rabbinic society of being a secret missionary of Sabbatarism, he travelled from one place to another. Weaned on the spirit of Rabbinic literature and steeped in the mystic doctrine of the Zohar and the Kabbalah, he continued the Messianic hopes of the Jews. He moved from Thessaloniki to Belgrade in 1683, and was captured by the Germans in Valona. After being freed, he returned to Thessaloniki. From 1698 to 1702 he lived in Nablus, Jerusalem and Sidon. He was exiled from Jerusalem, where the Rabbis proclaimed a *herem* on him. One of Nehemia Hayim's plans was to settle the disciples of Sabbatai in Tiberias. Despite his deep ties with Judaism and Israel's Torah, he continued his spiritual adventure in Europe and Northern Africa.

Alongside these controversial figures, there were also remarkable men of culture who were unanimously appreciated by the Jews. This was the case with David Pardo, the son of Venetian professor and rabbi Jakob Abraham, the author of *Shoshanim le David*, a commentary in two volumes on the *Mishna*; *Maskil le David*, an annotation of the exegesis of Rashi (printed in 1761); *Lamnatzeah le David*, which addressed the problem of property rights to land in the *Mishna*; and *Hasdei David* (the most important of his writings), an explanation of the *Tosephata* to which he dedicated the last twenty years of his life. According to Yakir Eventov, many of his poems were found in Spanish and Italian prayer books, being dedicated to Jewish holidays. He also visited Eretz Israel towards the end of his life, just like Nehemya Hayim, but, unlike him, he settled in the Holy Land. His departure was a festive occasion, and the approval of his Sarajevo co-religionaries is mentioned in the community's *pinakes* (from *pinkas*, meaning notebooks in Hebrew).[78]

Being present in more than one place at the same time, the Jew never forgets to be the measure of himself: 'Know thyself' is the supreme motto of his civilization. He is always turning to history, to his destiny. Braudel considers that it is the destiny of his diaspora. An agitation pushes him in the depths of his ego. He is aware of the spiritual remains of his forefathers which he bears inside himself, of that soul 'born of many selves.'[79] In Central Europe, home to some of the largest Jewish communities, the myth of the Golem was created, one of the most famous forms of the popular Judeo-Kabbalistic legends. As we have seen, as a result of being expelled from Spain, 'the pathos of Messianism' invaded the new Kabbalah in the sixteenth century: 'The beginning and the end were linked and understood together. The cataclysm received the value of salvation: it represents the pains at the birth of the Messianic age.'[80] It was in this context that the Prague ghetto became famous – the Golem, the clay statute created here by Kabbalist Rabbi Juda ben Bezalel Liva (also known as Rabbi Löw) is a phantasm of mankind's origins, the 'archetype', in Jung's terms, existing deep within the unconscious, profound, individual and collective, which unites all beings and all cultures beyond time and history.[81] In the Prague ghetto the Jew was a prisoner within the grey walls of a medieval-modern fortress, a place where the absurdity of existence forced him to attempt to surpass his own condition, asserting of the transcendental, without which escape from the labyrinth seems impossible: 'A repetition of the original creative act, the uninterrupted dream of the golden age of humanity.'[82]

The Golem thus becomes the symbolic defender of the Jewish people living as a diaspora, in the shadows of the ghetto where he must pace out his life. A name unknown to many today, but one that expresses the interior meandering of the soul on the road to self-knowledge. The meaning is at once abstract and magic. During this retreat, the Jew will become conscious of his own tragic destiny. In his exegesis dedicated to Meyrink, Michel Achard reveals to the reader the true initiatic, interior voice.[83] Essentially, it is the dialectics of transparence and the obstacle, of the pure and impure which is reached by this inevitable marriage of light and shadow, enabling us to summon the power necessary to penetrate another world, beyond death. Surprisingly, perhaps, such a doctrine may be closely related to gnosticism.

What is certain is that the two tendencies that manifest themselves so clearly in the Judaic diaspora, mysticism and magic, 'come closer and coexist as in the history of Jews. Most often, it seems to be placed outside time. Its dark exterior is a chance for interior light. Are we going too far if we suggest a comparison with the transcending universe of the blind, as the supreme expression of isolation and loneliness?'[84] Borges, analyzing Goethe's syntagm *alles nähe werde fern* (all that is close becomes distant), stated that when evening falls even the closest things grow in distance from our eyes, adding, 'in the same way that the visible world distanced itself from my eyes'.[85] The ghetto, as the loss of sight, is not a catastrophe or 'total disaster'. On the contrary, it is a new means of confirming one's own powers, intellectual and spiritual, capable of defeating the Minotaur at any time.

The last mystical movement in Judaism we shall consider is Hasidism, which appeared in Podolia and Volhynia. The founder of the movement, Rabbi Israel Baal Shem Tov ('The Teacher of Good Reputation' – Besht for short), neutralized Sabbatarian Messianism, abandoning the exclusivist system of a secret initiatic brotherhood (the traditional Kabbalah), promoting instead a mysticism which performed a social function. In his doctrine the ordinary man gained access to the spiritual discoveries of the Kabbalists. Its success was immense, and its most heroic and creative period was the second half of the eighteenth century. The limits of traditional Judaism were revived. As Eliade states, 'The place of the traditional Talmudist erudite or of that initiated in the classical Kabbalah was taken by the "pneumatic", the enlightened one, the prophet Tzaddik ("The Fair Man"), that is to say the spiritual master, most often becomes the example.' The important factor now was the behaviour of the 'holy' man, not the exegesis of the Torah or the esoteric character of the Kabbalah. Not all Jewish consciences evolved thus.

The strange Messianism I have described, as well as the 'archetype' presented above, can be associated with real philosophical reflections, some touching on scepticism and atheism. In this context the intellectual love of God professed by Leon Abravanel, and later by Spinoza, is highly relevant. But for those times and circumstances, religious superstitions and exaltations became a natural component of a community that found itself alone before an entire continent. It is no doubt desirable to distinguish between true and false metaphysics, since this will enable us to give a balanced judgement of the dominant tendencies at this point in history. In the case of ghetto Jews there was an alternation between light and dark, mixed with or accompanied by superstition, or even infused with metaphysical jargon. Nothing, however, was faked.

Was this a state? Perhaps it was more a popular philosophy, whose enlightenment touches us, offering a glimpse into the faculties of human intellect and its secret sources. In a region of great confluences, the transition zone from Central to Southeastern Europe – the region encompassing Dalmatia, Croatia, Serbia, Slovakia, Greece, Hungary, Transylvania and Banat – we will discover traits common to all ethnic groups, including the Jews, even if that Talmudic distinction is impossible to avoid. Impossible because Judaic civilization rejects true assimilation, and still practises a degree of forced or deliberate seclusion. The seventeenth century displayed the first signs of future emancipation, conditions in which the convergences would become numerous. At this point the Jew came into contact with, learned and mastered the Other's way of life, while transmitting his values, spiritual or material. Sometimes, though far less often, Jews became Christians.

The historical studies upon which I base my point of view, as well as the documents I have studied referring to cultural life, furnish sufficient supporting examples.[86] Let us keep a sense of proportion. What was happening in the West during the transition to the Modern Era or even earlier cannot be compared with the slow emancipation of the Central-Eastern nations. That mutations did take place in this part of Europe is obviously true. Without reaching Western levels of organized cultural and community life, the Jews of this region contributed to the development of 'corridors' through which information, ideas and scientific experiments were transmitted. Relations with co-religionaries remained interrupted and enabled the dissemination of teaching. Sometimes they achieved more than that: the study of Hebrew language and culture, which had become compulsory in Western universities, became a major bridge of communication. Books in Hebrew were brought by former students, colporteurs and merchants in general, and then acquired by private collectors and the libraries of colleges or monasteries. The Hebrew language became a subject of study for many other intellectuals of the times, belonging to other religions. Transylvanian humanist Nicolaus Olahus (Nicholas the Wallachian) was especially interested in mastering the language, his particular ambition being to achieve an accurate Latin translation of the Book of Daniel which, due to its 'hidden secrets', he wanted to approach and to interpret as objectively as possible. In his correspondence with Dutch philologist Johannes Campensis, a man steeped in Latin, Greek and Hebrew, Olahus states frankly that such 'scientific knowledge will not only be to his liking, but also to all those who study the Holy Scriptures'.[87] For his part, Campensis was clearly interested in maintaining ties with certain Jewish scholars from Germany and Italy, recommending to Olahus that he should consult Elias Levi (Elia Levi ben Asher), 'wiser than all the learned men who have lived in the past thousand years'.[88]

The Jewish communities possessed an encyclopedic culture which Jewish doctors introduced to the universities of the Czech lands, Slovakia, Hungary, Transylvania, Moldavia and Poland. Even in Spain, Jews monopolized the sciences, especially the medical arts.[89] The medical profession earned them a certain prestige during the fragile equilibrium of the European diaspora, a phenomenon that can also be observed in the continent's eastern hemisphere. There were many Jewish doctors at the princely courts, and, as documentary evidence shows, they were engaged in a broad range of activities. In the seventeenth century the Transylvanian princes benefited from these services, and granted certain privileges to doctors – these had some impact on other social categories of Jews. The convergences I have mentioned became possible as the old school of Alba Iulia was expanded and its library was founded, and transferred to Aiud (Nagyenyed) in 1662, but they came about especially as a result of many young people's studies in the great German, Swiss, Dutch, English, French and Italian universities. At the time when Martin Opitz was invited to teach at the Collegium Academicum, approximately one thousand Transylvanians were sent abroad to study.[90] The communities needed to establish a dialogue, often in dramatic circumstances. The Spanish tragedy, where the Jews found themselves among Arabs and Spaniards, was repeated in Hungary from 1593 to 1606, and from 1686 to about 1700 through the terror of being situated between the imperials and the Turks. This state made the Jews involuntary inheritors of the civilizations that surrounded them and whose goods they disseminated in one sense or another.

The eighteenth century brought changes to spiritual values that were seen as a necessity rather than a loss of identity. I will examine material and spiritual culture together, as we can observe authentic mutual influences between the two. Let us not forget that this was the century in which reason was elevated to the status of coordinator of all human actions. The Romantics were to follow one hundred years later, as well as nationalism. The German *Aufklärers*, the Jew Moses Mendelssohn among them, embodied the ideal of the emancipation of the European peoples – an emancipation that would also mark what history was to call the second Renaissance of the Jewish people. This emergence from the ghetto into the wider world had good and bad consequences, but as a historical turning point it was clearly brought about by encyclopedic and rationalist philosophy. It was a process of adapting as you go, a setting of the pace.

In *Jerusalem oder über religiöse Macht und Judenthum*,[91] Mendelssohn predicts a great progressive Reform, not just for the Jewish people, but for others as well. He was greatly appreciated for this by the most representative thinkers of the Enlightenment. Kant praises him for the religious reconciliation and freedom of conscience which he promotes, for his championing of the profound and necessary freedom to choose the way to raise oneself to divinity. 'Our Church,' he wrote, 'will finally have to think how to set aside everything that can be a burden and oppress its conscience.'[92]

The Viennese Empire instituted a civil or military administration in the territories conquered from the Turks, and attempted to obtain as exact an estimation as possible of the population of all localities. (We are now referring to the region around which so much gravitated, and which was to provoke long disputes among the three empires whose borders and interests met there: Turkish, Hapsburg and Tsarist.) Many Jews, finding it difficult to be admitted into cities, which they could achieve only in exchange for large taxes, decided to live on their outskirts. This ban was lifted in 1739, at least in Banat, Transylvania and Hungary (where I was able to consult data from published and unpublished archival documents). Furthermore, after migration from Central to Eastern Europe doubled and Ashkenazi Jews were admitted, the population lists show two separate groups, *Spanische Judengemeinde* and *Deutsche Jedengemeinde*.[93] This is also the case in the equivalent documents from Lugoj and Timișoara.

On other occasions, the administration provides us with tables, listing houses, the names of Jews, their number, the taxes they pay and the social categories to which they belong. This is the case of the institutionalized life of Jews in Carei (Nagykároly),[94] or, along the same lines, the division of Jewish taxpayers in some Hungarian regions such as Sopron, made available to us through the documents of the Alexander Scheiber edition.[95] In general, imperial rules were imposed, based on a detailed knowledge of precedents, such as the Transylvanian or Hungarian Diet debating the barring of Greek, Armenian, Jewish or Serbian from participating, according to their earnings, in public expenditure. Decisions were made by the seats of justice of the counties, through the municipal councils and magistrates. Many interdictions were issued, especially in Transylvania in the first half of the eighteenth century. Obligation to pay military tax along with the usual annual taxation was arbitrarily imposed; the same occurred when Jewish families expressed their wish to settle in as many towns as possible. In Cluj and Dej the formalities necessary to settle in the community were put off.

A document written in 1722 states that the arrival of outsiders would prejudice the town's inhabitants; the motive behind this statement was the sale of plum brandy, which caused the magistracy to limit their right to sell alcoholic beverages and forbade them from settling in the town.[96] A certain religious conscience lay behind some of these decisions, of course. These are not the only occasions on which the Jews were forced to live outside the town walls or in the countryside. In Alba Iulia, a petition addressed in 1729 by the Commercial Company of Jews to the Governor of Transylvania indicates other injustices as well, this time on the part of the judge and town council. An attempt was being made to drive the Jews from Alba Iulia, which was contrary to all princely dispositions and to Article LXXXII of the *Approbatae Constitutiones*.[97] Intervention by the Royal Gubernatorial Council, through the pen of a well-known scholar (Sámuel Köleseri), now acting as Gubernial Secretary, re-established the freedom to trade.[98]

As we know, however, much of the thinking behind these documents was still bound by medieval precepts, and so the version of events described by cabinet and chancellery papers was not always a true reflection of what was really taking place. Men often ignored papers, either in ignorance or with perfect awareness. Furthermore, the circumstances of the moment and even chance played their part, often encouraging a first step towards communication and understanding. This was true not only in Transylvania. In Banat, the absence of the privileged classes – or, to be more exact, their disappearance after becoming part of the Turkish Empire – as well as a linguistically and religiously diverse population, made exclusion impossible during the first century of Austrian rule.

By way of illustration, while in Dej clear restrictions were in place, in Timișoara the town administration invited the Jews Jakob, Moise and Abraham Köpisch of Pressburg to sign a contract for the installation of a beer factory.[99] They enjoyed a complete monopoly, and the economic results were remarkable: their first beer factory, founded here in 1718, went on to gain European renown. The export of this drink became legendary, if we are to believe the claim that the beer – which in those times must have been prepared using water from the Timiş river – reached Brazil.[100] In 1726 the production of beer and plum brandy was also granted to two Jews, Menczer Farkas and Schlesinger Levi.[101] Of course, in attempting to discover the causes of this phenomenon, we cannot rule out political interests or the desire to match the economic development of other provinces. Useful comparisons can be drawn between the socio-economic and institutional-political history of Transylvania and the Banat, comparisons that have thus far been ignored by historiographies dealing with the problem unilaterally.[102] Maramureş provides a special case for Jewish history.

One cannot ignore the whole here, either. What is certain is that there are more factors influencing the greater or lesser freedom accorded to the Jews. There are objective reasons as well. In 1738, plague was ravaging the empire, prompting Charles VI to try to check the danger by forbidding the access of Jews, Serbians, Romanians and Armenians to Hungary, Transylvania and Banat. Many places were contaminated by the epidemic and this appeared to be the only way of preventing it from spreading.[103] There were precise indications regarding the disease – suspected cases in Ocna Sibiului, Porumbacu and Guşterita, while in Alba Iulia two Jews originally from Ploieşti (in Wallachia) had died.[104] There were countless victims in Timişoara, where the entire population was affected between 1738 and 1740.

What were the origins of the Jews from Satu Mare (Szat-márnémeti), Arad, Bihor County (Bihar megye), and those from Hungary, Transylvania and the Banat? The conscriptions of the eighteenth century in the counties of Arad and Bihor and in the town of Satu Mare – contained in Spielmann's edition – show that they came from Moscow, Poland, Germany, the Czech lands and Hungary. In a document issued in Pressburg by the Hungarian Lieutenancy Council, the names of the aristocratic protectors of Transylvania are recorded: Counts Batthyány and Czobor, and Baron Palocsay. In other cases their foreign protectors are listed: Count Kaunitz and Prince Liechtenstein of Moravia, the Prince of Nikolsburg, Prince Visnyovszki of Poland,

Prince Dietrichstein of Frankfurt and so on.[105] The conscriptions of the counties of Hungary – reproduced in the Scheiber edition – give a much larger number of Jewish inhabitants, as well as their zigzag motion between Buda, Kismárton, Veszprém, Sopron and Tolna on the one hand, and Pressburg, Vienna, Lemberg and Frankfurt on the other.[106] We can easily deduce this from the name of the protector and the places of origin. In Alba Iulia, things are not quite the same. Besides the Jews arriving from Lublin, Lemberg, Cologne, Moravia and Hungary, those of Greece, Bulgaria, Wallachia and Moldavia settled here. Another *mixtum compositum*, in terms of linguistic and intellectual exchanges.

The condition of a wandering son is evident. By way of illustration, let us consider the declaration of Moses Judas, which was actually asked of all Jewish residents (and not only them) of Alba Iulia by the 'Royal Government and the Great Supreme Directorate of the Imperial-Royal Chamber of Transylvania, as a result of decisions taken of mutual accord':[107]

> M. J., about 28 years of age, originating from Turkey, namely from the town of Nikopolis, is in the company of Transylvanian Jews, and pays an episcopal tax, as well as the country's tax, of 30 Hungarian florins and 40 dinars. He does not contribute to any other Company, except the one already mentioned. As a taxpayer, he owns a house, whose communal taxes reach 30 Hungarian florins. He practises commerce, within the borders of Transylvania, with Turkish goods, but mostly with those brought from Vienna, whence he has a yearly profit of 2 thousand Hungarian florins. Subtracting the expenditures for his home, he was left with a net profit of 200 Hungarian florins this year.

Or another example: 'Aaron Isaac, about 48 years of age, originating from Moldavia, the town of Iași, of Jewish nationality, married. He has been in Transylvania for 40 years, and in Alba Iulia for 30 years.'[108] In Banat, Timișoara, Lugoj and Caransebeș, the Jews admitted as residents were former inhabitants of Belgrade and Ragusa, of Nikopolis and Rusciuk.[109] They were the first to settle here, a few families surviving the period of transition from the Ottoman regime to the Hapsburgs, as noted in the documents of 1716.[110] The Ashkenazi also reached this region, the conscriptions of 1742 signalling their organization as a distinct community. They originated from Hungary, the Czech lands, Moravia, the German principalities and Austria.[111]

Whenever Vienna stretched out its tentacles, its interests were plain to see. The limits of absolute thinking can be perceived everywhere and always: the direction of society had to be coordinated from Vienna. A significant piece of legislation for this new phase in the life of the Jewish diaspora was the 'royal resolution in the domain of the systematic rules of the Jewish nationality', a decree signed by Joseph II in 1783 and issued by the Hungarian Lieutenancy Council. It was valid in Hungary and Transylvania, across all the regions of the empire where Jews lived.[112] It declared that Jewish youths had the right to attend schools, to study in their own educational institutions, the school books being approved by imperial authorities. They had the right to attend institutions of higher learning, on the condition that they knew one of the official languages: German, Hungarian or Serbian. The Jewish language was to be used in religious processions and in the study of religious books.

Teachers could be Jews or could belong to other linguistic or religious groups.[113] Could this possibly have been in the empire's interest? Simply by pursuing apparently random fragments of the region's cultural history, we are able to judge things correctly – the Enlightenment brought a certain relaxation of rules to Transylvania, at least intellectually. Books, many containing echoes of the new era, became even more pervasive, thanks to students and professors, merchants and noblemen, and not least through the famous colporteurs of Cluj, Sibiu, Alba Iulia and Târgu Mureș (Marosvásárhely). Homo Religiosus was losing ground to scholars, writers, historians and philologists. Anti-dogmatism, so clearly asserted in the West, also reached Eastern court circles.[114] It filtered down, slowly but surely, on both the private and the public level, through Hebrew books of great value, books on Jewish history and culture. The collections of Teleki, Batthyány and Brukenthal were founded in Târgu Mureș, Alba Iulia and Sibiu respectively. And in Hungary, at Illésfalu, that of István Csáky, in Serbia, at Karlowitz, that of Stefan Stratimirović, in Buda, that of Ferenc Széchenyi. Some of these (or their families) had been protectors of Jews who, as we have seen, had settled in their domains. I have found Csáky and Batthyány in documents, as well as their predecessors.

We should not forget that as early as 1695, Sámuel Köleseri, a Calvinist theologist, but best known as a man of science and a specialist in Hebrew, acquired for his library a large number of Hebrew books published in the West, in Amsterdam, Frankfurt, London, Leipzig, Leiden and Basel. They included lexicons and dictionaries, books on grammar and practical rhetorics, volumes on monetary history, ancient history and Bibles. This information has reached us through *Conscriptio et Aestimatio librorum Samuelis quondam Köleseri de Keresér*.[115] The variety of titles can be explained by the encyclopedic character of the Transylvanian Enlightenment scholar's studies, though philology and history occupied pride of place. Ancient Oriental culture was one of his favourite subjects. At least in this way, more and more people came to know, and in some cases attain a deeper knowledge of the Babylonian Talmud, the Jews' religious and civil ceremonies, Biblical geography, the history of the great Temple of Jerusalem, the Judaic synagogues, the Old Testament, and so on.

Such ways of bridging the gaps were not isolated, and indicate the beginning of a new openness. Tipografia Universitatis Hungaricae Budae, whose modern activity began in 1777 (taking up the publishing activity which already existed here in the sixteenth century), published books in Hebrew, as well in German, Hungarian, Greek, Russian, Romanian, Serbian, Croatian, Bulgarian and Ukrainian. Titles included in *Index Librorum Selectorum* demonstrate the constant interest in the culture, religion and history of Israel. In those years, Buda had been two centuries ahead. *Systematica gentis Judaicae regulatio* granted Jews the right to settle in all free royal towns, except where there was mining, the right to pursue any economic, religious or cultural activity, and in return asked of them to respect their contacts, obligations, testaments, commercial books, documents and trial decisions. Jews were to respect these irrespective of the language in which they had been written: Hungarian, German or Latin.

It also decided that juridical acts and publications signed (by the leaders of the communities) in Hebrew were to be formally recognized across the entire empire. Restrictive steps referring to the wearing of beards or the Germanization of names cannot be ignored, however: these were applied with clear intentions, and their consequences would be felt later, during the process of assimilation that took place during the nineteenth and twentieth centuries. I will not dwell upon this, especially since the phenomenon of conservation, of maintaining identity, was at least as strong.

The regulations introduced by the Hapsburgs were not simply the result of principles derived from the policy of enlightened despotism, but also the consequence of collective memories, of opinions expressed by the leaders of communities and subsequently published. Evidence for this can be found in the circular edited at the end of the eighteenth century entitled *Opinio de Judaeis*.[116] In Transylvania, confined to the towns indicated by imperial decrees, and limited in 1650 by the *Aprobatae Constitutiones* to Alba Iulia, Jews sought over the next hundred years to obtain from the authorities the right to settle in all towns of the province (not just in villages), in the same conditions granted to Greeks and Armenians. Thus they numbered 2,000 in 1766,[117] doubling to 4,047 in 1782, and a few years later, in 1789, the figure reached 4,166.[118] The aforementioned document stresses the integration of Jews in the economic activities of the region, not only with regard to commerce, but especially to the manufacturing industry.

The new regulations also allowed Jews to practise agriculture.[119] This phenomenon is particularly interesting – and rare, as they acquired this privilege in very few regions – in Maramureș (Máramaros), where, having obtained land, Jews exercised the profession of farmers alongside Romanians. Rabbinic jurisdictions received the official resolutions and supervised the commercial companies led by Jews, in the same way as they coordinated synagogues and schools. Community members were allowed to attend Christian institutions of learning as well, on condition that they learned the language of the place where they lived. Thus, the communities of Alba Iulia, Cluj, Sibiu and Brașov, as well as those of Satu Mare, Oradea and Carei, went through dramatic changes.

Let us pause to discuss the case of Jews in Maramureș. They arrived here from Polish Galicia, but also from the other regions of Poland. They originated in Hungary as well, but in much smaller numbers. The Polish persecutions of the sixteenth and seventeenth centuries are well known, though the anti-Semitism of those times, which was proliferated by rulers and many noble families, was only one episode in a series of sad events. Over the broader course of history we can observe this identity crisis repeating itself constantly, the Polish Catholic conservative spirit doing away with the difficulty of false accusations and the misunderstanding of Judaism. The movement of Jews to neighbouring regions, then, was not accidental in the time of transition to the Modern Era.

In 1780, Karl Gottlieb von Windisch reckoned the Jewish population as 1,200 in the county of Satu Mare, 300 in Bihor and several hundred in Maramureș.[120] We know that at the beginning of the nineteenth century there was a synagogue, a rabbi and a Jewish national judge in Sighetu Marmației (Máramarossziget), thanks to information supplied by Johann von Csaplovics.[121] In the seventeenth and eighteenth centuries, the Jews frequently passed through Maramureș on their way from Poland towards Transylvania. Their number reached 30,000 annually. A minority of them settled in urban or rural areas. We should not forget that a centre such as Baia Mare (Nagybánya) was much appreciated by merchants for its great fairs – they visited from Leipzig in 1626, as well as from Vienna, Sofia and Cernăuți (Chernivtsi-Czernowitz).[122] However, our understanding of the administrative and political regime of such a town is qualified by the fact that the Jews were in no hurry to settle here: the town magistrate exercised judicial and executive powers to a dictatorial degree,[123] which could not have been to the liking of any Jew eager to exert his freedom of conscience. The drawbacks were obvious.[124] It was not until the nineteenth century, after 1850, that the Jews of Maramureș enjoyed a properly organized cultural, social and administrative life.

This was the time of the land grants I mentioned above. Jews now became farmers and shepherds, without giving up their previous occupations as merchants and artisans. They became masters of the land they bought in the mountains. They learned once again how to raise sheep from the Romanians of Maramureș, who had been sheep farmers for centuries. They built shelters for themselves in the Romanian fashion while tending their flocks, and prepared Kosher cheese, simultaneously becoming shepherds and specialists in the preparation of Kosher food. The interior of their shelters was constructed in the Maramureș style, and the exterior in the Someș style, with some variations according to specific conditions. Jewish shelters were situated in the valleys, while the Romanian shelters were found at higher altitudes. Sheds used for storing cheese and other sheep products also served as dwellings during pasturing. Despite these similarities, there were also differences between the Romanian and Jewish ways of raising sheep:

> Rennet from the Romanian shepherds is made from the stomach of a suckling lamb a few weeks old; the stomach is filled with regular milk or new milk (milk from sheep that have just lambed), then it is salted, the ends are tied together and it is put to dry next to the oven.

The Jewish shepherds only take rennet from Jews and it must be Kosher. The lamb or small calf is only slain by the Schachter and must be clean: this is confirmed by taking out the lungs and examining them. If there is no trace of illness on them, the animal is declared Kosher; the rennet is taken from the stomach and put in a vessel together with milk and salt. It is left thus until a large amount of milk evaporates; what is left is the Kosher rennet, to be used for making cheese. Jewish shepherds say a prayer before they start making the cheese, and on Saturday, when the law does not permit them to make cheese, they let one of the Romanian workers do it. The milk is thus left in the special vessel for 40 to 50 minutes.

When the milk has started curdling, it is 'broken' with a large wooden spoon. The curdled milk is well beaten with a special instrument until it becomes thin, and then the head shepherd puts his hands into the bottom of the vessel so that the part used for making butter is extracted.[125]

Jewish shepherds occupied the mountains until the beginning of the twentieth century, and in the regions of Maramureș and Bucovina they enjoyed great economic success. This phenomenon is unique to this part of Europe, one of the many specific traits of the Jewish diaspora. This was more than a mere attempt to recover their livelihood: having always been nomads, these Jews were attracted to shepherding, and quickly re-learned one of their principal activities during ancient times.

The knowledge we have of this historical movement can be connected to the century's intellectual revolution. Some of the references to Jews in Serbia, Bosnia, on the Dalmatian coast and in Thessaloniki are furnished by the so-called *pinakes* or accountant's books, but otherwise the only reliable sources during that period for news of important events in Moldavia or Wallachia are the most prominent Jewish writers, such as the Rabbi of Iași, Nathan Hannover, the author of an important dictionary, *Milon Safa Bérura*, in five languages, printed in Prague during the second half of the eighteenth century. It is worth emphasizing that the arts provide important primary historical sources right across the region: the costumes of women or folk objects from Sarajevo that preserve characteristic elements of Spanish folklore; the art of carving tombstones from Siret in Moldavia, where we find the symbols of great ancient civilizations; the majestic temples of Central-Eastern Europe, such as those of Buda and Oradea; and the splendid series of chandeliers which played various roles in the spiritual life of Jews in the Romanian principalities. Judaic art, like Jewish culture as a whole, while reminding us of the imperial emblems of Byzantine power and of the Hapsburgs and Romanovs, displays a unity in its diversity that the Jewish people created in Europe and then disseminated across the world.

Judaic civilization withdraws and opens out depending on the times and on the political, social, and cultural events it encounters. This conspicuous oscillation encouraged me to draw numerous comparisons with the Jewish people's movement from one end of the region to the other: this, I believe, is how one may discover the meaning of their wanderings. These wanderings repeatedly facilitated contact with Western cultural centres. This has enabled me to see afresh the characteristics of Judaism in Central-Southeastern Europe, describing them (as far as possible in this initial sketch) in relation to the links established with regions inhabited by Greeks, Turks, Serbians, Romanians, Poles, Hungarians and Germans.

Let us conclude that the Jews here, as in other parts of the world, continued to be bound to time and not to space; they were not sedentary, but nomads, and learning was a guide to them, so that they were never satisfied with the present, always seeing and thinking of the future. Our evaluation of Judaism should also be connected to our understanding of the ways of thinking among which it existed. For any Homo Europaeus in Eastern Europe, Judaism brings an extra sense of vigour through its love of books, of wisdom, of education and the perpetuation of beliefs. This explains the survival of the Jews during a long and difficult exile. The contacts they made and the directions they took cannot be understood outside the economic and commercial networks of Mediterranean, Central and Northern Europe. Jewish art, science and erudition reflect these convergences and, no matter where they made their presence felt, they defined essential elements of the Renaissance or the Enlightenment spirit.

Judaism carries within it a synthesis, combining the ancient oriental civilizations with those of the West, including echoes of life among the Balkan peoples in medieval and modern times. For example, the synagogue art of the lower Danube reminds us of Central European Baroque, of the Baroque of Constantinople, while the Jewish folk art of the Romanian principalities had its roots, as a well-informed contemporary researcher says, in the 'double level of

Romanian and Jewish interpretation of beauty, sometimes melting into unexpected syntheses, the result of centuries of living together, where the feelings of humanity, felt by both Romanians and Jews, was the fundamental mark of all works of art'.[126] In the same way, printing presses created by Jews across the entire continent also played a role in the European dialogue at the dawn of the modern age: they were famous for their ability to print books in different languages, and thus to adapt to the intellectual conditions in which they existed. And, since we spoke of Eastern Europe, we should acknowledge that, in the first decades of the eighteenth century, contact with the people of this region led to a kinship of spirit. This was the time of Enlightenment, and I believe that we will gain a better understanding of it by examining the ways in which Jewish organizational structures were incorporated into Christianity.

Perhaps the best way to understand the history of European Jews is to visit their graveyards, since these reflect an arc across time, a unity that was never shaken, a community that opened a dialogue with humanity, and withdrew in order to endure its times of crisis. And why do we mention gravestones? Probably because, behind their inscriptions and symbols, we can discover the great credo that guided Judaism through the millennia of diaspora. They enable us to see how it was possible to survive, to see the force behind that idea of oneness found in each individual, family and community. For example, the Jewish cemetery of Lugoj is evidence of a strong community, not so much in size, but rather in its social, economic, and political condition. The gravestones often indicate professions, functions, activities in Lugoj society during the period 1840–1940: lawyers, doctors, merchants, judges, pharmacists, landowners, factory owners. Some of the inscriptions date from the eighteenth century, indicating the first stage of their settlement in Lugoj. They are in Hebrew, German and Hungarian. Beginning with the nineteenth century, the majority are in German (unlike those of Cluj or other Transylvanian towns where they are most often in Hungarian). Hebrew inscriptions all belong to the Orthodox faith, which never abandoned its use of the language of the Torah.

We reproduce here some of the formulas used on the gravestones: *Hier ruhet in Frieden* (May he rest in peace), *Friede seiner Asche* (Peace to his soul), *Ehre seinem Angedenken* (Honoured be his name), *Szeretet egyesítő életükben méghaltukban sem váltak el!* (They loved their union during their lifetime and not even death could part them). Their conciseness reveals some of the fundamental meanings of the Judaic faith. They directly refer to the soul and the mind; the syntagms are a testimony to what the people were during their lifetimes and what they stood for. The cemetery not only shows the specific character of the faith and its traditions, but also the dimensions of a spirit turning towards its inner self. We find once again that closed civilization which, despite its ability to open up and communicate with other worlds, was directed towards the knowledge of one's own ego. In Timișoara, Arad, Oradea, Cluj, Bucharest, Budapest and Prague, graveyards are more than a collection of ornaments, more than an example of a particular art (however original) – they embody a multitude of traits uniting souls and consciences, transcending space and sometimes even suggesting an atemporal character. On each stone you read the importance given to the beauty and solidity of feelings which guided Jewish families.

The design of the wings on these graves, of the hands that embrace to symbolize the same vigorous trunk, define the idea of the family itself, the entwining signifying the orientation of the Judaic faith. The history of Judaism is not embodied by the leader of one or another, it is defined by the people as a whole. The overall impression one gains by visiting any Jewish cemetery is impressive, because in it lies all the suffering, but also the joy of seeing and meeting once again. This lies at the heart of the admirable convergence of East and West. We have seen Judaism not just as a faith or religion: it is a belief, and a philosophy as well, in the sense that what it propagates is strongly tied to what man is. Its aim is direct communication with God. How else can one explain the 'great duration' (two millennia) of a diaspora spanning the entire Earth? But what is the diaspora for the Jews? What does it represent on a spiritual level? Beyond political, economic and social circumstances, beyond the difficulties overcome, from pogroms to mass expulsions, we should acknowledge that the movement of the Jews from one region of Europe to another, and then across the world, represented a huge gain for the sum of human knowledge. Of course, not every period of Jewish withdrawal was followed by an opening out, and vice versa. Contact with other cultures, multiple connections with traditions (I have only mentioned a few in Central-Eastern Europe, but they can be observed in any part of the world), enriched Judaism, giving it a continuous opportunity to learn something new. The survival of the Jew himself required this, even if it only meant assimilating the language of the people among whom he lived.

From Mendelssohn to Canetti, we have many examples of this phenomenon just in the last centuries. In exile, the Jews bore a deep suffering, but the suffering of the wanderer set the spirit in motion, which in its turn created and disseminated ideas, both for itself and for others, becoming involved with others but never forgetting its own ego. Was survival guaranteed at the cost of loss of emancipation? What are we to think, looking again at the ghettos that were established in the large cities of Europe, the humiliation that these communities endured, but which they in a way accepted, as the only way to resist over the course of time? The leaving of the 'quartal'[127] could not come about without some form of sacrifice or renunciation, without communicating with the forms and structures of the town's organization, without fraternizing with human nature around them. Only thus, by proving their will, their power to create, by using their intellect on all occasions, could Jews really contribute to the edification of Homo Europaeus, and Judaism become a 'sustaining pillar' of universal culture, lending its rich experience of life and offering the world its wisdom and the music of its ancestral soul. Only through knowledge and communication was it possible to offer humanity some solutions for escaping the existential labyrinth. Only faith, paired with a correct understanding of the need for openness, enabled Jews to perform this crucial spiritual role.

And now, we might ask ourselves, to what extent does religion exert an influence on the thinking of modern Jewish intellectuals? Is religion a starting point, a source of inspiration? Does education play an important role in the formation of personality? Is it the legacy, the spirit of the eternal seeker, restless, never at peace with himself or with others? We are all born with a legacy, which is no merit of ours, but rather a gift of nature, akin to a talent. It is important to remember that Judaism bore and still bears a huge sacred tradition, whose bequests are no less sacred in the Modern Era (and not only to Europeans), and which, even when far removed from religion, even when assimilated, bears the mark of the Torah, and of the nation that gave birth to the Jewish people's parents and forefathers. There is a hidden symbolism here, concerning the rules of one's inner life and those of coexistence with others – like a ship on the waves, no matter how many storms bear down on it, it can never be abandoned. It is a will that cannot be shaken, a firm belief in human power, in its value, in the infinity of its existence.

Judaism considers that nothing is impossible for man. And perhaps this would be hard for us to believe, if we did not try to see things in perspective ourselves. It is probable that what we see beyond the immediate, beyond everyday life, beyond the here and now, was born with this vitality, with this temperament, with this instinct to survive. It is impossible to explain the continual evolution of the speed of thought, without believing in the ritualized activity of man. But if we go back to the era at the beginning of the diaspora, we will find in *Mishna* an answer to the question of what man can do: 'Man can set the world in motion the way God can.'

The tones of the sacred texts complement one another, sustaining one and the same belief: 'Listen, Israel, our God, the God, is one.' That ONE helped Judaism survive for almost six thousand years, granting it a world situated both in and beyond its earthly envelope. The modern Jew's aspirations will often follow this direction. His intellectual speculations have two sources: the Bible and Philosophy. Both nurture meditation and the transcendence of the spirit.

As bearer and emitter of the fundamental precepts of universal thought, Judaism profited from spiritual communions, unshackled by the servitude of administrative and political institutionalism. It made of God an ethical and social fact. In this context we might recall the thoughts of Rabbi Simon ben Iohai: 'The respect due to your father and mother is so important, that God even considered it above the respect due to Him.' Learned men have always tried to find in the words of the Bible that which corresponds to the needs of a more complex life. Professing an optimistic and meliorist concept of the world, Judaic philosophy spread ideas of the immanence of goodness and righteousness, and a set of symbols – the eagle, for example – connected to the relationship between man and divinity and the corresponding relationship between parent and child.

The symbol of the eagle operates at an educational level. Learning how to fly, a condition *sine qua non* of existence, is achieved by stimulation and care. The eagle appears in the Bible as an allegory of tact, of delicacy, of prudence, essential elements of harmony at both the family and the divine level. It is the intermediary between sky and earth, the symbol of man's spiritual journey, through which he aspires to a unitary destiny of planetary dimensions.

V

HOMO EUROPAEUS AND THE INTELLECTUAL REVOLUTION OF THE ENLIGHTENMENT

In the beginning there was the light of the Mediterranean and Europe half existed... Then the statues of Greece were lost in the northern fog and philosophy was born. And at sunset the Mediterranean light passed through the stained-glass windows of cathedrals. And the Gothic universe was born. And the light of Mediterranean painting enriched the shadowy depths and created Rembrandt and Vermeer. Then Europe left to work its miracle on all the landscapes of the Earth. But nowhere was the Mediterranean or its misty sister of the North to be found.

Eduard Pamfil

SOME ERAS OCCUPY A privileged place in the history of mankind. We look to them in order to understand the origins and meaning of our own existence, our reasoning, and the journey we have made towards the current expression of our spirit. Once identified, these periods enable us to rediscover what was essential to human becoming, and to see for ourselves the times of great metamorphosis, those immense leaps from old to new, and the admirable, open souls and consciences that made these great changes happen. It is not by accident that we are always invoking the great creations of the ancient world, of Biblical Israel, of Aristotelian Greece, of medieval Byzantium, and of the Renaissance, harking back to *Quattrocento* Italy. My intention over the next few chapters is to do something similar in the case of Enlightenment Europe, revealing the ideas, theories, books, institutions, personalities, indeed everything of value that helped to bring about the intellectual revolution at the dawn of the modern age.

I will attempt to present an original perspective on the subject. Moving beyond the fine studies by Ernst Cassirer or, more recently, Paul Hazard and Pierre Chaunu, I will present a broader picture of the cultural dialogue in Europe, revealing in greater detail evidence of the Enlightenment in Central and Southeastern areas, where the intellectual elite made many contributions of unquestionably universal value. I will describe some of the specific tendencies that originated in the great capitals of Western Europe in the eighteenth century – London, Paris, and Berlin – and then examine the smaller spiritual capitals of Central-Eastern Europe situated between Vienna, Buda, Karlowitz, Cluj, Bucharest, Petersburg, Athens and Constantinople. This approach will open up new perspectives, hitherto neglected in the study of European history.

I write as a Central-Eastern European historian, not in order to take issue with Western historiography, but rather to complete the picture of the history of the Enlightenment. Although economic and social infrastructure are important factors in defining the characteristics of an era or a region, scientific and economic considerations are not the subject of this study. I will refrain from any attempt at historical reconstruction, at bringing back to life Frederick II's Prussia or Catherine II's Russia, the Romanian principalities during the reign of the Mavrocordatos family, Serbia and Hungary under the Hapsburgs, francophone Greece, and so on.[1] Instead I will focus on Central-Eastern Europe and the Balkan region, where I have been able to consult primary sources, and gained access to less-known or even unknown sources of information that gave me the chance to analyze and interpret facts at first hand. Throughout my research I have kept an open mind about these older sources, generally preferring to reformulate the opinions they express or to offer a fresh point of view. My ambition is to present a coherent picture of the spiritual evolution of Eastern Europe. This is by no means a comprehensive account, but I hope it will help the reader towards a firmer grasp of the history of Enlightenment ideas.

Let us begin our account of Enlightenment thought by examining how states were organized and the idea of nation evolved, and within this wider context what spiritual conditions triggered a change in conscience immediately after the religious reforms of the seventeenth century, once Theophilos Corydalleus and Dimitrie Cantemir made their voices heard across Europe. If for the West 'the eighteenth century is a century of consolidation', as Pierre Chaunu puts it, for the East it was a new beginning of sorts. The French model of administrative monarchy was slowly spreading to the centre and east of the continent. The French language gained more and more ground, replacing Italian and Castilian in the South, and Latin in Hungary, the Scandinavian countries and the Netherlands. It became an international language, leading to the adoption of French culture in many states across the continent. The apogee of this French influence on the European elite was pinpointed by Chaunu as the decade 1760–70. Chaunu also states that the German language regained its 'rights within the empire and [began] the assault on the middle classes of all Danubian Europe' after 1770, but that

> the French position, which was incomparable to any other up to the end of the century, continued to assert the French model of administrative monarchy. One of the sources of inspiration of enlightened despotism is the French administrative monarchy, seen through the myth of Louis XIV. This is at the origin of much literature; the word, the problems linked to it, the interest in it, all originate in German historiography of the nineteenth century.[2]

Here the monarchical state appears to support Enlightenment thinking rather than the other way round – a formulation often found in eighteenth-century literature. In these conditions, those areas of Europe which had been slower to develop – Chaunu locates them within a triangle formed by the Danube, the Mediterranean and the East (meaning Russia) – began to develop somewhat earlier than the French historian leads us to suppose (1740). The first signs of transformation came around the first two decades of the eighteenth century, when superior forms of state organization were imposed in Russia by Peter the Great, in Moldavia and Wallachia under the rule of Greeks from the Phanar district of Constantinople, and in Transylvania and Hungary, and later Banat, Oltenia and Serbia by the change from Turkish to Hapsburg dominion. Of course, the rhythm of these political changes differed from one region to another, but the French conception of the state gained ground, as is clearly demonstrated by the examples of Bohemia, Austria, Hungary, Serbia, Banat and Transylvania.

The reality was complex, and I will attempt to show this from within, drawing on examples from intellectual life in Central and

Southeastern Europe. These regions experienced disturbances, crises of conscience, periods of hope and resignation. Modern institutional models and the legislation used by the Romanian and Russian princely courts already existed there in the seventeenth century: nothing is created in a vacuum, no evolution is possible without the proper conditions for changes in rhythm, without precedents. The ideas of Matei Basarab, Vasile Lupu, Peter the Great and Dimitrie Cantemir, and the systems of government proposed by Bethlen and Rákóczi, suggest that a significant chapter in the genesis of modern Europe took place outside the more developed world. The existence of Homo Ottomanicus is frequently invoked to explain a perceived backwardness in these regions, but this is only partly true: these historical conditions witnessed many successful developments in the evolution of thought. Decades before the Enlightenment, the autonomy of the Romanian principalities or the Greek diaspora encouraged the formation of an intellectual elite every bit as culturally sophisticated as Homo Europaeus. In the seventeenth century, humanism was professed in the schools of Târgoviște, in the Royal Academies of Bucharest and Iași, in the institutions founded in Athens and Constantinople, and in the urban architecture of old Novgorod or new Petersburg, by figures for whom distances had grown smaller, since they could convene in important cultural centres such as Padua, Venice, Leipzig, Uppsala, Krakow, Göttingen, Paris and Leiden.

The movement of political ideas is relevant here. For example, in Transylvania there was perfect continuity between the thinking of the seventeenth and eighteenth centuries. The principality bequeathed a code of laws, the *Approbatae Constitutiones*, which, along with the *Leopoldine Diploma* of 1691, lent Transylvania a special political standing that lasted 150 years. This was the context in which the great religious struggles emerged, and Romanians fought to assert their own dignity. In the first half of the eighteenth century, the appearance of a great political personality with an all-encompassing vision such as Inocențiu Micu-Klein had a great bearing on cultural activity in the region. His struggle – involving the interests of every stratum of society – 'represents first and foremost the striving of a social class that rises or aspires to rise by formulating its demands'. Micu-Klein's memoirs reveal him as a forerunner of the Romanian Enlightenment, for whom schooling, and indeed culture in general, were to be the principal means of developing the nation and, above all, its intellectual elite. As David Prodan writes:

To raise a new Romanian governing class that could take ownership of feudal domains that were disappearing, new aspirational strategies had to be found – cultural strategies. This objective was not to be achieved through the Catholic schools: Romanian schools needed to be founded, catering for the needs of the Romanian people, promoting their culture rather than estranging them from it and destroying their national identity. First and foremost, the clergy needed to be educated, so that it could in turn transmit culture. In [Micu-Klein's] view union itself was an instrument of culture, of raising the level of civilization.[3]

Inocențiu Micu-Klein's struggle made an impact at the European level, since its aim was the recognition of a nation. It is worth noting that it took place before the Enlightenment made inroads across Europe, preparing the ground for a historical, cultural and philosophical movement unique to Central, Eastern and Southeastern Europe: the Transylvanian School. It is, therefore, a clear expression of a wish for emancipation, for the strengthening of intellectual ties with the rest of Europe, and for modernization – new social structures, different political and religious hierarchies and a new education system. Banat was abreast of political innovations in Vienna from the beginning of Austrian rule, and conversant with the system of economic and social reforms proposed by the authorities in the Hapsburg capital. In the first decades of the eighteenth century there was no landed gentry in Banat,[4] and so, unlike the other provinces of the monarchy, the region experienced no conservative opposition to the rapid implementation of Austrian reforms. Banat enjoyed direct communication with Vienna's legislative, political, economic and cultural institutions. The consequences of this influence soon appeared, both in the emerging mercantile economy and the spread of Enlightenment ideas from Vienna, clearly inspired by the French despotic model. There were numerous examples of this influence, but we will confine ourselves here to those that reveal the European spirit evolving in a society which, though only at a preliminary stage in its development, was taking shape, asserting itself, maintaining a dialogue, making its presence felt, in short demanding its right to exist.

Progress was slow but genuine. Enlightenment despotism created new networks for the dissemination of books and ideas, of scholars and artists, so that by middle of the eighteenth century Central and

Central-Eastern Europe were ready and hungry for change. At this point Berlin became the capital of a twofold culture, encompassing both the European, francophone drive for emancipation, and the German Protestant *Aufklärung*. Similarly, Poland embodied the prosperity of Central-Eastern Europe, strongly influenced by the Febronianism coordinated by Chancellor Zamoyski. Vienna applied the ideology of the Enlightenment through the deeds of its great chancellors Hangwitz and Kaunitz, while Petersburg was the 'great lung' through which Russia breathed the air of the Enlightenment. Even as it spread and became universal, the Enlightenment spirit found specific forms of expression in each country – therein lay its richness and complexity. As Frederick II of Prussia stated:

> The good of society is your own. Without knowing it, you have strong ties with your homeland, so you cannot isolate yourself, nor separate yourself from it, without suffering because of your mistake. If the government is happy, you will prosper; if it suffers, its lack of success will impact on you… Love of your country is therefore not just something conventional, it really does exist.[5]

Studying the extraordinary transformations that took place during the Enlightenment, we can observe that the movement of ideas generated and developed throughout Europe, but also beyond (notably in the British colonies of North America), was initiated and then for a long time spearheaded by a group of intellectuals who for the most part came from religious backgrounds, and for whom dogma had become unbearable, like an ill-fitting garment. Emerging from a world of Protestant pastors, Anglican bishops, Lutheran teachers and, frequently, laymen, these thinkers declared a new vision of life and nature, advocating the power of the Enlightenment and of reason. There was only one temptation – liberation, specifically freedom of thought and action or, as Kant put it, the leaving behind of man's state of being a lesser being, unable to use his own intellect without being led by someone else. The new era was one of many talents, its champions in European intellectual circles including Michael von Loen, Peter Annet, Christian Benedict Michaelis, Johann Salomo Semler, Francisco Manuel do Nascimento, Warburton (bishop of Gloucester), Joseph Butler (bishop of Durham) and Benito Jerónimo Feijóo. Then there were other individuals, working in schools or churches, at their writing desks or in publishing houses, who prepared the ground for those who followed.

Assessing how Romanians and the other Southeastern ethnic groups – Serbs, Macedonians, Bulgarians and Greeks – felt the European impetus, Nicolae Iorga concludes that this not only facilitated 'the awakening of conscience, but also made possible the open declaration of a pride in the past, and the striving towards a better future'.[6] There is much written evidence from the eighteenth century to suggest that alignment of Central and Eastern European spirituality with the West was not accidental, even if differences were still apparent. The dialogue between East and West became permanent, creating a sort of pan-European communion, one soul tending in the same direction: this was the soul of Homo Europaeus, who had been present in the conscience of mankind since the time of Erasmus. His ideal, his dream, retained its deep symbolic value through the centuries and remains unfulfilled today, questioning our way of life and our beliefs, urging us to establish the true meaning of life while there is still time.

Modern thought is the result of strenuous efforts to form a clear idea of mankind's potential. In a famous study, Ernst Cassirer describes how the representatives of the Enlightenment tried to establish 'the relationship between ideas and reality', between 'law' and 'facts', at once demarcating these concepts and bringing them together. They believed that nationalism and history were strongly tied to and stimulated by the general movement of the times.[7] The Southeast was exposed to these ideas later than the West, but Enlightenment intellectuals who had settled in the region nonetheless enjoyed great success. The provinces of the Hapsburg Empire boasted some of the most diverse populations in Europe, and hence the greatest spiritual mix. Yet in these circumstances each nation fought to win or preserve its rights, freedom and spiritual identity. Romanians, Serbs, Croats, Hungarians and Slovaks all discovered the possibility of ties with Europe, gaining access to its literature and its political and religious ideas. Later, the reforms of Joseph II paved the way for the Enlightenment, introducing intellectual life to peoples who had hitherto been politically backward.[8] The new schools founded in Transylvania, Serbia and Hungary, and the founding of courses in great university centres such as Vienna, Rome, Göttingen and Lvov led to the formation of an elite spearheaded by teachers and the clergy.

These conditions saw the emergence of figures such as Samuil Micu, Gheorghe Șincai, Ioan Piuariu-Molnar, Petru Maior, Ioan Budai-Deleanu, Stefan Stratimirović, Iovan Raic, Dositej Obradović, Paisius of Hilandar, Anton Tomaž Linhart, Pavao Ritter Vitezović, Iosipos Moesiodax, Veniamin of Lesbos, József Podmánicky, Ferenc Széchenyi, Ignác Batthyány, Sándor Kőrösi Csoma, Samuel von Brukenthal, Ioan Teodor Callimachi, Paul Iorgovici, Gherontie Cotorea, Radu Tempea, Gheorghe Lazăr and many others. These same circumstances also fostered political and historical writing: for example, Inocenţiu Micu-Klein's *Supplex Libellus* was followed half a century later by two other important texts, *Supplex Libellus Valachorum Transsilvaniae* and the *Revendication of the Ilfyric Congress of Timişoara*.

The majority of the scholars listed above absorbed the new concepts of Western Enlightenment culture, and their individual efforts paved the way for the dissemination of Western writings, making clear that Central and Southeastern Europe needed to embrace the European Enlightenment.[9] Although they came from different ethnic and linguistic backgrounds, historical destiny brought them together: they had a shared vision in both their reception and their expression of Enlightenment culture, their unity of thought and feeling clearly demonstrated in their writings. Șincai's *Chronicle* belongs to both Southeastern and Central European historical literature, and can be compared with the Serb Iovan Raic's *History of Different Peoples, Especially of the Serbs, Bulgarians and Croatians* (Vienna, 1780) and the Bulgarian Paisius of Hilandar's *Istoria Slaveanobalgarsko* (1762): the latter work had a similar destiny to that of Șincai, circulating in manuscript copies. Furthermore, Șincai attended school in Central Europe and possessed a great deal of the Hungarian and Austrian spirit: his *Rerum spectantium ad universam gentem daco-romanam* is the result of his intellectual development during the years he spent in Pest. During this period he enjoyed a fruitful collaboration with György Kováchich in the study chambers of the library of Count Ferenc Széchenyi. There is also an interesting parallel between the historical works produced by the Transylvanian School and the writings of Metropolitan Stefan Stratimirović (especially his study *On the Wallachians*). We find in both a similar method of interpretation, with obvious models from Buda and Vienna, but most notably from Germany. It is probable that the Széchenyi Library or even Count Ferenc Széchenyi himself facilitated Stratimirović's access to Șincai's works, and those of the Transylvanian School in general.[10] The cultural and intellectual influence of the West, along with consistent communication within Central-Eastern Europe, stimulated great advances for society in the region.

What was the situation across Europe at the time when Central and Southeastern intellectuals came together in this way? What were their models, and what did these contribute to the formulation of their own feelings, values and choices? In terms of the masses, Pierre Chaunu is right when he states that of the 180 million people living in Europe during the eighteenth century, that of the Enlightenment, most did not subscribe to the ideals of Homo Europaeus the innovator: 'In the age of the Enlightenment, true Europeans – people who read, who thought, who expressed a coherent philosophical system – never numbered more than twenty million, nine-tenths of them concentrated in the densely populated median axis.'[11] Chaunu's analysis is an exemplary historical and historiographical study, combining the work of the statistician and demographer in order to reveal as accurately as possible the spiritual revolution of the times. Yet we should be cautious about drawing hasty conclusions from his assertions. Only in the last few decades have we begun to gain a clearer understanding of the historical and geographical factors we must take into account when studying Southeastern and Central-Eastern Europe – nuances that long eluded modern historiography. We now know that these areas of Europe were home to a highly original civilization that made great contributions to spirituality, the arts and politics, right up to modern times.

Let us now consider some of the directions taken by intellectual life at this time. In the history of thought, the Enlightenment differs from Classicism both by being the first truly pan-European movement of its type, and by giving a central role to history in the formation of national conscience. For all their regional differences, literary men, historians and philosophers adopted more or less the same ideas, convictions and expressions. The word Enlightenment became reality, and in Northern and Western Europe gave rise to great historical, philosophical and literary works which clearly laid out the objectives of the new thinking: the establishment of an anti-theological spirit, rooted in opposition to dogma, prejudice and superstition, and committed to the enlightening of the masses; the creation of a new political, social and economic order; and the spread of ideas concerning justice and liberty, demonstrating the universal character of reason. The enlightened minds of the new age thought on a universal scale, leaving behind previous narrow ways of evaluating relations between people, and abandoning the practice of labelling nations according to their language, religion and customs. These new moulders of conscience emerged rapidly and grew in influence throughout the eighteenth century: Leibniz, Rousseau, Diderot, Voltaire, Kant, Herder and Hegel arrived at a crucial moment, enabling the lesser-known regions of Europe to participate in the continent's collective intellectual development and thus opening up the great 'cultural channels' between East and West.

This process was initiated by the French, German, Austrian and Italian Schools, whose thinkers became acquainted with the Eastern and Southeastern reaches of the continent. Once they came into contact with the greatest minds of Europe, these societies tended to form their own schools. While Rousseau opened the eyes of the world to peoples whose existence had hitherto been unknown to them, Voltaire acquired a deep understanding of the civilization of the Balkans, the Turkish Empire and the Tsarist Empire of the East, where the enlightened figures of Peter and Catherine inspired him to reconstruct and explain the history of the region and its people. The Turks, for example, were known in the West through the work of Dimitrie Cantemir, but Voltaire renewed and deepened this acquaintance. *The History of Charles XII* (1728)[12] is replete with information on the state of the Ottoman Empire at the end of the seventeenth century, during its years of close contact with Sweden, providing details on the intrigues and ways of thinking at the sultan's court, descriptions of the army, and useful information on Constantinople's diplomatic relations across Europe, its central role in the great Christian negotiations, which Voltaire likens to that of Rome. In short, he presents an interpretation of the political situation in Turkey at the dawn of the Enlightenment:

> The erroneous policy of the Gate always to receive, out of vanity, the ambassadors of Christian princes in Constantinople, but not to tolerate the presence of any of its own diplomatic agents at the Christian courts, enabled the Christians to penetrate and even influence the most secret decisions of the Sultan, while the Divan knew nothing of events that were common knowledge in Christian lands... So great was the inertia and so deep the somnolence of this court, that if the Christian princes were to unite against it, their fleets would reach the Dardanelles

and their land armies the gates of Adrianople before the Turks even considered defending themselves. Yet the vested interests that always divide Christianity will save the Turks from a fate to which they would otherwise seem destined by their lack of political knowledge and their ignorance in war and navigation.[13]

Voltaire also identified the value of Petersburg and Moscow as key meeting points for trade, and left us a memorable sketch of Prince Cantemir, whose qualities he compares to those of the ancient Greeks, especially in his mastery of literature and arms. Most remarkably, he shows great tolerance in his analysis of religious movements, including those we have described above in terms of the reforms or crises of conscience experienced in the Southeast, or, in the case of Judaism, of the convergence of Eastern Europe. In *Essai sur l'histoire générale et sur les mœurs et l'esprit des nations depuis Charlemagne jusqu'à nos jours*,[14] Voltaire mentions the actions of the self-proclaimed Messiah Sabbatai Zevi (see above, pp. 129–30) in 1666 as an event that attracted the attention of Europe and Asia:

> His reputation spread across all of Europe; in the Dardanelles he received representatives of the Jews from Poland, Germany, Livorno, Venice and Amsterdam: the high price they were prepared to pay for the right to wash his feet is probably what saved his life. The Holy Land was quietly divided up in the Dardanelles castle. Further, the rumour of his miracles clearly spread far and wide, considering that Sultan Mahomet was curious to see this man and question him himself. He brought the king of the Jews to the Serai.[15]

Montesquieu also contributed to a better understanding of the European world, not by relaying facts about the continent, but rather by deciphering political and religious structures, revealing the principles of civil and canon law, and rediscovering the principles of political and natural law. He explained to his contemporaries how Islam related to Christianity, setting them alongside one another, comparing the laws preached by each and showing how they corresponded to the *forma mentis* of the Orient or of Europe. By this means, he fostered a greater understanding of territories and civilizations less known to Western Europe: Turkey, Greece, Egypt, the Middle East and China. Emphatically a political writer and less – if at all – a theologian, Montesquieu possessed a universality comparable to that of Leibniz in Germany, as demonstrated by his work of historical reconstruction *Considérations sur les causes de la grandeur des Romains et de leur décadence*:

> When the laws of a state consider it is necessary to tolerate more religions, they must also force them to accept one another. There is a principle whereby any religion that is persecuted becomes in turn a persecutor itself, since as soon as it escapes adversity, it attacks the religion that persecuted it, not as a religion, but as a tyranny. It is, therefore, beneficial for laws to demand that these different religions refrain not only from disturbing the state, but from disturbing each other. A citizen does not fulfil his duty towards the law simply by not producing disturbances within the state, he must also not disturb any other citizen, no matter who he be.[16]

This way of thinking is free from all dogmatism – it represents a freedom of reflection, a successful attempt to formulate a general political law whose ultimate purpose is the edification of mankind, 'the basis of all societies'. Montesquieu suggests the lifting of all barriers, the unanimous recognition of the right to life, to emancipation, to the free organization of nations. The ideas he expresses in *L'Esprit des lois* apply beyond the confines of Western and Central Europe, serving as a model for the East as well, and, as Ernst Cassirer has stated, expressing a historical vision that can counter the most ardent of adversaries and critics. Johann Gottfried Herder, though he frequently argued against Montesquieu's method and premises, admired his monumental undertaking, adopted it as a model and attempted to master its ideas. Herder's theories became some of the most important sources for men of culture in Central and Southeastern Europe, but we should not forget that his thinking derived not only from his compatriots Leibniz and Johann Georg Hamann, but also from Montesquieu and Rousseau. From this we may conclude that the most important and influential ideas are born from shared approaches, from communions of thinking. Montesquieu gave everything of value to the Century of the Enlightenment: he described different political regimes, the way Aristotle had done in ancient times, and analyzed the evolution of regimes, drawing on the sequences of events that gave rise to political change, but also on physical geography, climate, historical traditions and religions. His work does not include a scientific explanation for the development of society, but – together with the work of Rousseau, although different from it in many respects – denounces, in the name of reason, the absurdities and injustices he witnessed in the society of the time. *L'Esprit des lois* differs from Rousseau's *Contrat social* insofar as the latter sheds light on the morality rather than the science of politics. What brings the two treatises together and led to a growing interest in them is their examination of the universal value of political law. This is what led educated people of the East, some of whom achieved great intellectual distinction (notably the leading men of the Phanar district of Constantinople, the Phanariots who acted as 'mediators' in the European integration of the Southeast), to facilitate wider access to the writings of Rousseau, Voltaire and Montesquieu, and to Diderot's *Encyclopedia*.

August Ludwig von Schlözer, Johann Gottfried Herder, the Schlegel brothers and the Grimm brothers also applied serious historical, linguistic and folkloric research to the study of the East, revealing to Westerners remarkable facts, completely unknown until then, about material and spiritual life in the region. As historians and philosophers they served as brilliant examples for the intellectuals beginning to emerge in Central and Southeastern Europe: their studies, the ideas they disseminated and the political systems they devised formed the basis for the modernization of states. This time saw the emergence of the *Weltbürger* or citizen of the world, the individual convinced that his mission was no less than to serve all of mankind. Leibniz expressed this belief in a letter to Peter the Great: 'I am not one of those who are fanatic about their country or of a certain nation in particular, I serve all mankind, considering the sky as my homeland, and all people of good faith as citizens of this sky... My inclinations and my tastes urge me towards the good of the community.' [17] Similar ideals concerning world history and the borders and relations between nations were professed, for example, by followers of Rousseau, who advocated the creation of a constitution for Poland.

There was a further level of communication between West and East that should be emphasized, as it is relatively unknown. Enthusiasm for culture, educational reform and the establishment of new social and political structures are evident in the papers published in *Die Berlinische Monatsschrift* (1783–96). According to Dominique Bourel, this journal was the eventual fulfilment of Leibniz's wish many decades earlier of founding a quasi-official publication of the *Aufklärung*, where the most varied of tendencies could be set alongside each other.[18] It was the product of a much reflection within the *Mitwoch-Gesellschaft*, also known as the Friends of the Enlightenment. The intellectual atmosphere that inspired Central and Eastern Europe, a scholarly dialogue in perpetual refreshment and renewal, was born here in the writings of Johann Friedrich Zöllner, Johann Joachim Spalding, Johann Jakob Engel, Christoph Friedrich Nicolai, Moses Mendelssohn and others – the intimate circle of the 'lights of Berlin'. This second Athens rejected Bayle but rehabilitated Spinoza.

The Jewish-German philosopher Mendelssohn played a leading role in the history of ideas in the second half of the eighteenth century. He was not interested in partial history, in the history of a specific ethnic and cultural region, but was attracted by the refinements of the new current of thought. His profound intuition is displayed in *Phaedon oder über die Unsterblichkeit der Seele* (Berlin and Stettin, 1767) and *Jerusalem oder über religiöse Macht und Judenthum* (Berlin, 1783), which led to his recognition by Kant, Goethe, Hegel and even Hamann, who had no sympathy for Berliners or representatives of the *Aufklärung*. Mendelssohn was the first to draw attention to the theological origins of the term *Aufklärung* and the aspirations designated by this word. He does this in his work *Die Bestimmung des Menschen*, offering the first explanation of the ambivalent connotations of Enlightenment. He cites neither Aristotle nor Horace, but focuses solely on the *Mishna*, the most explicit treatise on the particularities of Judaism, for the description of the above-mentioned phenomenology of impurity and the ritual of washing hands (*jadayim*). Mendelssohn departs from his precursors, but the effect is not one of contradiction within his discourse. There are many important reasons why Europe accepted his views at that time and throughout the nineteenth century. His liberalism is still valid today,[19] since totalitarianism has not completely disappeared. According to Mendelssohn, natural law is man's protector against oppression, and no reason of state has the right to replace natural ethics with violence. Another reason why his work has been read and reread across Europe is his vision of the singularity of the Jewish people and its universal significance. He argues that to be with the nations of the modern world means to be for those nations, and that this is specific for the Judaic way of thinking. This entering of otherness is undertaken in order to understand it and adapt it for oneself (a way of thinking that appears to have influenced the philosopher Emmanuel Levinas).[20] For these reasons I was not surprised to discover Mendelssohn's books (in the original text or in translation) in the libraries founded during the Enlightenment or the Romantic Age in Transylvania and Wallachia, in Catholic, Greek Orthodox, Protestant and Jewish circles – for example, in the Brukenthal and Astra collection in Sibiu, among the books collected by the Unitarians in Cluj, as well as in academic societies (preserved in the Central University Library), in the Blaj collection (now at the local branch of the Library of the Romanian Academy), in the Bethlen collection in Aiud, in the Batthyaneum collection in Alba Iulia, among the books of the Metropolitan Neofit in Bucharest (part of which is in the Library of the Romanian Academy) and so on. In Austria and Hungary I found many copies of Mendelssohn's work in the Austrian National Library, in the old Széchenyi collection. The first Hungarian translation of *Phaedon* is dated 1793 – it was printed in Pest and then distributed to the most important libraries in Transylvania. The Paul Burian editions (Paul Burianschen Buchandlung) are the most important: printed in Pest and Oradea (1819–21), they reproduce in German the complete works of Mendelssohn. Some of these reached the Piarist School of Cluj (the Collegium Claudiopolitanum Scholarum Piarum), now preserved at the local branch of the Romanian Academy Library. For now, the impact of these texts was confined to closed religious communities, aristocratic circles and the scholars of Vienna, Halle, Göttingen and Pest: unfortunately, beyond the middle axis of Europe, most of the population remained illiterate for almost a century. The general absence of education, and in particular of lay institutions of middle and higher learning, gave rise to social stratification that had a negative effect on communication and mutual understanding within communities.

When Romanticism first appeared at the end of the eighteenth century Friedrich Schlegel, one of its most important founders, deliberately chose to analyze the history of Central and Southeastern Europe, as the Hapsburg monarchy provided a clear model of the idea of empire. Schlegel's choice of subject allowed him to formulate his own opinions on the emancipation of nations, which resulted in the rapid reception of his work in the cultural and political circles of the times, and in German and Austrian schools and universities.[21]

Contact between West and East increased significantly following the pioneering work of August Ludwig von Schlözer, who laid the foundations of the modern study of the past: in *Allgemeine nordische*

Geschichte he became the first scholar to apply the new methodology to the study of the history of Central and Southeastern Europe. He established the chronological development of the region and conducted research on ethnic questions, arousing the interest of Western scholars. Schlözer traced the relations between the South Slavs, and his historical and linguistic comparisons anticipated the method of Wilhelm von Humboldt. He studied the Hungarian language and displayed particular interest in the Transylvanian Germans, exerting a strong influence on the way their history was understood. His *Kritische Sammlungen zur Geschichte der Deutschen in Siebenbürgen* was known in the circles of Samuel von Brukenthal long before it was published (Göttingen, 1795–7, in three volumes) and provides an edifying example of bringing the two worlds together, of creating a dialogue between West and East as part of the intellectual revolution of Enlightenment Europe. He was interested in important medieval sources for the East such as Nestor's *Chronicle*, which he published in Göttingen in 1802 as *Russische Annalen in ihrer slavonischen Grundsprache vergleichen übersetzt und erklärt*. Among the key figures of Romanian culture, Dimitrie Cantemir was known to him via Western editions of the *History of the Growth and Decay of the Ottoman Empire*. Schlözer's role in the mobilizing of historians and the stimulation of historiography, and his influence on the constitution of the nations of Central and Southeastern Europe, are in my opinion just as important as Herder's. This said, there are significant differences between the historian and the philosopher, between Schlözer's pragmatic history, which expounds the generous ideas of the times, and Herder's philosophy, which includes not only the precepts of the Enlightenment, but also the vision that was to be embraced by Romanticism – a more profound way of thinking, an analysis and interpretation of tones, a history coupled with a philosophy of ideas which aims to discover the meaning of life. Despite these differences, their intellectual efforts basically shared a common aim: the birth of the new world, with a superior intellectual infrastructure and modern forms of organization, the society that was to come into being in the following century.

Schlözer's writings could be accessed directly at the famous school in Göttingen or via Vienna. The important factor in our discussion is the widespread understanding of his ideas, and his historical and linguistic works, across Central and Southeastern Europe. Serbian historians and men of letters took great interest in him, especially during the decades of the formation of national conscience, through the books of Stefan Stratimirović, Pavle Julinac and Jovan Rajić.[22] Josef Dobrovský introduced Schlözer's work to cultural circles in Prague, while Adam Kollár ensured its popularity in Slovakia.[23] There are indications that it may have been known to the professors of the Princely Academy of Iași, to Stefan Dungas and Dimitrie Govdelas, for example.[24] In Transylvania, Schlözer's work was embraced by the intellectuals of the journal *Siebenbürgische Quartalschrift*, notably its editor Johann Filstich, a former student at Göttingen, and Samuil Micu and Ioan Budai-Deleanu, the latter having recourse to medieval sources edited by Schlözer when writing his work *De originibus populorum Transylvaniae, commentatiuncula cum observationibus historico-criticis*. In Hungary, the dissemination of his works was mostly due to Ignaz Aurelius Fessler and Michael Horváth, and in Austria to Johann Christian von Engel.[25]

In conclusion, the importance of Schlözer's influence is due above all to the almost immediate adoption of many of his ideas in Southeastern and Central Europe, where intellectuals assimilated his social, political and historiographical concepts. The Eastern Enlightenment was in the process of rediscovering the historical nature of things, which explains the eagerness of writers in the region to embrace the directions that research was taking at the end of the eighteenth century and the beginning of the nineteenth. One of these directions was the study of sources, the attempt to clarify older chronologies and create a solid foundation for the articulation of national history, as was the case with Gheorghe Șincai in Transylvania, Stefan Stratimirović in Serbia and József Podmánicky in Hungary.[26] Another was the tendency of historians to depict ancient or medieval times in works written in the native language of their people, writing with a heightened level of pathos and passion, but also with greater creativity, giving impetus to political actions, as was the case with Petru Maior and Eftimie Murgu in Transylvania and Banat, Ignaz Fessler and György Bessenyei in Hungary, and Adam Kollár in Slovakia.

We have examined in detail the influence of Voltaire and other French Enlightenment thinkers on the great regeneration of the East, but it is important to balance this account with due recognition of the equally powerful influence of Johann Gottfried Herder. The German philosopher, a civilized European par excellence, won over many intellectuals with his theory of the history of mankind, and became a pivotal figure. Herder's triumph came not so much in the eighteenth century as in the century that followed, representing the peak of Enlightenment philosophy, exercising a dominant role in the development of historiography and implicitly ideological movements in an age of rising national conscience.

In assessing the outstanding qualities of Herder's work, its status as a milestone of modern historical literature, and the cultural influence it wielded in Central and Eastern Europe, we need to go back long before 1800, to Immanuel Kant's conception of the essence of the Enlightenment. To the question *Was ist Aufklärung?*, Kant wrote as follows:

> The Enlightenment is man's escape from the state of being a minor, a situation for which he himself was responsible. Being a minor means being unable to serve one's own intellect without being led by someone else. This state of minority originates in our own failings, if it is down to not a deficiency of the intellect, but a lack of courage to make use of it without someone else's leadership. *Sapere aude.* Have the courage to use your own intellect! This is the motto of the Enlightenment, because the Enlightenment needs nothing more than freedom, that is to say the least damaging of things that may be called freedom: the public use of reason in all its forms.[27]

Kant's motto, one of the most eloquent and convincing formulations of the new current of thinking, provided Herder – who had attended Kant's courses from 1762 to 1764 – with a starting point. Herder cultivated every field of study available to him: historiography, cultural history, linguistic history, and the history of the great cultures of Antiquity, the Renaissance and the modern age. He described his motivation as follows:

> My feeling for greatness is what directs my soul. My love, hate, admiration, my dreams of happiness and unhappiness, my intention of living in the world, my expression, style, carriage, my physiognomy, conversation, occupation, everything is directed towards it.[28]

This feeling, then, was what fired his spirit and guided his artistic and philosophical preferences. It also lay at the heart of his sympathy for the Jewish people, as well as for the Greeks, Egyptians, Celts, Scots, and the peoples of Eastern Europe. The attention he devoted to the study of languages and folklore was unprecedented in its influence and the emulation it inspired. This was a time when peoples across Europe were demanding their right to be recognized as a nation, and in Herder's work they had a foundation for the theory of nations, in which unity and diversity were upheld as the quality that characterizes every enduring work of nature. In each people Herder saw the need for the reign of reason and of justice, eliminating partiality and enthroning eternal good. He may also claim to have been the first to grasp the true political and cultural significance of language. In his view, language was a crucial unifying force for communities: 'If language is the organ of our spiritual forces, the means destined for culture and for our most profound education, then we can only be well educated in the tongue of our country.'[29]

The intellectual climate in his native Germany gave Herder a thorough grounding in the law of historical phenomena. He argued that deeds performed by living human beings were the moving force that shaped humanity's past, and that mankind's education and way of thinking were genetically determined. This observation gave rise to the theory of specific national characteristics – immutable qualities with roots going back to the oldest civilizations, and which could not possibly be subject to confusion. Herder yearned constantly for new horizons, his research being 'like the branches of a tree, which suddenly had to bear fruit in the midst of a storm'.[30] Living at the end of an era that revolutionized thinking, Herder was conscious of the falsity of political systems and the impossibility of adapting old habits to new theories, and hence he strove to establish a new faith, conceived in opposition to the medieval vision of the world: Homo Religiosus had to make way for Homo Europaeus, dogma had to give ground to the free communication of ideas and opinions. Where Giambattista Vico identified thought as the sublime essence of human activity,[31] Herder believed in a specific idea that was always present in one modified form or another – the idea of space enclosing within it the forces of creation, and time which perfects and develops those forces. From the plant that produces shoots and the bird making its nest to the most sophisticated social creatures, he saw the telos of everything as the flourishing of mankind, leading the world slowly out of chaos; and he believed that every organic being was creating, through a process of trial and error, the raw materials that the ensuing centuries would develop in their turn. Herder conceived this system in terms of two worlds, one emerging from the other, although Quinet rightly observed that they are one and the same thing. If the laws of physics built the universe, the laws of humanity built the world of history.[32] Herder anticipates Romanticism's conception of the living of history, which teaches us to understand facts in their historical framework; at the same time, he tries to destroy the faith of his contemporaries in absolute norms, replacing these with the diversity of historical and national relations.

A few examples from Central and Southeastern European historiography and ideology will demonstrate the ways in which Herder's work was received and disseminated, underlining the role he played in shaping the scientific and political tenets of the intellectuals of the Enlightenment and Romanticism. The current of thought created by Herder's philosophy can be detected in men of culture from Serbia and Hungary, from the Czech lands and Slovakia, from Transylvania, Banat, Wallachia and Moldavia, from Greece, Bulgaria, and Russia.

One of the first scholars to take up Herder's teaching and disseminate it across the region under Hapsburg domination was the Italian Alberto Fortis. A naturalist and passionate scholar of geography, geology and botany in the mode of Lazzaro Spallanzani or Charles Bonnet, Fortis ranged far beyond his professional interest in fossils, insects and marine micro-organisms, conducting research into Greek inscriptions, Roman coins and ancient Illyrian songs.[33] Herder's enthusiasm for the riches of local and popular culture were reflected in Fortis's special interest in Dalmatian life and the people living in this region. His books express the spirit of Enlightenment, inspired by German culture and by the ideas of the French Revolution.[34]

This enthusiasm for Herder was most prevalent in the first decades of the nineteenth century, when the concept of illuminating the masses became almost obsessive. In Hungary, István Széchenyi's writings were strongly influenced by Herder's ideas, in particular his theory that national character was closely tied to the development of language and culture.[35] These ideas can be found in Széchenyi's proposed reforms, intended to clarify the national problem.[36] The impact of Herder's ideas in Greece has been discussed by Constantin T. Dimaras, in particular their presence in the development and assertion of Neo-Greek ideology and culture.[37] Paul Cornea has analyzed the role of German culture in the Romanian revolutionary movement of 1848, focusing on common points between historical and literary works of the Romantic era and the precepts of Herder.[38]

Iosif Wolf also studied Herder's influence on Romanian ideology in 1848, concentrating on its representatives in Transylvania,[39] while Zoe Dumitrescu-Bușulenga has examined the same phenomenon in comparative research dedicated to the historiography of Romanian Romanticism in the European context.[40] I have attempted to complement the research of these scholars by describing further texts by Romantic historians influenced by Herder's concepts.[41]

The dialogue between East and West in Herder's work becomes explicit when he refers to Romanians in his discussion of the freedom of people to express themselves in their own language. In *Ideen zur Philosophie der Geschichte der Menschheit*, he claims that Wallachians and Albanians deserve special attention, being ancient European peoples rather than recent incomers.[42] These references possibly refer to the Romanians south of the Danube, probably Macedo-Romanian students at Halle or other European universities that Thunmann cites in his work *Untersuchungen über die Geschichte der Östlichen europäischen Völker*.[43] These references possibly explain why political and aesthetic ideas aroused such curiosity and even passion in the Romanian principalities. Herder's ideas were discovered there in the books and magazines circulating across Eastern and Southeastern Europe, in fragments translated first in the pages of George Barițiu and then in other periodicals, in the French edition of Herder (by Quinet) known in the principalities, and finally, in the case of Transylvania or Banat, through contact with German and Austrian cultural circles – examples include Alexandru Papiu Ilarian, Aaron Florian, Timotei Cipariu, Simion Bărnuțiu, George Barițiu and Vasile Maniu – or French influences, as in the cases of Nicolae Bălcescu, Mihail Kogălniceanu, Vasile Alecsandri, Alecu Russo and Constantin Alexandru Rosetti.

Romanian intellectuals, like Serbo-Croatians or Greeks, were influenced less by the books themselves and more by the changes the German Enlightenment brought about. Many Central and Eastern European historians of the revolutionary period of 1848 wrote about the past, proceeding from a philosophical standpoint derived directly from Herder. It is no less true, however, that the wealth of ideas propagated by Herder – a model not only for the East, but for all of Europe – stimulated the spirit of people looking for their own ideals, their own way to enhance the life of mankind. It is impossible to make a neat distinction between those ideas that were adopted in the original spirit of the Enlightenment and those that are specific to the activists of 1848, but this 'does not lessen the merit of the initiator's genius'.[44] Reciprocally, we should add that the power and presence of an Enlightenment precursor such as Herder in no way diminishes the individual efforts made by his followers. On the contrary, Herder's thinking stimulated works of great value on language, tradition, religion and philosophy. These became part of a pan-European humanism that Alexandru Duțu describes as follows:

> Cultural heritage was organized according to a plan devised by the champions of Enlightenment philosophy. With a predisposition to emancipation, accomplished through culture, Western civilization created its own exemplary works. The societies established in this part of Europe considered that humanism belonged to them, that powerful cultural movement that defeated the barbaric Goth and raised the great pantheon where man finds himself, surpassing his own works or those that held him in a familiar language.[45]

If we re-read carefully the works of those Eastern and Central European thinkers who propagated the ideas of the French Revolution, we may notice that they championed them too early for 'the darkness reigning in this country'. The reflections of Ignatz Joseph Martinovicz, the politician and scholar who was active in the Masonic and Jacobin groups of Vienna and Pest, provide a good example.[46] He laments the almost insurmountable obstacle posed by the ignorance not only of those 'at the bottom', but, most distressingly, of those 'at the top'. He dreams of a victory over the aristocracy and the priests, but is left with 'forlorn hopes' because even the laws promulgated by Joseph II have been deferred or circumvented. An ambassador of the new ideas in Europe, Martinovicz was privy to many secrets of the monarchs who were plotting against the French nation.[47] He maintained relations that encouraged dialogue between East and West. Indignant at the delays and obstacles invented by the chancelleries of the imperial courts, he took it upon himself to draft the constitutions of the future national states of Central and Eastern Europe, establishing fruitful communication between Vienna, Pest, Zagreb and Timișoara in the East, and Paris in the West. He imagined the coming together of the two forms of Enlightenment we mentioned above – the original spirit of the movement and its perversion as revolutionary ideology. He saw it as a spectacular matching of rhythms in the Europe of the future, and, in 1848, history to an extent proved him right.

The Risorgimento of Transylvania, Moldavia and Wallachia is similarly inseparable from Enlightenment thinking: the same period, from 1791 (the year the *Supplex* appeared), to 1848, ushered in a way of thinking that declared freedom as every individual's birthright. This was miraculous, to the extent that Romanians discovered (culturally speaking) the call for integration in a very short time – it was the call of universality, a new understanding of the status conferred by modern Homo Europaeus. Links with France became essential at this critical time, while intellectuals in the circles of the princes of Moldavia and Wallachia were instrumental in preparing the ground for the new order, even if its impact upon infrastructure was still some way in the future. This 'spring of the people' was confirmed by 1848, the year of the revolutions. From Constantin Stamati, secretary to Prince Alexander Ypsilantis, from his friends Dimos Stepanopoli (known as Barbo Dimo) and Daniel Philipides, up to the generation of Kogălniceanu and Bălcescu, we can observe the stimulus provided by the Western model, which was to take the conscience of cultures in this area in a new direction.[48]

Here we are almost certainly dealing with the birth of a political language which, although inevitably uneven, came to dominate the world right up to the present day. In the same way that there is a 'plurality of revolutionary heritage', there is a coexisting unity and disparity within the ideas proposed in 1789.[49] These tensions are the origin of the division of opinions to the right and left. It is a spectacular inheritance, creating new horizons for mankind and history, but it opens up a very complex future, hard to control and to organize. Its ideological origins can be found in Diderot's *Encyclopedia*, a work which profoundly influenced magistrates, clerks and local dignitaries, the section of society who led the French Revolution. The presence of the Encyclopedists among the official intelligentsia in France indicates a spirit of continuity between 1780 and 1800,[50] one that was replicated between 1790 and 1848 in Eastern Europe. In short, however, it is a political heritage that – wherever we are in Europe – we cannot ignore if we are to understand ourselves in the present day.

VI

'CULTURAL CHANNELS' IN EAST-CENTRAL EUROPE: BOOKS AND LIBRARIES IN TRANSYLVANIA, BANAT, HUNGARY AND SERBIA

The library defends itself, it is as impenetrable as the truth it possesses, as deceiving as the lies it keeps. The labyrinth of the mind is an earthly labyrinth as well. You can enter, but you cannot leave...

Umberto Eco

MORE THAN THIRTY years ago, the historian Răzvan Theodorescu proposed a theory that is as complex as it is attractive: the 'cultural channels' of Southeastern Europe during the Middle Ages. He returned to the subject in a paper delivered at the Romanian Academy,[1] in which he went back further, to pre-medieval times and even as far as Antiquity. His pioneering work enables us to understand a certain spiritual geography, revealing that the Balkan 'channels' merit close study, the cultural links they represent defining geopolitical unity in the region as well as shaping the major historical changes that have occurred there. My aim is to build on this research, drawing on written culture, and in particular the activities of libraries and of people who propagated books, information and ideas, in an attempt to reform society. In previous chapters I have described the 'channels' that facilitate communication from Göttingen in the North to Transylvania in the East, from the Flemish world to Austria, Hungary and the

Danubian principalities, from the academic and intellectual circles of Halle and Berlin to those of Buda, Karlowitz, Sibiu, Blaj, Iași and Bucharest, and beyond to Russia in the time of Peter the Great and to Athos in Greece. We have followed the routes mankind took on its long quest to establish liberal thinking. These 'great durations' will allow me to decipher the modern dimensions of Homo Europaeus in his Eastern incarnation.

Public and private libraries are a key element in the culture of all peoples. They reveal to us the history of a community across an extended period of time, enabling us to assess the character of an individual civilization, and, in the case of this study, its relationship with modern Europe. The general characteristics of a community can be identified by studying its cultural institutions large and small, since these are true repositories of information that show us the movement of ideas. As we look more closely at the tumultuous history of the eighteenth century, these institutions offer precious insights, since they were a key destination for man in his quest for knowledge, as he attempted to adopt the intellectual system created by Enlightenment Europe.

In the course of my research in a number of old libraries in Transylvania, Banat, Hungary and Serbia, I attempted to understand the nature of intellectual ties between Central and Western Europe, and to identify evidence of these contacts through books. In an investigation of this nature, the book that is selected, bought and read symbolizes the interests and tendencies of the *Aufklärer*. My intention is to use these documents to reveal ideals that were shared across different ethnic and spiritual groups: a firm grasp of the scale and reach of these ideals will help us to define the European character of culture in the East.

A library is not merely a collection of books or a reading room, nor is its value confined to the community of readers who have access to it – it can also be seen as an institute of learning that transmits ideas and propagates culture. In this regard it functions like other institutions: school and church, printing press and publishing house. Its activities are supported by a team of teachers and students, priests and librarians, and its patron is often a representative of the new aristocracy, or of the Greek Orthodox, Greek Catholic, Roman Catholic or Protestant clergy. In the face of apparently conflicting tendencies – ideologies, traditions and so on – libraries establish enduring communication and even a sense of emancipation, bringing the communities of the world together. I will demonstrate that in Eastern Europe as elsewhere, intellectuals were able to engage these institutions in their desire to create bridges, triggering a rapid and spontaneous period of development at the end of the eighteenth century and in the first decades of the nineteenth.

In Transylvania and Banat, libraries were the principal means of access to European culture, and they played a central role in the establishment of modern man in the region. Large and small towns actively competed to communicate with Enlightenment Europe. In Sibiu (Hermannstadt in German, Cibinium in Latin), Blaj (Balázs-falva in Hungarian), Alba Iulia (Gyulafehérvár in Hungarian, Alba Carolina in Latin), Târgu Mureş (Marosvásárhely in Hungarian) and Aiud (Nagyenyed in Hungarian), Cluj (Kolozsvár in Hungarian, Klausenburg in German), Oradea (Nagyvárad in Hungarian, Gross-wardein in German, Magnovaradinum in Latin), Sfântu Gheorghe (Sepsiszentgyörgy or Szentgyörgy in Hungarian), Braşov (Kronstadt in German), Arad, Radna and Timişoara (Temeswar in German, Temesvár in Hungarian, Temišvar in Serbian), books were introduced by intellectuals, aristocrats, political leaders, and through the activities of merchants crossing the continent, from the Franco-German West to the Russian East and from the Polish North to Southern Constantinople. It was in these circumstances that Brukenthal founded in Sibiu a public library to match those of Central Europe, and that the libraries created in Blaj in 1747 broadened the horizons of Romanian national schools with the ideas of the Enlightenment. In Alba Iulia, Bishop Ignác Batthyány founded one of the most beautiful and valuable collections of documents in Europe. Ecclesiastical institutions competed to obtain books, as was the case of the Franciscan monasteries in Arad, Radna, Deva, Cluj and Timişoara, while in Oradea, under the patronage of Iosif Vulcan, the Greek Catholic episcopate was enriched with valuable donations and acquisitions of documentary and historical material. The library of Sámuel Teleki in Târgu Mureş made an important contribution to the European character of the region. There are many such examples of this attempt to clarify the new way of thinking and reorganize the cultural and political landscape, and they will enable us to understand how knowledge increased with the circulation of books and the growth of the global mass of information. On the subject of knowledge, Pierre Chaunu states that philosophical judgement itself

is confronted with a major problem, that of constructing a valid theory of knowledge that meets the need for a geometrical

SPIRITUAL INFLUENCES IN CENTRAL AND SOUTHEASTERN EUROPE

How important is the West's influence on Central and Southeastern Europe? Although most new ideas emanated from Paris, Vienna and Rome, we have tended to regard the continent as a single spiritual construct, as an organization that survived the Byzantine-Orthodox and Catholic worlds, the two halves of the old Roman Empire. They were accompanied by the contributions of the North, which the empire never managed to control and which later became the territory of the Reformation.

progression of knowledge, on the one hand because this is the essential problem of the eighteenth century, but also because knowledge – for which the eighteenth century sacrificed everything – is the great disturbance in Enlightenment thinking. Here, at this central level of human activity, the eighteenth century needs certainty.'[2]

Let us begin with books and the people and entities that brought them to life. Blaj, for example, had a Romanian library that owed its existence to the educational institutions which developed there. Its schools and seminaries were institutions of the first rank, their activities shaped by a generation of Enlightenment scholars including Grigore Maior, Leonte Moschonas, Silvestru Caliani and, later, Ioan Lemeni, Timotei Cipariu, Ioan Moldovan, Nicolae Pauleti and others. Already armed with an estimable collection of European books, the teachers of Blaj travelled around both the neighbouring cultural area and more distant regions, amassing an encyclopedic collection of texts as they went. Learned Greek scholars maintained relations with Buda, Vienna, Lviv, Kiev, Bucharest, Râmnicu Vâlcea and Galaţi, while the historian and philologist Gheorghe Şincai was in close contact with Buda, Grigore Maior with Vienna, Ioan Budai-Deleanu with Poland, and Timotei Cipariu with Bucharest and Râmnicu Vâlcea.[3] The private libraries that were created as a result of these cultural contacts prove the vibrant presence of Enlightenment culture in East-Central Europe.

These collections, which were eventually brought together in Blaj, are mentioned in documents written in 1747, 1777 and 1830. Iacob Mârza[4] has examined the three inventory catalogues in the Cluj branch of the Library of the Romanian Academy – *Inventarium Librorum Balasfalvae in Residentiae Episcopali 1747* (MS Lat. 550), *Inventarium Seminarii Dioecesani Balasfalvensis de Anno 1777* (MS Lat. 257) and *Catalogus Bibliothecae Monasterii Balasfalvensis ad Sanctissimam Trinitatem 1830* (MS Lat. 435) – and revealed the didactic literature from both Romanian and Latin that was studied in the cultural heart of Transylvania. These works include Emmanuel Alvarus' grammar and Cyprianus Soarius' rhetoric; editions of classical literature (Cicero, Livy, Ovid, Cato the Elder, Aesop, Juvenal and C. Julius Phaedrus); historical works by Johann Christoph Gatterer, Charles Rollin, Johann Hübner, Károly Ferenc Palma, György Pray, Martin Felmer, Hendrik Nieupoort, Stephanus Schoenwisner, Philippus Hollius, Claude-François-Xavier Millot, Márton Bolla, Samuil Micu and Petru Maior; mathematics and physics textbooks by Johann Ignaz von Felbiger, Maximilian Hell, Ambrus Ambrosius Hornyay and Adam Tomtsányi; and collections of philosophical works by Immanuel Kant, Wilhelm Traugott Krug, Stephanus Márton and Joseph Calasanz Likavetz. The collections also display an impressive interest in books by intellectuals such as Ioan Giurgiu Patachi, Petru Pavel Aron, Samuil Micu, Petru Maior, Gheorghe Şincai, Ioan Halmagi, Ioan Bob, Ioan Alpini, Ioan Turcu and others.

There was also a printing house in Blaj, created to serve the spiritual interests of the Romanian linguistic community. It supported the efforts of the seminary to instruct its students and contributed to the promotion of didactic literature. The printing press was introduced to Blaj in 1738 by Inocenţiu Micu-Klein, and commenced operations in the time of Bishop Petru Pavel Aron. Its activities bore comparison to presses further west, thanks to the fruitful exchange of cultural values and technical know-how between Romanians and Hungarians. For example, Zsigmond Jakó has gathered evidence demonstrating the collaboration between Aron and Gherontie Cotorea (the *inspector Typographiae*) and the typographer of the Protestant College in Cluj, István Székely Páldi, who had been trained in Holland and continued the work of the famous Miklós Misztótfalusi Kis, the man who laid the foundations of the artistic printing of letters in the eighteenth century. This is a significant instance of spiritual convergence, of cultural development in the region through communication, for the benefit of the community as a whole: due to the efforts and experience of Homo Novus, the Romanian art of printing in Blaj reached the same level as other Transylvanian printing houses:

> In carrying out this plan [which involved an alliance with the Roman Catholics and the introduction of Latin printing characters to Romanians] the bishop [Aron] received material support from treasurer Ignác Bornemisza, the protector of the Unified Church, and from Friedrich Wilhelm Dietrich, counsellor of the Aulic Chamber and of the Treasury.[5]

What does this raising of standards prove? First of all, the broader range of education available. Works were now printed specifically for their educational content: *Doctrina christiana ad usum hujus scholasticae juventutis* (1757), *Questions about the Holy Union. Selected from Church Books* (1780), Samuil Micu's *Moral Theology*, I–II (1796) and *Dogmatic and Moral*

Theology about Ever-Present Secrets (1801), *The Dogmatic Theology*, I–III (translated by Dimitrie Caian and others, 1804–11), Ioan Bob's *Book of Christian Teachings* (1805–6), Samuil Micu's translation of Thomas à Kempis' *Imitation of Christ* (1812)[6] and *The Great Catechism, or Christian Teachings with Questions and Answers* (1836).[7] The dates, names and titles listed here reveal much about this age of the spreading of knowledge, this historical crossroads in which Transylvania also played a key role in the dissemination of new ideas. The complex educational programme which lay behind the printing of these books was shaped partly by Western ideas and partly by writings and attitudes characteristic of the region.[8]

It is clear that the atmosphere engendered by the crises experienced in Western Europe after 1760 – the critical moments faced by the old feudal monarchies that culminated in the French Revolution – had a decisive impact on the East. From West to East, the mood became agitated, and everywhere opposition arose to the development of the new civilization. Historians Franco Venturi and Pierre Chaunu have both identified the need to re-evaluate French culture during the period 1760 to 1790 in this context,[9] and a similar reassessment of the development of culture is necessary for the so-called periphery of Europe, where spirits were reawakened by the philosophy of the century, fostered by enlightened despotism. For example, in Transylvania – but also in Hungary, Serbia, Moldavia, Wallachia, Russia and Greece – Homo Novus strove to change the nature of cultural and political life, unaware that the goals of the imperial courts in Vienna and Petersburg were merely economic. As a result, Romanian intellectuals felt great frustration, and vented their disillusionment – they needed the kind of scholarly, institutional framework that would enable them to emulate the fine achievements made in the West a couple of decades earlier, through the work of Diderot, d'Alembert, Voltaire, Maupertuis and their peers. The moment finally came with the publication of the *Supplex Libellus Valachorum*, to which the scholarly circle of Blaj made a telling contribution. This emancipation, in which the language and ideas were identifiably European, was brought about primarily through books and their function as bridges of communication. As such, it was the achievement not only of writers and thinkers, but of all who made the effort to acquire books. Blaj, aptly nicknamed 'Little Rome', actively participated in this dissemination of knowledge, and became the principal cultural centre for Romanians, their equivalent of imperial Byzantium, Renaissance Florence, Golden Age Castile or Buda in the times of Matthias Corvinus. Here, Rome is of course synonymous with Europe, a remarkable development given that the typical intellectual from the banks of the Târnava, however open to universal ideas, would have been steeped primarily in national scholarly traditions.[10]

Returning to the subject of libraries, in Târgu Mureș this irradiation of culture was made possible by the institution founded by nobleman Sámuel Teleki, which represented a new link with Europe, transforming intellectual life in the city. Teleki's library followed the Viennese model, and Teleki himself was a specialist acquainted with all the latest methods of Enlightenment librarians. He embodied a certain type of Transylvanian noble, who embraced the European cultural model partly because it was fashionable, but also for genuine moral and spiritual reasons. In the 'Praefatio' to his library catalogue (1796) Teleki stated that his passion should be used to benefit his country, or, in his favourite formulation, 'for the advancement of the sciences among my community and my homeland'. His aspirations, typically for an enlightened Transylvanian chancellor, went beyond any single linguistic community or ideological or religious group, and envisaged the education of society as a whole in the spirit of German and Austrian *Aufklärung*. He compiled catalogues of his books himself, having learnt in great detail the techniques used in the imperial court libraries. His clear intellectual vision resulted in the first fully scientific and systematic library catalogue to be printed the region.

Intellectuals were the main beneficiaries of this success, in Târgu Mureș and other centres of learning, leading to the conscious sense of an elite among Transylvanian scholars, whether Romanian, Hungarian, German or Jewish. The library's encyclopedic character and immense spiritual riches gave each of them a deeper understanding of the history and development of their particular ethnic group, as well as an interest in other peoples. This nurturing of the culture of Enlightenment and liberal Romanticism gave rise to brilliant works by Gheorghe Șincai, Ioan Budai-Deleanu, Gheorghe Barițiu, Gábor Döbrentei, Ferenc Széchenyi, István Széchenyi, Stefan Stratimirović, Ferenc Kazinczy, József Kemény, Anton Kurz, Stefan Ludwig Roth and Constantin Danil Rosenthal.

In the same preface to the Teleki library catalogue[11] the reason for the foundation of the collection is explained, namely the stimulation of society by reading the words of 'true men' who gave mankind ever-lasting works – here Teleki first mentions the names of ancient Greeks such as Socrates, Xenophon and Pericles, and the Romans Octavian, Antonius, Lucullus, Fabius and Marcellus. In particular, he stresses the importance of the work of Plato, establishing parallels between ancient and Renaissance thought and showing the contribution of each to human progress. Teleki's conception of the Enlightenment comes into sharp focus when he speaks of the principles of the modern world embraced in England, France and Germany, under the influence of the ideas of Francis Bacon or Hugo Grotius.[12] He also emphasizes the importance of the great libraries founded during the Renaissance, not only the famous institutions of the Vatican or Florence during the time of the Medici family, but also those of Central-Eastern Europe during the *Quattrocento*, most notably the illustrious example of Matthias Corvinus.[13]

The fact that Transylvania lagged behind Western Europe by almost one hundred years can be explained by the Tataric and Turkish invasions it endured. As I have mentioned, religious reform was the spark for the region's intellectual revival, bringing it more into line with Hungary in the time of Matthias Corvinus and enabling intellectual life to prevail over medieval barbarism. This process began not with Prince Gabriel Bethlen, but with John II Sigismund in the second half of the sixteenth century. Bethlen built on this legacy by giving greater authority to the cosmopolitan circles of Alba Iulia. These developments occurred in an intellectual atmosphere inspired by Erasmus and the 'heretical' Protestant humanists (such as Giorgio Biandrata, Johann Sommer and Ferenc Dávid), as Teleki acknowledges, even if he does not trace the itinerary of these influences correctly. The radical reformism professed at the court of John II Sigismund, which typified the Protestant faith of Anti-trinitarians in permanent contact with Italy, was proof of a religious tolerance that fostered dialogue with the great courts and ruling houses of Europe. This dialogue gave rise to a rich and varied cultural life which was of great benefit to Transylvanian intellectual circles.[14]

Teleki was rightly convinced that libraries have always played a crucial role in the education of youth. It is in this context that he describes the contents and the destination of Bethlen's collection, which was to become such a significant assertion of European spirituality. The presence of schools, colleges and printing houses explains the appearance of the first public library in Alba Iulia, a rich repository of rare books from Europe – as Teleki knew, since he clearly consulted part of the collection which had been moved (after a fire) from Alba Iulia to Aiud.[15] This development in Alba Iulia is clear from the inventory registers of its documentary fund. The eighteenth-century Transylvanian historian Wolfgang Bethlen compared this treasure with that of the Corvina Library in Buda, and this influential assessment of the Aiud collection may have stimulated Teleki's work towards obtaining a system of classification for his books. The catalogue is the best proof of this, demonstrating the unarguable rigour with which he assembled and conserved his collection. This is mentioned in Teleki's preface, but can also be inferred from the four volumes of the catalogue itself (1796–1819), as well as those elements of the original collection that remain part of the library today, and are still arranged according to the structure conceived during the Enlightenment.

Books were bought from every corner of Europe and in all fields: rhetoric, grammar, philosophy, mathematics, canon law, mythology, medicine, ethics, geography, economics, history, music, astronomy, the art of war, oratory and theology. The Teleki collection includes many famous works produced during the Renaissance and the Enlightenment, primarily masterpieces of typography from the latter period – monographs, syntheses, encyclopedias, lexicons, dictionaries and atlases – and works by political, military and cultural figures, such as a valuable manuscript copy of the work of Eugene of Savoy produced by a Viennese scribe of the Imperial Chancellery, which demonstrates Teleki's interest in rare books.[16] This passion for books was itself the reason for producing the catalogue, which mirrored similar productions in Western Europe at the time – it was a formula propagated by men of culture across the continent that helped to break down age-old barriers.

Sámuel Teleki's merits stem from his commitment to culture and the benefits he brought to book collectors.[17] He valued his contemporaries Brukenthal and Batthyány for their efforts to enrich the spiritual life of Transylvania: we have concrete evidence of his esteem for their achievements in the halls of his library, where their portraits are prominently displayed. He invested a considerable fortune in assembling the collection, its 60,000 volumes requiring an expenditure of 800,000 forints[18] in order to secure the work of the best publishing houses. While his library reveals the interests of a specific, wealthy social class, it is nonetheless indicative of the extent to which European culture was implanted beyond the median axis of the continent. Teleki's scholarly activities embody the way of life of a certain kind of European bibliophile of his time. His abilities and refined taste led him to gather books of unquestionable documentary value during his visits to Vienna, where many of the new publications from Germany, France, Italy and England could be obtained. In addition, his enterprise was facilitated by his fortune and public office:

> He could buy the greatest printed works of Bodoni, the famous publisher of Parma, he could buy the Corvinian codices discovered in Strasbourg, and the hound dogs of imperial censorship could not stop him from buying the forbidden works of the Enlightenment and the French Revolution for his library.[19]

The example provided by Teleki is similar to that of Brukenthal, Batthyány or, later, Cipariu, of István Csáky and Ferenc Széchenyi in Hungary, or of Stefan Stratimirović in Serbia. They all represent a social class for whom mankind's great hope lay in an intellectual revolution – not the ideas of Revolutionary France or the Napoleonic epic, but rather the necessary steps towards the progress of 'Light'. Their ideal was a Homo Novus of the Western type, a reforming force whose actions were only possible in a context of enlightened despotism. These latter-day revolutionaries were all disciples of the Enlightenment, and 'Enlightenment is not revolutionary and does not prefer revolutionary methods': though the Romanian activists in Transylvania in 1791 foreshadowed the seismic changes of 1848, they were 'not revolutionaries either'.[20] This was emphatically the case with Count Teleki. The famous collective memorandum *Supplex Libellus Valachorum* entered his library, followed by the works of Samuil Micu, Gheorghe Șincai and Petru Maior, and these were his sources when the emperor looked to him for his knowledge, reflected the limitations of his thinking, on the one hand respecting their social status, while on the other inhabiting a political position strictly dependent on Vienna. This attitude ultimately led him to reject the theses of the *Supplex*, turning his back on the European cosmopolitanism that had interested him for so long, and revealing in him a fear of ideas that were too advanced, too new, and liable to create a political storm. He was unwilling to challenge the artificial boundaries imposed from without, and as such proved to be as conflicted and undecided as the era itself. In the final analysis, Sámuel Teleki turned out not to be the forerunner of the liberal István Széchenyi, but his library survived him, setting his name among those of the worthy scholars of this era of change.

The book collection of Samuel von Brukenthal, the former governor of Transylvania (1777–87) and councillor of Maria Theresa, also became a successful public library.[21] It was housed in Sibiu's impressive Palace of Cavaliers, which Brukenthal had built in late Baroque style with obvious Viennese influences. Brukenthal (1721–1803) was a contemporary of Teleki (1739–1822), and also drew inspiration for the organization of his collection from Vienna, bringing in a specialized librarian named Samuel Hahnemann who devised the scientific basis of the institution and gave it its Austrian appearance. The library was inaugurated with 15,872 volumes, 76 incunabula and about 200 manuscripts, and was soon enriched with donations: it acquired the Kapellenbibliothek collection, whose history goes back to around 1300,[22] as well as a number of other collections belonging to prominent figures in Transylvania.

The history of the Brukenthal Library is inseparable from the life and travels of its founder, whose activities were emphatically those of a modern Homo Europaeus. He was educated in the German universities of Halle and Jena, where he studied law and political sciences, general and Transylvanian history (a course taught by Martin Schmeizel of Brașov, who in the first decades of the eighteenth century had also held the position of councillor of the Prussian court),[23] philosophy and theology. Even during this early period of his life Brukenthal established many contacts among the higher echelons of Western society, and became conversant in the good manners of Franco-German intellectual life – a far cry even from the most refined of Transylvanian German circles – and eventually gained entry into the spiritual world of the German Enlightenment. These were the middle decades of the century of Enlightenment, in which the achievements of Frederick II's Prussia bore comparison with the work of the French Encyclopedists. French-speaking Europe was gaining ground, and the German Protestant *Aufklärung* suddenly came into contact with the ideas of Maupertuis, d'Alembert, Diderot, Helvétius, La Mettrie and Voltaire.

It was no mere coincidence that the Northern German intelligentsia were receptive to the influence of the French spirit and the contribution of the Jewish intellectual bourgeoisie, headed by Moses Mendelssohn. Both played a beneficial role in the region's change of conscience, which paved the way for great scholars such as Alexander and Wilhelm von Humboldt. Nor was it simply by chance that the area maintained lines of communication with the East, especially contact with Transylvanian German intellectuals. In addition, Freemasons were very influential, their ideas having considerable impact on academic and political circles. Even the 'active tolerance' of the royal and imperial courts brought unexpected changes in the century's way of thinking.

Freemasonry in particular was a significant means of communication for Easterners, establishing a network of contacts capable of kickstarting the spread of new ideas. It was of use to Brukenthal, who during the years 1740–50 became a member of the Halle branch of the Berlin lodge 'Zu den drei Weltkugeln', and later *maître députe* of the Halle lodge 'Aux trois clefs d'or'. He was described by the Freemasons of Berlin as a *très digne et très respectable frère* [most worthy and respectable brother],[24] and by those of Sibiu, immediately after returning from his studies, as a *von Wissenschaft und feiner Kultur glänzeuder junger Mann* [brilliant young man of science and high culture]. In record time, Brukenthal climbed the social and political ladder and became governor of Transylvania and one of the great personalities of the Hapsburg Empire. His repeated trips to Vienna and the close relations he maintained there with the court, especially with Empress Maria Theresa who appreciated and supported him greatly, encouraged him to carry out his intellectual and scholarly projects. Beyond politics[25] – which can never be entirely separated from Brukenthal's activities – culture attracted him from his youth to the end of his life. He was convinced that his example could have an influence on his contemporaries, at least those who were broadly of his social class, and his political actions were always underpinned by the aim of attaining knowledge in various scientific fields and collecting works of art, books, coins, antiquities and minerals.

Both Brukenthal's personal collection and the books he subsequently acquired for his library required considerable financial investment and an enduring commitment to the arts and sciences. To this end he surrounded himself with a group of specialists who included, in addition to Hahnemann, a number of librarians, bibliophiles, artists and scholars. It has been said of Brukenthal:

> His activity as a collector is not a goal in itself; it is on the contrary directed towards gaining knowledge of his homeland – both its past, its history from the oldest of times, and its natural riches – and the encouragement of artists and scientists in Sibiu.[26]

Brukenthal demonstrated the kind of enthusiasm and spiritual vigour that, as we have seen in the case of Chancellor Teleki of Târgu Mureș, was appreciated in the Transylvanian nobility both by clerics and, above all, intellectuals who realized that important aspects of Transylvania's traditions were being saved and preserved by his actions. These conditions fostered important developments in historiography, numismatics, heraldry, diplomacy, chronology and genealogy: historians, many of them encouraged by Brukenthal, studied the history not only of their own community, but of the Romanians and Hungarians as well. References to the history of the Romanian community, for example, can be found in the works of Johann Filtsch, Daniel Filtsch, Johann Michael Soterius von Sachsenheim, Georg Hirling and Michael Conrad von Heydendorff. Brukenthal himself, in his petitions and memoirs, displays his own predilection for a certain type of historiography. The stamp of Homo Europaeus could be felt throughout the palace in Sibiu, among all of Brukenthal's coterie. The books and paintings housed in the palace embodied the extent to which the Enlightenment had now entered Transylvania. Theological literature, which had been predominant in the preceding century, slowly made way for the sciences – geometry, geology, medicine, geography, astronomy, micro-technology and optics – while local languages increasingly replaced Latin as the medium of communication. This phenomenon was made possible by the ending of Jesuit censorship and the separation of religion and state during the time of Joseph II. By the end of the eighteenth century, Transylvanian intellectuals were planning the foundation of a 'Philosophical Society' and a 'Societas philohistorum Transylvaniae', whose aim was to enlighten the people with 'teachings from the present sciences, from the fields of physics, geography and other sciences which would benefit the economy'.[27]

The champions of the German pre-Enlightenment and Enlightenment, from Samuel von Pufendorf to Friedrich Gottlieb Klopstock, were well received in the East against a backdrop of interest in Transylvanian German culture. The region's bibliophiles, however, were drawn to rarities, such as the printed editions of Aldus Manutius the Elder and Younger, and the translations of Robert Estienne produced by the famous Elzevir publishing house (over one hundred volumes). Manuscripts and incunabula increased the value of Brukenthal's collection and enhanced its credentials as a research library, its treasures including the *Brukenthal Breviary* (fifteenth century), *Codex Altenberger* (fourteenth century), *Liber missorum* (1394), *Psaltirium Davidis* (fourteenth century), Haydn's *Sibiu Symphony* (the name originates from the town where it was discovered), a fifteenth-century antiphonary and many acts of donation (the oldest of which is dated 1223), as well as first editions of Thomas Aquinas, Petrarch, Albrecht von Eyb and others, all dating from before 1500.

The library placed an equal emphasis on history, and especially Transylvanian cultural history: one of its sections was entitled Transylvanica and was doubtless a principal area of interest for the intellectual group around Brukenthal, since it formed one third of the entire collection. It included many edifying works that reflected the distinctly European character of the region's historiography at this time: Laurentius Toppeltinus' *Origines et occasus Transylvanorum seu Erutae Nationes Transylvaniae* (Vienna, 1762),[28] Nicolaus Olahus' *Hungaria et Attila sive de originibus gentis, regni Hungariae situ, habitu, opportunitatibus et rebus bello paceque an Attilae Gestis* (Vienna, 1763),[29] *Epistolae Mathiae Corvini* (Košice, 1743),[30] the anonymous *Historica Hungarica. De septem primis ducibus Hungariae* (Kolozsvár, 1747),[31] and Johannes Filstich's *Schediasma Historicum de Valachorum Historia Annalium Transilvanensium multis in punctis Magistra et Ministra* (Jena, 1743).[32] In addition to these books, this section of the library also contained a large number of works by Transylvanian representatives of the Enlightenment, both Transylvanian German historians such as Martin Schmeizel, Daniel Flistich and Martin Felmer, and important Hungarian humanists including Péter Bod, Sámuel Köleseri and Péter Pázmány. Brukenthal even encouraged the writing of some of these books: for example, the notable historian József Benkö expresses his gratitude to Brukenthal for facilitating his research in the preface to his work *Transsilvania sive magnus Transsilvaniae Principatus olim Dacia Mediterranea doctus orbi nondum satis cognitus* (Vienna, 1778). All the authors listed above strove to present a thorough and detailed history of the region, but also of Moldavia, Wallachia and other East-Central and Southeastern European territories. This fostered a sense of emancipation and progress within each linguistic community.

Brukenthal selected the texts for the Transylvanica part of his library with great care, in the hope that they would be of benefit to cultured society, even if politicians proved unreceptive to them. Political interests were never far away, especially during Brukenthal's tenure as governor of Transylvania, and the information contained in his library was often put to use in this context. During the uprising of

Horea (1784), he drew on his expertise in the region's social history and delivered an official presentation to the imperial court of the living conditions of the Romanian peasants from Transylvania and their state of servitude compared to the other communities: 'Now and later on, he drew clarity from his own observations rather than those long "descriptions of the country" made by generals or higher imperial dignitaries, descriptions that abound in this period.'[33] In general, knowledge was driven by political interests, whether as a result of direct orders from Vienna or in order to fulfil the aspirations of the intellectual classes. These considerations, coupled with the ideals of the Enlightenment, can be found in all Brukenthal's works, in a manner consistent with the tenets of Austrian enlightened despotism, and they led him to support efforts to research and document Transylvanian history.

The centre of Transylvanian German historiography now moved from Brașov to Sibiu, and a collection of Transylvanian German documents was gathered under the stewardship of the great Göttingen historian August Ludwig von Schlözer, which was to form the basis for the *Urkundenbuch zur Geschichte der Deutschen in Siebenbürgen* produced by historian Franz Zimmermann from the second half of the nineteenth century. Schlözer himself published the *Kritische Sammlungen zur Geschichte der Deutschen in Siebenbürgen*, with which the Transylvanian Germans were acquainted before it was printed, as Schlözer had sent the manuscript to Sibiu for review by the town's historians. Schlözer's knowledge of the region between the Carpathians and the Danube was second hand, as is demonstrated in this and other writings, and he knew little of the problems faced by the Romanian people, but the model of his endeavour was adopted not only by German intellectuals but also by Romanian scholars who read the *Siebenbürgische Quartalschrift*.[34] Romanian historiographers who came into contact with Transylvanian German and Hungarian intellectual circles were inevitably exposed to the modern historical techniques proposed by Schlözer: this was the case with Samuil Micu, Budai-Deleanu and Petru Maior. Although they identified errors in the German professor's interpretations, some of them exonerated him of blame: 'Schlözer's opinions,' writes Budai-Deleanu, 'even if surprising, are such that he cannot be accused of partiality.'[35] These points of contact were numerous, especially when historians were attempting to gain recognition for the scientific validity of their work. They were less evident when the climate was more overtly political, as was increasingly the case when the foundations were being laid for the historicism of the nineteenth century. Yet the tense coexistence of these two tendencies, scientific and political, did not exclude overlap in their ideas and methods. Both national political programmes – Romanian, Hungarian and Transylvanian German – and theoretical scientific study shared common sources of information and interpretation. This was the case, for example, with natural law, Enlightenment philosophy and historical law. We should not be surprised that they all draw on the same sources, appealing to Schlözer, and then to Herder and Michelet, since historiography itself laid the foundations of political programmes: 'National rebirth favoured the historical perspective of contemporary times and the resurrection of national political traditions.'[36]

Sibiu was aware of developments across the Romanian territories as a whole, which were increasingly lending momentum to the movement of ideas. In the governor's library people could access the data gathered by Sámuel Köleseri in his *Auraria Romano-Dacica* (Sibiu, 1717), Michael Schendo's book *Historico-Phisica Topographica Valachicae Austriae Subterraneae Descriptio* (Alba Iulia, 1720), as well as the newspapers and magazines of the day describing, for instance, the uprising of Horea (hence Brukenthal's court was aware of how it was reported in Europe), just as the appearance of the *Supplex Libellus Valachorum* excited much debate among Transylvanian German intellectuals in the years following 1791. The Romanian national conscience was well known in the circles of Sibiu, as was the economic interdependence between Transylvania, Wallachia and Moldavia, subjects which had been tackled by Transylvanian German chronicles since late medieval times. Romanian culture, religion and traditional customs were also widely known, the result of long cohabitation and exchange of values. This tradition of communal existence could not be wiped out by the eighteenth century, and its spirit can be found in the work of Johann Filstich of Brașov.[37] Brukenthal himself accepted this dialogue with Romanian intellectuals, and in 1779, for example, had an audience with the great Moldavian scholar Gheorghe Saul.

The atmosphere created by Brukenthal's patronage was by no means replicated among the German community from the Royal Lands (*Fundus Regius*) of Transylvania. The Enlightenment 'transplant', though done with the best of intentions, was not understood by Transylvanian German feudal and bourgeois society. Collections of books, paintings and minerals served only a small section of society,

Plate 1
The town of Karlovy Vary

Plate 2
Old market in
Frankfurt am Main

C. Andelfinger & Cie., Kunstanstalt, München. Nr. 145. Nach der Aufnahme des k. k. Hofphotographen Erdélyi, Budapest.

Budapest, Kilátás Budáról — von Ofen aus gesehen.

Plate 3
University of Halle

Plate 4
View of Budapest

Plate 5
Hungarian Parliament
in Budapest

Plate 6
Szeged Synagogue

Ljubljana - pogled z Marijínega trga na ljubljanski grad

Miskolcz Széchényí utcza

München.

Altes Rathaus.

Marienplatz mit Mariensäule.

Plate 7
Central square in Ljubljana

Plate 8
Széchenyi Street in Miskolcz

Plate 9
Central square in Munich

Plate 10
Novi Sad/Újvidék

Plate 11
Central square in Oradea/Nagyvárad

Plate 12
Central square in Krakow

Plate 13
Prague Astronomical Clock

Plate 14
Romanian Athenaeum
in Bucharest

Plate 15
Batthyaneum Library in
Alba Iulia/Gyulafehérvár

Kassa   Székesegyház a Szent Mihály kápolnával

I. Biblioteca Universitátei din Jași

TEMESVÁR   Megyeháza - Comitatshaus

Temesvár
Ferencz József liget

Plate 16
St Michael's Square in Cluj/Kolozsvár

Plate 17
University Library in Iași

Plate 18
Queen Mary Street in Lugoj

Plate 19
Governor's Palace/County
Government Building/Art Museum
in Timișoara/Temeswar

Plate 20
Franz Josef Theatre in Timișoara/
Temeswar

Temesvár, Jenő herczeg tér. — Prinz Eugen Platz

Kiadja a Polatsek féle könyvkereskedés Temesvár.

19-6-06

Souvenir de Salonique

Vue générale de l'Hôpital Municipal

Editeur: J. S. Varsano, Salonique

Sarajevo   Begova Moschee - Begova Džamija.

Софiя, Народния театъръ.   Sofia, le Théâtre National.

Mala Luka.   Split. — Spalato.

Plate 21
Prince Eugene Square (Liberty Square today)
in Timișoara/Temeswar

Plate 22
Municipal Hospital in Thessaloniki

Plate 23
Neighbourhood in Sarajevo

Plate 24
Sofia National Theatre

Plate 25
Harbour in Split/Spalato

Szabadka — Városháza

CONSTANTINOPLE — Corne d'Or et Stamboul

Constantinople — Palais Impérial de Dolma Bagtché — Bosphore

Plate 26
City Hall in Subotica/Szabadka

Plate 27
Constantinople/Istanbul

Plate 28
Imperial Palace in Constantinople

Plate 29
Stock Exchange Square in Trieste

Plate 30
Aerial view of the city of Višegrad

Plate 31 (next spread)
Johannes Honter (1498–1549),
untitled map of Eastern Europe
from *Rudimenta Cosmographica*
(first edition Brașov 1542, this
copy from 1558 Zurich edition),
woodcut, hand coloured and
with manuscript annotations
(probably 17th century),
Ovidiu Șandor collection

Gruß aus Višegrad, Bosnien

Leopo
Barisa
Ri.dom.
Cassonia
Carpatus m.
Cremnicia
Agria
Posonium
Vacia
TRA
Debricia
VNGARIA
Strigonium
Buda
Varadi
Colocia
Ticia fl.
Alba regalis
Segedinum
Quinque ecclesiæ
D
Drauus fl.
Peta
Bellograd
Sauus fl.
BOSNA
Orbelus m.
Scardona
Scardus mons
DALMATIA
MARE
Ragusium
Haliacmon fl.
MACE
Dyrrachium
ADRIATICVM
PA

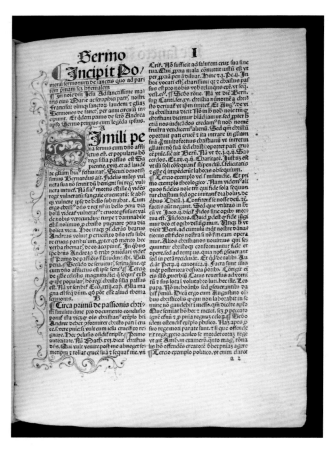

Plate 32 (left)
Johannes Honter (1498–1549),
Rudimentorum Cosmographicorum
(1552, title page of first
Antwerp edition), 10 x 15.5 cm,
Ovidiu Şandor collection

Plate 33 (above)
Pelbartus Ladislaus of Temesvár
(1435–1504), *Sermones pomerii fratris
Pelbarti de Themeswar diui ordinis
Santi Francisci de Sanctis incipiunt feliciter*
(Hagenau, 1499), printed page
with manuscript decorations,
15 x 21 cm, Ovidiu Şandor collection

and although Western visitors on the eve of the nineteenth century were impressed by the refinement and taste found in Transylvanian court circles, and even by the European dress sense depicted by Martin van Meytens in his paintings of the founder and his wife,[38] all this was far removed from the life of most Transylvanian Germans, who were unable to understand or participate in Brukenthal's spiritual project. Even musical and literary soirées were rejected by the local bourgeoisie. Society as a whole was not ready for the innovations of Homo Europaeus, and so 'Only those collections having an obvious traditional Transylvanian German slant on the interpretation of the past had great influence in the cultural life of Sibiu at the time of Brukenthal'.[39] Another century would pass before his thoughts and work were truly understood, and the museum in Sibiu which bears his name would realize its founder's dream of a cultural centre with European values.

In Alba Iulia the traditions came from earlier centuries, when John II Sigismund facilitated the link with Renaissance humanism, or, as we have seen, Gabriel Bethlen opened new windows on the civilization that was changing Europe. It was only to be expected that the intellectual circles of these earlier times would exert an even greater influence in the field of culture during the Enlightenment, especially in literature. In the middle of the fortress recently built by Charles VI in Alba Iulia (whence its name at that time, Alba Carolina),[40] not very far from the imposing Roman-Catholic cathedral, the bishop of Transylvania, Ignác Batthyány (1741–98), intended to found an academy of sciences, as well as a number of related institutions. His great ambitions were beyond his powers, and the project was limited to a library, a small museum of antiquities and mineralogy and an astronomical observatory. This institute, which quickly established a reputation way beyond the borders of Transylvania, was known as the Batthyaneum. Installed in a former Trinitarian church, the book collection was opened to the public in 1798. In his eagerness, Batthyány used Gutenberg's printing press to set the enterprise in motion himself. His passion for knowledge had possessed him since his studies in Graz and Rome – he spent many hours in the Vatican Library, where he acquired his love of books and old manuscripts. His studies laid the foundation for his future historical writings and, eventually, the creation of his collection. He gathered many old manuscripts and codices in Rome, but especially the incunabula that were to form the most prized part of his library. Successively canon of the diocese of Esztergom (1767), church dignitary in Esztergom and Eger (1773) and Roman Catholic bishop of Transylvania (1780), Batthyány travelled extensively and collected books wherever he went. His frequent visits to the diocese of Eger resulted in important acquisitions of religious books, including sixteen volumes of papers and original letters and copies belonging to Sámuel Dobai Székely, the collections of the library of Löcse, manuscripts from Szepes, and valuable books from Cassa and from the parish of Bártfa. In 1786 he made an extraordinary acquisition, the library of Count Christopher Migazzi, cardinal of Vienna and bishop of Vácz. This collection brought 8,000 volumes to Alba Iulia, although after many years they could no longer remain there, when Joseph II put a stop to the accumulation of duties and Batthyány lost his position as a bishop.[41]

A first catalogue compiled in 1824 by András Cseresznyes shows that Batthyány's library contained 18,201 volumes, the most important element being the collection of 1,230 manuscripts: most of these were sumptuous medieval codices, beginning with the so-called *Codex Aureus* (also known as the Lorsch Gospels), a staggering monument to European culture that combines Byzantine, Anglo-Irish and Carolingian traditions.[42] From the outset Batthyány possessed one of the richest collection of Bibles in Europe, as well as a great number of books published by the most prestigious houses across the continent, covering everything from medieval Christianity to the evolution of the sciences from the fifteenth to the eighteenth century. The library also contained 530 incunabula obtained from famous printing houses, especially in Germany and Italy – for example, Nicolaus Jenson Gallicus from Venice, Anton Sorg from Augsburg, Anton Kobeyer from Nürnberg and Aldus Manutius from Venice – which published works by many great writers, such as St Augustine, Marsilio Ficino, Flavius Josephus, William of Ockham, Pico della Mirandola, Thomas Aquinas and Lorenzo Valla.[43] Batthyány was attracted to every type of rare book, whether its interest lay in the execution of the printing or its contribution to European culture, and his thirst for the acquisition and communication of knowledge confirms him as a true Homo Europaeus. His ambition was no less than to create, through his astronomical institute and library, the first centre of scientific research in Transylvania – a vision that was already clear during his academic training, when he kept company with linguist Adam Kollár (then director of the Imperial library of Vienna) and historian Dániel Cornides (librarian and university professor in Pest).

Batthyány was interested in the scientific study of medieval texts, analyzing rare books from a philological and historical perspective. His activity as a collector was of secondary importance, the principal focus of his work being the foundation of methodical Hungarian codicology and textology.[44] Batthyány's creative cultivation of the sciences came at a turning point for Central and Eastern Europe, as the region was beginning to embrace modern ideas, and his efforts led to the foundation of the Scholarly Society (*Societas Assiduorum Litteraria*), an 'aristocratic scientific workshop' for the study of early medieval history, the analysis of contemporary Western literature, the reappraisal of both the sacred and lay texts of clerical life, and the interpretation of the ecclesiastical laws of Hungary and the prerogatives of the bishops of Transylvania. Batthyány's own works in these subject areas include *Acta et Scripta S. Gerardi episcopi Csanadiensis hactenus inedita cum serie episcoporum Csanadiensium* (Alba Iulia, 1790), *Edictum episcopale circa regulationem cleri* (Sibiu, 1781), *Leges ecclestiasticae regni Hungariae*, tomes I (Alba Iulia, 1785), II and III (Cluj, 1827), *Homilia ad clerum* (Sibiu, 1781), *Prerogativa episcoporum Transilvaniae in excelso regio gubernio* (Alba Iulia, 1791) and *Norma vitae cleri* (Sibiu, 1780). Two works that remained in manuscript form, *Dissertationes de rebus gestis inter Ferdinandum et Sigismundum Zapolya regem* and *Isabellam reginam et Georgium Martinusium episcopum Magno Varadiensem, ejusque cede in Alvincz*,[45] relate essential aspects of the political and religious history of Transylvania during the Reformation, showing how Batthyány's historiographical interests led him to a careful reconsideration of old texts. His Scholarly Society was a first-rate institution whose standards of research, editing and publishing rank alongside those of any modern university. Its printing house was founded in 1785, for the purpose of publishing the findings of the Batthyaneum group.

In founding his library, Batthyány drew on the experience he had acquired as librarian of Sant'Apollinare College in Rome. He conceived the rules by which the collection was acquired and organized, and devised the arrangement of the reading rooms. The result is a kind of labyrinth that teaches us much about the circulation of books generally, and those of the Enlightenment in particular. Many valuable works reached Transylvania by means of the Batthyaneum, some of which are indicative of the local elite's interest in the new European Man. In Alba Iulia, as in Buda or Vienna, intellectuals were reading Erasmus, Luther, Rousseau and Voltaire, and these authors were supplying the discourse for the kinds of debate that had begun to appear in Central-Eastern Europe. The route taken by these books, whether bought by Batthyány, his collaborators or the bibliophiles who donated them later, was far from straightforward. At that time copies of books could be purchased from publishing houses, printers or bookshops, and a glance at the stamps and written notes on these books reveals a tortuous route from the creator to the reader. A number of examples from Batthyány's collection will illustrate this.

It should come as little surprise that copies of Erasmus' work passed through many homes and libraries in the course of their journey between Holland or the German principalities and Transylvania. For example, *Colloquia nunc emendatiora cum omnium notis*, printed in 1560 in Amsterdam by Elzevir, passed through the Catholic abbeys of Central Europe before it entered the possession of Christopher Migazzi and was then acquired by Batthyány.[46] *Opus de conscribendis epistolis*, published in Cologne in 1554, was obtained in the town of Ingolstadt by Michael Fogarassy, a Catholic priest from Transylvania who studied in the West, whence it passed into Batthyány's collection, indicating a possible itinerary from Ingolstadt via Vienna, Buda and Cluj to Alba Iulia.[47] *De duplici copia verborum ac rerum commentarii duo, multa accesione novisq. formulis locupletati*, published in Cologne in 1540, bears the signature of Luther and the name of a Prussian owner, Boegle, as well as an Ex libris *Bibliothecae Fogarassyanae*, which proves that Transylvanians systematically acquired bibliographical rarities.[48] *La Paraphrase d'Erasme divisée en deux tomes, dont le premier contient l'Exposition des quatre Evangélistes et des actes des Apostres. Nouvellement translatées de Latin en Françoys*, printed by Johann Froben in Basel in 1563, bears a handwritten note, *Ex libris Antony Siskovich de Ontopa*, which tells us that the book was owned by an Eastern European intellectual who spoke French, but also reveals another important fact: despite the traditions of his culture, this Transylvanian nobleman, like many others, was seduced by the ideas of the first great modern Homo Europaeus.[49] *Colloquia familiaria*,[50] published in Ulm in 1747, is another admirable example of the way this generation acquired books: along with Batthyány's library stamp (*Gyula Fehérvári Grof Batthyány püspöki könyvtár*), we find the cognomen 'Joh. Aemilii Buczy', which belonged to a scholar well known in the religious circles of Alba Iulia, Cluj and Bistriţa as well as the academic society of Buda (of which he was an active member), a leading representative of the era of transition towards the new world.[51]

It would be an exaggeration to claim that this constant return to Erasmus reflected some kind of crisis of conscience. The intellectual elite of Southeastern, Central-Eastern and Central Europe were always searching for models, and the figure of Erasmus loomed large in history, a brilliant mind who encapsulated the profound social changes that had taken place during the Renaissance and the centuries that followed. Like Galileo, Erasmus was a pivotal figure between two eras, who wished to bring about change through reform rather than war and revolution. In this respect he coincided with the spirit of Enlightenment despotism, which was deeply embedded among Transylvanian intellectuals, as it was in the other Romanian principalities, in Serbia, Greece, Hungary, the Czech lands and Croatia. However, it would be a distortion to say that Erasmus was read purely for his broad European perspective: in elite Protestant circles he was valued for his confrontations with Luther. Protestant colleges acquired his works, but restricted access to them – on some copies the phrase *inter prohibitas primo classis* indicates that Erasmus' truths were not for universal consumption.[52] This was not the case in Jesuit colleges, where a growing interest was shown in his work.[53] This response to Erasmus during the last years of the eighteenth century suggests a search for fresh beliefs, the hint of a vision permeating through the 'cultural channels' inhabited by the owners of the Dutch scholar's works.

Another important figure in the spread of knowledge was Martin Luther, a focus for both religious and cultural interests who also reveals much about the communication between West and East. The Batthyaneum held a number of sumptuous copies of Luther's Bible, but also in editions intended for study in schools and colleges. Printed in Wittenberg, Dresden, Frankfurt and Jena, re-edited in the first half of the eighteenth century both across Germany and in the printing centres of Danubian Europe, among them Buda and Brașov, Luther's books reached all the major court circles of the Enlightenment. Catholics also played an important role in the reception and circulation of books, as one might expect given the diversity of Hapsburg society during the Enlightenment – a principle enshrined in the Edict of Tolerance of 1781, whatever its limits and hidden intentions. However, the 'sincere Catholicism' and openness of Joseph II was not enough in itself to raise Central-Eastern Europe to the level of the West. As Pierre Chaunu says, 'Consciences cannot be governed. He did not understand the value of Baroque Catholicism, its perfect coordination with the knowledge of the traditional culture of the villages. In order to use this wealth you first had to understand how to love.'[54] There was a genuine change of rhythm and reading became more diversified, but its impact was initially experienced only among the intellectual and social elite, and some time passed before its influence permeated the deeper fabric of society. For now, the East remained handicapped, but it would gain greater self-knowledge during the ensuing century of national consciousness.

Luther's presence in the libraries of Transylvania during the Enlightenment indicates how religious liberalism influenced the new current of thought. The principal Evangelical universities had to an extent brought together scientific humanism and Evangelical theology, while the modern centres of learning in Protestant Germany, of which Halle and Göttingen were the eighteenth century's most brilliant examples, displayed great openness and understanding. This attitude allowed both science and theology to be studied not only by ethnic Germans, but by Croats, Hungarians, Slovaks and Romanians. The intellectuals of these linguistic communities came into contact with the teachers, libraries and universities of the Protestant North. There are no traces of religious indoctrination here: in this atmosphere of learning, intellectuals were not exposed to dogmatism, but could explore the ideas within Lutheranism that connected them to the new principles of European politics and culture. Many adopted a qualified form of belief that developed into Christian patriotism or ethical humanism – this was the case with Klopstock, Schiller, Goethe and Wilhelm von Humboldt – while G. E. Lessing rejected Protestant Orthodoxism. Historian Werner Conze concludes that this was a 'Protestant movement specific to Germany whose climax, from a philosophical point of view, was Kant and Hegel, and from a theological one, Schleiermacher'.[55] A brief foray into the work of Herder – for example, *Ideen zur Philosophie der Geschichte der Menschheit* – shows us that writers and philosophers of this new generation were paving the way for the Romantic conception of history and political reality.

The institutions of Central-Eastern Europe wished to emulate these feats, and it is in this spirit that national literature, theatre and education emerged in the region. The importance for intellectuals in this part of Europe of the corridor linking Vienna to Alba Iulia is illustrated by the many books by Martin Luther rediscovered in the Transylvanian town, which offer a *sui generis* panorama of the ways and communities of this cultural corridor. Examples include *Biblia*.

Das ist die ganze heilige Schrift. Deutsch von Dr Martin Luther (1563) from the Migazzi collection[56] and *Epistolarum reverendi patris Domini D. Martin Lutheri* (Jena, 1556),[57] the first page of which bears many notes indicating the cardinal's interest or that of his group of collaborators in the work; the main body of the book is also filled with marginal notes of a scholarly rather than polemical nature, including a mention of the famous critic Pierre Bayle, author of the celebrated *Historical and Critical Dictionary* and an important figure in pre-Enlightenment thought. There is also another volume of *Biblia. Das ist die ganze heilige Schrift* (Frankfurt, 1572),[58] bearing a few handwritten notes, one of which stresses the fact that the volume comes from a Jesuit college, probably in Transylvania, from where Batthyány obtained it, using his authority as a bishop.

A copy of *Die Haupt Artikel des christlichen Glaubens wider den Papst und der Helen Pforten zu erhalten* (Wittenberg, 1557)[59] indicates that it had been owned by a certain 'Mich. Heyndel', a (presumably eighteenth-century) Lutheran from the Royal Lands (*Fundus Regius*), before passing into the Batthyaneum collection. There is a copy of *Die Propheten alle Deutsch. Doct. Mart. Luther* (Wittenberg, 1546) with a splendid *ex libris* of Christopher Migazzi,[60] and another book that belonged to him, *Assertio septem sacramentorum adversus Martinum Lutherum, aedita ab invictissimo Angliae et Franciae Rege Do. Hyberniae Henrico eius nominis octavo* (1573),[61] that contests the Theses of Wittenberg, demonstrating the appetite for knowledge of Catholic society in Vienna and Transylvanian Alba Iulia. Further proof of Luther's appeal to both Homo Religiosus and Homo Novus are the various translations of his writings, for example one into Hungarian[62] that was circulated in numerous editions.[63]

The Lutheran Church embodied the Great Western Schism. Its challenge to Catholicism contributed, however unconsciously, to a new fragmentation of Europe, or the creation of new cultural and ideological nuclei. Originating in the need for freedom of religious expression, and coinciding to an extent with the idea of social emancipation, Luther's reforms were essentially confessional in nature.[64] What do Lutheranism, Calvinism and Anglicanism mean? A return to the sacred texts; salvation through religious calling (unlike Catholicism, where it is to be found in faith and traditions); the reduction of the sacraments from seven to three (Baptism, Holy Communion, Confession); consubstantiation rather than transubstantiation, meaning the presence of Jesus Christ in the Eucharist, in which the substance of bread and wine endures; the translation of the Bible into German, a language closer to that spoken in everyday life, and the corresponding abandonment of Latin as the language of the religious service; the church as a place of prayer, divine communication and communion, not a hierarchical institution. Beneath all of this lies the vehement protest of the North against the Roman Church. At its origins this divergence was understood only by theologians, but once it was propagated, it became an unprecedented fanatical struggle, with consequences that can still be felt, involving innocent people whose grasp of the matter is as far from the original faith today as it was centuries ago.[65]

The new Church was not aristocratic or intellectual in character – it was the Church of the lower and peasant classes. Luther himself was the son of a miner. His Bible makes no attempt to follow the ancestral sources – it is an adaptation, a simplification for his fellow countrymen. The Lutheran theses speak of a 'fluid' descending from the preacher to the masses, who embrace him as their representative and follow his ideology, with no notion of their destination. A new Jesus appears before the eyes and in the hearts of the many. They follow him, because Luther promises a battle for their rights. Lutheran dialectics emerged victorious, but only in a formal religious and political context (the Reformation was a gift for the prince electors, especially the Hohenzollern family, who supported Luther during the disputes). Luther was less successful at a more profound level, as religious feeling remained largely misunderstood, and although the North became Protestant, intellectuals did not join him.

The eighteenth century erased much of the prevailing dogma while maintaining a critical view of the European schism produced by the Reformation. The *Aufklärer* had little time for Lutheran doctrine, although by birth and education many of them came from Protestant families. Even the translations of the old sacred texts were amended in light of new interpretations. This was the case with Moses Mendelssohn's German edition of the Psalms of David (*Die Psalmen*, Berlin, 1783). The result of ten years' work, Mendelssohn's Psalms were intended to give Christian Europe a clearer picture of the secular poetry of the Jews. His translation is infused with the spirit of the Orient, but is also testament to the aesthetic sense of a master of the Hebrew language who was able to capture the tone of the old Jewish texts.

Luther was interested only in the immediate need for freedom of expression and resistance to the imperial Catholic oppressor, and his doctrine appeared to deny individual differences in the way of communicating with the Divine. This inflexibility was encapsulated in Luther's own words at Worms in 1521: *Hier stehe ich. Ich kann nicht anders. Gott hilfe mir. Amen!* [Here I stand. I cannot do otherwise. God help me. Amen!] This intransigence, perpetuated in the radical form of Reformation championed by John Calvin and his Geneva University, became intensely provocative. It was mirrored by violent reprisals from the Catholic authorities. The deists of the eighteenth century responded to the crimes perpetuated by both sides by devising new paths to universal knowledge, creating their own philosophical and religious doctrine without imposing it on others. English civilization of the seventeenth and eighteenth centuries was a fine example of this tendency: Judaism had influenced the Catholic and Anglican movements there, bringing about great philosophical and organizational changes on both sides. Similarly enlightened thinking could be found among the French Freemasons and in the intellectual society of Berlin, where Lessing and Mendelssohn played a predominant role, and, in America, in the case of Benjamin Franklin and the Philadelphia lodge.[66]

Alongside the texts of Erasmus, Luther and others, many valuable books by Transylvanian Reformation writers appear in the Batthyaneum's collection – works by Nicolaus Olahus, Johannes Honter, Christian Schesaeus and Pelbartus Ladislaus of Temesvár. There are two books by Olahus, both of which display the true European spirit of Enlightenment Transylvania. *Catholicae ac christianae religionis*,[67] printed in Vienna in 1561, enjoyed an immediate and enduring success in Austrian, Hungarian and Romanian religious circles, and from Vienna reached Alba Iulia via Trnava and Esztergom. *Hungaria et Attila*,[68] which earned Olahus fame as a historiographer, was widely read at this time thanks to the edition of *Aufklärer* Adam Kollár, published by Thomas Trattner in Vienna in 1762, a copy of which is in the collection at Alba Iulia. This work helped to cement Olahus' place in European culture of the Renaissance and Enlightenment. Kollár's was the second edition to appear during the eighteenth century, following one produced by Mathias Bel in Bratislava in 1730. Kollár's enthusiasm for Olahus stemmed from his sense of the public's appetite for new translations, which in this case led to the publication of a precious source for Central-Eastern European history. The demand for such a work among elite intellectual circles of the region is revealing in itself. The book contains extensive descriptions of the region's geography, its political institutions and its riches, and offers detailed information on the inhabitants of Transylvania – Hungarians, Szeklers, Transylvanian Germans and Romanians. Indeed, this is the first explicit reference to the Romanian linguistic community, which is placed alongside the other three populations for the first time: *In hac sunt quatro diverso genere nationes: Hungari, Siculi, Saxones, Valachi.*[69] The origins and traditions of each people are accompanied by erudite details on their names, demographic situation, communities, fortifications and occupations, and followed by a comprehensive overview of the Banat region and Pannonia. In his preface, Kollár comments on the elegance and ingenuity of Olahus' writings and the universal character of his ideas, giving further endorsement to a book that had already entered the canon of Enlightenment historiography.

The Batthyány collection has only two volumes of a single work from the vast oeuvre of Olahus' contemporary Johannes Honter, *Rudimenta cosmographica*, in an edition printed in Zurich in 1573.[70] We do not know exactly when this copy reached Alba Iulia, and it is likely that the bishop-scholar's circle came across it by chance. Their interest is probably explained by Honter's fame as an encyclopedic scholar, who made important contributions to the development of Transylvanian and European culture, rather than the value of the *Rudimenta cosmographica* itself. The two books in the library – volumes I and III of this four-part work – contain an image of the obsolete geocentric universe of the Middle Ages, rather than the heliocentric system of Copernican theory, and the geographical information included in volume III (as well as in the missing second volume) had been discredited by the discoveries of the sixteenth century. The only book of the *Rudimenta cosmographica* that was accurate by eighteenth-century standards was the absent fourth volume.[71]

Ruinae Pannonicae, the most important work by Christian Schesaeus of Mediaș, can be found at the Batthyaneum in an edition published in Sibiu at the end of the eighteenth century, in which Carl Eder's notes reproduce the 1571 Wittenberg first edition. Of the seven books of the twelve-book work initially printed (I–IV and IX–XI), only the fourth[72] is included: the rest were considered to be lost during the Enlightenment, but have been discovered relatively recently in libraries in Brașov, Mediaș, Cluj, Budapest, Krakow and Oxford.[73] This impressive historiographical poem, which I have compared to the most sophisticated texts produced in Central-Eastern Europe during the transition from the medieval to the modern age, displays intellectual qualities that were obviously scrutinized by the intellectual circles of Enlightenment. At once a poetic work and a chronicle of events, *Ruinae Pannonicae* is also a living picture of the way of thinking of Schesaeus' Transylvanian contemporaries, allowing us an insight into the region's dialogue with Europe at this time.

The library collection in Alba Iulia contains many editions of Pelbartus Ladislaus of Temesvár's work, including the *Expositio compendiosa et familiaris sensus liberale et mystici complectes*.[74] Pelbartus was a popular preacher of the Oradea Franciscan monastery, an expert in literary theology, philosophy, natural sciences and astrology, and he provides a useful reference point for the intellectual and spiritual life that gave rise to the Franciscan presence in Oradea. It is an indication of the Counter-Reformation in action. The Batthyaneum copy of his book shows us that his work was read in Alba Iulia and in the Catholic circles of Central Europe, and the handwritten notes added to the book indicate that it travelled from Hungarian Cassovia (Košice) to the towns of Transylvania.

Having considered Erasmus and Luther, as well as a number of Transylvanian writers, let us now examine how the new theories of the Enlightenment from the West were disseminated in Central-Eastern Europe. Despite the practical obstacles, eighteenth-century libraries proved remarkably resourceful and receptive. We have emphasized the influence of French thinkers such as Voltaire and Rousseau over the more moderate German-Austrian *Aufklärung* embodied by Leibniz, Christian Wolff and Pufendorf, but it should not surprise us that Transylvanian noble circles felt a greater affinity with the moderate Enlightenment of Berlin and Vienna where cultural questions were more important than social and political problems.[75]

Yet the elite of the West, among whom the French held the greatest appeal, managed to reach a privileged audience beyond the German Alps, in Hungary, Serbia, the Romanian Principalities, Greece and Russia. We find the works of Voltaire in most of the cultural institutions founded in Central-Eastern and Southeastern Europe, including several dozen in Alba Iulia and an impressive number in Aiud, Târgu Mureș, Cristuru Secuiesc and Sibiu. Research[76] has revealed the special relationship between Voltaire and Transylvania, and the Batthyaneum alone includes a sizeable collection including *Eléments de la philosophie de Newton* (London, 1791), *Histoire de Charles XII, roi de Suède* (Basel, 1782), *La Henriade de Voltaire avec les variantes* (Paris, 1800), *Romans de Voltaire* (Paris, 1800), *Essai sur les mœurs et l'esprit des nations...*, tomes I–VIII (Paris, 1817) and *L'Oracle des nouveaux philosophes* (Berne, 1760).

Voltaire's influence on Transylvanian intellectuals is clear, and examples abound. Count Ioan Lazăr's manuscript *Tractatus de Tolerantia* (1767) is a Latin translation of Voltaire's famous *Traité sur la tolérance*; Budai-Deleanu had Voltaire firmly in mind when he wrote his *Țiganiada*, where he discusses the concept of freedom in the spirit of the French Enlightenment and anticipates new forms of government; Petru Maior owned a copy of the *Lettres philosophiques*, and Emil Buczy possessed the German edition of the *Anti-Machiavel*. Martin Hochmeister, a printer and merchant from Sibiu who possessed a remarkable book collection,[77] was one of the most important recipients of these works; the purchase and dissemination of many valuable copies that reached the public and private libraries of the times were due to him.[78]

Noblemen, teachers, priests and freethinkers were not the only people who read Voltaire. As we have seen, the ordinary bourgeoisie, here represented by publishers and booksellers, acquired a taste for history through the works of the French Enlightenment. Voltaire's approach to history, typified by the *Mélanges historiques*, was entirely new: he analyzed his subject in both European and universal terms, bringing together history and philosophy. Like other Enlightenment writers, he did not subordinate history to the imperatives of philosophy, but combined the two disciplines in order to achieve richness of vision and detail. This stimulating way of understanding and rewriting history inspired intellectuals in Central and Eastern Europe, just as it gripped the rest of the continent. As Ernst Cassirer states:

> In the same way that mathematics became the prototype of the exact sciences, so history was now the methodological model to which the eighteenth century gave a new, deeper understanding of its universal calling and its structure, specific to the human sciences. The first step had to be emancipation from its subordination to theology. By gradually allowing the historical method to be introduced into its own sphere, and itself becoming a history of dogma and the Church, theology had suddenly acquired an ally that was soon to prove stronger than it, and in the end was to dominate it on its own turf. Friendly competition turned into a conflict that involved the new form of history and humanist sciences in general.[79]

Voltaire offered the world a new vision of human existence, in which reasoning was the guiding force. In Central-Eastern Europe his historical writings in particular left their mark upon the new ideas. Reform, like revolutionary thinking, drew great inspiration from Voltaire.

Rousseau also brought the reasoning of the Enlightenment to the East. The number of volumes to reach Alba Iulia was more modest, although the political ideas they communicated were just as influential. The Batthyaneum has two copies of works by Rousseau, *Lettres de deux amants, habitants d'une petite ville au pied des Alpes* (Amsterdam, 1792), and *Du contrat social ou principes du droit politique. Avec les considérations sur le gouvernement de Pologne et sur sa reformation projetée* (Rouen, 1792), received after the bishop's death.[80] More important than the number of copies available was the extent to which Rousseau was read, and evidence suggests an uncommon interest in his writing. The dissemination of his books across Transylvania originated not only from Alba Iulia, but also from Sibiu, Blaj, Arad, Târgu Mureș and Cluj. On the evidence of records listing which volumes were consulted in the Teleki library, it is clear that readers preferred Rousseau to Voltaire and Montesquieu. This can probably be explained by the profound influence of Rousseau's notion of the 'social contract': the notes on the Batthyaneum copy reveal that it was previously in the possession of Fogarassy, demonstrating that it had been circulated widely. Rousseau was invoked less in Transylvanian Cluj than in the Hungarian territories, but he was nonetheless well known to a fairly large number of Romanian scholars, and in the text of the *Supplex* he is mentioned nine times. David Prodan notes that 'The deduction of the Romanian petition is a direct reference to Rousseau's contract'.[81] It is worth mentioning that the Transylvanian School displaced Rousseau's idea of the 'contract' from a social to a national context, applying it to the specific concerns of the region rather than the political identity of the time.

Looking more closely at the text of *Du contrat social*, Rousseau states in his reflections on Poland that an outsider can only give a general view of a state's problems, but they are useful provided they lack prejudice, vested interest or a subjective viewpoint. In his enthusiastic support of the Polish people, Rousseau recommends drawing on examples of history in order to modify the Constitution, but with circumspection:

The immediate future will bring many advantages, which will be keenly felt. Put the law into man's hands so that it may be compared with the area of a circle in geometry. Solve this problem correctly and the government that results will be a good one, a government that will not abuse its power.[82]

This nobility of thought was welcomed all across Europe, but especially in the East, where emerging nations were faced with exactly this kind of situation for a century. Rousseau's deism, founded on intuition and personal experience, contrasted with the rationalist deism professed by Voltaire or the empiricism devised by Montesquieu. Rousseau 'sees a distinction between the religion of man (theism) and the religion of the citadel'.[83] The profound aspirations – which were not without contradictions – that formed the foundation of Rousseau's system led Ernst Cassirer to consider him the leading figure of the Enlightenment. Rousseau's concepts set great minds in motion from Eastern Prussia to the Romanian principalities, from the intellectual elite of Königsberg (Kaliningrad), where around 1760–70 Hamann, Herder and Kant met to discuss his work, to the intellectual society of the Southeast, where Neo-Hellenism propagated the values of French Enlightenment culture. Everywhere, Rousseau's ideas galvanized those who had been deprived of freedom: while Voltaire was a phenomenon of his time, Rousseau lives on in us all.

Another great name whose writings were embraced in Central-Eastern Europe as well as the West was Dimitrie Cantemir, whom we discussed in an earlier chapter. Batthyány's library held a copy of Cantemir's *Historisch-Geographisch und Politisch. Beschreibung der Moldau* (Frankfurt and Leipzig, 1771),[84] in which annotations indicate that the book circulated in Transylvania among Romanian and Hungarian intellectual circles. One of these notes mentions the name of Iosif Meheși, the Enlightenment scholar who presented the *Supplex* in Vienna: *Inscriptus catalogus libror[um] Josephi Meheși*. Another refers to Elek Horányi, a specialist in ancient Greek and in theological literature, teacher at the Piarist School in Cluj: *De Auctore Horany Memoriae Hungarorum, Part. II, pag. 227*. Son of a priest from Mănăștur, councillor of the Imperial Chancellery of Vienna, Meheși contributed directly to the drafting of the *Supplex*, the fundamental political document of the Romanian population of Transylvania, a task which required close study of many historical and philosophical books. In these conditions, the work of Cantemir provided more than just encouragement:

it offered valuable arguments that helped to define the Romanian community of Transylvania. It is certain that Meheși read Cantemir during the years in which he participated in the collective preparation of the *Supplex*, alongside Ioan Para, Samuil Micu, Petru Maior, Ignatie Darabant, Ioan Piuariu-Molnar and Gheorghe Șincai.

The pageant of books offered by the Batthyaneum collection is a good illustration not only of Alba Iulia's status as a cultural and administrative centre, or of the extent of Ignác Batthyány's scholarly circle: it is an important testimony of Transylvanian spiritual life and, more than any other cultural institution in the region, proof of the relationship between man and book, creator and receiver. The *Codex Aureus*, the jewel of the collection, cements Transylvania's standing in European cultural history. The manuscript survives in two separate halves, one in Transylvania, the other in Rome: this symbolizes not a rupture, as we might be initially tempted to conclude, but the unity of the continent, fittingly since the work was conceived during the time of the Carolingian Renaissance.

In Aiud, the tradition of the previous century was upheld: its college and library had been compared, even in Bethlen's time, with the Corvina in Buda. The library was far more important than the school, a distinguished spiritual institution for Transylvania from the seventeenth to the nineteenth century, and home to the richest scientific collection of the Hungarian Reformers. Today, its collection comprises 65,000 volumes, including manuscripts and incunabula, as well as many rare bibliophile copies. Damaged in 1658, 1704 and 1849, the library was reborn again and again; during the eighteenth century it received some substantial donations, first from politician and historian Imre Mikó, founder of the Transylvanian museum of Cluj (Kolozsvár in Hungarian).[85] This explains how the library managed to retain its masterpieces from Antiquity and the Renaissance and attract Transylvanian humanists from the sixteenth to the eighteenth century, whose writings paved the way for the age of Enlightenment. *Catalogus Alphabeticus Ilustris Collegii Alba N. Enyediensis Renovatus Anno MDCCLII Diebus Novembris*, the oldest manuscript inventory in the Bethlen Library (compiled by the librarian who worked there in the middle of the eighteenth century), lists the great works in the library's collection at that time, many of which have since disappeared: among the ancients, Aristotle, Aristophanes, Pythagoras, Pliny the Elder, Plutarch and Ptolemy; from the Renaissance and post-Renaissance, Erasmus'

Epistolarum liber, Encomium Moriae, Apologia, Colloquia, Apophthegmata, Adagiorum Epitome and Rhetorica, Richard Simon's Historia Critica, Pufendorf's De habitu religionis christianae ad vitam civilem, Dissertationes Academicae, De statu imperii germanici and De rebus gestis Friderici Wilhelmi Magni electoris Brandenburgici, Johannes Leunclavius' Annales Sultanorum Othmanidarum, Johannes Oecolampadius' Exegemata in Iob et Daniel and Pelbartus' Opera varii Argum. Among the beautiful bibliophile editions that were useful to the school's pupils (in general, youths who were educated during the Enlightenment and Romantic ages, and who therefore did not benefit from the Mikó donation, which only reached Aiud in 1863) were books that revealed European learning in mathematics, medicine, astrology, philosophy, geography and mechanics. Three especially impressive volumes of this type are Coloniae Agrippinae Typis Bertram Buchholtz (a donation made by Dénes Bánfi in the eighteenth century, as indicated by a handwritten note alongside an ex libris of Imre Mikó), De re metallica and Cosmographia Petri Apiani.[86]

The atmosphere generated by this library was enjoyed by Sándor Kőrösi Csoma at the beginning of his intellectual development. He is a symbol of Transylvanian Enlightenment and Romanticism culture, a true example of Homo Europaeus. We discover from Regestrum piarum fundalionum et Protocollum designationis beneficiorum Collegii evang. reformat Alba-Nagyenyediensis[87] that he first attended the college in Aiud on 31 January 1809. The period he spent here was decisive for his future career. Kőrösi learnt a number of languages, including Romanian and Latin, and in the library he encountered the writings of well-known contemporary scholars. In his last years at the college he studied the reformers of Hungarian culture, Sámuel Gyármáti,[88] Gábor Döbrentei and Ferenc Kazinczy. He became the protégé of Mihály Kenderessy, an enlightened and broad-minded man who moved in all the major cultural circles of the area, and then attended Göttingen University, where he finished his research in classical philology and history and began the work in Oriental studies which would make him famous. Kőrösi studied the works of Ignác Einhorn in history, Christian Gottlob Heyne in philology and hermeneutics and Johann Friedrich Blumenbach in comparative anthropology. His Tibetan–English Dictionary (Calcutta, 1834), Tibetan Grammar (Calcutta, 1834), Sanskrit Tibetan–English Vocabulary (in manuscript form) and Tibetan Studies (in Asiatic Researches and Journal of the Asiatic Society of Calcutta, 1834), were unanimously praised. In the year these books were published the most important Buddhist university of the time, Taisho in Tokyo, sang the

Lotus song to Kőrösi, considered the supreme recognition that can be bestowed on a mortal, confirming him as a *bosatsu* (bodhisattva).[89] These works were available to intellectuals in Transylvania through the great private library of Timotei Cipariu and the college library of Odorheiu Secuiesc (Székelyudvarhely in Hungarian), the most important Szekler library beyond Târgu Mureș (Marosvásárhely in Hungarian). Cipariu, a friend of Kőrösi, and also interested in Oriental languages and phenomena, paid close attention to his work. One of the first editions he received as a gift (*Donavit Seminario Alexander Cs. de Kőrösi*) contains many underlined Sanskrit words, proper as well as common nouns. Cipariu also collected dictionaries and books documenting the history, geography and ethnography of Asian peoples, making the Oriental section of his library one of the finest of his day.

Kőrösi's alma mater in Aiud offered an austere education typical of Reformed colleges, where teachers took their role in moulding consciences very seriously. Importantly, both the teachers and the library staff at the college were characterized by a tendency towards Europeanization, inspired by Bethlen's legacy. Sándor Kőrösi Csoma successfully drew on elements of the approach of each of his tutors, but deeper moral and intellectual influences can be attributed to Ferenc Benkö, a renowned teacher of natural sciences, József Hermányi Denes, a priest best known for his collection of anecdotes, István Tőke M. Vásárhelyi, a teacher of philosophy and mathematics, and above all Ferenc Pápai Páriz, the scholar who at the end of the seventeenth century introduced from Western schools the noble aspiration of contact with the wider world. These ideas also influenced his Romanian friend and colleague, Mihail Halici.[90]

The scholars of the college in Aiud – *Illustri Collegio Nagy-Enyediensi Professor Publicus* as they were called at the time – were learned men whose surviving works include Ferenc Pápai Páriz's *Dictionarium Latino-Hungaricum, succum et medullam purioris Latinitatis, eiusque genuinam in Linguam Hungaricam conversionem, ad mentem et sensum proprium scriptorum classicorum*, published in 1801, the result of a collaboration between two publishing houses in Central-Eastern Europe, Johann Michaelis Landerer de Fuskut from Bratislava and Martin Hochmeister from Sibiu, featuring a preface by Enlightenment scholar Petru Bod;[91] *Pax Corporis*, also by Pápai Páriz (Cluj, 1764);[92] *Institutiones philosophiae naturalis dogmatico-experimentalis, quibus veritates physicae luculentis observationibus et experimentis illustratae ac confirmatae, nexu scientifico* methodice proponantur, by István Tőke M. Vásárhelyi (Sibiu, 1736);[93] Erköltsi Antropologia, a textbook of anthropological ethics for students, by Sámuel Köteles (Târgu Mureș, 1817);[94] Dissertatio Juris publici de Jure quod dicitur postliminii, by Michael Tsomós (Cluj, 1857);[95] Erdélyi Féniks Tótfalusi Kis Miklós. Avagy Profes. Pápai P. Ferenc-nek a Könyv-nvyomtatás mesterségének találásáról, es folytatásáról, a Tótfalusi Kis Miklós emlékezetére irott versei (Pápai Páriz's homage as a poet to the printer-artist Miklós Misztótfalusi Kis), in an edition that belonged to Petru Bod and was published in 1767;[96] A bányász tudomány és a lipsiai gazdaságról ertekező tudós társaság nemes tagjának, Ferenc Benkö's Hungarian translation (Cluj, 1784) of Werner's work published in Göttingen in 1782, which includes a dissertation on the science of mining and the economy of Leipzig, intended for a scientific German readership.[97] These are just a selection of the books that illustrate the channels through which ideas were transmitted from one end of the continent to the other. They demonstrate the influence of the Western European humanism under which Transylvanian culture asserted itself.[98]

Funds for books increased and private and public collections developed rapidly in Cluj, Oradea, Sfântu Gheorghe, Blaj, Târgu Mureș, Brașov and Sibiu. Although new Protestant public libraries were not created, the number of volumes in existing collections rose, often by incorporating books from elsewhere. This was the case of the library of the Unitarian college in Cluj, which was based on the older collection of the local sixteenth-century Dominican monastery, or that of the Reformed college in Târgu Mureș, which took over the collection of the town's Franciscan monastery. In Oradea, the life of its equivalent institution was interrupted in 1660, when the town fell into the hands of the Turks. More modest, by no means insignificant, were the libraries of the Reformed schools of Sighetu Marmației, Zălau (Zilah in Hungarian) and Orăștie. The value of the Zălau library was due to Sámuel Gyármáti's collection, which contained interesting books on the history of science, while, until its destruction in the Second World War, the Orăștie library housed the remarkable volumes gathered by Mihail Halici.[99]

Steeped in religion, science and art, studious youths from the colleges and libraries of Transylvania headed west. Culture changed direction as they became conscious of the benefits of contact with the universities of Europe. Dutch researcher G. Henk van der Graaf has demonstrated the impressive number of Transylvanian Protestant students enrolled in well-known institutions of higher learning: these include József Benkö, the future historian, in Utrecht in 1751; Petru Bod, the Enlightenment scholar, in Leiden in 1717; István Ágh, who became Unitarian Bishop of Transylvania, in Amsterdam in 1734; János Baty, a well-known medical doctor and university professor, in Utrecht in 1775; József Bodoki, teacher of history and Oriental languages at the college in Cluj, in Leiden in 1759; and Zsigmond Borosnyai Nagy, who was associated with the college in Aiud, in Leiden in 1731, Frankfurt in 1734 and Utrecht in 1735.[100] These examples indicate progress in both religious and scientific learning, which gave rise to a methodological leap in writing from Transylvania.

This phenomenon is well illustrated by the historiographical activity of Josephus Aloysius Kereszturi, a teacher in Oradea who published his innovative ideas in *Compendiaria descriptio fundationis ac vicissitudinum episcopatus et capituli M. Varadiensis* (Oradea, 1806), a documentary and interpretative history of the bishopric and chapter of Oradea from its beginnings to the end of the eighteenth century. Oradea's past is presented in connection with that of other towns in Transylvania, Banat, Hungary and Serbia. The book is based on medieval chronicles, first-hand sources (by György Pray, Miklós Istvánffy and György Kováchich) and documents preserved in the archives and library of the bishopric. Beyond its account of an ecclesiastical institution, this work enables us to appreciate Kereszturi as a representative of the Enlightenment, receptive to the different manifestations of the movement across the continent. In this respect he bears comparison with his compatriots Petru Bod and József Benkö, while his flexibility is redolent of the Italian historian Francesco Griselini.

Catholic schools and monasteries, too, founded many libraries across Transylvania and Banat. Most were monastic in character, but they reveal links with the rest of Europe, and some were receptive not only to purely religious influences, but also Enlightenment literature of a rationalist and encyclopedic nature. As Zsigmond Jakó states:

> After 1773, following the dissolution of the monastic orders, they suffered great losses. Only the libraries of the Catholic high schools of Odorhei [Székelyudvarhely in Hungarian] and Miercurea Ciuc [Csikszereda in Hungarian] survived in a more or less satisfactory state. Among the collections that were destroyed, that of the library of the minorities of

Arad is especially regrettable (some of the copies are still preserved in the local county library), as is that of the former Premonastratensian high school of Oradea [Nagyvárad in Hungarian] which inherited the wealth of books of the Jesuit school and house in the town. A grave loss for the patrimony of our country's libraries was the scattering of the book collection of the Catholic seminary of Oradea, which had been enlarged in 1789, and which had also included the books left by historiographer György Pray, as well as the 30,000 volumes of the Catholic bishopric collected at the end of the eighteenth century.[101]

We could complete this picture by mentioning that a small number of books from the collection of the convent of Hunedoara (Vajdahunyad in Hungarian, Eisenmarkt in German) can be found in the Regional Museum of Deva: one of its most prized volumes is an edition of Thomas Aquinas' work *Commentaria in octo libros politicorum Aristotelis* (Paris, 1645), with a surprising *Ex libris Constantini Cantacuzini* and the indication of a year, 1740, when the book probably entered the convent's collection.[102] In Radna, the old convent of St Mary has preserved a wonderful library collection, while in Timișoara, the books of the Trinitarian Order of Misericordians are of considerable interest: they are scattered across the libraries of the Banat Museum, the Timiș County Library and the Radna library, as well as in the care of the Roman Catholic Church, along with the books of the bishopric of Timișoara and Cenad.

The Catholic Church's influence remained strong throughout the eighteenth century, especially in Central and East-Central Europe: its patronage is evident in monastic buildings such as the Franciscan monastery of Radna, built in 1756 in a style suggestive of German-Austrian Baroque, and a visible echo of Catholic imperialism. The setting of the church itself on the hills surrounding the small town, its robust towers soaring towards the sky and housing two belfries, its two massive annexes where the library and school are located, its apparent harmony with the surrounding nature – reminiscent of the monumental abbeys of Melk and Pannonhalma, though without matching their architectural standards – all suggest the continuing vitality of Catholicism in a region where Orthodoxy was challenged. With its impressive bastion, the church also suggests, albeit on a modest scale, Catholicism's ability to dominate the masses – a spiritual battle in which it did not always prevail.

Founded in the eighteenth century, the library of the monastery of Radna amassed nearly 6,000 books, mostly dating from the sixteenth to the nineteenth century. The collection is principally made up of religious works – Bibles, dogmatic tracts, canon law, ascetics, books of Mariology, sermons – but also books on history, literature and cartography, lexicons, grammars and dictionaries. Numerous notes in the library's collection reveal the people and communities that came together in this place of pilgrimage, the roads they travelled across Europe, and their religious and ethnic affiliations. The books also indicate the ideas that aroused people's interest in the region and constituted the dialogue between East and West we have been discussing.

The old catalogue[103] of the library indicates the majority of volumes it acquired up to the beginning of the twentieth century. These include sixteenth- or eighteenth-century editions of ancient authors such as Cicero, Ovid, Flavius Josephus, Horace, Seneca, Sallust, Aristotle and Caesar; important treatises on diplomacy or great volumes on the chronology and political history of individual regions of Eastern Europe (Dalmatia, Slovenia, Transylvania, Hungary, the Ottoman Empire, Poland and Russia); biographies of Western European political and religious personalities of the medieval and modern ages; historical books, some by well-known writers, such as *Regnum Hungariae* by Miklós Istvánffy (1724), *Tabulae Hungariae Regni* (1702), *Mursensis Columna* by Petar Katančić (1782), *Napoleon Bonaparte* by Walter Scott (1828), *Königreich Neapolis* by Germanus Alderhold (1702), *Liebens und Tod Inocentii XIII* (1688), *Series Romanorum Pontificum* by Gregor Kolb (1733) and the undated Series *Banorum Slavoniae*; textbooks and other valuable books for study by different religious orders, Catholic, Reformed and Orthodox sermons, and dictionaries and lexicons for the study of mythology, history and modern languages, such as *Manuale Confessorii* (1765), *Manuale Missionariorum* (1726), *Manuale Rhetorum* (1718), *Lexicon mythologicum* (1741), *Libri miraculorum* (1500), *Lucerna Mystica* by José López Ezquerra (1733), *Lux Evangelica* (1648), *Historischen Lexicon* (1730, 1740), *Konversations-Lexikon* by Johann Hübner (1777), *Augustini Sermones* (1560), *Izraeliták és keresztény-eskölesei* (originally *Mœurs des Israélites et des Chrétiens*) by Claude Fleury (1802), *Nouveau Dictionnaire* by D. Voyageur (1732), *Religio Reformata* by Laurent Tapolcsani (1714) and *Predicationes Illiricae* (undated manuscript, probably from the eighteenth century).

My research at the library also uncovered a number of important books on geography, especially atlases acquired for the pupils of the Franciscan school, some of which had been circulated across different

RELIGION AND CULTURE: THE LIBRARY OF THE CONVENT OF ST MARY IN RADNA

With space for storing and reading books, the library of the Franciscan Monastery in Radna (Arad County, Banat region) has acquired about 6,000 volumes in its nearly two centuries of existence.

Illustration concept: V. NEUMANN | Layout: D. PENTELIUC-COTOŞMAN | Background map engraved by W. CHAPIN in 1779 | Shutterstock SL Licence- ID: 1193586

'CULTURAL CHANNELS' IN EAST-CENTRAL EUROPE: BOOKS AND
LIBRARIES IN TRANSYLVANIA, BANAT, HUNGARY AND SERBIA   215

regions of Central and Central-Eastern Europe. Among them, I identified an excellent *Atlas compendiaris seu ita dictus scholasticus minor in usum erudiendae juventutis adornatus Excudentibus Homanianis Heredibus*, published in 1758. It is a compelling example of the way atlases were used to encourage young people in the region to enlarge their horizons and discover the most important cultural, religious, scientific, economic, political and administrative centres of Europe and the wider world. This particular atlas draws on the scientific discoveries of the Enlightenment, including excerpts and reproductions of famous works of the time, maps drawn according to precise rules, with stereographic projections obtained by modern observations, and indications of the location of ancient monuments. The map of Europe is the work of Jean Matthias Has, first published in *Les Héritiers Homann* in 1743.

A considerable number of books in the Radna collection were donations from different places. For example, *Divi Aurelii Augustini Hipponensis episcopi operum* (ninth volume),[104] published in Venice in 1584, reflects the region's interest in the thought of St Augustine, in which two directions of ancient meditations come together, the sacred Hebrew texts and Greek metaphysics, while also demonstrating the circulation of this valuable book along one of the main 'channels' between Italy, Croatia, Banat and Transylvania. In the seventeenth century this book was in the Jesuit library of Zagreb (it bears the note *Collegii Soc. Jesu Zagreb Catalogo inscript.* 1629), a donation from a private collector (*Ex dono D. Patri Szinicza Cussodie*), but at the end of the eighteenth century or, more likely, the first decades of the nineteenth, the volume reached Radna, probably through a monk or a Croat priest who had visited on a pilgrimage. The collection also includes an edition of the first volume of *Disputationes in Aristotelis Logicam* from Buda, originally printed in Venice in 1727 and bearing the notes *Fr. Adallbertus a Buda* and *Conventus Radnensis*, which reveal the volume's transfer from one centre to another during the Enlightenment. From the library of the Franciscan monastery in Vienna (*ab bibliotheca Viennae P. S. Franciscane*) comes a work containing the complete theological lectures of Honoré Tournely (published in 1726 in Cologne), 'doctor of the Parisian University' and 'professor emeritus of the Royal Society of the Sorbonne'. There is a copy of Franz Xaver Widenhofer's *Sacrae Scripturae Dogmatica Polemica Explicatae* from Wallachia (1755), with the notes 'Dono oblatus a Pre. Francisco Subotim Ministro Provinciali Provia Bulgaria. Patri Luca Ruszinowich ejusdem Provia Alumno 779 (1779) A. Carolina' and 'Pro usu Pios Fris. Luca Ruszinovich Ord.

Min. Provia Valachico Bulgariae. Anno D-ni 779 (1779)', which prove the presence of the Franciscan Friars Minor to the south and north of the Danube in the second half of the eighteenth century. From Craiova (Conventus Crajovensis) comes *Concionis Tergeminae rusticae, civicae, aulicae, in omnes dominicae Festa totius Anni* (Cologne, 1709), belonging to the same Bulgarian community that we find later in Vinga, in Banat, where it was permitted to settle via a decree by Maria Theresa (the town was invested with the rank of free royal town and named Theresienstadt or Teresiopolis); it came into the possession of the Radna monastery library towards the end of the century of Enlightenment. The faithful of Vinga donated many other books to the Radna collection, some of which suggest the existence of private collections: for example, the volume *Institutiones doctrinae christianae sive compendium theologiae dogmaticae et moralis* by Petro Ludovico Danes Castelano (Venice, 1733) was in the possession of a certain Ambrosy Bogdanovich in 1763, while *Biblia Sacra* (Augsburg, 1730) passed through the Bogdanovich collection in 1766, and *Promptuarium morale super Evangelica Dominicalia totius anni* (Antwerp, 1593), was with Bogdanovich in 1786. Other libraries that operated in Banat in the eighteenth century belonged to the Orthodox bishop Petar Petrović, the Jewish intellectual Hirsch Levi and the German journalist Mathäus Heimerl.

The European dialogue conducted through books was already well established in Transylvania, so it is little surprise that in the middle of the Enlightenment countless cultural contacts were forged between the monastery of Radna and the intellectual and religious societies of Arad, Cenad, Oradea, Timișoara, Cluj and Deva, along with its connections with the evolving world of Central Europe: Slovenia, Hungary, Bosnia, Poland, Serbia, Italy and Dalmatia (as we understand, for example, from the manuscripts *Necrologium Aradiense* and *Ordinationes Provincialis Aradiensis 1754–1765*, which bear the note *Conventu Nostro S. Antonio Paduani*). It is no accident that among the Radna collection I discovered a number of books bearing annotations that signified an exchange of spiritual values: in the specific conditions of the time, Homo Religiosus understood that he needed to gain knowledge in other humanistic subject areas, including the exact sciences. The ideals of the Enlightenment often led him to abandon Church controversies in favour of a free, rational form of thinking. The appearance of literary, historical and philosophical works in the region, the genesis of the Transylvanian

School and the emergence of personalities with a European culture required these steps to be taken by the representatives of the Church. Their emancipation led to the secularization of culture and enabled modern forms of thinking to thrive. The monastery of Radna was in this respect a centre of ideas and cultural convergence in exactly the same way as the institutions we have examined in Blaj, Sibiu, Târgu Mureș, Aiud, Cluj and Oradea.

This vibrant cultural climate of was also felt in Greek-Catholic and Greek-Orthodox Romanian circles. During the years 1790 to 1840 in Banat and Transylvania these Church communities were represented by teachers with a thirst for knowledge and the desire to bring about positive change. The bishoprics of Ignatie Darabant (1788–1805) and Samuil Vulcan (1806–39) served the Enlightenment, their administrative and political aims accompanied by a wish to spread the ideas of the Reformation. A seminary was founded in Oradea and a high school in Beiuș, both educational institutions that did great service to the process of emancipation. The movement around the *Supplex* reaped the rewards of this progress, Samuil Micu and Gheorghe Șincai finding support and understanding for all branches of their literary and historical activities from the bishops and Church dignitaries of Oradea. This was a true friendship, a communion of souls and minds eager to put behind them the problems of the past. Romanian intellectuals were especially helpful in fostering and supporting the historical spirit, while the publishing of books was sustained by court circles in Oradea, and Romanian books and manuscripts were circulated among the city's library and archives as part of everyday cultural life. During the Enlightenment Oradea received 287 volumes (including thirty-three works in forty-four volumes) and eleven leaflets and letters from Samuil Micu; eight works in thirty-nine volumes and seven letters from Șincai; nine volumes from George Farcaș; four leaflets on the *Supplex Libellus Valachorum*; and two volumes from the correspondence of Inocențiu Micu-Klein.[105] It is easy to imagine the great distances crossed by the volumes reaching Oradea, with Romanian scholars travelling between Blaj and Rome, and stopping over in Oradea, Buda and Vienna. This helped to maintain contact with the ideas emanating from Western Europe and encouraged the implementation of an advanced cultural programme in the East-Central European lands. Books and textbooks on philosophy, such as those by Friedrich Christian Baumeister and Karl Steinkellner, reached Romanian intellectual circles in

Transylvania, and both original writings and translations – such as those of Samuil Micu – were produced as a result of this absorption of European spiritual values. Micu and Șincai also worked with the great publishing institution of Buda (Typographia Universitatis Hungariae Budae), acting respectively as censor and proof corrector. Petru Maior played a similarly important role in this process of cultural mediation. Romanian-language publications, as well as works in Hungarian, German and Serbian, became very well known, and accounted for a significant proportion of the books needed not only by intellectuals, but by the middle class as well.[106]

In Banat, books were acquired by the educated classes, by teachers and priests, officers of the border guards, future professors of the Preparandia (college) of Arad, and scholars who wished to strengthen their relations with the Romanian principalities: these were the same educated sectors of society that sent writers and men of ideas to Buda, Vienna and Karlowitz, great minds that flourished by producing their own original works under the influence of *Aufklärung*, but also that of the national historiographies of Europe. Initially only the intellectual elite was attached to the European ideals, while the intermediate social classes followed the traditional culture. Yet the temptation of communication became stronger for this latter group, and outside influences were brought to bear.[107] Banat became a leading zone for the fruitful exchange of values, and the eighteenth and nineteenth centuries nurtured countless examples of the *Erweiterung des Bewusstseins* (expansion of consciousness). Intellectuals continued to read old Romanian books, acquire the typographical works produced in Râmnicu Vâlcea and maintain enduring links with similar institutions in Blaj, often at the request of readers from Banat. Books in Romanian, as well as those in German, French, Hungarian, and Serbian, also came from Vienna or Buda. This attitude stemmed from the universal spiritual values without which an intellectual elite could never form in the first place. In multilingual Banat, it was inconceivable that figures such as Paul Iorgovici, Moise Nicoară, Dimitrie Țichindeal, Damaschin Bojincă, Constantin Diaconovici Loga, Paul Vasici and Eftimie Murgu did not learn, even in childhood, two or more languages. Attending schools in the region, as well as in Central Europe, broadened and strengthened this multilingual approach, which was vital for the assertion of their political interests, since they could achieve nothing without the ability to communicate in German, Hungarian and

Serbian. Even the priest Nicolae Stoica of Hațeg often used German, and his manuscripts include texts written in the official language of the time. This comes as little surprise when we observe the extent to which the lower categories of society used the language as well: as a result of living side by side, even the Romanian peasantry from the villages of the Timiș plain came to learn the language of the Banat Germans, as is proved by the fact that to this day many families continue to speak both Romanian and German dialect. This prompts us to go beyond the narrow historicism of the nineteenth century and recognize the cultural complexity of the social, political and economic structures of the Banat community.

Books know no borders. They were brought to Banat from Wallachia, Transylvania, Serbia, Hungary and Austria. Churches and schools acquired them for village communities; officers and under-officers of the border region bought books for themselves and their families; and townspeople made an equally important contribution, 'generically referred to as *jupân* [master] in the handwritten notes added to designate a book's owner'.[108] Booksellers also contributed to the movement of publications, passing from one side of the Carpathians to the other, travelling to Vienna and back. Books that circulated in this fashion include *The Pentecostary* (Râmnicu Vâlcea, 1743 and 1767), *Sermons* (Râmnicu Vâlcea, 1748), *Apostle* (Bucharest, 1748), *Gospel* (Râmnicu Vâlcea, 1746 and Bucharest, 1750, 1775), *Triodion* (Râmnicu Vâlcea, 1761), *Anthology* (Râmnicu Vâlcea, 1745, 1752 and 1786), *Collected Sermons* (Vienna, 1793), *Liturgy* (Sibiu, 1798), *The Bible* (Blaj, 1795) and the liturgical book entitled *Mineie*, which was published in Râmnicu Vâlcea in many editions between 1776 and 1800, and reissued (in twelve volumes) by Ioan Piuariu-Molnar in Buda in 1804–5.[109] Many of these books feature annotations that reveal their origin and circulation, political and economic events, the names of their owners, the social groups they reached and the cultural interests of society more generally. These, though, were religious books, and a spiritual rebirth that followed the innovations of the Enlightenment required something more: without neglecting valuable traditions, Europe's example had to be followed, and this was soon understood by the Romanian scholars of Banat.

Dimitrie Țichindeal and, not long after him, Constantin Diaconovici Loga conceived a plan for enlightening the region's population that was more in line with developments elsewhere in Europe. Translations and originals gradually emerged in the books published by Novacovici and Kurzböck in Vienna, at the Buda University Press. Paul Iorgovici and Ioan Teodorovici became emissaries of the movement, working as censors in the Austrian and Hungarian capitals. 'We should endeavour to make books of all kinds,' Diaconovici Loga wrote, 'to take them from other languages, as well, then to have them printed without delay,' and 'every man must lend a hand according to his own powers: for this is how the altar of our people is built, the gift of the light can be gained from the efforts of many.'[110] Diaconovici Loga's own books combine the legacy of the past and the tendencies of modern educational science, demonstrating that his interests ranged from the cultivation of his mother tongue and the unity of his people to the 'happiness of human society' which depended on the quantity and quality of knowledge, and the value and progress of communication. His works in this spirit include *Abecedar* (*Primer*, 1824), *Chiemare la tipărirea cărților românești* (*Call for the Printing of Romanian Books*, 1821), *Gramatica românească* (*Romanian Grammar*, 1822) and *Ortografia sau dreapta scrisoare a limbii românești* (*Spelling or Correct Writing of the Romanian Language*, 1818). He nonetheless continued to print religious books, conscious that the learning of new ideas should be balanced with the dignified, civilized practice of religion. The bishops were delighted to discover and support such inspiring work, aware of the value of disseminating books. In their view, too, albeit from a more conservative perspective, the function of the written word was to enlighten: the people needed the old texts, otherwise they could not be instructed in traditional ways of behaviour. Supported by Maxim Manuilovici, bishop of Vârșeț, and Nicolae Stoica the 'protopresbyter' of Mehadia, the *Octoih* of Diaconovici Loga could now be acquired by the communities of Banat:

> This book, *Octoih Tipicon*, copies of which you received in August 1821, you must show which church asks for one copy, and which for two; and if anyone else should want one or two copies, then write it down. In the shop I will show you where you must write one or two, 1 or 2, and then soon after despatch copies to each.[111]

This is a fine illustration of the close collaboration between clerical and secular intellectuals, between teachers in the towns' schools and educators in the villages who were working together to develop cultural life, gradually shifting the focus of learning towards the kind of diversity characteristic of the Encyclopedists. This time saw a revolution in the organization of schools, the criteria for the selection of their directors and teachers, the scholars' erudition and the standards they introduced. Banat came to know Europe, multiplying its ties with Transylvania, the Romanian principalities, the countries of Southeastern Europe, and the peoples and cultures of the Centre and West of the continent. Books were the principal mediators of the new culture, and the institutions that produced, propagated and preserved them rose to new heights, establishing bridges across time and space. The new spirit is encapsulated in the following extract from a document outlining the duties of the director of schools in the territory of the Romanian-Illyrian Regiment:

> The duties of this director of schools will cover schools in the Romanian-Illyrian Regiment. The plan is for him to be present twice each year to inspect the schools and to be here at examinations, to promote the schools and their teachers, to improve methods in the schools and finally to take care of the good teachers, to prepare them... It is also required of this director to know the Serbian, German and Latin languages, and to be able to prove that his life until now has been without blemish or foolishness.[112]

The authorities found their man. The person who met these requirements was one of the teachers of the Arad Preparandia, an individual who connected the Romanian conscience to that of Europe – none other than Constantin Diaconovici Loga himself. In 1830 he assumed leadership of the Romanian and Serbian national schools in the border regions of Banat.

The impetus given to educational institutions and their teachers was stimulated by the libraries around them, which represented a reflection of the interests of the region's intellectuals. They were neither numerous nor wealthy institutions, but they transmitted something significant for the generations to come: the work behind the books, work that was intended to serve the public good. The library of the Arad Preparandia, the private library of Nicolae Stoica of Haţeg, the library of Mesić monastery and the library of distinguished scholar Damaschin Bojincă are just a few examples illustrating how the imperatives of knowledge operated in Banat, for both Romanians and Serbs. I will not elaborate on their collections – these have already been described in detail by Nicolae Bocşan[113] – but should emphasize that they indicate, in this region more than any other, the two cultural strands that attracted scholars: Central European and Southeastern post-Byzantine. In conclusion, Banat provides a compelling example of the way a closed culture and the old medieval forms of civilization were brought to an end. Romanian intellectuals shaped their own destiny, and books, which favoured the absorption of the great ideas of Europe, offered an atmosphere conducive to the genesis of modern man.

Moving from Banat to Serbia, we discover a community going through the same process of rediscovering its conscience and clearing a path towards the new civilization. I have examined some aspects of this elsewhere in my study of Karlowitz, which during these decades of profound change was dominated by the personality of Stefan Stratimirović.[114] Let us now analyze it in the context of the multitude of channels by which written culture was able to reach the region. The founding of the Serbian libraries is tied to the history of the first churches and monasteries, in the same way that the life of the Serbian state cannot be fully explained without reference to Greek and Slavic Orthodoxy. The Christian East achieved unity through the cultivation of religious education, and collecting medieval books was a noble tradition taken up and continued by the intellectuals of the Enlightenment and Romanticism. During the Middle Ages almost every Serbian religious community benefited from the presence of books, and collections large and small proved to be of great educational value. Some of these old Serbian collections have been lost, due to wars or poor conditions of preservation. The construction of more suitable buildings came at the beginning of the modern age, as the Enlightenment elevated the status of libraries. This process was begun by the Belgrade Patriarchate in 1690, when Metropolitan Arsenie III Crnojević saved a considerable number of books from the Church of Peć: this became the so-called initial collection of the Belgrade Patriarchate of today. The privileges granted by Emperor Leopold I to the archbishop and bishops 'according to the Serbian custom' allowed the teaching of language and the dissemination of knowledge across the parishes and the people in general,[115] and books were held in high regard once more. In 1706 the first catalogue of the Patriarchate's library was compiled. In 1737 Metropolitan Mojsije Petrović decided to move the collection to Sremski Karlovci (during the time of the

Hapsburgs the town was known as Karlowitz), and shortly afterwards conferred on it the title of Metropolitan Library. From this point the collection was enlarged with numerous acquisitions, possibly as a result of the fiscal system and the considerable autonomy granted by Vienna even in 1720. Mojsije Petrović enjoyed the same rights as the Catholic bishop of Cenad and Timișoara, Count Ladislau Nádasdy, enabling him to wield the authority of the Church in both the kingdom of Serbia and Banat of Timișoara.[116] Books circulated in the towns and villages subordinated to Karlowitz; many of them ended up back in the Metropolitan Library, since instructions issued in 1769 made the return of volumes compulsory on the death of a hierarch.

The century of Enlightenment left its mark on the collection through the variety of acquisitions made by Stefan Stratimirović. He bought 2,072 books for the Metropolitan Library and donated his own collection of 2,480 volumes and over 200 maps and drawings. For over four decades he maintained numerous links with Buda, Vienna and Göttingen, establishing a lively dialogue with the West. Historical works, old source texts published by Austrian and German scholars, bibliographies, catalogues of great libraries, the literature and philosophical writings of the German and French Enlightenment, all were of constant interest to him, and acquiring copies through booksellers and antiquarians, by direct exchange and through mediators sent to the capitals of Europe on special book-buying missions, Stratimirović acquired a significant collection of the most important books of the European world.

Seduced by Western Europe, Stratimirović became a member of the Scientific Society of Göttingen University and distanced himself from the East, understanding, like his compatriot the writer Dositej Obradović, that only thus would the Serbs emerge from their semi-feudal captivity and re-enter the community of free European peoples from which historical circumstances had excluded them five centuries ago. His position as Metropolitan did not favour this task, but the limits imposed by the rank did not prevent him from expressing himself as a secular man and a true representative of the Enlightenment. He carried out his duties very differently from his predecessors, accepting into his inner circle not only the best ecclesiastical minds, but all who showed an interest in art, science and humanist culture. He was impressed by the library of Count Ferenc Széchenyi in Buda, appreciating its organization and cataloguing system, as well as the acquisitions it had made in order to remain in touch with universal values.[117] Stratimirović was eager to see some of the history books gathered in the Vienna imperial library, and on this subject his correspondence with historian Johann Christian Engel is edifying. He was also interested in obtaining editions of medieval source texts produced by German scholars at that time, such as the famous edition of the *Chronicle of Nestor*. In this manner, the collection of the Metropolitan Library was assembled. Its development marks the beginning of the history of modern libraries in Serbia as a whole.[118]

The cultural channels through which Serbia consolidated its ties with Enlightenment Europe cannot be understood without reference to the extraordinary contribution of Dositej Obradović. A contemporary of philologist and linguist Vuk Stefanović Karadžić, Obradović embodies the second phase in the assertion of Serbian culture after Sava Nemanjić (St Sava). He tackled the great problems faced by his community at this time – how Serbia could be freed from its backward social and political structures, how it could achieve economic and spiritual liberalization for the good of its people, and what were the most efficient means of communication with the rest of Europe. Preferring to serve his people rather than God, Obradović – a true European, steeped in Byzantine culture but profoundly influenced by the rationalism of his times – succeeded in communicating his thinking in an accessible manner. His writings, published at Buda University between 1806 and 1829,[119] present the philosophical, educational, social, political and cultural ideas of the eighteenth-century Enlightenment, adapted to current concerns. He constructs a coherent framework for his analysis of mankind, using logic, epistemology, politics and aesthetics. His task was facilitated by his command of many languages – Greek, Latin, Slavic-Serbian, Italian, Romanian, French, German, English, Albanian and Russian – which allowed him to travel from one cultural region to another and examine, for example, the concepts of the English thinkers, creating analogies between the thinking of ancient authors and the philosophers of the Renaissance and post-Renaissance periods. He became acquainted with the metaphysics of Gottfried Wilhelm Leibniz and Christian Wolff, and thus managed to present classical logic and the ethical principles of rationalism to the Serbian people. He read Thomas Hobbes, John Locke, Joseph Addison, Richard Steele and Vicesimus Knox with passion and discernment, including their observations on morality in his teachings. Andrija B. Stojković rightly associates

Obradović's activities with the initial attempts of the Serbian people collectively to adopt a modern view of the world.[120] In this endeavour he can be compared with his compatriot the poet Lukijan Mušicki and his Slovene mentor, Jernej Kopitar.

In Hungary, the Enlightenment was strongly influenced by the French spirit, supported by the books and libraries of Humenné (Homonna) and Pest and the efforts of the Buda publishing establishment. This was a time of new cultural activities following the movement of Francis Rákóczi in the first decade of the eighteenth century. New ideas emerged everywhere, as the Hapsburgs and the resurgent Jesuits worked together to achieve progress in education and culture. In this context the intellectual elite, in Hungary as in France and England, gave their support to the efforts of Enlightenment despotism to assist people on the periphery of society.[121]

In Humenné, the family of Count István Csáky founded a splendid *bibliotheca dominialis*. The count and countess were great enthusiasts of Western literature, and during the time of their studies in Vienna acquired a considerable number of volumes in French and German. Countess Iulia Csáky in particular was an avid reader of the works of the French Enlightenment. The literary salon at their castle was comparable to that of the Marquise du Deffand in Paris, while on their Illésfalu estate the family installed an English park, named the New Sans-Souci. The park was designed by István Csáky, influenced by what he had seen in Austria, and conceived as an idyllic world incorporating classic French style. This *Novum Sans Souci receptaculum philosophi, liberarum artis, solitudinis, pacis et libertatis amatoris*[122] included a pine forest, the castle, a guest house, a chapel, a dome, a space for riding horses, dedicated space for sporting activities (for example, a hill for javelin-throwing) and a re-imagining of the peak of the Muses. It epitomized a new openness to culture from outside Hungary, and in particular a passion for the French school of ideas.

Returning to the Csákys' library, it seems remarkable that several thousand volumes in French reached Humenné in spite of the strict imperial censorship, which forbade the importing of any of the books on its well-known *Catalogum librorum prohibitorum*. The only explanation is that merchants were able to bring these books into the country along with their usual merchandise. Later, during the time of Joseph II, the rules were relaxed somewhat, and books could travel from Paris to Central and Eastern Europe in a relatively short time. A

Specificatio librorum from 1777 lists the French books that were collected at Humenné by the family of Count Csáky. The library inventories themselves are dated 1790, 1792, 1805 and 1807. In the year it was put up for sale (1808), the Csáky library contained about 5,000 volumes, of which 3,600 were in French; a considerable number were in Latin and German.[123] It was purchased by Péter Atzel (the nephew of palatinal judge István Atzel) who had received land at Șicula-Ineu, close to Arad; at this point the collection was not available to the wider public and could only be consulted (as it was on rare occasions) by the owner and his family. Fortunately, the collection has survived thanks to its incorporation into the Arad County Library.

The combination of a *Catalogue des livres français et italiens* cited by Sándor Eckhardt and my own consultation of books in the collection has enabled me to assess exactly what was being read in Humenné, how it reflected the tastes of Hungarian intellectual circles and to what extent these had embraced the political and cultural ideas of the time. The *bibliotheca dominialis* is well stocked with French literature of all kinds: bibliographies, grammars, dictionaries, pedagogy, plays, writings from periodicals (after the English manner) and literary criticism (Charles Rollin, Charles Batteux, Père André). There is also an almost complete collection of the philosophical writings of the French Enlightenment: the works of Voltaire (many of them in first editions), some of the writings of Rousseau, the *Encyclopedia* and philosophical works of Diderot, books by Maupertuis, La Mettrie, Helvétius, Buffon, d'Holbach and Condillac, political manifestos for and against the French Revolution, and literature on the different forms of state, government, monarchy and religion.[124]

One remarkably well-preserved book bearing the *ex libris* of István Csáky is a history of the Hungarian revolution which includes the memoirs of Prince Rákóczi, *Histoire des Révolutions de Hongrie où l'on donne une idée juste de son légitime Gouvernement avec les Mémoires du prince François Rákoczy* (1739).[125] Some of the French periodicals in the Csáky library (including items gathered by Péter Atzel and Ferenc Vörös) offer a fascinating picture of the interests of their owners and the channels of communication they enjoyed with the West: *Magazin historique pour l'esprit et le cœur* (Strasbourg and Paris, 1764), *L'Année politique contenant l'Etat présent de l'Europe, ses Guerres, ses Révolutions, ses Sièges, ses Batailles* (1758), *Mercure historique et politique contenant l'Etat présent de l'Europe* (1765–8), *Journal historique* (London, 1773), *Journal littéraire dédié au roi par une Société d'Académiciens* (1776), *Correspondance littéraire secrète: Annales politiques, civiles et littéraires du dix-huitieme siècle* (1777), *Tableau Raisonné de l'histoire littéraire du dix-huitième siècle* (1779), *Courrier de l'Europe. Gazette anglo-française* (vol. 17, 1785), *Journal des Révolutions de l'Europe* (1786), *Révolutions de Paris...* (1789–90) and *Courrier politique et littéraire des deux nations* (1789–90).[126] This list indicates how fashionable the French language was at the time, and demonstrates the esteem in which French civilization and ideas were held – not only in Northern and Central Europe, but also in Central-Eastern and Eastern Europe. Hungarian culture embraced the influence of Enlightenment France, and many of its representatives became attracted to the ideas of the Revolution: the extensive infiltration of magazines into the country, often disguised correspondence to avoid censorship, eventually led to the Jacobin movement of Pest at the end of the eighteenth century.[127]

Count Ferenc Széchenyi laid the foundations of the famous library that bears his name, creating a cultural institution that was both a hub for Central-Eastern and Southeastern Europe and a place for the lively exchange of cultural values with the West.[128] As well as all the essential texts of the Enlightenment, the library was home to the historical and philological studies of the early nineteenth century by György Kováchich, and it was under this roof that the foremost scholars of the Enlightenment in the East met. The institution also made remarkable contribution to the research and modernization of the Hungarian language. The Széchenyi collection impressed its most eminent visitors.[129] Stefan Stratimirović wrote as follows:

> Your highness's library will be extremely useful to posterity, and to the advancement of science and education, thanks to your understanding of the enlightenment of the people. You can be satisfied, dear Count, and happy with the contribution that you have made to the formation of future generations. Unto the joy of the spirit and unto your honour, I am convinced that your personal contribution is a great one and it is with these thoughts that I remain sincerely yours, Stefan Stratimirović.

The correspondence between Széchenyi and Stratimirović gives us a privileged insight into how individuals saw the destiny of their people collectively. There are comparable examples in Romanian, Russian and Greek intellectual circles. The desire to spread knowledge and defeat ignorance brings these great minds together, and is what prompted Széchenyi to propose to Stratimirović a debate on the language and alphabet used in Serbian, Romanian and Russian books, to which the Metropolitan answered:

> Thanks to the attention that your highness pays to me, I had the honour of receiving with great joy the three volumes of the *Bibliotheca Hungarica*. As a token of my sincere thanks to your highness, in this letter I will respond to your request regarding the language and the characters used with great honour through the ages in our Church books.[130]

Both men were driven by their erudition, their superior understanding and their wish to foster and maintain dialogue.

Gheorghe Şincai worked in the Széchenyi library as Kováchich's first collaborator. The corpus of documents entitled *Rerum spectantium ad universam gentem daco-romanam* is the result of the Transylvanian scholar's activities in Pest. His work in the Hungarian library brought him into contact with the new historiography and gave him valuable experience of the techniques used in the editing of sources. He will have made use of the *Index alter libros Bibliotechae Hungaricae Széchenyiano regnicolaris in scientiarum ordines* (3 volumes, Pest, 1807–8) that Alexandru Papiu Ilarian and August Treboniu Laurian consulted in their later research.[131] This excellent catalogue lists the titles of all the writings that entered the Széchenyi library at the beginning of the nineteenth century, organized by subject: general cultural history, Church history, geography, hermeneutics and Hungarian and world literature. It includes books acquired from the great publishing houses in the majority of European languages, and many in Oriental languages. A remarkable collection for its time, it drew many intellectuals from both within and outside the empire, who benefited from its commitment to promoting the Enlightenment in art, science, politics and economics. We should remember that Ferenc Széchenyi was also the founder of the Hungarian National Museum, another institution that helped to prepare minds for the impact of European culture. Count Ferenc Széchenyi's philosophy was echoed in his son, István, who upheld the family traditions with considerable brilliance, striking fear into the old conservative order with his courageous support of the great liberal concepts of Western Europe, and bringing hope to those who had been deprived of basic human rights. He became the foremost thinker of post-Enlightenment Hungary. Although István Széchenyi's reforms did not have the political impact he would have wished (this did not come until revolution, inspired by the radicalism of Robespierre), his influence was felt in the Academy of Sciences, in the modernization of the economy, even in the urban architecture of Buda and Pest, which came together as Budapest thanks to his engineering projects, which resulted in the construction of bridges across the Danube.

The publishing house of Buda University was another vital Hungarian institution at this time, a focus for the social, political and cultural life of the modern linguistic communities of Central and Southeastern Europe that played an important role in the gathering and dissemination of knowledge in the period from 1777 to 1849. It traced its origins to the sixteenth century, when it served the Catholic Church and then Buda University, founded in 1635. The university library and the publishing house were closely associated and shared the same patron, the university chancellery and senate.[132] By the end of the eighteenth century the publishing house had fully embraced the ideology of the Enlightenment, whose reforming influence directed all its printing activity, in conditions specific to the regions of Central-Eastern and Eastern Europe.

An Education Edict of 1777 granted the publishing house the privilege of printing textbooks for all the peoples of the region, extending its reach beyond Hungarian readers to include Serbs, Croatians, Slovaks, Romanians, Bulgarians, Greeks, Jews and Ukrainians. From 1779 it printed primers, spelling guides, grammars and books on mathematics, geography and natural history in all the languages of these territories. Authors included Miklós Révay, Károly Luby, Gáspár Pál, Daniel Mitterpaher and Antun Mandić. The publishing house's widened remit was especially important in the context of the generalization of education in the different mother tongues and the application of new educational methods: its books mirrored the progressive teaching policy of Josephinism. For high schools, it produced textbooks on the natural sciences, arithmetic, geometry, physics, natural history, logic and natural law. It also printed books for university, often associated with the scientific research of the professors.

Since the Enlightenment in this region encouraged the promotion of native languages, the publishing house's grammar books and dictionaries were of great importance. They included the Slovak grammar of Anton Bernolák, the Romanian grammar of Gheorghe Şincai, the Hungarian grammar of Ferenc Verseghy, the Slovenian-Serbian grammar of Avram Mrazović, the Ukrainian grammar of Mykhailo

Luchkai and the Bulgarian grammar of Christaki Pavlović Dupničanin. There was also the *Lexicon Budense*, a great Romanian–Latin–Hungarian–German dictionary, whose main editor was Petru Maior, a Slovak–Czech–Latin–German–Hungarian dictionary by Anton Bernolák and a Latin–Italian–Illyric (Croatian) dictionary of Joachim Stulli.[133] The publishing house produced books in the field of historiography and universal history, such as the works of Johann Matthias Schröckh in Romanian, Serbian and Bulgarian, but national histories, too: Petru Maior's history of the birth of the Romanian people in Dacia, Vuk Stefanović Karadžić's monograph on the Serbian prince Miloš Obrenović, Ján Kollár's history of the Slovaks and Slavs, Jovan Rajić's synthesis of the evolution of the Southeastern Slavic peoples, and histories of the Hungarian people by István Katona and György Pray. There were also short popular science works on horses, bees, silkworms, industrial plants, fruit trees and the growth of tobacco, as well as books on the development of medicine. Publications were often distributed free of charge through the Council of Lieutenants, their printing financed by contributions from religious or secular communities or central administrative institutions.

It would be fair to say that the publishing house of Buda University was emblematic of the way in which cultural dissemination had evolved in Central-Southeastern Europe. It was also indicative of the spiritual communion of the region, a meeting point for ideas of freedom and equality in everyday life. The different national theories propounded in its publications – the Czecho-Slovak doctrine of Kollár, the thesis on Daco-Roman continuity by Maior and Murgu, the Pan-Slav doctrine of Berkel, the conception of Serbian nationality by Obradović and Karadžić – envisage not only the emancipation of each linguistic community, but mutual cooperation between them all. The publishing house supported and even encouraged the multiplication of the 'channels' linking East and West, promoting books that advocated the reforming influence of the Enlightenment.[134] It enjoyed a certain independence, and frequently published its books and collections without seeking approval from the authorities. It also provided a context for fruitful collaboration across borders, and the correspondence between Hungarian, German, Romanian, Slovak and Serbian intellectuals shows that differences in language and culture did not imply tension or conflict.

'The truth is common to all nations and all religions,' writes Ferenc Kazinczy in a letter to Lukijan Mušicki, 'and it is found wherever there are good and wise people. Unhappy is the man who allows himself to be shocked by dress or language. So let us love each other, dear Sir, for we feel that we are the children of truth.'[135] Similarly, representatives of the Transylvanian School enjoyed close relations with the Hungarian scholars of the time: this was the case with Samuil Micu when he was writing his *Dictionary* with Benedek Virág and András Haliczky, and Șincai and Kováchich enjoyed a similar friendship, the latter assuring Șincai's living conditions for six months in exchange for the help given by the Romanian in the editing of his works and the organization of the Széchenyi library. When Șincai was appointed proof corrector of the publishing house instead of Ioan Onișor, he was recommended by the scholar from Buda as *clarissimus vir* [a most outstanding man]. Petru Maior maintained close contact with historians György Pray, József Benkö and Daniel Cornides, and was well rewarded, receiving the considerable sum of 1,253 florins for two of his publications.[136] There was also fruitful correspondence, which had begun in the context of the publishing of their work, between Constantin Diaconovici Loga and Dimitrie Țichindeal, Dositej Obradović and Lukijan Mušicki, and many others.

Although there are differences between the Western and Eastern Enlightenment, we can see in both cases that whenever new ideas are able to spread, the momentum builds from one decade to next with almost incredible vigour. Economically and socially, the countries of the Central-Eastern and Southeastern region were lagging behind, but a vision of Europe was instilled in the hearts of those who had been inspired by books and libraries, schools and universities. The ideas of the century of Enlightenment advanced from one end of the continent to the other, transforming whole societies, conferring a dynamism that influenced first ideology and then the conditions of material existence. Intellectuals with progressive views gradually extended their influence and authority, founding libraries, literary salons, scholarly societies, clubs for political debate, and organizations promoting the great books of the Enlightenment and the journals prohibited by the monarchic censorship introduced by Emperor Francis I. They sought unity, a gathering of forces, for which knowledge was essential, but also the forging of contacts between people. I have shown in this chapter how different cultures and ways of life were brought together under a single system of ideas in order to serve truth, good and beauty, to give meaning to life. This was a different direction to that offered by the Church. A need for a radical change was felt among the people of

Central and Southeastern Europe. They faced great obstacles during the period from the middle of the eighteenth century to the third and fourth decades of the nineteenth, but ultimately the intellectual elite succeeded in propagating the ideals of the new age, largely through written culture. The channels through which books were disseminated played a crucial role in the establishment of liberal innovations, taking the civilizing influence of the Enlightenment beyond the densely populated heart of Europe to its Southeastern fringes.

VII

BANAT DURING THE EIGHTEENTH CENTURY: A MEASURE OF CIVILIZATION IN CENTRAL AND SOUTHEASTERN EUROPE

The ideas of a historian of human life, like those of a historian of nature, are first and foremost his interpretations...

Nicolae Iorga[1]

WHY BANAT AND NOT SOME OTHER REGION? Given that it is my birthplace, I could understandably be accused of bias. However, Banat really does have a special atmosphere, and it would be no exaggeration to claim it as a unique case in the historical geography of Central and Southeastern Europe. I have followed its repeated European temptations, and if I have dared to introduce a more personal element to the discussion at this point, it is because I feel it will help to bring this complex subject to life in a more interesting and engaging way. My aim in this chapter is to describe the civilization that was established here in the eighteenth century, creating a precedent for the following century: its metallurgical industry, mines, river transport and canal system, its commercial entities, press and publishers, and its innovations in agriculture, food preparation and hygiene, all fostering the beneficial exchange of values and even setting the standard for Central and Southeastern Europe.[2]

I will examine in depth Banat's social hierarchy, both the upper and lower echelons. As Iorga states:

> The lives of individuals within a community are in a state of constant mutual interdependence... The same warmth, winds and rains swell their waters, which then grapple with the same obstacles posed by the earth, eroding river beds and taming the rocks at their bottom, breaking them down into the sands with which they will play. And though they might flow far from each other, these waters in turn make the sky clear or cloudy, open up the way for the winds and determine the quality of the air, continuously influencing one another.[3]

Banat at the time of the Enlightenment offers a fine example of this interdependence, displaying a wealth of contacts and convergences between different communities, ideas and technical innovations, religions and languages – countless forms of progress born under the same roof, contributing to material and social benefits shared in common. Situated at the meeting point of the trade routes linking Central Europe with the Mediterranean South, between two worlds with different infrastructures and resources, Banat may be seen to represent a locus of continental unity from any geographical perspective. As such it transcends the sorts of labels and divisions that compromise our understanding of Europe as a whole. While the actions of State and Church gave rise to ethnic and linguistic realities that might encourage some to separate East and West, geography and anthropogeography tell a different story, reflecting the fundamental truths of history. Braudel saw in the Mediterranean and the world that surrounded it the bridges uniting territories and people, the channels through which knowledge could be exchanged – its gulfs, isthmuses and passes. He discovered unity in diversity, not simply in terms of relief or climate, but of nature as a whole and its impact on mankind's existence. By accepting this conception of geography, we no longer see Banat as a square of earth bordered by the Mureș, Tisa and Danube, nor simply as the description of its plains, hills or mountains, or its natural riches above and below ground. This approach also encourages us to avoid drawing illusory, reductive conclusions, and makes us mindful that however ample the data amassed now and by our predecessors, this alone can never tell the full story. We need to shift across space and time, studying the geography of the present in order to rediscover permanent values, 'the organization of a settlement according to the perspective of the guiding line of greatest duration'.[4]

The world of Banat is a rich one, and its geography has contributed positively to its history. The topography encourages you to linger in the region's towns and villages, among the ruins of its buildings and fortresses; to travel across its hilltops and mountain paths; to bear the heat of the summer sun beating down on the banks of the Timiş, Bega, Mureş and Criş; to admire, while journeying by car or train, the barely perceptible variations in relief; to cross on foot the huge green central plain, situated between Caransebeş and Ineu, tasting the sweetness of the Mediterranean fruits of the Caraş region; to see the patriarchal agricultural techniques still used by the peasants of Banat; to try to understand how their occupations depend on the soil and climate, and on those ancestral tools preserved in museums; to enter the vineyards of Miniş or on the Mocrea hills, and enjoy wine prepared according to age-old methods; to discover the wooden churches of the Făget region, or those built in the mountainside along the Cerna gorge, where the climate is by turns moist and dry, but the temperature is never very low. The earth, or rather varieties of earth here cater to every human need. In short, with its plenitude of physical and human characteristics Banat is, if not a complete *Mitteleuropa*, then at least a *Kleineuropa* that unites Eastern and Western civilization.

Banat is both mountainous and flat, hence its settlements differ in appearance. The region possesses villages large and small where the houses crowd against one another up steep slopes, melting into a whole that resembles a redoubtable fortress, with the wealthiest and most densely populated areas at the lowest levels, mirrored in the sluggish waters below that suggest an unhurried communion with nature. Changes in relief characterize the transitions from one part of the region to another: the gorges of the south and east enable contact with Severin County, Oltenia and Wallachia (from where the heart of the Balkans is accessible), the lands around Haţeg and all of Transylvania; plateaus covered with forests and crossed by rivers such as the Bârzava permit access from Caransebeş to Vršac and on to Karlowitz and Belgrade; while the straight lines of the plain favour long journeys, to Lugoj, Timişoara, Arad, Buda and Vienna. This landscape, like any landscape, has a profound influence on the character of its inhabitants. In the case of Banat its communities have had to adapt to the very different circumstances of living in the mountains and on the plain.

Let us now compare how the region has been described, in the seventeenth century and then the eighteenth, by two eyewitnesses, Evliya Çelebi and Francesco Griselini. The Ottoman explorer Çelebi (1611–82) marvels at the rich, green land, on which parks and gardens bloom; at the 'life-giving' River Timiş; at the plains that spread in all directions, feeding horses, oxen, water buffalo, sheep and other animals; and at the wealth of fruits, notably the 'varieties of sour cherries'. His description of the fortress of Timişoara itself suggests a construction in the middle of an island, a simple but solid building, pleasing to the eye, with gates connected by mobile bridges – probably similar to those of Central and Eastern Europe during the Middle Ages – and arches and towers of birch with sharp peaks, 'covered with planks', on which flags are raised. Çelebi also turns his attention to the palace, the main square covered with a 'hard layer of mortar', the dwellings, streets, shops and warehouses in which the inhabitants go about their business – a peaceful population of simple folk, soldiers and merchants, who live happily and wisely in the gentle Adriatic climate. In particular, Çelebi focuses on what people eat in Banat, and how the region's produce extended its influence across the Balkans and Europe further afield. The region was fed on wheat, bread and pasta – which he refers to respectively as 'little breads', 'butter pie', and 'honey pie' – information which gives us clues about the economic level of Banat's citizens, since wheat, flour and bread are key indicators of the living standards of a community. The region's richness is also illustrated by its production of butter, honey, meat and milk, commodities that earned it considerable prestige a century or two later when it began to export agricultural goods in great quantities. 'The honey and the butter produced here are famous the world over,' Çelebi states, a view endorsed by other writers.[5] Çelebi's picture of Banat will have remained more or less unchanged by the middle of the eighteenth century, when other sources appear.

The naturalist Francesco Griselini (1717–87) came from a completely different intellectual background: he was an *Aufklärer*, a Venetian scholar and citizen of the Austrian monarchy whose fame had spread across Europe. His picture of Banat is comprehensive and accounts for the wealth of the region. The province had come under Vienna's control in 1718, following the Treaty of Passarowitz, and its new masters wished to understand the potential usefulness of the new southeastern corner of their empire. In this context, Griselini aimed to offer 'true and exact' facts which would allow Vienna to evaluate the region's material and spiritual qualities:

Europe still has many countries that are little known, whose true description, compiled with a discerning spirit, could be edifying to scholars, and would satisfy all seekers of knowledge and those whose job it is to identify subjects that could be of use to society generally – even persons of great station. Among these lands, the Banat of the Timișoara region should be considered an important province.[6]

The region's fertile land was beneficial to the economy, manufacturing and trade, and well suited to raising livestock; its mountains, covered with forests, provided all the wood its inhabitants required; its waters were rich in fish and gold deposits; below ground, it abounded in minerals and waters with curative powers. Griselini is impressed by the baths of Mehadia, dedicated by the ancient Romans to Hercules, and by the villages, towns and castles that by the end of the eighteenth century had made Banat an especially beautiful region that bore comparison with other parts of Europe both in fertility and quality of life. Griselini studied Banat in situ for almost three years, analyzing its geography and climate, its demographic and ethnographic makeup, its religious, ethical and linguistic characteristics. His discoveries were considered a revelation at the time, and today they give us an insight into the atmosphere and mentality of an era. Of course, travellers often deem things extraordinary when they observe them for the first time, and on occasions when they list archaeological finds, describe landscapes and human types, and map out ancient and medieval monuments, their enthusiastic subjectivity lapses into excessive claims and interpretations. Our job is to compare sources critically and systematically, and it is with this perspective that we should approach the works of Çelebi, Griselini, Johann Jakob Ehrler, Nicolae Stoica of Hațeg and many others.

Banat was under the direct administration of Vienna between 1718 and 1779, and organized in districts.[7] During Maria Theresa's reign it was annexed by Hungary and divided into three counties: Caraș, Timiș and Torontal. Its border regiments were permanently administered by the Imperial War Council. The province was coordinated by a *Landesadministration* headed by a military or civilian governor, and later run by the Hungarian Lieutenancy Council. Vienna's power was wielded through the Aulic Chamber, the Neoaquistic Commission and the aforementioned Imperial War Council. Banat was considered a domain of the Crown and the Chamber (*Reichsunmittelbare Kron- und*

Kammerdomäne), a newly acquired property (*neoaquisitum*) occupied by right of war (*jure belli*), and no legislation covering the private or public sphere prior to 1716, when the Turks had been masters of the region, had any legitimacy.[8]

The Austrian Empire exploited the resources of the countries and regions in its dominion as it saw fit, in its own political, strategic and economic interests. The Chancellery in Vienna was concerned almost solely with expansion and power, and gaining as advantageous a position as possible over its European rivals. Every corner of the empire was administered in the service of the Hapsburgs, and subject to their way of life, economic planning and social stratification. Politically, too, the regions had to conform to the system devised by Austrian ideologists and statesmen. From the beginning, the judicial status of Banat imposed by Eugene of Savoy in 1717 reflected the need for political stability on the empire's eastern border that had led to the conquest of the region in the first place. The emperor exerted *dominium altum*, sovereignty of state, won through *jus gladii*, the right of the sword, and a *dominium secundum terrestrae* as a feudal landowner, according to which everything in Banat came under the juridical power of Vienna. A strong and well-organized administration with competent law enforcement can guarantee state security and enable powerful leaders to act freely and exploit the means it possesses, and these qualities made Austria an imperial bastion comparable to the Vatican. The programme of uniformity introduced across the imperial territories presupposed Vienna as the epicentre, the place from which ideas were transmitted and where they were to return once they had materialized. An absolute and totalitarian monarchy in essence, it took the form of enlightened despotism when Western Europe was swept by the earth-shaking changes of spirit and crises of conscience we have described in this book. It was a time of revolution, of uncertainty and of apparently limitless possibilities, from which there was no turning back. This tide of events is demonstrated by Austrian imperial history from 1800 until about 1850, but prior to this, the Hapsburgs glimpsed the danger and sought to shelter themselves from the seismic events initiated and driven by the bourgeoisie. During the eighteenth century no one dared entertain the thought that the empire might end, and in Banat – as evinced by its level of civilization at this point – a series of initiatives were undertaken, intended as a new beginning for the region that would see development across a wide field of activities. Within this programme, mercantile policy was reformed again and again. Idealistic Austrian and Austro-Hungarian historians of the time subordinated their learning to the imperatives of official history, seeing themselves as mere instruments and Banat as a test case within the wider context of the empire's aims and needs. I have discussed this phenomenon elsewhere, with reference to the writings of Johann Heinrich Schwicker, Johann Nepomuk Preyer, Samu Borowsky, Jenő Szentkláray, George Popoviciu and Ioan Dimitrie Suciu.[9] What really interests us here is to understand the realities of the times, both in terms of the objectives set by Vienna and, above all, of human nature and the destiny it forged with its own way of thinking.

The population of eighteenth-century Banat – who brought such rapid progress to the region through their ability to bridge social, linguistic and geographical divisions – is registered in a 1774 a survey by Johann Jakob Ehrler, an administrative official. Ehrler tells us that there were 220,000 Romanians, 100,000 Serbs, 53,000 Germans, 2,400 Hungarians and Bulgarians, and 340 Jews. To this we can add a relatively small number of Spaniards, who settled in the first decades of the century at Becicherecul Mare, then called New Barcelona (today Zrenjanin): their disappearance from there was explained by their inability to adapt to the relatively difficult living conditions in that part of the region. During his travels through Banat, Griselini did not encounter them. Other linguistic groups that were even less numerous made their presence felt in one way or another. The statistics present us with a demographic reality, but they do not constitute history in themselves. These figures, however authentic, reveal nothing of the soul, thoughts and feelings of these groups, nor do they tell us to what extent these inhabitants felt, consciously or not, that they were part of the great family of Banat.

The best starting point is to analyze the lower rungs of society as well as the elite, since the people's traditions, beliefs and occupations offer a better indication of the character of the community as a whole. Ehrler states that 'The Romanians and the Serbs are by nature supple, tall, strong and beautiful'.[10] They were overwhelmingly Greek Orthodox, although a few were converted to Catholicism – for example, the inhabitants of the village of Slatina, in the Caransebeș district[11] – while in the early decades of the nineteenth century others accepted the transition to Greek Catholicism, in which Eastern and Western Christianity mingled. However, Orthodox beliefs held sway both in everyday life and in the dissemination of ideas. The priests and bishops upheld Orthodoxy at every level, and even the United Church exercised restraint in order to conquer the region – making far fewer impositions than in Transylvania – in spite of an imperial rescript on the founding of the Greek-Catholic bishopric issued in 1738.[12] Opposition to unification was strong, beginning with Visarion Sarai and his disciples, who operated at the borders of Banat and appear in official documents as early as 1742.[13]

While the Hapsburg missionaries were unsuccessful in their attempts to convert the population, they found the Romanians and Serbs more receptive when their beliefs were not challenged and their occupations were nurtured and supported – peasant households raised cattle and undertook mining activities, metalworking and forestry, all of which made a fundamental contribution to the economy. Romanians played a key role in working the mines of Bocșa and Reșița, and in the production of wood and coal necessary for furnaces and metalworking. The craftsmen coming from Wallachia to Banat were accepted – with some reticence by the authorities – and made an energetic contribution to the material civilization of Banat. Similarly, Romanian families such as the Brediceanu, Broșteanu, Cioroianu, Diaconovici, Gropșianu, Grozescu, Izverniceanu, Nemoianu and Telescu, all hailing from Oltenia, played an important role in the region's intellectual life and cultural emancipation.[14]

The majority of the Romanian and Serb peasantry in Banat – those who owned only divisions or fragments of land, as well as serfs and other workers – took up new agricultural practices and made use of the latest developments in science and technology. The wooden plough was widespread both among the native population and the German colonists. Influenced by German settlers, farms across Banat acquired all the necessary tools and resources for the working of the land: axes, hoes, spades, pitchforks, ploughs, harrows, shovels, scythes, harnessed carts, horses, oxen, cows, seeds and fodder.[15] Griselini provides further compelling examples of these developments:

> During the time when Count Clary was president of the Banat administration, a glassworks was built in Slatina, in the Caransebeș district. The Romanians immediately appeared and, under the guidance of a master glassblower, learned the art of making bottles, glasses, etc., which Banat now produces in quantities sufficient for its own use. Also, in the mining operations across the four mountain ranges of Banat, for example at Ciclova and Bocșa, alongside the German workers

are many Romanians, who lack neither skill nor experience. Also, the current owner of the rice farms of Omor reports that Romanian workers produce the best results.[16]

These Romanians and Serbs were also experienced in the arts of dyeing, painting (which they carried out in the Byzantine manner) and printing, and contemporary sources bear witness to their ingenuity. Alongside these skills, they preserved ancestral traditions in their everyday lives, for example in their love of dancing.[17] The Romanian diet was based on a sort of polenta (mămăligă) made of corn, while the Serbs used ordinary homemade bread. Both peoples took great pleasure in eating raw bacon, smoked in the open air, a practice shared by the Hungarians and Germans of Banat. Similarly, all of these communities had similar methods for preserving meat, especially pork. Exchanges between these different groups, in which each borrowed from the other, led to the development of a distinct regional cuisine. The Romanians drank răchie, 'a liquid resulting from the fermentation of wild plums', while the Germans drank wine. These drinks were produced in great quantities in Banat – all communities learned how to produce them, and their consumption became a regular leisure activity across the region.[18]

Looking at the Serbs in particular, while their presence in the region goes back to the fifteenth century and the time of Count Pavel Chinezu (Pál Kinizsi), their numbers increased after the Austro-Turkish wars at the end of the seventeenth century and the beginning of the eighteenth. They were good farmers, accomplished artisans and reliable soldiers, and as we have seen, they shared many characteristics with the native population. An industrious and devout people, they had a similar approach to Church and school as the Romanians, and the Austrian political system treated them in a similar fashion. The Serbs enjoyed a degree of privilege, since the Karlowitz Metropolitan was the only leader of the Greek Orthodox Church recognized by Vienna. This advantage favoured their social and intellectual emancipation, and earned them greater recognition across Europe.

The presence of Germans in the Banat region colonized by Charles VI and Maria Theresa created complexities at all levels – socio-economic, political and legal – as part of a wider clash between the intentions of the Austrian officials and the way of thinking of the resident population. The Austrians' aim was to raise the province to the standard of Central Europe, which triggered an awkward period of transition and adaptation in which different religions, languages, traditions and habits were forced together. While this could have been disastrous, the population successfully maintained broadly harmonious relations, in which the generally tolerant outlook of the Romanians and of Greek Orthodoxy played a significant role.

The Germans, meanwhile, were an important component of Banat society, influencing everyday and intellectual life. Culturally they were far removed from the Viennese: many came from Alsace, and hence had closer linguistic ties with the French[19] than with the Austrians, an affinity dating back to the Middle Ages which was peculiar to the western extremity of the German lands. While their activities in trade and agriculture followed the instructions of the Austrian officials, this was mostly the result of age-old habits. They were a diligent, disciplined and organized people: eager to learn, they readily acquired new skills in any domain they considered of benefit to themselves and others. They were generally well integrated into Banat society, participating in their own festive days and traditional celebrations, but also in those of the Romanians, Serbians, Hungarians and Jews. On the whole they were multilingual, proficient speakers of Romanian and Hungarian, and sometimes of Serbo-Croatian as well (as was the case with the Germans of Bela Crkva/Biserica Albă). Indeed, very soon after settling in the region the Banat Germans considered themselves citizens of this land, and they were accepted as such by the native population – an almost incredible idea, rarely seen elsewhere. There were the occasional, inevitable misunderstandings, but crucially, the land that was given to them did not impinge on the agricultural activities of the Romanians and Serbs:

> All of the land not used for agriculture was given over to grazing, and in these conditions the territory granted to the colonists for arable farming in no way affected the land used by Romanian farmers – it merely reduced an extensive and inefficient way of grazing. The instructions issued by Joseph II regarding the administration of the region mentions that 'the division of land will be made according to the number of working members of the families without regard to which of the three nations of Banat they belong to'.[20]

The villages of German colonists, much more numerous in the central-northern and western parts of Banat, were founded as specific projects. Eighteenth-century maps of the villages of Banat provide an exact picture of these communities: the configuration of the spot, adjoining economic and agricultural areas, water resources, mineral deposits and roads. The authorities kept records of land ownership and taxable revenues. These maps also include village streets, family farms, churches, schools, landowner's and priest's residences, centres of law enforcement (the hussars), taverns and cemeteries:

> The imperial administration introduced the so-called sys-
> tematization of the territory in the villages of German colo-
> nists by drawing up streets perpendicular to each other, a
> method of systematic street planning also introduced in some
> of the old Romanian villages, such as Alioș in 1785, Balinț
> in 1776–1817 and Bara in 1828, replacing the old traditional
> Romanian arrangement.[21]

While economic wellbeing was especially important to these German settlers, their intellectual life was also rich and vibrant. German clerks, priests, printers and teachers all spearheaded their cultural activities. In 1771, *Temesvarer Nachrichten* records that publisher and editor Mathäus Heimerl had gathered a circle of scholars including Johann Jakob Ehrler (who held a senior position in the Banat admin-istration), Clemens von Rossi (first canon and head of the parish of the cathedral, former priest of the Italian settlers in Merțișoara), Wolfgang von Kempelen (counsellor of the administration), Gottfried von Bretschneider and many others, including disciples of Goethe who were rivals of Christoph Martin Wieland's followers.[22] Even a humble merchant could aspire to a spiritual existence.

The Church remained a great rallying point, despite the growing popularity of the ideas of the Enlightenment. The Roman Catholic bishop, along with the members of the cathedral chapter, held sway in all of Banat's religious disputes – indeed, the jurisdiction of the cathedral chapter of Cenad also extended into Hungary. In 1774, there were seven Catholic churches in Timișoara alone, as well as three monasteries, two Franciscan and one Minorite.[23] The Roman Catholic cathedral – 'a splendid building', as Ehrler calls it – and the smaller copies found in the German Banat villages reflected the alliance between political and ecclesiastical power. The Catholics differed from Greek Orthodox believers: their traditions and customs, from the marriage ceremony to funeral rites, were characterized by a certain austerity that became all-pervasive. Their representatives even gained control of administrative power in Banat, a predilection inspired by the Vatican itself. At first, Orthodoxy and Catholicism coexisted awkwardly in the region, but eventually a tacit accommodation and mutual respect prevailed. The fundamental inflexibility of Homo Religiosus meant that in the long run he lost ground, as ideas of working for the good of the majority took root, and the population of Banat favoured friendship over division.

The Hungarians also played an integral part in the region's history. They had lived alongside the native linguistic groups of the region since the Middle Ages but, unlike in Transylvania, this cohabitation was disrupted by the period of Turkish domination in Banat. Only a relatively small number lived alongside the Romanians and Serbs during the time between the Battle of Mohács and the treaties of Karlowitz and Passarowitz. This may be because the towns of Lugoj and Lipova in autonomous Transylvania were more integrated than the towns administered directly by the Turks. An even more plausible explanation is that the Hungarian class system, basically comprising nobles and serfs, could not survive under Turkish domination, a problem that did not occur in Transylvania. The eighteenth century saw the re-establishment of connections that had been lost under the Ottomans. The agricultural proletariat reappeared in the villages, and an industrial proletariat slowly formed, along with the foundation of mines and the development of manufacturing. Political conditions had changed, and social classes were more heterogeneous. The end of feudalism triggered a change in the people's aspirations, and the Hungarians gratefully returned to Banat and its new leadership, becoming integrated in everyday life and spreading their language. The Jews and Germans were the first to learn Hungarian: the Jews, because some of them arrived from Hungary or Austria, and because the learning of new languages was a fundamental trait that helped them survive in any land or region of the globe. For the Germans it was more of a practical necessity, as they sought collaboration with the Hungarians in trade, agriculture and the production of food.

Before the rise of nationalist ideologies and the age of revolutions, the citizens of Banat lived together peacefully. Even thereafter they preferred harmony and understanding to conflict, hence the social relations between the peasants of Banat and those of Transylvania.

This was also the case among merchants, publishers, printers, even intellectuals who were fighting for the emancipation of their own ethnic group, as they understood that they could not succeed by doing injustice to others. Cultural contacts with the institutions of Timișoara, Arad, Buda, Vienna and Karlowitz brought enlightenment, and while it is true that the French Revolution embodied the impulses of the moment (the cases of Nicolae Bălcescu and István Széchenyi are examples),[24] Banat always looked after the interests of wider society. Hence the Hungarians were integrated into its socio-economic life.

Jews and Bulgarians, although smaller in number, made important and frequently exotic contributions to the character of the Banat region. Elsewhere I have described[25] the universal characteristics of the Jewish diaspora, with particular attention to its role in the history of Central and Southeastern Europe, and suggested that the Jewish past in Banat was worthy of a study in itself. Their number was small during the seventeenth and eighteenth centuries, just a few hundred families in the second half of the century of the Enlightenment[26] who lived in the towns of Arad, Timișoara, Lugoj, Caransebeș and Vršac. Unlike the Romanians, Serbs and Germans, they possessed no land. They were tolerated, even accepted (subject to certain obligations) by the Austrian imperial officials. As the main intermediaries between Vienna and Constantinople, they played an important diplomatic role that attracted both sympathy and hostility. As merchants, they travelled from one region to another, disseminating not only goods, but ideas and books as well. In the towns and villages of Banat we find them as tavern-keepers, small tradesmen, booksellers, printers and publishers. There were also a number of Jewish intellectuals in the region: rabbis, teachers, doctors and apothecaries.

The Jewish community in Banat was both Sephardic and Ashkenazi, and displayed great spiritual unity. As well as adapting to the locality and learning its languages, they took steps towards embracing the Central European Enlightenment. This modern outlook, which partly explains their survival, continued with the ideological changes of the nineteenth century, even bringing some religious reforms to the life of the Jews. In Arad, Rabbi Aaron Chorin encouraged a transitional form of religious emancipation, which contributed to the political freedom of Jews in the Austrian Empire. It was a bold step forward, but one which can be seen to have paved the way for some of the persecutions endured by the Jews in the twentieth century.

The last community we should mention is the Bulgarians of the villages of Vinga and Dudeștii Vechi. They were Catholics, so-called Paulicians (having been converted by the monk Paul of Samosata at the beginning of the Middle Ages), and came from the villages around Vidin. Encouraged by the Austrian victories over the Turks and following failed uprisings in their homeland, this community left its native region to settle in Southern Transylvania – in Deva, Sibiu, Vinţu de Jos and Alba Iulia – at the end of the seventeenth century, then in Oltenia, Craiova, Brădiceni and Râmnicu-Vâlcea after 1718, and then in Banat, after the retrocession of Oltenia by the Hapsburgs in 1737–9. These Bulgarians, primarily farmers and artisans, obtained permission from the authorities to found communities that became economically robust. During the reign of Maria Theresa, Vinga – called Theresienstadt at the time – numbered approximately 8,500 inhabitants. The privileges they obtained, not without considerable effort, were a reflection of the greater integration they achieved within the civilization of Banat.[27]

The civilization of Banat I have described above is a mosaic, of which I have captured only the essentials and not the fine detail. What should emerge is the special makeup of the region between the Danube, Tisa and Mureș, an area that has rarely been properly apprehended and has therefore suffered from unjust neglect by scholars. A buffer between two empires, a region that belongs culturally to Romania and is therefore a place of transition from Central to Southeastern Europe, Banat fuses two worlds and as such provides something of a measure or yardstick of civilization. I should add that the diversity of linguistic groups living alongside the majority native population and the multitude of religious beliefs – there was even a small Muslim presence – helped to foster the continuous dialogue between Central Europe and the West, the Balkans and the Byzantine world, which is the central theme of this book.

As I have mentioned above, the French Revolution of 1789 was one of the great changes in rhythm, one of the spectacular points of articulation in the history of mankind. To differing degrees the shockwaves of the event were felt everywhere. The extent to which the Romanian principalities came under the influence of the liberalism championed by the French revolutionaries differed from one region to another, but on either side of the Carpathians the great ideas of liberty, equality and fraternity stirred feelings of national reawakening. The great powers, including France, were turning their attention to the east, since this was the meeting point of three empires: Turkish, Tsarist and Hapsburg. The Southeast was about to become a focal point for all of Europe.

Wars of ideas evolve over decades, and so events in Paris continued to shape life in Europe and beyond right up to the middle of the nineteenth century. Similarly, these seismic events are fomented over a long period, and a stimulus to revolution had come in earlier years from the enlightened absolute rules of Frederick II, Joseph II and Catherine II. The great French Revolution and the era of Napoleon that followed distilled elements of the spirit of Enlightenment, extending its insistence on renewal, modernization and integration into Europe's social, economic and political relations, its institutions and culture. Then, as David Prodan asserts:

> All these were superimposed on a specific state of flux that already existed in the East, which itself was no stranger to Europe, to humanism, to the cult of one's own history, and the regional patriotism of such great names as Grigore Ureche, Ioan Neculce, Miron Costin, Spătarul Milescu, Cantacuzino Stolnicul and Dimitrie Cantemir.[28]

This was the moment when Banat, like Transylvania, made a great contribution to the assimilation and application of Western political concepts. Their reception in the Southeast depended to a great extent on the success with which Romanian representatives could outwit their Austrian masters in the political and diplomatic game. In Banat, these ideas passed along the well-established channel Arad–Timișoara–Caransebeș–Karlowitz–Buda–Pressburg(Bratislava)–Vienna, from where Western ideas were absorbed or applied by Germans, Hungarians, Serbs, Croats, Slovaks and Romanians.

We have already discussed the routes taken across Europe by the ideas emanating from France, communicated via books, schools, societies, secular and Church institutions, and enlightened individuals. What interests us here is to examine the form these ideas then took, and what original features they displayed alongside their more general European character. In Banat, echoes of the French Revolution had a considerable influence on the way different social classes saw the world, not in the form of revolutionary violence, but rather in an atmosphere of enthusiasm and invigoration, especially among intellectuals. By the last decades of the eighteenth century, both before and during the Revolution, the region seemed well on the way to emancipation:

Romanian priests and teachers from Transylvania not only had the right to settle in Banat, they could also hold religious services in their mother tongue and teach in the Romanian schools of the region.

This inclination by Vienna towards the principles of the Enlightenment triggered a good deal of fruitful activity among the clerics of Karlowitz, Vršac, Timișoara, Caransebeș and Lugoj. The Hungarian Locotenential Council asked the Metropolitan of Karlowitz to push for the introduction of primary education in Banat according to the decrees of 1779, 1782 and 1784, a move that supported the need for education but was also in the social and political interests of Transylvanian and Banatian Romanians at this point. The bishop of Vršac, Iosif Ioanović Sakabent, communicated to all the parishes under his control the need to build Romanian schools, offering the support of Romanian priests and teachers from Banat and the territories to the south of the Carpathians that were under Turkish domination. He ordered that churches in Romanian villages within his diocese should hold their religious services in Romanian, while those with a mixed population of Romanians and Serbs should use both languages.[29] Reports on school activities at the turn of the nineteenth century refer to the privileges granted to those who work for the development of education, and to the conditions that must be met by all candidates taking the entrance examination. New presses founded for printing religious books and schoolbooks are listed, steps taken to organize education in the Romanian regiment are described, and school directors are named. Nicolae Stoica of Hațeg, sensing this change in atmosphere, praises the utility of culture and asks intellectuals to support institutions founded for the cultivation of the spirit: 'We can see that it is in school that men of all nations stand to gain and become prosperous. Education enlightens, raises men to the stations they had hoped for. It makes good and stalwart Christians.'[30] The journal of inspection of Grigore Obradović (who became director of the national schools of Banat in 1808), records that there were 189 schools in the county of Caraș, 15 in Timiș and 23 in the district of Timișoara. One year later, Bishop Petru Ioanović Vidak announced the inauguration of the clerical school of Vršac, while the Metropolitan of Karlowitz, Stefan Stratimirović (whom we have already encountered several times in this study), urged the priests of Timișoara to encourage citizens to send their children to school, especially the three schools that were founded (beginning in 1811) in Arad, Pest and Sânandrei.[31] These conditions produced intellectuals of great eminence in cultural and political life: Paul Iorgovici, Constantin Diaconovici Loga, Moise Nicoară, Dimitrie Țichindeal, Eftimie Murgu, Damaschin Bojincă, Teodorovici Nica and others.

While all this was going on, the Romanian and Serbian populations of Banat were beginning to meld – their destinies seemed interconnected, their ideals were uniting, fostering anti-Hapsburg and anti-clerical attitudes. Ideas of freedom and independence, which eventually provoked the population to insurrection, can only be explained by the influence of France – this led, for example, to the 1808 uprising of Romanian and Serbian border soldiers who planned insurrection right across Banat. Their leaders, Pârvu Jumanca, Toma Scripete, Petre Stoica and others, were in the main former prisoners from the conflicts between Austria and France.[32]

There was panic within the Church. Although its schools had served as the main vehicle for Enlightenment ideas, they had confined themselves to modifying traditional precepts and stopped well short of the kind of radical changes occurring in Paris. However, we hear the echo of the Revolution in the reaction of the clergy: Church documents relate that the spreading of the ideas of the 'French rebels' is causing terror, also fuelled by the presence of concentration camps for French prisoners within the territory of Banat. As one document states: 'The French people who usurped civic laws, who crushed the churches and altars of God, who have forsaken the Christian faith... are putting into the ears of the stupid and unthinking people their unclean thoughts.'[33] The Church and the intellectuals of Banat were clearly far apart in their reaction to French revolutionary ideas.

The grammarian and political writer Paul Iorgovici, who would have a profoundly beneficial impact not only on Banat and its people, but on Romanian spiritual life as a whole, was in Paris at the time of the Revolution. The events he witnessed made a great impression on him and directly influenced his subsequent activities, for example his collaboration with Piuariu-Molnar in founding the Philosophical Society of the Romanian Nation in the Principality of Transylvania (which brought together cultural personalities from Wallachia and Moldavia) and their 'Announcement' of the forthcoming publication of a journal by the Society (which unfortunately never came into being), and his introduction into elite European ideological circles, such as a society allied to the Freemasons whose influence reached Sibiu.[34] Later, his work *Observații de limbă românească* (*Notes on the Romanian Language*, Buda, 1799), a synthesis of the philosophical and linguistic ideas of the Enlightenment, was the fruit of his Italian and French studies, and his direct contact with the major works of Western thinkers. It displayed the outlook of a 'philosophical scholar', as a modern publisher of his work has stated.[35]

His sojourn in the European capitals of Vienna, Rome, Paris and London gave him a thorough grounding in the new ideas of liberty. As a man of culture he was able to understand – especially during the three years he spent in Paris – the discrepancy between the freethinking of the Enlightenment philosophers and the 'novices' who were currently direct-ing political life. He was abreast of revolutionary movements in Central Europe when, shortly after finishing his studies, he held the position of Imperial Chancellor and *Hofconcepist* in Vienna.[36] We may assume that, having come into contact with Freemasonry, he was acquainted with the democratic ideas championed by scholars such as Ivan Drasković, Baltazar Krčelić, Maximilian Vrhova and Nikola Škrlec Lomnički, and was aware of the struggle of the Jacobin rebels led by Ignatz Martinovicz, in which the Croats played an important role by founding Freemason lodges in Hungary and Croatia. This familiarity seems all the more likely when we consider that the project of Martinovicz and his associate Ivan Lacković, published in Pest in 1793 in the form of a manifesto, was to form a new federal republic comprised of four parts – Hungary, Illyria, Slovakia and Moldavia – each with its own parliament, conducting business in its own language.[37] Movements such as these deepened his sorrow about the 'division of the Romanian nation' among Austrians and Ottomans. Though he confined himself to writing and never attempted direct action, he nonetheless created a precedent, and his work pointed the way for the scholars of the revolutionary generation of 1848. He is an important figure in the struggle for cultural progress and political recog-nition in Eastern Europe.

A similarly influential personality in the fight for nationhood was Moise Nicoară, a learned, energetic man with a good command of several languages (German, Hungarian, French and Latin) who travelled widely in the region between Vienna and Constantinople. Enthused by the exciting atmosphere of the Enlightenment and the transition of the region from the medieval to modern era, he proved an accomplished and persuasive diplomat. He is known for his activ-ities on behalf of the Church, specifically his campaign for the right of Romanian Greek Orthodoxy to appoint its own leaders, but prior to this Nicoară was a spokesman across Europe for the desires of his compatriots. In 1805, while a student at Pressburg University

(Bratislava), he sent French minister Talleyrand a note entitled 'All Romanians'. Unfortunately, this text has not survived, but other articles, kept in the Nicoară Collection of the Romanian Academy, offer a glimpse of what he said in the document addressed to Talleyrand: in a discussion he had in 1849 in Constantinople with Ion Ghica, Nicoară recalls how in the same city in 1814 he strove to communicate his aims to the leading diplomat of Napoleonic France and the Ambassador in Vienna, General Antoine-François Andréossy.[38] His optimistic vision was nothing less than the national unity of all Romanians. As historian Cornelia Bodea observes:

> In other words, while in Pressburg and other European diplomatic talks the Romanian principalities were part of negotiations intended to satisfy individual ambitions, resolve battles for supremacy or achieve balance in Europe, the Romanians in 1805, as in subsequent moments, had a completely different perspective. The message was the same as in 1849: they wanted a unitary state, a new Dacia with a united historical conscience that linked older events with more recent developments in Transylvania during the time of Horea.[39]

Nicoară was wholly devoted to this new ethno-national ideal, conscious that it required someone to sacrifice himself in the name of his people, to convey their sorrows and hopes, protect and perpetuate their beliefs, educate them out of ignorance and lead them to international talks where they could assert their historical, legal, political and religious rights. In short, he saw himself as the unofficial representative of his community. He was well placed to fulfil this role, being thoroughly acquainted with the political climate in Vienna and possessing an intimate knowledge of religious life in Central-Eastern Europe, where Catholicism and Orthodoxy interacted. He professed a liberalism whose roots lay in Enlightenment thinking, inspired by the French Revolution. An impassioned champion of reform and an overwhelmingly revolutionary spirit, Nicoară wrote the following in 1817–18:

> Since my early youth, I have known no passion as strong, none that has taken over my soul so completely, as the love for my people and my care for their happiness, that they might escape the yoke that has oppressed them, and wash away the stain that

has besmirched them in the eyes of other peoples. This yearning within my soul led me for the first time to take up a cause that was never going to bring me any personal gain. It was a great misfortune in itself, one that might bring unhappiness to others, but to me truly it was not, because I was following my own beliefs.[40]

His intention was to broadcast his ideas not only to the intellectuals of Banat, Crişana, Transylvania, the Romanian principalities and Europe more generally, but especially among the masses whose destiny he shared. With time he came to understand the complications of imperial policy, and his manuscript reveals his shifting position towards Vienna, in which he had initially placed his hopes for change. In his later years he abandoned the dispute with the Serbian religious hierarchy that had occupied him previously, and focused exclusively on the real meaning behind the politics of the Hapsburgs:

> We have reached a point where the Romanians have been fooled and no longer know what to do. They have been deceived with the hope that the Emperor would set things right, when the sole intention was for the Romanians to pay expenses, and they were tricked again when strict orders were given for no money to be given to anyone for paying these expenses. This order was given by their rulers in the name of the Emperor, and the unfortunate Romanians were deceived into thinking that the Serbs were the cause of this.[41]

Nicoară was driven by the desire to raise public conscience through schools and learning, hence his direct attacks on the emperor, whom he held responsible for the state of ignorance in which the border regions of the empire were being kept. Although he does not openly call for revolution, the idea is implicit in his writings.

Nicoară's successors Dimitrie Ţichindeal, Eftimie Murgu, Damaschin Bojincă and Diaconovici Loga followed the same path towards emancipation. This was increasingly true of Banat generally, where subscriptions to Romanian periodicals, such as those of Gheorghe Bariţiu in Transylvania, were on the rise. Ties between the intellectual elite and the masses were close, since the majority of priests, teachers and scholars came from humble families.

Historical and literary works written by the representatives of the Enlightenment and the Romantic movement sought to identify and understand the past, and played an essential role in uniting the population and establishing a wide communion of the spirit. The Moldavian historian Damaschin Bojincă offered a synthesis of the prevailing ideas on the Roman origins of the Romanian people in his *Animadversio in Dissertationem Hallensem*, in which he attempted to awaken the conscience of the Romanians. Bojincă drew on many of Petru Maior's ideas, and the first part of his book borrows extensively from Petru Maior's *History of the Beginnings of the Romanians in Dacia*. The second part is more interesting because it discusses a number of new ideas concerning the Roman origin of the Romanian people. Bojincă collaborated closely with Zaharia Carcalechi on *Biblioteca românească* (*The Romanian Library*), the oldest Romanian-language literary magazine, and in the foreword of the periodical he is referred to as a 'scholar, burning with the light of our people'. His liberal convictions chimed with the atmosphere of the times, and his most enduringly valuable articles tackle educational themes addressed to a wide readership.

The aforementioned Eftimie Murgu also exerted a progressive, civilizing influence, fighting against attempts to halt the cultivation of the people, against ignorance and hostility towards other languages and nationalities,[42] while Dimitrie Țichindeal is especially important for his reception of the events of the French Revolution and the Napoleonic Wars. Nicolae Bocşan[43] has demonstrated that a German translation of the book *Întâmplările războiului franțozilor şi întoarcerea lor de la Moscova* (*Happenings from the War of the French and Their Return from Moscow*, Buda, 1813), signed Alexie Lazaru, might in fact have been written by Țichindeal. The 'Notice' in the book's appendix is especially valuable: it informs readers of a future periodical in the Romanian language, and champions the role of the press in crossing distances in space and time within Europe. As we have already seen, the Buda University Press performed this function for the Romanians and indeed for all the peoples of Central and Southeastern Europe. Intellectuals in Banat and Transylvania made an important contribution to these activities and, as we have seen, the number of books published in Buda between 1799 and 1846 reflects a spiritual awakening across all strata of society.[44] In addition to the major printing operations taking place in Buda, the increased dissemination of books was also a result of individual or institutional contacts established with Vienna, Berlin, Halle, Göttingen, Venice, Zagreb, Karlowitz, Cluj, Râmnic and Bucharest, as well as libraries belonging to private individuals and churches.[45] As I have mentioned, these religious and intellectual contacts came to light during my research of the eighteenth-century collection at Radna monastery.[46]

The swiftness and efficiency of these new means of communication were demonstrated by the Pan-Romanian movement of 1834–5. The ambition of this secret society was to unite all Romanians, and it relied on close links between Banat, Transylvania, Bucovina, Wallachia and Moldavia, and the circulation of people, ideas, leaflets, books and newspapers with a clear revolutionary orientation, especially those from France. A denunciation communicated to Colonel Roth, the commander of the Banat border regiment, states as follows:

> In order to support the plan, it is considered especially useful to consolidate ties with the most important people in Wallachia, so that Wallachia has the necessary time to strengthen itself, and the literary press that publishes Wallachian newspapers can serve this purpose and French works may be translated into Wallachian, works showing the breath of freedom, and such publications may be distributed across the Wallachian nation of Banat and Transylvania.[47]

A general revolt was launched, carefully timed to coincide with wider attempts at emancipation in Central Europe, in order to catch the Austrian police off guard. In Banat, propaganda was disseminated by teachers: the denunciation above cites the case of the teacher Maran from Dognecea. The 'Marseillaise' was translated into Romanian and learned by the people, appealing to their dissatisfaction and will to revolt. Chancellor Metternich wrote in a report to Count Sedlnitzky, the chief of police: 'The intention of their leaders is to carry out, without interference, their plans in this neighbouring territory [Wallachia], and to achieve results across our dominions, so the state administration must follow their movements very closely.'[48] Under the new emperor, Vienna was worried by the propaganda movement in Banat and Transylvania, and rightly so, since the Pan-Romanian movement, based on the model of the Freemasons of Galicia which brought together Romanians and Poles, had a democratic character. Its aim was to create a republic according to the principles of the French Revolution: equal rights, universal suffrage, equal access to all offices, freedom to work, the abolishment of the nobility, freedom of education, equality of all religions, the emancipation of peasants, land reform and so on.[49]

Western influences, and especially the new ideas from France, unquestionably played a role in the different intellectual movements that burgeoned in the East. They were accommodated within age-old peasant traditions of Slav or Byzantine origin. The new political conditions and the French Revolution in particular made possible a new type of dialogue between East and West based on ethnicity and nationhood. The result of this dialogue was a transformation in thinking across Eastern and Southeastern Europe.

AFTERWORD
CONCEPTUALIZING MODERNITY IN MULTI- AND INTERCULTURAL SPACES: THE CASE OF CENTRAL AND SOUTHEASTERN EUROPE[1]

'CENTRE' AND 'PERIPHERY'? SOME PRELIMINARY REMARKS ON A SERIES OF CONTROVERSIAL NOTIONS

Is it possible to explore and assess Europe via the notions of 'centre' and 'periphery'? What do these terms denote? What can we infer from them? Are they of service to the study of history? Do they imply partisanship? How can one establish the centre and the periphery of a cultural space? Are these notions interchangeable? Provided that we agree on the importance of a civilization's structure, what is the point of introducing a 'centre' versus 'periphery' distinction into cultural-historical investigation? Might it not be an illusion, leading us to imagine relations within a continent in terms of formulas derived from geography, an illusion that can ultimately be reduced to the notional pair 'we' and 'you'? Or does it carry an ideological message in which the concepts of 'Europe' and 'the Other Europe' imply the advanced state of certain European regions and the backwardness of others, thereby highlighting socio-economic inequalities and their consequences?

Such questions are legitimate since these notions reflect differences rather than similarities: they suggest contradictions between two or more cultural geographies rather than unity in diversity across a single continent. In political discourse, notions of 'centre' and 'periphery' are apt to be invoked by those seeking to impose their own interpretation on a range of cultural phenomena, for example languages. In an academic context such an approach could be limiting and even harmful: it might give voice to prejudices, and its results become subordinated to transient ideological interests. Time and space have been differently interpreted depending on individuals' religious beliefs, cultural-historical traditions, specific notions and languages: the categories of space and time therefore signal the existence of certain specificities. However, this does not justify their use by historians as tools of investigation. Eschewing the dichotomous approach inherent in these notions of an alleged 'centre' and an imaginary 'periphery', a number of seminal studies over the past couple of decades have adopted an innovative perspective on Eastern Europe and the culture of identity across Europe as a whole, casting doubt on the limiting approach I have described. While a culture manifests itself in a certain socio-political context to which it is related,[2] history is the result of interpretations that facilitate the understanding of that particular culture, its people and its system of values. History, then, can enable us to identify individual and collective mentalities specific to a particular era or location. It can be a narrative about the past, but it is not linear, nor is it hindered by religious, ethno-cultural, national or economic prejudices.

The champions of Romanticism and their disciples took political communities backwards and laid the groundwork for an anachronistic view of nationhood and the nation state. Their ideas were adopted during the conceptualization of modernity, and hence – not for the first time – the technical and economic advancement of humankind was not accompanied by an inclusive vision of cultural diversity within communities. It is impossible to establish a clear definition of 'centre' and 'periphery' acceptable to the majority of European cultures. When these notions are invoked, their meanings vary across different people and communities, since they are not anchored in fixed, unchangeable points of reference. It would be more accurate to speak of intertwining

spiritual, social and economic factors that show who we are at a particular moment in time – an idea well described by Giambattista Vico.[3]

Put differently, in the case of Europe 'centre' and 'periphery' are
figments of our imagination. A remarkable example of this can be
found in English and American literature, which has constructed an
imaginary geography of the Balkans.[4] In her book *Inventing Ruritania*,
Vesna Goldsworthy explores the archetypes of the Balkan Peninsula
and its worlds disseminated through long-established literary and
film productions by famous Western artists. These archetypes
emerged in the nineteenth century and have percolated in society ever
since. Used by politicians and by the mass-media-grounded 'industry
of consciousness', these archetypes not only function as clues towards
the falsification of realities, but also reveal the manner in which the
Balkan region has been exploited as an object of dominant cultures'
dialogues about themselves. As a result, the societies – and especially
the elites – of the Balkan region have had to learn not only the vocabulary of the West but also the stereotypes it has assimilated. Apparently
exonerated of any possible accusation of racism, the cultural and
political language of the West has created through the notion of the
Balkans an 'other' that could be blamed for anything.[5] In response,
Goldsworthy argues convincingly that the Balkan Peninsula is part of
Europe despite the fact that the adjective 'Balkan' has commonly been
invoked to mean the opposite of European. Meanwhile, the practice of
using the 'Balkan' adjective to refer to one's neighbour has often been
the result of ignorance and bigotry.

Deploring nationalist interpretations, conceptual history promotes a comparative and transnational approach to intellectual life by
trying to decode both the shared and the distinct meanings of notions
from one language to another, exploring the transfer of ideas between
cultures and examining both genuine and false notions contained
within languages, discourses and texts. In the case of Central and
Eastern Europe, conceptual history is a particularly innovative research
method since it has to confront the above-mentioned stereotypes that
have been widely perpetuated over the course of time. Europe is a
mixture of political and economic systems whose origins lie in multiple religious and cultural values which, in their turn, are a function of
the location in which they initially emerged and were later developed.
The specificities of Europe derive from its multitude of allegiances,
including Catholic Rome, Orthodox Byzantium, the Protestant North,
the Mediterranean South, the Anglo-Saxon or French–Dutch West and

the Russian East. Religion has undoubtedly played an important role in these areas. While they evolved from a variety of historical legacies – oral languages and written texts, old and new religions – they are associated in a shared concept of Europe. Similarly, modernity is not only defined by its disjuncture with the Middle Ages, but also by continuities – values that were perpetuated from one historical era to another and bestowed a sense of authenticity on people and the places they inhabited. By examining these latter aspects, we can establish the set of values that permitted the construction of a civilization and, eventually, of a corresponding identity.

The foundation of identity-based culture was established at a time when Europe was organized in principalities, kingdoms and empires, and intellectuals imagined cities and regions inhabited by several linguistic and religious groups living free from prejudice and aspiring to build a *sensus communis*. Modern Europe, which long pre-dates the idea of the 'nation', was founded on knowledge of the transnational condition and a grasp of the continent's history. On the other hand, we must acknowledge that each region of Europe is also defined in terms of the traditions, historical legacies and mental reflexes it has acquired. To these we should add the experiences of political life and the notion of a state functioning according to natural law and established covenants – a logic based on a constructed rational apparatus and a cultural framework that presupposes a heightened level of legal constraints.[6] The concept of the state should also be understood in relation to culture, as a creation of free people beyond socio-economic constraints. As for the concept of culture, it is fundamental not only because it fosters social cohesion, as Reinhart Koselleck has observed, but also because it allows us to decode the peculiarities of communication and representation among different human beings according to their location in time and space.

The conceptualization of modernity is not confined to a particular time and geographical area, just as it is not limited to a single model of social existence. During the transition towards modernity, but especially after the Modern Era had begun in earnest, the social and liberal understanding of the concept of culture became relatively similar all over Europe. However, in this process intellectual circles in Central, Eastern and Southeastern Europe played a different role from their counterparts in the West, since in these regions modernization occurred in the absence of a sophisticated administrative and juridical system. The dissemination of new ideas relied on encyclopedic minds and the contributions of a series of remarkable and innovative personalities who championed both traditional spiritual values and new intellectual principles, seeing no contradiction between them. The Russian intelligentsia, for example,[7] perfectly illustrates this tendency since, on the one hand, its members were influenced by and in contact with Western ideas while, on the other, their ideas combined their own culture and its historical-religious and identity-related views with radical, critical viewpoints.

THE SPECIFIC REALITIES OF CENTRAL AND SOUTHEASTERN EUROPE: MULTICULTURALITY AND SOCIOCULTURAL HETEROGENEITY

Frontier cultures and cross-border cultures should not be analyzed solely in relation to their geographical coordinates, just as they should not be associated with the traditional medieval idea of statehood or with that of the nation state as it was constructed and understood in the West. What are the coordinates that define Europe? Where is its centre located, and where is its border? Do we conceptualize modernity in relation to space, or only in relation to time? If the latter, how do we define geographical areas? What degree of importance do we bestow on meeting places or points, transit areas between Western and Eastern Europe? Could we, for instance, analyze modernity in the regions and sub-regions of Central and Eastern Europe via the notion of liminality, an idea derived from the Latin term limen (and, ultimately, the Greek λῐμήν) and signifying a threshold, the meeting point between the earth and the sea, the idea of a harbour, a transit area, or a so-called grey zone?[8]

There are regions and cities whose histories, cultural-juridical evolution and administrative structures do not overlap with those of the 'centre' or the 'periphery', their demarcation lines being arbitrary. Bohemia, Silesia, Moravia, Slovenia, Banat, Transylvania and Bucovina are all conspicuous areas of transit, whose multifarious character provides an extremely fertile context for communication between communities, for the formation of collective consciousness, and individual or collective cultural creations. These areas illustrate why the conceptualization of modernity can be examined at once in relation to an area's geography and to the results of the cohabitation of two or more linguistic and religious communities within it. This is not a case of mere speculation in the absence of history, nor is it based on hypotheses intended to enrich the cultural memory of the present day. Rather, this approach involves the explanation and conceptualization of modernity in relation to social and cultural signposts, real behaviours and a plurality already in existence when the modern world emerged. It is less a new theory than a theorization of realities. Following this approach, the multiculturality of Central and East European spaces should no longer be viewed simply as something that existed before the Modern Era, but as a key factor contributing to the conceptualization of modernity.[9] This conceptualization derives from a state's form of organization and administration, its reforms and political philosophies. It is not a completely new type of construction, but a rethinking of past legacies in the context of a strong yearning to be integrated into Europe's system of values at that particular time. In the case of Central and Eastern Europe, the multicultural configuration of the area and its hybrid identities continued to represent a reality that could not be ignored, either by imperial administrative powers or by the ideologists of the ethno-nation. This is one reason why, once ethno-national ideas became widespread, the conceptualization of modernity and models of political and societal thought had to accommodate different meanings and types of discourse as well as a series of ideological contradictions.

Is the concept of multiculturality itself a problem of interpretation derived from socio-communitarian and cultural-linguistic experiences? Are there contradictory meanings inherent in the concept? Long-lasting imperial administrations – as well as conceptual historians following in their footsteps – have admitted that all cultures, irrespective of the time of their genesis or their evolution in different periods of time, should benefit from some sense of integrity, and enjoy respect rather than being silenced on the basis of territorial criteria or numerical strength. Individual and societal ideals bear the traits of the place in which they were formed. They absorb external influences but also maintain cultural-historical legacies. The genesis of modern thought sprang largely from the psychological traits of regional communities. As for the thorny question of traditional societies, they differ from liberal-democratic societies in that the former tend to foster older types of multicultural cohabitation while the latter are permanently preoccupied with settling potential conflicts between communities. In this latter case, the difficulties to be broached include the need to reconcile the idea of (allegedly) superior cultures with the duty to treat all human beings as equal.[10] This argument is used by Charles Taylor to show that the birth of modern identity was prompted by changes that brought about the end of social hierarchies. He considers that the recognition of differences from one group to another laid the groundwork for asserting collective identities.[11]

The example of North America is enough to demonstrate that this theory cannot be applied universally. More generally, the act of differentiating between one group and another by no means presupposes respect for the other, nor does one's identification with one group or another necessarily entail the embracing of a nationalist ideology. In order to understand the idea of cohabitation involving two or more cultures in the context of emerging modernity, it is important first to decode the meanings ascribed by various cultures to notions of ethnicity, nationality and nationhood. Once understood, these notions allow us to avoid the kinds of linguistic errors that have propagated ethnocentric and nationalist ideologies, while the concepts of multi- and interculturality can help to explain what constituted modernity for the inhabitants of Central and Eastern Europe.

The ethno-nation and the ethno-national state were products of the nineteenth century, emerging under the influence of the revolutionary and reformist ideologies of France and Prussia. Given their position as a geographical crossroads, Central and Eastern European regions cooperated sometimes with the East and at other times with the West, borrowing sets of values from both cultures and civilizations, giving rise to ties or conflicts with both, while constructing their own identity in terms of intercultural harmonies or disharmonies. Hence in order to conceptualize modernity in Central and East-Central Europe, we first need to examine the politics of the Hapsburgs and the Austrian Empire in the eighteenth and nineteenth centuries, since these regions had been disputed for centuries by three great empires: the Hapsburg, the Tsarist and the Ottoman. As a result, these societies possessed multiple legacies that intertwined various languages and cultures, a melting pot that became increasingly evident at the beginning of the Modern Era, when the circulation of people was triggered by territorial conquests, administrative reorganizations, economic progress and colonization. Note that none of these changes was related to ethnic divisions, which had played no major role in these regions' affairs before the 1800s. Rather, a certain tension in relations characterized the inhabitants of these spaces during a long and complicated process of emancipation and modernization, one which cannot be confined to a single moment in time.

There was no sense in this part of the world that it represented a 'periphery' – it was part of Europe. Many of the technical innovations, literary and artistic creations and administrative-political realities of the eighteenth, nineteenth and twentieth centuries proved not only these regions' closeness to the West, but also their openness to experiment and innovate on their own initiative. This, too, is a reason why we should avoid determinist assessments that claim that socio-economic or political phenomena are the key to tracing differences between one region and another.[12] Many Central European cities were comparable to their Western counterparts despite differences in administrative and economic structure. They were, and have largely remained, the cultural products of the Austrian Empire, and as such represented a standard of civilization that was emphatically not lower than that of medieval or modern Europe. These cities may have had their regional peculiarities and possessed an appetite for borrowings and crosscurrents, but they did not differ fundamentally from Western urban structures.

The cities of Prague, Budapest, Bratislava, Novi Sad, Gorizia, Trieste, Krakow, Lemberg/Lviv, Timișoara/Temeswar and Cernăuți/Czernowitz evolved into modern, self-sufficient entities thanks to multilingualism and religious convergences between Catholic and Protestant, Orthodox and Catholic (the case of Greek Catholics), Jew and Christian, and Muslim and Christian. In other words, they became part of modern civilization thanks to their multiple-coded cultural inheritance. Consequently, they shared many similarities with neighbouring Western European cities, while concurrently developing numerous exotic characteristics generated by the impact of Enlightenment ideas. Hence we can conclude that the modernity of the region coincided with new scientific, technical and industrial discoveries, competition in trade, and avant-garde literary, artistic and musical movements, all of which propagated unity in diversity. In their turn, Southeastern European cities such as Bucharest, Belgrade, Sofia, Sarajevo and Thessaloniki defined themselves by the cohabitation of various religious communities and not only by their geographical position. They had rarely invoked the term Balkans in their self-definition, nor did they see themselves as an outpost of European Christianity or a defensive fortress impeding the advance of Ottoman civilization. Instead, they constructed their identity by the conservation of traditions, long-term transitions from one historical era to another, and by experimentation and innovation.

Analyzing the Modern Era through the lens of multi- and interculturality offers a different perspective on social and intellectual history, since it allows us to conceptualize modernity on the basis of cultural transfers and the transnational meaning of urban and regional identities. Moritz Csáky has demonstrated the deep connection between the world of officialdom and politics and the life constituted by diverse cultural, artistic, literary, historical and philosophical forms of expression.[13] This was a fundamental aspect of the social evolution spanning the eighteenth and nineteenth centuries as Central and Eastern European regions transitioned to the Modern Era. These communities defined themselves by behavioural peculiarities transmitted from one generation to another, but they were also receptive to change. Their search for identity was of great importance to them, but it was also problematic, and our understanding of their individual and collective mentality must take into account the new contexts of their cultural creations – in literature, music and art. Even when these changes are part of, or have given rise to, the spread of ethno-national and national ideas, we must be aware of the geographical and historical specificities of the region under consideration, especially any ambivalences within its cultural heterogeneity.

'Ambivalent cultural legacies'[14] and creations have survived to this day all over Europe. In Central and Eastern regions they are an intrinsic part of identity, originating in the great bureaucratic reforms of the Hapsburg state that resulted in a shared culture of 'Austrian Germanness'; institutions that led to the formation of behavioural reflexes; empirical terms indicating administrative-juridical, economic and political subordination; the establishment of the ruling royal house as a reference point and a symbol of citizenship; and a German language peppered with expressions originating from the languages of several communities, especially Czech, Polish, Hungarian and Italian – in short, plurilingualism. All these aspects show how individuals and collectivities from these areas acquired similar models, since their politics, justice and economy were based on similar principles. Their evolution demonstrated the success of the reforms conceived by the Emperor Joseph II from as early as

1765, later accepted by Maria Theresa and eventually implemented by the State Council. These reforms were the result of long-lasting disputes that remodelled the system Haugwitz had introduced in 1749.[15] In this socio-political context, shared inherited characteristics of the empire's populations were coupled with newly imposed administrative and financial changes. The fruit of radical reformist ideas, these developments first occurred in Bohemia, and later in Hungary, Banat and Transylvania. At first, during his 1773 trip to Banat and Transylvania, the emperor gathered data about the state of the civil and military administration of the regions, their financial situation and the manner of collecting taxes. He then formulated the programme of reforms, which prioritized the introduction of the civil and criminal codes; reform of the magistrature; the establishment of the real-estate register; archiving of documents and medical checks; regulation of the activity of representative institutions and their clerks, and of the functioning of craft guilds; the setting up of manufacturing and factories depending on the raw materials that were exploited; a rise in clerks' wages and the abrogation of the peasants' obligation to provide their upkeep.[16] In this respect, similarities were stronger than the differences across the regions under discussion, and these reforms themselves constituted the early stage of modernization.

Over the course of the nineteenth century, the emergence of nationalities, nations and nationalist stereotypes was accompanied by a wish, expressed by many intellectuals and politicians, to highlight 'the motley kaleidoscope represented by the mixture of peoples' as a positive quality. Literature, historiography, political philosophy, music and visual arts of the times focused on the question of cultural amalgamation – an aspect of life that has bestowed an air of exoticism on the regions of Central and Eastern Europe. Undoubtedly, the modernity of these places was due, on the one hand, to the reception of Western ideas and, on the other, to the conception of a different kind of statehood than that of Western Europe. Multiculturality was a reality in Central and Eastern Europe, not a utopia or a myth devised by the Hapsburgs. It was grounded in historical realities and closely tied to a 'heterogeneity of the cultures'[17] specific to these areas.

Consequently, any theory aimed at the conceptualization of modernity in Central and Eastern Europe must take into consideration the geography of the place, and distance itself from interpretative models borrowed from postmodern schools or from those subordinated to ethnicist and nationalist ideologies. The analysis of multi- and interculturality should be an essential part of any historical investigation into these areas, but it is often ignored by studies whose analysis proceeds from the present-day configuration of states and politics. Located between the East and West, Central and East European regions have benefited from the influences of both civilizations, with Western influences prevailing over Eastern ones during the course of the Modern Era. Some historians have identified these complex sets of influences in the region's organizational structure and socio-economic life, while others have indicated their presence in cultural ideas or in the values pertaining of various religious and linguistic communities.[18] Most importantly, the conceptualization of regional modernity must take into consideration the contributions of the state's administration to the region's socio-economic and organizational progress, as was the case with the House of Hapsburg, the Austrian Empire and the Austro-Hungarian monarchy. There are plenty of other examples proving that the Ottoman and Tsarist empires also reformed the state, drawing inspiration in their endeavours from Western changes that occurred during the Modern Era. Regardless of which of these political structures we refer to, we can ascertain that they were not the cause of Central and Eastern Europe's backwardness, as has often been contended.[19]

ENLIGHTENMENT AND MODERNITY

In an article dedicated to the concept of the Enlightenment and the meaning Reinhart Koselleck attributed to it in his book *Kritik und Krise*, Hans Erich Bödeker notes that the absolutist state has been interpreted by historians in highly problematic ways,[20] because the conceptualization of the Enlightenment, and, by extension, of modernity, presupposes a type of understanding that takes into consideration political, social, cultural and civic realities. Unfortunately, at times Koselleck himself extrapolated the data and knowledge he had acquired about the German principalities, France and other Western countries to wider areas which had evolved differently. Regarding the state's agency during the eighteenth century, rather than stressing, as Koselleck did in *Kritik und Krise*, the dialectics between morals and politics, we might instead focus on the ambivalence of Enlightenment ideas. At the beginning of the eighteenth century, the Hapsburgs still treated the Roman Catholic Church as a state religion – for instance, in the conservation of traditions and in efforts to improve society by combating illiteracy. The Hapsburg colonizations of the eighteenth century were carried out with the help of Catholic populations, whose integration was projected and realized on the basis of religious and moral connections linking the holders of imperial power with the representatives of the Roman Catholic Church. This was carried out extensively in Banat and Bucovina. The Hapsburgs also considered establishing a new Church in order to subordinate their newly conquered territories and populations to the representatives of the administration and their interests. Following this line of thought, the Greek Catholic Church was established in Transylvania – a Church subordinated to the Vatican but founded on the basis of mixed Orthodox and Catholic values. This is an instance of the cross-fertilization of doctrines, a less familiar concept in the West, but one which ensured social peace and political stability for some time in the region we are discussing. This phenomenon resulted from close cooperation between the state and the Church. The same imperial representatives had spread Enlightenment ideas in a top-down manner, thereby maintaining control over their consequences. In this equation, the emperor had to heed Church-imposed norms, natural rights and traditional juridical conventions all at once. The autonomy of the Lutheran and Calvinist communities, for example, would not have survived in the eighteenth century had the Hapsburgs not continued to observe old juridical norms, the region's specific form of organizing religious life, or the specifics of its social and institutional hierarchies that had been founded in the previous centuries. In other words, in the regions of Europe that were integrated into the Hapsburg Empire and in which progress was only partly indebted to Enlightenment ideas, the conceptualization of modernity has to be understood as a mixture of discontinuities and continuities in relation to structures of medieval thought, and not just as the outcome of discontinuities in a vacuum.

It would be misleading to assume that radical, revolutionary views took hold across all of Europe and led to its modernization: it would be truer to say that in many communities the lure of modernization became a reality only through the intervention of an organizing power. That is the reason why intellectuals often cooperated with the absolutist state, hoping thereby to impose their reformist programmes regarding law, the economy and politics. Friends of the nobility, the clergy, lay intellectuals and merchants were all increasingly in favour of promoting education and emancipation. The books they read, the institutions they founded and the keen interest they showed in new ideas were all reflections of their high level of education, thinking and behaviour, and indications that they were conscious of entering a new historical era. At the same time, a certain strain of Enlightenment politics encouraged kings and emperors to embrace mercantilism, rather than revolutionary thinking which was considered dangerous or counterproductive. This was the policy of many despots across eighteenth-century Europe, including those of France, Prussia and Austria. They were generally in favour of reform and against revolution or revolutionary reform as imagined by radical Enlightenment thinkers. Of course, differences arose between the various states across Europe, as is clear by comparing the politics of the rulers in Vienna or the Frankfurt Parliament of 1848 with the regime in Paris either in 1789 or in 1848. In contrast to Paris, the politics of Vienna and Frankfurt had not been genuinely revolutionary at either of these two pivotal historical moments. Nevertheless, despite these differences, a desire for renewal was prevalent during those times in all regions of Europe. It had been facilitated by the 'cultural channels' created by the colonizing empires, and by the administrators, merchants and intellectuals who had circulated through the continent and opened up a dialogue between the West, the Centre and the East of Europe.[21]

We have mentioned the attitude of the Hapsburgs towards the Roman Catholic Church in the early eighteenth century.[22] This new imperial consciousness implied another form of communication and a different *sensus communis* that was to be constructed by the Catholics. Its intention was to make the inhabitants of the region adhere to a single code of cultural and civilizational values. It was implemented slowly, over the course of the entire eighteenth century. Although Latin was the language of the Catholic Church and the Imperial Chancellery, in the second half of the eighteenth century the process of integration was conducted in the regions of the empire via the German language. This made communication easier with the various populations of the empire, ensuring that communities were not divided on linguistic lines. The ethno-national idea only appeared later, at the time when Romantic literary and historical works were being read and adapted to the local context. It benefited from the innovations of the Enlightenment movement but was opposed to its aspirations. Yet, for a long time, multicultural realities continued to exist as a matter of course and were not hindered in any way by official politics; during this time, the German language successfully disseminated culture and conveyed the shared interests of the region's inhabitants. The empire was preoccupied with the organization of its subjects, their activities and religion, and therefore needed diverse means of communication. Consequently, education and religious practices were established in various languages and plurilingualism became a way of life for the populations of Central and Eastern Europe in the eighteenth and nineteenth centuries.

In this way, enlightened despotism created the 'corridors' for the percolation of books, scholars and artists into the Central and Eastern European regions. To this end, Vienna enforced several reforms in keeping with the ideology of the Enlightenment, which can be attributed directly to some of its chancellors.[23] Among the Hapsburg rulers, Emperor Joseph II was considered to be the most radical reformer of the eighteenth century, and in these circumstances it is not easy to understand the inherent contradiction suggested by the term 'despot' that is associated with him, and especially the title 'enlightened despot' by which he came to be known. Joseph was 'a revolutionary on the throne': he introduced a new vision to politics, redefined the function of the elite and campaigned for a change in mentality, cultivating social relations enlightened by the philosophical ideas of the times. He imposed his point of view on his subjects because he believed it was the only way to reform his empire with any swiftness. The ideas of the Enlightenment as he understood them undoubtedly redefined the dynamic between the emperor and three key institutions – the papacy, the monasteries and the Freemasons.[24] This universalization of modern philosophical ideas existed alongside certain local peculiarities, for example the activities of noblemen who read, wrote and collected books and pictures, bypassing the imperial censorship that had banned the circulation of all art and literature connected to the French Revolution. These initiatives by the nobility were complemented by the actions of individuals within the educational and cultural sectors that fostered the rise of intellectual elites across all the regions we are discussing.[25]

For these intellectuals the attraction of the Enlightenment was the lure of high culture and the support it offered for their literary, historiographical, philosophical and artistic creations. They were not seduced by the concept of the nation as championed by

Revolutionary or Napoleonic France: they were interested in the idea of 'enlightenment' itself and their ideal was a Homo Novus that could only be attained through the top-down changes enacted by enlightened despotism.[26] In Central and Eastern Europe these were the ideas embraced and spread by Joseph II, hence this current of thought came to be known as Josephism or Josephinism. In contrast to Western Europe, it was a radical reformist movement with no revolutionary connotations.

Modernity and multiculturality were promoted across the cities of the empire under Vienna's cultural influence. School textbooks from the first half of the nineteenth century written by German-language writers such as Alfred von Luschin-Ebengreuth, Alfred Dopsch and Ludwig Gumplowitz, as well as books written by Hungarian-language or Czech-language authors like Victor Hornyánszky and Vaclav V. Tomek, claimed that the unity of the empire was based on its linguistic and cultural-communitarian diversity rather than on the myth of the Hapsburg dynasty. These writings evidently ran counter to anti-monarchic and nationalist thinking. Vaclav Tomek, for instance, maintained that the monarchy as a political structure resulted in multiple inter-crossings, intermarriages and a multicultural consciousness, which sustained a shared ideology.[27] The Austrian state was undergoing a genuine cultural hybridization, and its highly diverse components differed from its Western European counterparts. This dynamic facilitated the emergence of several urban centres where a symbiosis of cultures was evident both in social relations and in architectural, artistic, musical, literary and philosophical creations. These centres included Brünn/Brno, Prague, Bratislava/Pressburg, Buda/Ofen, Cernăuți/Czernowitz, Novi Sad/Neusatz, Pécs/Fünfkirchen and Timișoara/Temeswar, and their influence spread widely to villages across the regions that functioned under the administration of the Austrian Empire.

The religious life of the region was also conducted in several languages. In the eighteenth and nineteenth centuries, the different Churches promoted a multicultural and transcultural mentality. For example, the region of Banat in the southeastern corner of the empire registered 1,302,807 inhabitants in 1834, of whom 366,841 were Roman Catholic. These Catholics lived alongside 867,287 Orthodox followers, 26,643 Reformed Church followers, 22,299 Evangelicals, 12,242 Greek Catholics and 7,495 Jews. The statistics compiled by the old episcopate of Csanád/Cenad (Temeswar/Timișoara) concerning the Roman Catholic churches of the area inform us that its various religious communities spoke a variety of languages – German, Hungarian, Serbo-Croatian and Romanian. In fifty-seven of the Catholic churches that were situated in Banat in 1834, religious services were performed simultaneously in two or three languages.[28] Similarly, Catholic schools in the border counties, functioning under the patronage of the same episcopate, were largely plurilingual and instructors taught in German, Hungarian, Serbian, Czech, Romanian and Slovakian.[29]

These activities in the border regions of the empire typify the cultural plurality that was understood and promoted in both urban and rural environments. Despite their centralism and Roman Catholicism, the House of Hapsburg in the eighteenth century, the Austrian Empire in the nineteenth century and the Austro-Hungarian monarchy in the second half of the nineteenth century all cultivated multiculturality, striving to maintain or build bridges of communication between communities. The successive Hapsburg governments appreciated the need to protect local languages, religions and cultures as part of their programme to integrate the empire's administrative-juridical structure. At the same time, loyalty to the emperor was recognized as the expression of a citizenship shared by all his subjects. The concept of modernity was therefore nurtured and developed within the framework of empire, with the different Churches and the state acknowledging and promoting multi- and intercultural traits as manifestations of the peaceful coexistence of its inhabitants.

Vienna's politics aimed not only at consolidating power in the territories annexed to the empire after the wars with the Ottomans, but also at maintaining peace. In places where communities were well organized and believers of various faiths adhered to their established practices, the authorities tolerated the existence of non-Catholic Church hierarchies. This was the case with the Slavonian/Serbian-language Church, whose metropolitan seat in Karlowitz/Sremski Karlovci was recognized by the Viennese authorities as the official representative of the Orthodox Christian creed within the empire. In turn, for all its attachment to religious dogma the Orthodox clergy was enthused by scientific study and receptive to new ideas, and as a result they made their own contribution to the formation of modern thought. Their support for the cultivation and emancipation of the individual, their peaceful cohabitation and their acceptance of and contribution to political reforms, conferred a new status on Churches in the eighteenth century. Since they were spread throughout the empire, the Austrian Enlightenment was omnipresent, which explains why many of the era's scholars frequented Hungarian, Austrian and German schools, corresponding with one another and writing academic studies inspired by the most prominent representatives of the Enlightenment. Metropolitan Stefan Stratimirović (1790–1836), whom we have encountered throughout this book, was one of them: he participated actively in cultural and political changes as well as in intercultural and plurilingual communication (in Slavic-Serbian, Hungarian, German and Latin). His writings reveal a constant interest in studying the history of his own community, its connections to neighbouring groups and the relationship between the local and the universal.[30]

Jews represented another major group in Central and Eastern Europe promoting dialogue between cultures; they were a significant presence among the creative elites of the area and the social groups receptive to renewal. Their contribution was made in a context of tolerance, in which the practice of the Judaic faith was accepted in the regions under Hapsburg and Ottoman administration, Sephardim and Ashkenazim rites having been observed in these areas from the sixteenth to the nineteenth century.[31] Reciprocally, Jews were a unifying factor everywhere, since they tended to integrate into society, especially after the Austro-Hungarian monarchy had recognized their rights to citizenship. Jews did not develop ethno-nationalist claims as other communities did in the course of the nineteenth century of nationalities: instead, they were encouraged to assimilate by the laws of the dualist monarchy.

ROMANTICISM AND THE QUESTION OF IDENTITY: CONTINUITIES AND DISCONTINUITIES IN MULTICULTURAL SPACES

Where the Enlightenment had been characterized by a spirit of reform and a desire to maintain equilibrium between the local and the universal, Romanticism in Central and Eastern Europe expressed a strong desire for rapid change, fuelled by ideals that bore little resemblance to reality. Philologists, historians and philosophers were detached from the pulse of everyday life. Hegel paid little attention to history proper in compiling his doctrine about the past, while Herder described the relationship between humankind and political thought, but not that between the idea of nation and political practice. Karl Popper would later call this way of understanding a 'strange story', 'the story of the rise of German nationalism'.[32] Possessing encyclopedic knowledge and drawing inspiration from Enlightenment thinkers, Herder formulated and popularized the ethno-nationalist theory in the most accessible terms. Invoking the concept of *Volksgeist* (people's spirit), Herder impressed a large number of intellectuals with his development of Leibniz's idea of the monad. Herder's originality lay in his application of a biologist doctrine to history. Along with the concept of *Volksgeist*, Herder advanced a vitalist view of the world with teleological connotations. He also articulated a theory of the evolution of human history as the repository of overarching meaning.[33] Among his fundamental conclusions – some of which proved attractive to the learned revolutionaries of 1848 and later nationalists – was to regard the history of humankind as stemming from a supernatural force. Following this line of thought, only the intervention of divinity could inculcate a new life into dead matter at a critical moment.

The existence of independent principalities as a legacy of the Middle Ages and a privileged space for civil society and the urban bourgeoisie was inconceivable for ambitious politicians intent on domination. Herder had anticipated this state of affairs and argued for giving up obsolete forms of administration. Feeling the pulse of the era, he identified himself with the forces of change and those who he believed gave a voice to feelings and consciousness. Yet this type of change did not tally with the British liberal ideal or British nationalist aspirations that seemed to belong to another historical age. Nor did it correspond to the spirit of post-revolutionary and post-Napoleonic France. Those were different ideas[34] that gave rise to different policies. While in German culture the Enlightenment would above all represent a time of transition (the *Sattelzeit* identified by Koselleck with the period from 1750 to 1850), the transition to modernity in the regions of Central and Eastern Europe bore above all the imprint of the *place* where it occurred – a place characterized by the high status of the Catholic Church, the practice of plurilingualism, the heterogeneity and exoticism of cultures, and the omnipresence of ambivalences. In this sense, Stefan Jordan is right to state that many scholars have been too easily inclined to adapt or transfer to other areas and cultures a concept like that of *Sattelzeit*, whose character was vaguely defined even in its original conception.[35] In fact, if we compare the aspirations of the German and French Romantics, we can see that each had their own set of ideals regarding emancipation. We need therefore to understand the importance of investigating and assessing history from the point of view of geography and not only time.

Herder believed the ethno-national question had arisen within the scope of invented laws, hence he spoke of the emergence of a 'fictive ethnicity'.[36] His aspirations belonged to the idealistic monism professed by the Romantics. He professed that only poetry could tell the highest truth and inspire people with its 'sweet tinkling' (*süßes Geklingel*).[37] Herder's truth, in this case, was one according to which individuals had to obey the collectivity. For that to be possible, one had to create a people as an ideal form embodying the idea of unity. Formulated by the chosen few of the species, this idealism was meant to solve centuries-old frustrations. The poet alone had the power to turn a people's heart in the right direction, and Herder credited him with the role of opinion-maker. As a result, an individual's culture, reason and responsibilities as conceived by Enlightenment figures were abandoned in favour of dreams that had to be turned into reality, but which at that time bore no relation to social realities, the administration or the status of any individual or community. Thus the Romantics had ushered in a second paradigmatic change, in which their speculative ideas concerning identity created many discontinuities in European cultures, especially in the political cultures of the Central and East European peoples. In their vision, the poet was a god on earth, and the nation was regarded as a poet's creation, its purity equated with a 'true', 'simple', 'divine', even 'pure' poem. Implicitly, this idea was a response to the French Encyclopedists, to the French ideals championed by materialist scholars, and to the programmatic ideas of the 1789 Revolution. The Romantics maintained that if the *Volk* agreed to be guided by the masses' chosen one, their future was secure. This view replaced the concept of the political and democratic nation with that of the organic nation. The idea of the *Volk* – understood as a tribe, a community or an organic representation of a collective being – came to embody the future nation. Yet the argument that the 'great therapy' of humanity was, as Herder thought, 'a violent revolt',[38] makes no distinction between good and evil. To claim that power is based on violence and exalted feelings is tantamount to saying that reason has no role in human actions. For Herder, the state's constitution and legislation was to be grounded not in reason, but in piety, religion and chivalric honour. He believed in the irreducible specificity of each community and advocated a mystical metaphysics.[39] This speculative type of thought ran parallel to reality, replacing the idea of the rational administrative body that had been promoted by Josephinism. In this new perspective, the nation was an ethnic community, and statehood was conferred on the nation-ethnicity that represented the majority of the inhabitants of a particular area.

IN LIEU OF CONCLUSIONS: THE CONCEPTUALIZATION OF MODERNITY

The earliest conceptualizations of modernity in Central and Eastern Europe were made possible under the influence of Enlightenment ideas. Churches, schools, erudite circles, libraries, publishing houses, books, and especially curious, well-instructed people who were constantly moving from one end of the continent to the other, explored and became acquainted with each other's territories. Latin, Slavonic, French and German were means of communication through which ideas and discoveries circulated, and knowledge and values were disseminated. The relationship between transmitter and receiver was fundamental to these changes. In this way the Enlightenment era gave rise to a type of cultural elite in which the differences and contradictions between various regions seemed to be levelled. In the case of Central and Eastern Europe, the cooperation between the Austrian state and the Roman Catholic Church ensured a sense of balance, even at moments when the penetration of new ideas in society clearly indicated the need for reform. The Enlightenment cosmopolitanism of the Austrian Empire found its complement in local organizations. The multiculturality of these areas created a horizon of expectations in which the vocabulary of literary, historical, philosophical and political texts indicated the aspirations of the times. The elites of these regions conceived their new condition and status in terms that coincided with the cultural and political ideas percolating in society, especially the zeal for change. This was also the era in which Central and Eastern Europe drew inspiration from local values and the pre-existing cultural heterogeneity of the area. The idea of an inclusive society, considered a principle on which the existence of the empire depended, had practical results throughout the eighteenth century. The divergence between multicultural inclusion and ethnocentric exclusion that emerged in the following century deeply affected the second stage of modernity.

The Hapsburgs allowed communities to define themselves on the basis of their wealth and religious allegiance, respecting the role of the nobility and clergy. Yet, starting with the spread of Herder's texts and ideas, cultural differences among communities were encouraged at the expense of convergences, divisions that were then aggravated by the intellectual activism of each community in turn. Meanwhile, the German language and Protestant educational institutions, writers and scholars from the principalities outside Austria played an increasingly important role in the ideological training of the elites from Slavonia, Silesia, Bohemia, Hungary, Transylvania, Banat and Bucovina. German (and not French) had always been essential in these regions' sense of identity, but 'Austrian German' was gradually replaced by cultural-ideological messages given in 'Prussian German' and, later, in 'the German of Germany'. This process fuelled ethno-communitarian feelings and instincts.

Herder's theories had thus anticipated an ideal that was re-thought within a very short period of time, compressing the stages of modernization. His ideas spread across Central and Eastern Europe through the circulation of some of his works, through translations and popularizations published in the written press, and through seductive speeches that encouraged people to develop their own culture and specificity on the grounds of linguistic or dialectic particularities, and especially their origins, history, folklore and established residence in one territory. In these circumstances, over the course of the nineteenth century the new elites were often confronted with a choice between either a monocultural or traditionally multicultural point of view. Faced with the idea of the supremacy of one cultural ethno-nation over another, and recognizing that in the new Europe they would have to choose between inclusion or exclusion, these elites and the communities to which they belonged remained non-committal, accepting ambiguity and recognizing themselves both as an ethno-nation and part of the multicultural state. After several decades, this act of contesting multicultural realities led to a break of huge proportions, which found its most obvious expression in the events of the First World War, a conflict arising from extreme nationalisms. In the interim, the ideologies that encouraged separation and competition among groups gradually gained momentum, and the exotic and warlike theories of identity invented by the Romantics imposed themselves across Central and Eastern Europe to the detriment of communitarian plurality and peaceful cohabitation. Despite this tragic course of events, and despite the tensions resulting from the flawed management of relations between the majority and the minorities of ethno-national states, multiculturality survived throughout the twentieth century. It was, and largely remained, a uniquely fruitful source for all sorts of creative activity, and maintained bridges of communication among the various cultures and states of these regions. For this reason, multicultural history can make a significant contribution to a more objective understanding of Central and Eastern Europe in the modern age.

NOTES

Chapter I

1 Leo Frobenius, *Paideuma. Schiță a unei filosofii a culturii (Paideuma. Outline of a Philosophy of Culture)*, trans. Ion Roman (Bucharest, 1985), p. 147. (Originally *Paideuma. Umrisse einer Kultur- und Seelenlehre* (Düsseldorf, 1953)).

2 Ernst Robert Curtius, *Literatura europeană și evul mediu latin*, trans. Adolf Armbruster (Bucharest, 1970), p. 25. (English translation: *European Literature and the Latin Middle Ages*, trans. Willard R. Trask, introduction by Colin Burrow (Princeton, 2013).)

3 Ibid., pp. 14, 18.

4 Lucien Febvre, *Le Problème de l'incroyance au XVIe siècle. La religion de Rabelais* (Paris, 1962).

5 Ibid., p. 491.

6 Ibid., p. 497.

7 Bernard Voyenne, *Histoire de l'idée européenne* (Paris, 1964), pp. 6–7.

8 Ibid., p. 64.

9 Fernand Braudel, *Mediterana și lumea mediteraneană în epoca lui Filip al II-lea*, trans. Mircea Gheorghe, foreword by Alexandru Duțu (Bucharest, 1985). (*La Méditerranée et le monde méditerranéen a l'époque de Philippe II* (Paris, 1949; 2nd edn 1963, 3rd edn 1976, 4th edn 1979).)

10 See also his second work, *Civilization matérielle, économie et capitalisme, XVe–XVIIIe siècle*, Tome I, 'Les Structures du quotidien: le possible et l'impossible', and Tome II, 'Les Jeux de l'échange' (Paris, 1979).

11 Braudel, *La Méditerranée*, vol. I, pp. 240–41.

12 Emmanuel Le Roy Ladurie, 'Braudel le novateur', in *L'Express*, no. 1796, 13 December 1985, pp. 58–60.

13 Paul Zumthor, *Viața de toate zilele in Olanda din vremea lui Rembrandt*, trans. Ileana Littera and Alexandra Cuniță (Bucharest, 1982). (English translation: *Daily Life in Rembrandt's Holland*, trans. Simon Watson Taylor (Stanford, 1994).)

14 Jacob Burckhardt, *Cultura Renașterii în Italia*, vols I–II, trans. N. Balotă and G. Ciorogaru, foreword, chronological tables, notes by Nicolae Balotă (Bucharest, 1986). (English translation: *The Civilization of the Renaissance in Italy*, trans. S. G. C. Middlemore, ed. Peter Murray, introduction by Peter Burke (London, 1990).)

15 José Ortega y Gasset, *En torno a Galileo* (Madrid, 1976).

16 Paulino Garagorri, 'Nota preliminar' in Ortega y Gasset, pp. 9–11.

17 Ortega y Gasset, pp. 13–24, the chapter 'El galileismo de la historia'.

18 P. P. Negulescu, *Filosofia Renașterii* (*The Philosophy of the Renaissance*), vol. I (2nd edn, Bucharest, 1945), p. 74.

19 Johan Huizinga, *Amurgul evului mediu. Studiu despre formele de viață și de gîndire din secolele al XIV-lea și al XV-lea în Franța și in Țările de Jos*, trans. H. R. Radian, foreword by Edgar Papu (Bucharest, 1970). (English translation: *The Autumn of the Middle Ages* (Chicago, 2004).)

20 Ibid., p. 502.

21 Nicolae Iorga, *Histoire de la vie byzantine: Empire et civilization d'après les sources* (Bucharest, 1934); *Essai de synthèse de l'histoire de l'humanité I–IV* (Paris, 1926–9); *Byzance après Byzance: Continuation de l'histoire de la vie byzantine* (Bucharest, 1935); *Generalități cu privire la studiile istorice* (*Generalities Regarding Historical Studies*) (3rd edn, Bucharest, 1944).

22 Idem, *Bizanț după Bizanț* (*Byzantium after Byzantium*), trans. Liliana Iorga Pippidi, afterword by Virgil Cândea, (Bucharest, 1972), p. 7.

23 Victor Papacostea, *Civilizație românească și civilizație balcanică. Studii istorice* (*Romanian Civilization and Balkan Civilization. Historical Studies*), ed. and notes by Cornelia Papacostea-Danielopolu, introductory essay by Nicolae-Șerban Tanașoca (Bucharest, 1983).

24 Radovan Samardžić, 'Les idées du siècle des lumières et l'éveil national des peuples yougoslaves', in *Les Lumières et la formation de la conscience nationale chez les peuples du sud-est européen, Actes du Colloque international organisé par la Comission de l'AIESEE pour l'histoire des idées, sous les auspices et avec le concours financier de l'UNESCO, Paris, 11–12 avril 1968* (Bucharest, 1970), pp. 101–14; *The Balkan Urban Culture (15th–19th Centuries)* (Belgrade, 1984); 'The Jews of Dubrovnik in the Trade of the 16th and 17th Centuries', in *Zbornik*, 1 (*Jevrejski Istorijski Muzej*) *Studije i grada o jevrejima Dubrovnika* ((*Jewish History Museum*) *Studies on the Jewish History of Dubrovnik*) (Belgrade, 1971), pp. 21–40.

25 Ilia Konev, *Balgarskato vazrazdane i prosvestenieto* (*Istorija, istoricesko saznaieyzaimodeistvie*) (*Bulgarian Revival and Enlightenment (History, Historical Knowledge)*) (Sofia, 1983); Veselin Traikov, *Curente ideologice și programe din mișcările de eliberare națională din Balcani pînă în anul 1878* (*Ideological Currents and Programmes of the National Liberation Movements in the Balkans to 1878*), trans. Constantin N. Velichi (Bucharest, 1986).

26 Paul Cornea, *Regula jocului* (*The Rule of the Game*) (Bucharest, 1980), pp. 198–208.

27 Ilia Konev, 'Școala ardeleană și istorismul sud-est european' ('The Transylvanian School and Southeastern European History'), in *Transilvania*, no. 8 (1980), pp. 57–9.

28 See Traikov, especially the first two chapters: 'Apariția primelor programe și curente ideologice în mișcările de eliberare națională în Balcani pînă la crearea primelor state naționale' ('The Emergence of the First Programmes and Ideological Currents in the National Liberation Movements in the Balkans until the Creation of the First National States'), pp. 19–50, and 'Apariția primelor curente ideologice și a programelor în mișcările de eliberare națională din Balcani la sfîrșitul secolului al XVIII-lea. Influența revoluției franceze' ('The First Ideological Currents and Programmes in the National Liberation Movements in the Balkans at the End of the 18th Century. The Influence of the French Revolution'), pp. 51–92.

29 C. T. Dimaras, *Histoire de la littérature neo-hellénique* (Athens, 1966); *Neoellinikos diafotismos* (Athens, 1977).

30 Domokos Kosáry, *Művelődés a XVIII-ik századi Magyarországon* (*Culture in 18th-Century Hungary*) (Budapest, 1980).

31 Similar to this study are other equally remarkable works by Sziklay László, Péter Király and Emil Niederhauser, gathered in the volume *Les Lumières en Hongrie, en Europe Centrale et en Europe Orientale* (Budapest, 1971,

1975, 1977), the collected papers of the colloquia of Mátrafüred in Hungary.

32 *Typographia Universitatis Hungaricae Budae,* ed. Péter Király (Budapest, 1983).

33 David Prodan, *Supplex Libellus Valachorum* (Budapest, 1984); see also Victor Neumann, 'Supplex Libellus Valachorum' in *Romania literară*, no. 8 (1985), p. 5, in which I analyzed the conceptual and methodological aspects of the Romanian scholar's work.

34 Fritz Valjavec, *Der deutsche Kultureinfluss im nahen Südosten* (Munich, 1960).

35 See *The Balkans in Transition: Essays on the Development of Balkan Life and Politics since the Eighteenth Century,* ed. C. Jelavich and B. Jelavich, (2nd edn, Berkeley, 1974).

36 Emil Condurachi, Răzvan Theodorescu, 'Europa de est, arie de convergenţă a civilizaţiilor' ('Eastern Europe, Area of Convergence of Civilizations'), in *Revista de istorie* (History Magazine), nos. 1 and 2 (1981).

37 Ibid., no. 2, p. 194.

Chapter II

1 Huizinga, p. 31.

2 Negulescu, vol. I, p. 123.

3 See Louis Bertrand, *Histoire d'Espagne* (Paris, n.d.), ch. IV, 'Le gouvernement de Philippe II. La monarchie absolue, L'Inquisition', pp. 438–49; see also the analysis and interpretation of this problem in Febvre, pp. 490–500.

4 *Între Antichitate şi Renaştere. Gîndirea evului mediu. De la începuturile patristice la Nicolaus Cusanus (Between Antiquity and Renaissance. Thinking of the Middle Ages. From the Patristic Beginnings to Nicolaus Cusanus)*, trans., selection, bibliography and notes by Octavian Nistor (Bucharest, 1984), vol. II, p. 38.

5 Thomas Aquinas, *Summa Theologica* I, question LXXIX, 'Despre puterile intelective' ('On Intellectual Powers'), in *Între Antichitate şi Renaştere*, vol. II, p. 50.

6 Octavian Nistor, 'Toma din Aquino', in *Între Antichitate şi Renaştere*, vol. II, p. 50.

7 'Moşe Ben-Maimon', in *Între Antichitate şi Renaştere*, vol. I, pp. 293–6.

8 Moses ben Maimon, 'Călăuza şovăielnicilor' ('Guide for the Perplexed'), part III, ch. XI, in *Între Antichitate şi Renaştere*, vol. I, p. 303.

9 See Negulescu, vol. I, pp. 159–62.

10 Ibid., p. 163.

11 Cusanus' notable scientific works include *De transmutationibus geometricis, De arithmetricis complementis, De quadratura circuli, De mathematicis complementis, De mathematica perfectione, De una recti curvique mensura, De figura mundi, De ludo globi, Compendium* and *De apice theoriae.*

12 See the excellent chapters on the origins of the Florentine Academy in 'Originile Academiei platonice din Florenţa' ('Origins of the Platonic Academy in Florence') and 'Întemeierea Academiei Platonice din Florenţa' ('Establishment of the Platonic Academy in Florence') in Negulescu, pp. 225–41 and 270–78.

13 Plethon, 'Traité des lois ou recueil des fragments, en partie inédits, de cet ouvrage, précédé d'une notice historique et critique et augmenté d'un choix de pièces justificatives, la plupart inédites, by C. Alexandre', trans. A. Pellissier. See Negulescu, pp. 241–2.

14 C. Noica, 'Cuvînt prevenitor' ('Argument'), in Plato, *Opere V (The Republic)*, trans., interpretation, preliminary considerations, notes and appendix by Andrei Cornea, ed. Constantin Noica and Petru Creţia (Bucharest, 1986), pp. 9–10.

15 For Marsilio Ficino's text, see Negulescu, vol. I, p. 299.

16 Ernst Cassirer, *Individuum und Kosmos in der Philosophie der Renaissance* (Leipzig and Berlin, 1927), p. 4. The book was translated into English by Mario Domandi as *The Individual and the Cosmos in Renaissance Philosophy* (Oxford, 1963).

17 Huizinga, p. 519.

18 Andrei Oțetea, *Renașterea și Reforma* (*Renaissance and Reform*) (2nd edn, Bucharest, 1968), p. 24.

19 Pico della Mirandola was one of the first European humanists who studied the old books of Judaism, assisted in this direction by Jewish scholars who taught him Hebrew: Jochanan Alemanno, who had emigrated from Constantinople, Flavius Mithridates and Elia del Medigo, who gave public Hebrew lessons in Padua; cf. Negulescu, vol. I, p. 355.

20 George Uscătescu, *Erasmus* (Bucharest, 1982), pp. 96–7; for eras and movements, personalities and masterpieces of world music, see George Bălan, *O istorie a muzicii europene* (*A History of European Music*) (Bucharest, 1975), the chapter 'Bach, Händel și umanizarea divinului' ('Bach, Handel and the Humanization of the Divine'), pp. 108–14.

21 Erasmus, *Elogiul nebuniei sau cuvîntare spre laia prostiei*, trans. and notes by Stefan Bezdechi, introduction by Constantin Botez (Bucharest, 1959), pp. 3–4. (English translation: *The Praise of Folly* (Princeton, 2015).)

22 Huizinga, p. 55; see also idem, *Erasmus*, trans. H. R. Radian, foreword and chronological table by Cornelia Comorovschi (Bucharest, 1974), ch. IX, pp. 106–20. (English translation: *Erasmus and the Age of Reformation. With a selection from the Letters of Erasmus* (Princeton, 1984).)

23 Stan Velea, *Istoria literaturii polone: Renaștere, Baroc, Secolul Luminilor, Romantism* (*The History of Polish Literature: Renaissance, Baroque, Enlightenment, Romanticism*) (Bucharest, 1986), pp. 14–15, 21, 29.

24 Neumann, 'The Enlightened-Romanticist Mixture: The Case of Transylvania', in Victor Neumann and Armin Heinen (eds), *Modernity in Central and South-Eastern Europe. Ideas, Concepts, Discourses* (Bucharest, 2018), pp. 139–55.

25 Curtius, p. 39; see also Jean Delumeau, *La Civilisation de la Renaissance* (Paris, 1967); Alberto Tenenti, *Die Grundlegung der moderner Welt, Spätmittelater, Renaissance, Reformation* (Frankfurt am Main, 1967); Bernard Topfler, 'Zur Frage nach dem Begin der Neuzeit', in *Zeitschrift fur Geschichtwissenschaft*, VI (1986); for Central-Eastern Europe see the detailed studies of Kazimierz Lepszy, *Die Ergebnisse der Reformation in Polen und ihre Rolle in der europaischen Renaissance*, and *Renaissance und Humanismus in Mittel und Osteuropa* (Berlin, 1962); Francisc Pall, 'Fragen der Renaissance', in *Forschungen zur Volks – und Landeskunde*, no. 2 (1966), pp. 5–27.

26 Viorica Guy Marica, *Pictura germană între Gotic și Renaștere* (*German Painting between Gothic and Renaissance*) (Bucharest, 1981), pp. 261, 265, 267.

27 Ștefan Bezdechi, *Nicolaus Olahus, primul umanist de origine română* (*Nicolaus Olahus, the First Humanist of Romanian Origin*) (Aninoasa–Gorj, 1939), p. 13.

28 *Istoria Clujului* (*The History of Cluj*) (Cluj, 1974), pp. 146–7.

29 Ádám Dankanits, *XVI századi olvasmányok* (*16th-Century Readings*) (Bucharest, 1974), pp. 18–20. The author considers that the great turning point in the life of Transylvanian intellectuals is due first of all to ties with the land; he speaks of the consolidation of the bourgeoisie, of the decisive role it played in the economic development and spiritual movement of this century. But the unions of artisans or corporations of merchants of Brașov, Sibiu, Mediaș, Cluj, Bistrița and Sighișoara were far removed from the capitalist model of political economy. The situation was similar to that of Central and Southeastern Europe: it was only in some regions of the West that the sixteenth century showed early signs of the future capitalist system. Of course, its origins can be discovered here and there in medieval society, and even in

Roman antiquity and earlier. But this is not the essence of mankind's evolution in the transitional period from the medieval to the modern era. Downplaying the religious element and the horizontal and vertical dimensions of reform and humanism, Dankanits – like A. Oțetea in *Renașterea și Reforma* (1st edn, Bucharest, 1941; 2nd edn, Bucharest, 1968) – does not notice that behind the multitude of cultural, philosophical, literary and musical books published in the West and in Transylvania was a complex mechanism geared towards the proliferation of theses and ideas that, in turn, would not only stimulate enlightened minds but also the way of thinking of people collectively. Despite the wealth of data that he gathers from documents found in the great libraries and archives of those times, he does not grasp the genesis, the sense and the duration of crises of conscience, simply because he is unsure how to interpret archival sources (in the last decades of the century) when they cease to offer a means of understanding events from the perspective of economic history. What is to be done in this case? A sociological history, a history of ideas? Probably both.

30 Kisfaludy Katalin, *Matthias Rex* (Budapest, 1983), pp. 109–42; see also Karl Nehring, 'Mátyás Külpolitikája' ('Matthias's Foreign Policy'), in *Történelmi Szemle* (*Historical Magazine*), nos. 3–4 (1978); Horváth János, *Az irodalmi műveltség megoszlása. Magyar humaniszmus* (*Distribution of Literary Work. Hungarian Humanism*) (Budapest, 1935); Csapodi Csaba-Csapodiné, Klara Gárdonyi, Tibor Szánta, *Bibliotheca Corviniana* (Budapest, 1967); Zsigmond Jakó, *Philobiblon transilvan* (Bucharest, 1977), pp. 13–72.

31 Johannes Honter, *Odae cum Harmoniis*, introduction and ed. Gernot Nüssbacher and Astrid Philippi (Bucharest, 1983).

32 See *Encyclopédie de la musique*, vol. I (Paris, 1958); *Dizzionario Ricordi della musica e dei musicisti* (Milan, 1959). For his works as a composer see *Intabulatura Valentini*

Bacfarc Transilvani Coronensis Liber primus (Lyon, 1952); *Valentini Grefi Bacfarci Pannonii Harmonicarum Musicarum in usum Testudinis Factorum. Tomus primus* (Krakow, 1565). We are grateful to Nicolae Boboc for pointing our research in this direction.

33 Christian Schesaeus, *Ruinae Pannonicae* (Wittenberg, 1581); see also the edition published in 'Cibinium' (Sibiu) in 1797. Another, less well-known work by this Transylvanian German scholar is *Epithalamium in honorem nuptialem magnifici domini Gaspari Bokes de Korniat S .R. I. supraemi Cubiculari, eiusque Sponsae Generosissimae Annae, Egregij Domini Wolffgang de Harinna filiae scriptum* (Alba Iulia, 1667), which can be consulted at the Central University Library Cluj, Special Collections section, no. BMV 388. In the magazine *Manuscriptum*, no. 3 (1985), the original text and Romanian translation of the chapter 'De re Transilvania' of *Ruinae Pannonicae* was published, along with an article by George Togan; see also Ilona Bitay, 'Christian Schesäus irodalmi munkásságának magyar vonatkozásai' ('Hungarian Aspects of Christian Schesäus's Literary Work'), in *Művelődés történeti tanulmányok* (*Cultural History Studies*) (Bucharest, 1979), pp. 70–77.

34 See Gáspár Heltai, *A Bibliának első része, az az Mózesnek ött könyve* (*The First Part of the Bible is the Book of Moses*) (Cluj, 1551), *A Jézus Christusnak Uj Testamentuma magyar nyelvre fordítatott* (*The New Testament of Jesus Christ Translated into Hungarian*) (Cluj, 1572); collections, BMV 215 and 366a; *Cronica* by Tinodi Sebestien, which appeared in in 1554, can be consulted in this library at BMV 240.

35 Tonk Sándor, *Erdélyiek egyetemjárása a középkorban* (*Transylvanian Students in the Middle Ages*) (Bucharest, 1979), p. 168. The author gives very precise statistics of the places of origin of the students, identifying the name of each, the university he attended, as well as the type of study he undertook; the author also reveals the

material conditions of the students and their social origin.

36 Togan, *op. cit.*

37 Coresi, *Psaltirea slavo-română (1577) în comparație cu psaltirile coresiene din 1570 și din 1589 (The Slavic-Romanian Psaltery (1577) compared to the Psalms of Coresi from 1570 and 1589)*, ed., introduction and notes by Stela Toma (Bucharest, 1976).

38 *De la Honterus la Oberth… Studii (From Honterus to Oberth… Studies)*, ed. and introduction by Hans Barth, in Romanian by Peter Sragher, foreword by I. M. Ştefan (Bucharest, 1985), pp. 21–50 (originally *Von Honterus zu Oberth. Bedeutende siebenbürgisch-deutsche Naturwissenschaftler, Techniker und Mediziner* (Bucharest, 1980)); see also Gernot Nussbächer, *Johannes Honterus* (Bucharest, 1977) and Karl Kurt Klein, *Der Humanist und Reformator Johannes Honter* (Sibiu, 1935). Applied studies of great documentary value were published by Lidia A. Demény and Demény Lajos in *Carte, societate și tipar la români în secolul al XVI-lea (Romanian Books, Society and Printing in the 16th Century)* (Bucharest, 1986).

39 Iorga, *Istoria românilor și a civilizației lor (History of the Romanians and Their Civilization)*, trans. from French by A. Lascarov Moldovanu (Bucharest, 1929), p. 159. (Originally *Histoire des Roumains et de leur civilisation* (Paris, 1920).)

40 See, for example, the splendid books with sixteenth-century engravings in the Bethlen Collection of the Aiud documentary library, books that were in circulation in Transylvania at that time and came into the library's collection a century or so later: for example, a book of great beauty is *Cosmografia – Petri Appiani Per Gemman Frisium, Bassiliensi, Giorgio Bonito*, MDL no. 33.

41 Condurachi and Theodorescu, pp. 201–2.

42 Dragoljub Dragojlović, 'Printing and Transcribing of Cyrillic books in Balkan towns of the Turkish Empire' in *Balkan Urban Culture (15th–19th centuries)* (Belgrade, 1984), pp. 169–80.

43 Zavane Crnja, *Histoire de la culture croate* (Zagreb, 1966),'Les perspectives protestantes,' pp. 207–32.

44 See Nicolaus Olahus, *Corespondență cu umaniștii batavi și flamanzi (Correspondence with Batavian and Flemish Humanists)*, foreword, anthology, notes and bibliography by Corneliu Albu, translation of Latin texts by Maria Capoianu (Bucharest, 1971).

45 Levinus Ammonius (1485–1556), monk, scholar, admirer of humanism and one of the important personalities of the era.

46 Nicolaus Olahus to Levinus Ammonius, in Olahus, pp. 23–4, and Ammonius to Olahus, ibid., p. 16.

47 The monograph by Huizinga, *Erasmus*, brings out the thinking of Erasmus that found an echo that was at once immense and of great duration in European society, exerting at the same time a considerable influence upon the development of civilization.

48 Businessman and Erasmus' main courier.

49 Erasmus to Nicolaus Olahus, in Olahus, pp. 94–5.

50 Radovan Samardžić, 'On Urban Civilization in the Balkans from the 15th to the 19th Centuries', in *Balkan Urban Culture (15th–19th centuries)* ed. Verna Han (Belgrade, 1984), pp. 9–17.

51 Braudel, *La Méditerranée*, vol. I, pp. 232–3. The French historian argues continually for a balance between the two times, for continuity between the Middle Ages and the Renaissance, both before and after the sixteenth century.

52 See Oțetea, p. 278.

53 Ortega y Gasset, *op.cit.*, 'La estructura de la vida sustancia de la historia'.

Chapter III

1 Paul Hazard, *Criza conștiinței europene, 1680–1715*, trans. Sanda Șora, foreword by Romul Munteanu (Bucharest, 1973), p. 95. (English translation: *The European Mind. The Critical Years 1680–1715* (New York, 1990).)

2 Febvre; Hazard; Braudel, *La Méditerranée*; Jean Delumeau, *Frica în Occident (secolele XIV–XVIII). O cetate asediată*, trans., afterword and notes by Modest Morariu (Bucharest, 1986). (Originally *La Peur en Occident (XVIe–XVIIIe siècles)* (Paris, 2011).)

3 C. T. Dimaras, *Istoria literaturii neogrecești* (*The History of Neo-Greek Literature*), trans. Mihai Vasiliu (Bucharest, 1968), p. 75. See also editions cited in Chapter I, n. 29.

4 Răzvan Theodorescu, *Civilizația românilor între medieval și modern* (*Romanian Civilization between the Medieval and Modern Periods*) (Bucharest, 1987), vols I–II.

5 *Philocalia*, vol. VII (Bucharest, 1977).

6 Ibid, p. 229.

7 Virgil Cândea, introduction to Dimitrie Cantemir, *Divan sau gâlceava înțeleptului cu lumea* (*Divan, or the Wise Man's Quarrel with the World*) (Bucharest, 1969).

8 See 'Învățăturile lui Neagoe Basarab către fiul său Teodosie' ('The Teachings of Neagoe Basarab to His Son Theodosius'), in *Cronicile slavo-române din secolele XV–XVII* (*Slavonic-Romanian Chronicles of the 15th–17th Centuries*), edition revised and completed by P. P. Panaitescu (Bucharest, 1959); 'Din învățăturile lui Petru Movilă către fratele său Moise, domnul Moldovei' ('From the Teachings of Petru Movilă to His Brother Moise, Prince of Moldavia'), in G. Mihăilă, *Contribuții la istoria culturii și literaturii române vechi* (*Contributions to the History of Old Romanian Culture and Literature*) (Bucharest, 1972), pp. 195–6.

9 Mircea Păcurariu, *Istoria Bisericii Ortodoxe Române* (*History of the Romanian Orthodox Church*) (Sibiu, 1978), pp. 166–7.

10 I. Dumitriu-Snagov, *Românii în arhivele Romei* (*Romanians in the Archives of Rome*) (Bucharest, 1973), p. 81.

11 Prodan, p. 136.

12 See I. Dumitriu-Snagov, *op. cit.*, pp. 83–9, a certified copy of the Act recognizing the sovereignity of Rome.

13 Prodan, p. 150.

14 Paul Cornea, 'Romantismul sud-est european. Schiță de caracterizare zonală' ('Romanticism in Southeastern Europe. Character Sketch of the Area'), in *op. cit.*, p. 199.

15 Cornelia Papacostea-Danielopolu and Lidia Demény, *Carte și tipar în societatea românească și sud-est europeană (secolele XVII–XIX)* (*Book and Print in Romanian and Southeastern European Society (17th–19th Centuries)*) (Bucharest, 1985), pp. 65–6.

16 Sándor Szilágyi (ed.), *Monumenta Comitialia Regni Transilvaniae* (Budapest, 1882), p. 96; see Jakó, pp. 13, 433.

17 See the preface by Petru Bod to the writing of Ferenc Pápai Páriz, *Dictionarium Latino-Hungaricum, Seccum et medullam puris Latinitatis ejusque geminam in Linguam Hungaricam convertionem ad mentem et sensum proprium Scriptorum Classicorum* (Bratislava and Sibiu, 1801), tome I, p. 6, in the old books collection of the documentary library of the Bethlen School in Aiud, no. 7269.

18 Jakó, 'Biblioteca Colegiului Bethlen din Aiud', in Jakó, *op. cit.*, p. 145.

19 Papacostea-Danielopolu and Demény, pp. 52–3; see also P. P. Panaitescu, *Contribuții la istoria culturii românești* (*Contributions to the History of Romanian Culture*), ed. Silvia Panaitescu, foreword, notes and bibliography by Dan Zamfirescu (Bucharest, 1971), pp. 390–477; Iorga, 'Dezvoltarea literaturii românești în veacul al XVII-lea' ('The Development of Romanian Literature in the 17th Century'), in *op. cit.*, p. 181; Victor Papacostea, pp. 247–83.

20 See N. Drăgan, appendix to 'Codicele pribeagului Gheorghe Ștefan, voievodul Moldovei' ('The Codes of Gheorghe Ștefan, Voivode of Moldavia'), in *Anuarul Institutului de Istorie Națională* (*Yearbook of the Institute of National History*), III (1926), pp. 245–9.

21 Victor Papacostea, pp. 260–61.

22 Virgil Cândea, *Rațiunea dominantă. Contribuție la istoria Umanismului românesc* (*The Dominant Reason. Contribution to the History of Romanian Humanist Culture*) (Cluj, 1979), p. 67.

23 Konrad Onasch, *Civilizația marelui Novgorod. Istoria culturală a unui vechi oraș rus și a ținutului lui de colonizare* (*The Civilization of Novgorod the Great. Cultural History of an Old Russian City and Its Colonization*), trans. D. Marian, foreword by Dan Zamfirescu (Bucharest, 1975), 'Renașterea culturală și noua erezie' ('The Cultural Renaissance and the New Heresy'), pp. 146–57, and 'Cântecul de lebădă al marelui Novgorod' ('The Swansong of Novgorod the Great'), pp. 158–86.

24 Constantin Velichi, *România și Renașterea bulgară* (*Romania and the Bulgarian Renaissance*) (Bucharest, 1980), p. 37.

25 Cornelia Papacostea-Danielopolu, *Intelectualii români din Principate și cultura greacă, 1821–1859* (*Romanian Intellectuals from the Principalities and Greek Culture, 1821–1859*) (Bucharest, 1979), p. 20.

26 Victor Papacostea, p. 263.

27 Cleobule Tsourkas, 'La vie et l'œuvre de Théophile Corydalée (1574–1646)', in Theophilos Corydalleus, *Introduction à la logique*, trans. Constantin Noica (Bucharest, 1970), p. xiii.

28 E. Benz, 'Wittenberg und Byzanz. Zur Begegnung und Auseinandersetzung der Reformation und der Östlich-orthodoxen Kirche' (Marburg, 1949), in Victor Papacostea, p. 263.

29 C. Noica, 'Avant propos' to Corydalleus, p. xi.

30 Corydalleus, p. 2.

31 Idem, *Commentaires à la Métaphysique*, trans. and introduction by Constantin Noica (Bucharest, 1973), p. 2.

32 C. T. Dimaras, *Istoria literaturii neogrecești*, the chapters 'Începuturile pe ruine. Grecia în timpul stăpânirii otomane' ('The Beginnings on the Ruins. Greece during Ottoman Rule'), pp. 73–95, 'Semne de sărbătoare' ('Signs of Celebration'), pp. 96–121, and 'Elenismul în străinătate' ('Hellenism Abroad'), pp. 122–35. See also the excellent study by Victor Papacostea on 'Originile învățământului superior în Țara Românească' ('The Origins of Higher Education in Wallachia') in *op. cit.*, pp. 259–82, in which the author supplies valuable information, analysis and interpretation enabling us to reconstruct the history of the Schola Graeca et Latina in Târgoviște, where Ligarides made a major contribution.

33 Alexandru Duțu, *Literatura comparată și istoria mentalităților* (*Comparative Literature and the History of Mentalities*) (Bucharest, 1982), p. 203; see especially the chapter 'De la formă la model: Cultura postbizantină' ('From Form to Model: Post-Byzantine Culture'), pp. 191–249; see also Mircea Muthu, 'Amintirea Bizanțului în literaturile sud-est europene' ('The Memory of Byzantium in Southeastern European Literature'), in *Revista de istorie și teorie literară* (*Journal of the History and Theory of Literature*), no. 4 (1985), pp. 45–50.

34 Neumann, *Convergențe spirituale* (*Spiritual Convergences*) (Bucharest, 1986), pp. 11–16, 17–38.

35 See Romul Munteanu, *Cultura europeană în epoca luminilor* (*European Culture in the Age of Enlightenment*) (Bucharest, 1981), p. 50.

36 Dimitrie Cantemir, *Istoria Imperiului Otoman*, Preface, in *Manuscriptum*, no. 2 (1985), pp. 23–39. There is still no published version of this Preface or of the entire work in the original Latin, and it has been only partly published in Romanian translation.

The discovery in Harvard's Houghton Library of the Latin manuscript containing *The History of the Growth and Decay of the Ottoman Empire* in its final form was made by historian Virgil Cândea, and the Preface was translated into Romanian by Latin language specialist Dan Sluşanschi. Thanks to *Manuscriptum*, this work is finally beginning to emerge, after being known only through incorrect copies of incomplete translations; see also Dimitrie Cantemir, *Monarchiarum phisica examinatio* (1714), ed. I. Sulea Firu, in *Studii şi cercetări bibliologice* (*Bibliological Studies and Research*), vol. V (1961), pp. 269–76; idem, *Sacrosanctae scientiae indepingibilis imago* (1700), ed. N. Locusteanu (Bucharest, 1928); idem, *Sistemul sau întocmirea religiei muhammedane* (*The System or Elaboration of the Mohammedan Religion*), trans., introduction and commentary by Virgil Cândea (Bucharest, 1977).

37 Al Zub, *Biruit-au gândul* (*The Triumph of Thought*) (Iaşi, 1983), p. 69.

38 Virgil Cândea, introduction to *Divan*, p. liv.

39 Cantemir, *Divan*, pp. 28–30.

40 Ibid.

41 Idem, *Sistemul sau întocmirea religiei muhammedane*, p. 455.

42 *Bibliothèque Germanique ou histoire littéraire de l'Allemagne et des Pays du Nord*, vol. 8 (1724), p. 196; see Grigore Ploeşteanu, 'Alte ecouri europene ale operei lui Dimitrie Cantemir', ('Other European Echoes of Dimitrie Cantemir's Work') in *Vatra*, no. 2 (1985), p. 179.

43 *Le Journal Universel ou Mémoires pour servir à l'histoire civile, politique, ecclésiastique et littéraire du XVIII siècle* (The Hague), 1743, pp. 439–43, and 1744, pp. 182–6.

44 See Ploeşteanu, 'Noi mărturii privind ecoul operei lui Dimitrie Cantemir' ('New Testimonies of the Echo of Dimitrie Cantemir's Work'), in *Vatra*, no. 12 (1984), p. 165.

45 See Iorga, *Relations entre les Serbes et les Roumains* (Bucharest, 1922), and 'Operele lui G. Brancovici', in *Revista istorică*, III, nos. 1–6 (1927); other works that refer to Romanian–Serbian contacts, including those between Branković and Cantacuzino, include Silviu Anuichi, *Relaţii bisericeşti româno-sârbe în secolele al XVII-lea şi al XVIII-lea* (*Romanian–Serbian Church Relations in the 17th and 18th Centuries*) (Bucharest, 1980), pp. 31–2.

46 Aron Densuşianu, 'O nouă cronică românească' ('A New Romanian Chronicle'), in *Revista critică literară* (*Literary Critical Review*) (1893), pp. 366–96; see Anuichi, p. 31.

47 See Anuichi, p. 31. The original manuscript of the *Great Chronicle* is kept in the Library of the Serbian Patriarch of Belgrade, MS no. 90.

48 Constantin Cantacuzino, *Istoria Ţării Rumâneşti întru care să cuprinde numele ei cel dintâi şi cine au fost locuitorii ei atunci* (*The History of the Romanian Country, including Its First Name and Its Inhabitants at That Time*), edition based on an unknown manuscript, ed. N. Cartojan and Dan Simionescu (Craiova, undated).

49 Andrei Pippidi, *Tradiţia politică bizantină în Ţările Române în secolele XVI–XVII* (*The Byzantine Political Tradition in the Romanian Principalities in the 16th–17th Centuries*) (Bucharest, 1983), pp. 120–22.

50 Febvre; see also Braudel, *La Méditerranée*.

Chapter IV

1 Marc Bloch, *The Historian's Craft. Reflections on the Nature and Uses of History and the Techniques and Methods of Those Who Write It* (Manchester, 1992).

2 I have consulted collections of books and old manuscripts in the following institutions: the Library of the Romanian Academy in Bucharest; Cluj University Library; the Library of the Brukenthal

Museum in Sibiu; the Batthyaneum Library in Alba Iulia; the Library of the Cluj branch of the Romanian Academy; the Timișoara State Archives; the Archives of the Jewish Community of Timișoara; the Timiș County Library; the Archives of the Arad City Library; the Archives of the Timișoara City Library; the Archives of the Lugoj Library; the National Széchenyi Library in Budapest; the Museum of the Bucharest Jewish Communities; the Archives of the Federation of Jewish Communities of Romania; the Hungarian National Archives in Budapest; the Archives and the Library of the Budapest Rabbinic Seminary; and the Museum of the Jewish Community of Belgrade.

3 Simon Dubnov, *Istoria universală a poporului evreu (Jewish World History)*, abridged and revised in German by the author with A. Steinberg, with an introductory essay by Jean Cohen. Romanian version by S. Bainglass (Bucharest, 1946). (German translation: *Weltgeschichte des Jüdischen Volkes*, trans. A. Steinberg (Berlin, 10 vols, 1925–9).)

4 This point of view is inspired by Leo Frobenius: see *Paideuma* (Düsseldorf, 1953). I have studied the Romanian edition, translated by Ion Roman, with a foreword by Ion Frunzetti (Bucharest, 1985). Modern European historiography offers opinions and concepts of undisputable value, notably those of Marc Bloch, Lucien Febvre and Fernand Braudel. In Romanian historiography, I have drawn on important ideas in the works of Răzvan Theodorescu, Alexandru Zub, Alexandru Duțu, Paul Cornea and others.

5 Yakir Eventov, *A History of Yugoslav Jews*, I: *From ancient times to the end of the 19th century*, ed. Cvi Rotem (Tel Aviv, 1971), pp. 6–8.

6 Silviu Sanie, *Cultele orientale în Dacia romană*, I: *Cultele siriene și palmiriene (Eastern Cults in Roman Dacia, I: Cults from Syria and Palmyra)* (Bucharest, 1981). These include a ringstone discovered in Sarmisegetuza

(p. 161); an altar with a votive inscription dedicated to the god 'Theos Hyppsistos' by Aelia Cassia, possibly a Jew discovered in the same place (pp. 274 and 286), on a slate tablet etched with Judaic symbols discovered in Transylvania during the nineteenth century (p. 161–2); and a votive inscription discovered at Porolissum left by a Roman decurion with a *cognomen* of Judaic origin (p. 292). For other discoveries see *Inscripțiile Daciei romane (Inscriptions from Roman Dacia)*, vols I and III (Bucharest, 1975 and 1977). For the Simon bar Kokhba coins, see Nicolae Gudea, 'O interesantă descoperire arheologică în județul Caraș-Severin' ('An Interesting Archaeological Discovery in Caraș-Severin County'), in *Revista cultului mozaic (Magazine of the Mosaic Religion)*, XVII (1972), p. 271.

7 The first written evidence of a Jewish presence in the Pannonian Plain, which dates back approximately two thousand years, is displayed in the Hungarian Jewish Museum, which is located in the left wing of the Great Synagogue of Budapest.

8 I maintain that any man has the right to aspire to godhead according to his own convictions. I believe that this process is an all-embracing whole, in which communication is just the form, not the essence of belief. However, individual forms of expression have most often tried to assert themselves to the detriment of others, and in this conflict true knowledge always lost out. It is my conviction that, in various forms, we all tend towards one and the same expression of the Absolute, and thus a shared tolerance is not only possible but necessary – only thus can we express our unity, which is in the depths of our spirit and human soul.

9 Eventov, p. 8; see also Ármin Kecskeméti, *A zsidók egyetemes története. A Babilóniai fogságból való visszatéréstöl napjainkig (The Universal History of the Jews. From the Babylonian Captivity until Today)*, vol. I (Budapest, 1927), pp. 212–19. The author's understanding of

the restrictions placed on Jews is based on the *Collectio Constitutionum ecclesiasticarum tripartita (578–610)*, a compendium including the saddest of regulations regarding the Jews of Byzantium.

10 Spanish Jews are known as Sephardim, speaking the Ladino language, a mixture of Hebrew and Spanish; their territory was the Iberian Peninsula, but we also find them in the region of Northern Africa and, beginning with the twelfth and fifteenth centuries, in France, Italy and the Netherlands. German Jews are known as Ashkenazim, speaking the Yiddish language, a German-Hebrew idiom; their territory was approximately situated between Berlin, Prague, Vienna and Krakow, extending later to include all of Central Europe, as well as the north and northeast of the continent.

11 Eventov describes both external factors that affected the Jewish communities in the south of Slovenia and Jewish events generally that shaped the course of their history.

12 Robert de Beauplan, *Le Drame juif* (Paris, 1939), p. 10.

13 See Braudel, *La Méditerranée*. I believe that Braudel's chapter on Jews fundamentally changes our understanding of the history of Judaism and its European diaspora. Indeed, the entire conception that Braudel conveys in his history books and his volume on the theory of history, *Ecrits sur l'histoire* (Paris, 1969), reflects a transition that is as surprising as it is important to the development of modern historiographical thinking. It raises historiography beyond the narrow compass of its research to the status of a discipline that grasps, in all its complexity, the most universally valid human phenomena. The historian thus becomes a *spiritus rector* in which his traditional strengths are enhanced by a new clarity of vision. Braudel analyzes the comparative history of European communities, without concentrating on any one in particular. He examines the ways in which Jews have thrived across all

of Europe, revealing their economic, social, and intellectual ascension, the moments of great tension, regression and withdrawal, and the ways in which faith has guaranteed their survival.

14 See Victor Eskenasy, *Izvoare și mărturii referitoare la evreii din Romania (Sources and Testimonies concerning the Jews in Romania)*, vol. I (Bucharest, 1986), p. 3. Eskenasy took the fragment from J. Starr, *The Jews in the Byzantine Empire, 641–1204* (Athens, 1939), but this version of the text can be attributed to N. M. Adler, *The Itinerary of Benjamin of Tudela* (London, 1907). I will often refer to the Victor Eskenasy and Mihai Spielmann (vol. II, Bucharest, 1988) edition of different documents, since the two historians establish an important documentary and scientific foundation for the history of Jews in Romania. Some of these documents also refer to the situation of Jews in neighbouring territories – Hungary, Russia, Bulgaria, and Greece. I will also include documentary evidence from other editions, such as the comprehensive source entitled *Monumenta Hungariae Judaica*, which now runs to nineteen volumes.

15 Răzvan Theodorescu, *Bizanț, Balcani, Occident la începuturile culturii medievale românești (secolele X–XIV) (Byzantium, the Balkans and the West at the Beginning of Romanian Medieval Culture (10th–14th Centuries))* (Bucharest, 1974). See the chapter '"Coridoarele culturale" și începuturile civilizației medievale românești' ('"Cultural Corridors" and the Beginnings of Romanian Medieval Civilization"'), pp. 339–48.

16 Eskenasy, docs 3 and 4, pp. 4–6.

17 Sándor Márki, *Arad vármegye és Arad szabad királyi város története (History of Arad County and the Free Royal City of Arad)*, vol. I (Arad, 1892), p. 482; see also note 1, at the end of document no. 3 of the Eskenasy edition.

18 Braudel, *La Méditerranée*, p. 184.

19 Eskenasy, doc. 5, p. 6.

20 Ibid.

21 Ibid.

22 During the time of Louis I, the zealous king who wished to 'convert to Catholicism and gain unto Christ the Jews', retreat towards Austria and Bohemia also became a solution, at least for the moment. See Eskenasy, doc. 10, p. 11.

23 See above, ch. II, p.60.

24 I owe this information to Mrs Ilona Benosovski, director of the Hungarian Jewish Museum in Budapest, for which I remain grateful.

25 Fernand Braudel, *La Méditerranée*, p. 180.

26 Aurel Decei, *Istoria Imperiului Otoman până la 1656* (*History of the Ottoman Empire until 1656*) (Bucharest, 1978), p. 220.

27 I used a well-documented study in this direction, which includes data on the majority of Balkan Jewish communities gathered by Lazăr Rosenbaum, his information originating for the most part from Pierre Belon du Mans, Nicolas de Nicolay, Ogier Ghislain de Busbecq, Gabriel Luetz Baron d'Aramon, Pierre Gilles, Francesco Sansovino, Philip Lonicer, Bartholomew Georgiewicz, Luigi Bassano da Zara and others. See Lazăr Rosebaum, *Călători apuseni în Peninsula Balcanică. Știri despre evrei în prima jumătate a secolului XVI-lea* (*Western Travellers to the Balkan Peninsula. Jewish News from the First Half of the 16th Century*), a work that was left in manuscript and kept in the personal archives of historian Victor Papacostea. We take this opportunity to thank the historian's daughter, Mrs Cornelia Papacostea-Danielopolu, who gave us access to the above-mentioned document. See also Joseph Nehama, *Histoire des Israélites de Salonique*, vol. III (Thessaloniki, 1935).

28 Eskenasy, doc. 38, pp. 30–31.

29 S. Panova, 'The Jewish Population of the City of Sofia (during the XVIIth century)', *Annual*, XV (Sofia, 1980), p. 45; see also C. Cabalov, H. Duda, *Die Protokollbudier des Kadiumtes* (Sofia and Munich, 1960), and Eskenasy, p. 31, note 2.

30 Eskenasy, doc. 42, pp. 34–5.

31 For detailed information on the social, economic and cultural life of Balkan communities, besides the sources already cited we should also mention J. S. Emanuel, *Histoire des Israélites de Salonique* (Paris, 1936), and Israel M. Goldman, *The Life and Times of Rabbi David Ibn Abi Simra. A Social-Economic and Cultural Study of Jewish Life in the Ottoman Empire in the 15th and 16th Centuries as Reflected in the Response of the RDBZ* (New York, 1970).

32 Eskenasy, doc. 41, p. 33.

33 Ibid., doc. 43, p. 35.

34 Ibid., doc. 39, p. 32.

35 Ibid., doc. 48, pp. 39–40.

36 Andrei Pippidi, *Hommes et idées du Sud-Est européen à l'aube de l'âge moderne* (Bucharest and Paris, 1980), pp. 41 and 261–2; on the documentary value of the studies included in this volume I expressed my opinion in an article in *Vatra* magazine (Târgu-Mureș), no. 2 (1984), p. 155.

37 Eskenasy, doc. 50, p. 41.

38 Ibid., doc. 51, pp. 41–2.

39 Ibid., doc. 55, p. 43.

40 Ibid., doc. 17, p. 17.

41 Ibid., docs 19, 20, 21, 29, pp. 18–19 and 25; on the commercial relations of Transylvania with the Balkan-Levantine world, as well as extra data on the movements of Jewish merchants, see the studies of Samuel Goldenberg (former Professor of Byzantine Studies and Universal Medieval History at the Babeș-Bolyai University of Cluj, presently living in Canada, from whose courses, information and methodology I benefited during and after my university studies),'Der Südhandel in den Zollrechnungen von Sibiu (Hermannstadt) im 16. Jahrhundert', in *Revue des Etudes Sud-Est Européennes* (RESEE), II, nos. 3–4 (1964),

and 'Le commerce balcano-levantin de la Transylvanie au cours de la seconde moitié du XVIe siècle' (in collaboration with M. Dan), in RESEE, V, nos. 1–2 (1967).

42 Spielmann, doc. IV, p. 185, and doc. VII, pp. 187–8.

43 Ibid., doc. XIX, p. 195; for the situation of the Jews in Constantinople, see Robert Mantran, *La vie quotidienne sous Soliman le Magnifique et ses successeurs* (Paris, 1970).

44 Eskenasy, p. 36, note 2; see also doc. 44, p. 36, which includes the report compiled by imperial agent Belsius for Maximilian of Hapsburg, mentioning Juan Miguez (Josef Nassi).

45 Ibid., doc. 76, p. 52.

46 Ibid., doc. 101, p. 76.

47 Ibid., doc. 118, p. 89.

48 Regarding the question of the British Jews in the sixteenth and especially the seventeenth century, see Antonia Fraser, *Cromwell, Our Chief of Men* (London, 1973).

49 *Monumenta Hungariae Judaica/Magyar Zsidó Óklevéltár*, VII, pp. 259–60, reproduced in Romanian translation by Eskenasy, doc. 119, pp. 89–91.

50 Neumann, 'Tentaţia lui Homo Europaeus. Geneza spiritului modern în Europa central-estică' ('The Temptation of Homo Europaeus. The Genesis of the Modern Spirit in Central-Eastern Europe'), in *Românii în istoria universală* (*Romanians in World History*), coordinated by G. Buzatu, V. Cristian, I. Agrigoroaiei, I (Iaşi, 1986), II (1987).

51 *Monumenta Hungariae Judaica/Magyar Zsidó Óklevéltár*, XVIII, docs 92 and 93, p. 74; the first is also reproduced in Eskenasy, doc. 137, p. 100.

52 Eskenasy, doc. 159, p. 116.

53 *Monumenta Hungariae Judaica/Magyar Zsidó Óklevéltár*, XVIII, doc. 78, pp. 62–5; see also the statistics given in the same volume, p. 19.

54 See Izsák Schulhof, *Budai kronika* (*Buda City Chronicle*) (Budapest, 1979).

55 Pierre Belon du Mans, *Les observations de plusieurs singularités et choses mémorables trouvées en Grèce, Asie, Judée, Arabie et autres pays étrangers en trois livres par...* (Paris, 1586), pp. 180–81, in which the author shows two important directions of Jewish migration, from Spain and Portugal and then from Germany, prompting their growth in numbers in Southeastern Europe; see also Braudel, *La Méditerranée*; d'Aramon, *Le voyage de Monsieur d'Aramon ambassadeur pour le Roy en Levant. Ecrit par noble homme Jean Chesneau...* (Paris, 1887), p. 31; Rosenbaum, *op. cit.*

56 Elias Canetti, *Die gerettete Zunge. Geschichte einer Jugend* (Munich, 1977), trans. E. Viorel (Cluj, 1984).

57 A situation similar to that of the Armenians was created. I should add that following the great Cossack persecutions under the leadership of Hetman Bogdan, Ukrainian and Polish Jews were looking for a haven in the south of Poland and in Moldavia. Beyond this, the Jews' own troubles led them to attempts to find better, less humiliating living conditions. The migration to Moldavia continued throughout the century, so that during the next century the Jews came to be considered subject to the Raia; see Neumann, 'Evreii ţările române în secolele al XVI-lea şi al XlX-lea' ('Jews of the Romanian Lands in the 16th and 19th Centuries'), in *Equinox*, no. 10–12 (Cluj, 1982); Iorga, 'Documente istorice relative la Petru Şchiopul şi Mihai Viteazul' ('Historical Documents related to Petru Şchiopul and Mihai Viteazul'), in *Analele Academiei Române. Memoriile secţiei istorice* (*Annals of the Romanian Academy of Sciences. Memoirs of the Historical Division*) (Bucharest, 1898), II, t. XX, pp. 1–4.

58 See Paul Petrescu, 'Istorie şi simbolistică în arta populară a evreilor din România' ('History and Symbolism in Romanian Jewish Folk Art'), *Secolul XX* (*20th Century Magazine*) 282–3 (1984), pp. 117–29. His

research is among the most important on Romanian historiography, and displays a firm grasp of the role of the Jewish communities in Wallachia and Moldavia.

59 Spielmann, doc. XXXVI, p. 210.

60 Eskenasy, doc. 144, pp. 104–5.

61 Ibid., doc. 146, note 10, p. 109.

62 Ibid., pp. 107–8.

63 Ibid., doc. 142, p. 103.

64 M. A. Halevy, *Comunitățile evreilor din Iași și București până la 1821* (*The Jewish Communities of Iași and Bucharest until 1821*) (Bucharest, 1931), p. 16.

65 See, for example, Spielmann, doc. LXXIII, pp. 232–3.

66 This information was supplied by historian Andrei Pippidi, whom I would like to thank here again.

67 See Spielmann, doc. LIV, pp. 220–21; on the personality and activites of Daniel de Fonseca, and his meeting with Nicholas Mavrocordatos, see Pippidi, *Hommes et idées*, pp. 237–52; the patent of the French ambassador to Constantinople, Jean-Louis d'Usson (Marquis of Bonnac) was edited by E. Hurmuzachi, *Documente privitoare la istoria românilor* (*Documents on the History of Romanians*) (Bucharest, 1887–1913), V, p. 444, reproduced by M. A. Halevy, *Médecins juifs d'origine hispano-portugaise dans les Pays Roumains* (Paris, 1957); see also Spielmann, pp. 33–4, and relevant notes, based on archive studies.

68 Pippidi, *Hommes et idées*.

69 David Jacoby, 'Les juifs à Venise du XIVe au milieu du XVIe siècle', in *Venezia – centro di mediazione tra Oriente e Occidente (secoli XV–XVI). Aspetti I problemi* (Florence, 1977), pp. 163–216.

70 Toma Popović, 'Dubrovnik i Ankona u Jevrejskoj trgovini XVI veka' ('Dubrovnik and Ancona in Jewish Trade of the 16th Century'), in *Zbornik*, I, *Studije i grada ojevrejima Dubrovnika* (*Studies and Structures of the Jews of Dubrovnik*) (Belgrade, 1971),

pp. 41–54. Based on research of the documents, the author specifies the nature of the exchange of products carried out by Jewish companies: 'Jewish merchants exported from the Balkan market through Dubrovnik to Ancona the products of the textile and leather industry, including rasa (a kind of thick woollen cloth), mohair, ginger, carpets, oat-bags, coverlets, horsecloths and all kinds of tanned hides. In the traffic of these products they competed successfully with the merchants of Dubrovnik.'

71 Radovan Samardžić, 'Dubrovački jevreji u trgovini XVI i XVII veka' (The Jews of Dubrovnik in the Trade of the 16th and 17th Centuries), in *Zbornik*, I, pp. 21–39; on the social, economic and cultural life of the Jews in Dubrovnik, see Jorjo Tadić, *The Jews of Dubrovnik until the Middle of the 17th Century* (Sarajevo, 1937).

72 See the set of papers, namely the passports of Jews (eighteenth century) discovered and published by B. M. Nedeljković and in idem, 'Putne isprave Dubrovačkih jevreja' ('Passports of the Jews of Dubrovnik'), in *Zbornik* magazine, I, pp. 128–33.

73 Eventov, pp. 12–18.

74 See Jorjo Tadić, 'Aran Koem' ('Aaron Cohen'), in *Zbornik* magazine, I, pp. 313–22.

75 The new Kabbalah became known as Safed. Its masters were Moses ben Jacob Cordovero and Isaac Luria. The former produced a considerable body of work, including a personal interpretation of the Kabbalah and, in particular, of the Zohar.

76 Dubnov, vol. VII (1947), p. 14.

77 Eventov, pp. 29–31; the founding of a community in Sarajevo dates back to 1565.

78 Ibid.

79 Gustav Meyrink, *Der Golem* (Leipzig, 1915; Romanian translation, Bucharest, 1989).

80 Mircea Eliade, *Istoria credințelor și ideilor religioase*, vol. III (Bucharest, 1986), p. 181. (English translation: *A History of Religious*

Ideas, trans. Willard R. Trask (Chicago, 1978–85).)

81 Michel Vital le Bossé, foreword to Michel Achard, Aux frontières de l'au-delà... Le Golem, l'initiation au Ghetto (Caen, 1986), p. 9.

82 Ibid.

83 Achard.

84 See Eliade; Vital le Bossé.

85 Jorge Luis Borges, Cărțile și noaptea (Iași, 1988), p. 25. (English translation: Borges at Eighty: Conversations, ed. and with photographs by Willis Barnstone (Bloomington, 1982).)

86 Neumann, 'Reforma religioasă și criza de conștiință. De la Theophil Corudaleu la Dimitrie Cantemir' ('Religious Reform and the Crisis of Conscience. From Theophilos Corydalleus to Dimitrie Cantemir'), in Românii în istoria universală; see also chapter III of the present volume.

87 Spielmann, doc. V, pp. 185–6.

88 Olahus came into contact with Elias Levi in Transylvania, as mentioned in S. Kohn, Die Sabbatharier in Siebenbürgen (Budapest and Liepzig, 1894), p. 16. See also Spielmann, p. 186, note 4.

89 Valeriu Marcu, Die Vertreibung der Juden aus Spanien (Amsterdam, 1934), p. 49.

90 Neumann, 'Reforma religioasă'.

91 Moses Mendelssohn, Jerusalem oder über religiöse Macht und Judenthum (Frankfurt and Liepzig, 1787).

92 Immanuel Kant, Werke (Leipzig, 1842), band IX, p. 17; in Romanian see the micro-monograph by Lazăr Sain (Șăineanu), Moise Mendelssohn. Viața și activitatea sa. Studiu bibliografic (Moses Mendelssohn. His Life and Activity. Bibliographical Research) (Bucharest, 1880).

93 Monumenta Hungariae Judaica/Magyar Országos Levéltár, Budapest (National Hungarian Archives). Levéltári leltárok. Zsidó összeirások és a zsidókon vonatkozo egyeb iratok (Conscriptio Judaeorum) (Archival Inventories.

Jewish Census and Other Documents Related to Jews (Conscriptio Judaeorum)), 1725–67. E. 303, 13 csomó (packet 13).

94 Spielmann, doc. MCX, pp. 92–6.

95 Monumenta Hungariae Judaica/Magyar Országos Levéltár, vol. XVIII (Budapest, 1980), docs 544–55, pp. 236–45.

96 Spielmann, doc. LVII, p. 40.

97 The article shows that Jews were granted the freedom to trade across all Transylvanian territory and to live as tenants, on condition that they caused no harm to the towns or the established state. This article formed the basis of the juridical state of Jews in Transylvania during the eighteenth and nineteenth centuries.

98 Spielmann, doc. LIV, pp. 37–8.

99 Jenő Szentkláray, Száz év Magyarország újabb történelméböl (One Hundred Years of Hungary's Newest Spirit) (Timișoara, 1879), p. 144.

100 Lajos Kakucs, 'Dezvoltarea economică a Banatului în secolele XVIII–XIX' ('The Economic Development of the Banat Region in the 18th–19th Centuries') (doctoral thesis, Cluj, 1984), information received from the author during an academic presentation in Timișoara, 1984.

101 Szentkláray, Mercy kormányzata a Temesi Bánságban (Mercy's Government in the Banat of Timișoara) (Budapest, 1909), pp. 109–12.

102 See above. I have also taken up some aspects of this question in my book Convergențe spirituale (Spiritual Convergences) (Bucharest, 1986).

103 Spielmann, doc. CIII, pp. 87–8.

104 Ibid., doc. C, p. 83.

105 Ibid., doc. XCI, pp. 72–3; doc. XCVI, pp. 76–8; see Monumenta Hungariae Judaica, vol. XVII (Budapest, 1977), doc. 290, p. 207.

106 Monumenta Hungariae Judaica/Magyar Országos Levéltár, vol. XVII, pp. 207–26.

107 According to the decision of the Vienna Aulic Chamber, taken on 6 June 1735, the Transylvanian government asks for all counties to report the situation of Bulgarians, Armenians, Greeks and Jews up to 1 September 1735; see Spielmann, p. 72, note 1.

108 Spielmann, doc. XC, pp. 68–72.

109 *Magyar Országos Levéltár* (*Hungarian National Archives*), E. 303, 13 csomó (packet 13), pp. 7–12; 13–19; 20–23; 26–8; 34–9.

110 Lajos Baroti, *Adattár Délmagyarország XVIII századi történetéhez* (*Directory of 18th-Century Southern Hungarian History*) (Timișoara, 1893). See also László Marianucz, 'Administration, Colonization and Culture' in Neumann (ed.), *The Banat of Timișoara. A European Melting Pot* (London, 2019), pp. 77–103.

111 *Magyar Országos Levéltár*, E. 303, 13 csomó (packet 13), pp. 13–19.

112 I discovered one of these documents, addressed to Caraș County, in the archives of the Metropolitanate of Banat in Timișoara, doc. 51, Oradea collection. I have seen an identical resolution in the collection of the Cluj branch of the Romanian Academy Library. They were brought to my attention by my colleague Mihai Alin Gherman, for which I thank him. The resolution we are referring to was printed by Scheiber Sandor (Alexander Scheiber) in *Monumenta Hungariae Judaica/ Magyar Zsidó Óklevéltár*, vol. XVIII (Budapest, 1980), pp. 347–53.

113 Ibid.

114 Neumann, 'Les corridors culturels en Europe Orientale-Centrale. Livres et bibliothèques en Transylvanie à l'époque des Lumières', *Cahiers roumains d'études litteraires*, no. 4 (1988).

115 Spielmann, doc. CCIV, pp. 165–70; for the Buda publishing house and the Hebrew books printed there see 'Index Librorum Selectorum in Typographia UHB 1777–1848 Impressorum', in the volume *Typographia Universitatis Hungaricae Budae 1777–1848*, ed. Péter Király (Budapest, 1983), pp. 482–3.

116 I discovered such a document in the Cluj branch of the Romanian Academy Library; it comes from a collection whose inventory has not been compiled.

117 *Encyclopedia Judaica*, vol. XV (1978), p. 1342.

118 *Opinio de Judaesis*, file A.

119 Ibid., file B.

120 Karl Gottlieb von Windisch, *Geographie des Königreichs Ungarn* (Pressburg, 1780), vol. II, pp. 136–56.

121 Johann von Csaplovics, *Topographische statistisches Archiv des Königreichs Ungarn* (1821), vol. I, p. 401: see Tiberiu Morariu, 'Câteva contribuții la oieritul evreilor maramureșeni' ('Some Contributions to the Sheep Herding of the Maramureș Jews'), in *Lucrările Institutului de Geografie al Universității din Cluj* (*Papers of the Institute of Geography of the University of Cluj*), vol. IV, 1928–9 (Cluj, 1931), pp. 183–203.

122 Radu V. Meruțiu, 'Regiunea Baia-Mare – Baia Sprie. Istoricul chestiunii, Bibliografie' ('The Baia-Mare – Baia Sprie Region. History of the Subject. Bibliography'), in *Lucrările Institutului de geografie al Universității din Cluj*, vol. VI (Cluj, 1938), pp. 71–146.

123 A woman convicted of uttering incantations was burned at the stake in 1650, a year which saw four executions in the town. False oaths carried heavy sentences, such as the cutting out of the tongue or fines of up to 100 florins. Anyone who spoke critically or inappropriately to the town magistrate was also severely punished. A dishonest family life could be punished by death; see Meruțiu, *op. cit.*, p. 93.

124 Braudel, *La Méditerranée*, vol. IV, p. 182.

125 Morariu, p. 197. During the 1930s the author undertook a systematic programme of research, his information being correct with regard to the shepherds' flocks, their number and placement, as well as the types of activity in which shepherds were engaged. I have only used the positive data of the study, since his interpretation shows how Judaism can be misunderstood when it is viewed from the outside. The opposite extreme also does no service to the objective understanding of the subject.

126 Petrescu, p. 122.

127 This was the term used in the documents of the imperial Hapsburg administration to designate the place where Jews had the right to settle after having paid their taxes, after a thorough check by the officials. These documents were kept in the archives of the prefectures of free royal towns in the Banat and Transylvania, for example, the archives of the Timișoara prefecture, in the city's State Archives.

Chapter V

1 In this chapter I have made use of work already published in my book *Convergențe spirituale* (*Spiritual Convergences*), pp. 16–103, where necessary expanding my arguments by bringing into discussion books to which I have had access more recently.

2 Pierre Chaunu, *Civilizația Europei în secolul Luminilor*, trans. and foreword by Irina Mavrodin, vol. I (Bucharest, 1986), p. 247. (Originally *La Civilisation de l'Europe des Lumières* (Paris, 1971).)

3 Prodan, p. 191.

4 Nicolae Bocșan, *Contribuții la istoria Iluminismului românesc* (*Contributions to the History of the Romanian Enlightenment*) (Timișoara, 1986), p. 83. Bocșan rightly argues that the barring of noblemen with immunity from settling in the region was due to the special juridical status of Banat as a domain of the crown, the Chamber being in this case the main landowner. Only workers in the local administration or senior military officers attained noble status, and they were few in number. In Banat, unlike other regions, this class represented not an obstacle, but an instrument that was easily handled by Hapsburg politicians.

5 Frederick II, *Scrisori despre dragostea de patrie sau corespondența dintre Anapistemon și Philopatros* (*Letters on Love of Country, or the Correspondence between Anapistemon and Philopatros*), 1779, in Paul Hazard, *Gândirea europeană în secolul al XVIII-lea* (Bucharest, 1981), p. 437. (English translation: *European Thought in the Eighteenth Century*, trans. J. Lewis May (Harmondsworth, 1965).)

6 Iorga, *Etudes roumaines. Idées et formes littéraires françaises dans le Sud-Est de l'Europe* (Paris, 1924), pp. 29–43, 87–100.

7 Cassirer, *La Philosophie des Lumières* (Paris, 1970), p. 207.

8 Prodan, 'Transilvania sub regimul absolutismului luminat' ('Transylvania under Enlightened Absolutism'), in *Istoria României* (*Romanian History*), vol. III (Bucharest, 1964), pp. 731, 740.

9 Neumann, 'Reflecții proprii și repere apusene în gândirea istorică luministă a centrului și sud-estului european' ('Reflections on Western Landmarks in the Historical Thinking of Central and Southeastern Europe'), in *Convergențe spirituale*, pp. 18–19.

10 See my comments based on the correspondence between Romanian, Serbian, Hungarian, Russian and Austrian scholars in *Convergențe spirituale*, pp. 71–84.

11 Chaunu, p. 291.

12 Voltaire, *Istoria lui Carol al XII-lea*, trans. N. Roșca, in Voltaire, *Opere alese*, introductory study by N. N. Condeescu (Bucharest, 1957), pp. 155–235. (French edition: *Histoire de Charles XII*, preface by Yves Lemoine (Paris, 2002).)

13 Ibid., p. 217.

14 Idem, *Essai sur l'histoire générale et sur les mœurs et l'esprit des nations, depuis Charlemagne jusqu'à nos jours*, tome IV (Paris, 1756), pp. 276–80.

15 Ibid., p. 279.

16 Montesquieu, *Despre spiritul legilor*, trans. Armand Rosu, vol. II (Bucharest, 1970), p. 195. (English translation: *The Spirit of the Laws*, trans. Anne M. Cohler, Basia C. Miller, Harold Stone (Cambridge, 1989).)

17 Romul Munteanu, *Cultura europeană în Epoca Luminilor* (*European Culture in the Age of Enlightenment*) (Bucharest, 1981), p. 50.

18 Dominique Bourel, *Qu'est-ce que les Lumières?* (Paris, 1978), p. 13.

19 See Emmanuel Levinas, preface to *Jerusalem, ou pouvoir religieux et judaïsme*, ed. Dominique Bourel (Paris, 1982), pp. 19–20.

20 Idem, *Totalité et infini* (The Hague, 1961).

21 Friedrich Schlegel, *Werke* (Berlin, 1980).

22 Neumann, *Convergențe spirituale*, pp. 33–4, notes 13 and 22, as well as the entire chapter dedicated to scholar and historian Stefan Stratimirović.

23 On the Czech and Slovak reception of Schlözer's work, see J. Delansky, 'Die tschechische Slawistik des 18. Jahrhunderte und Schlözer', in E. Winter, *Lomonosov, Schlözer, Pallas. Deutsch-russische Wissenschaftsbeziehungen im 18. Jahrhundert* (Berlin, 1962); see Iosif Wolf, 'Repere europene în istoriografia Școlii Ardelene' ('European Landmarks in the Historiography of the Transylvanian School'), in *Stat. Societate. Națiune. Interpretări istorice* (*State. Society. Nation. Historical Interpretations*), ed. Nicolae Edroiu, Aurel Răduțiu and Pompiliu Teodor (Cluj, 1982), p. 281.

24 A. Camariano-Cioran, *Academiile domnești din București și Iași* (*The Royal Academies of Bucharest and Iași*) (Bucharest, 1971),

pp. 85–104; idem, *Les Académies princières de Bucarest et Jassy* (Thessaloniki, 1974).

25 On Engel's role as a mediator between German historiography and that of the Southeast, especially between Schlözer and Stratimirović, see also Neumann, *Convergențe spirituale*, pp. 71–83, where I demonstrated the importance of this relationship using correspondence discovered in the SANU Archive in Belgrade and in the manuscript section of the Széchenyi Library in Budapest.

26 For the state of Hungarian historiography during this time, see H. Balázs, 'A magyar jozefinisták külföldi kapcsolataihoz. Schlözer és magyar tanitványai' ('Foreign Relations of the Hungarian Jozsefinists. Schlözer and his Hungarian Followers'), in *Századok* (*Centuries*), no. 3, 97, (Budapest, 1963), pp. 1187–1204; see also Kosáry pp. 126–9.

27 Immanuel Kant, *Werkausgabe*, ed. W. Weischedel, vol. XI (Berlin, 1978).

28 Johann Gottfried Herder, *Scrieri* (*Writings*), trans. and foreword by Cristina Petrescu (Bucharest, 1973), p. 181. (English translation: *Philosophical Writings*, ed. Desmond M. Clarke and Michael N. Forster (Cambridge, 2007).)

29 Ibid.

30 Idem, *Scrisori* (*Letters*), trans. and notes by Cristina Petrescu (Bucharest, 1981), p. 10. (English translation: Clarke and Forster.)

31 In the *Scienza nuova*, which Jules Michelet translated into French the same year Edgar Quinet published the first French translation of Herder's work, *Ideen zur Geschichte der Philosophie der Menschheit*.

32 Edgar Quinet, introduction to J. G. Herder, *Idées sur la philosophie de l'histoire de l'humanité* (Paris, 1834).

33 Andrei Pippidi, *Hommes et idées*, p. 10.

34 Alberto Fortis, *Viaggio in Dalmazia* (Venice, 1774).

35 Herder, *Scrieri*, p. 167.

36 István Széchényi, *Közjóra való törekedések* (*The Pursuit of the Common Good*) (Budapest, 1981).

37 C. T. Dimaras, *Neoellinikos diafotismos* (*The Modern Greek Enlightenment*) (Athens, 1977).

38 Paul Cornea, 'Pașoptismul și cultura germană' ('German Culture in the Time of the 1848 Revolution'), in *Revista de istorie și teorie literară*, nos. 3 and 4 (1984).

39 Iosif Wolf, 'Die rumänische Herderrezepzion im Vormärz und Perspektiven', in *Cahiers roumains d'études littéraires*, no. 2 (1979), pp. 44–54.

40 Zoe Dumitrescu-Bușulenga, 'Herder și pașoptiștii români' ('Herder and the 1848 Romanian Intellectuals'), in *Valori și echivalențe umanistice* (*Values and Humanistic Equivalences*) (Bucharest, 1973), pp. 21–7.

41 Neumann, *Convergențe spirituale*, pp. 177–207.

42 Victor Morariu, 'Herder despre români' ('Herder on the Romanians'), in *Făt-Frumos*, XII, nos. 9–12 (1937), pp. 188–91.

43 Cristina Petrescu, foreword to Herder, *Scrisori*, p. 30.

44 Paul Cornea, 'Pașoptismul', vol. II, p. 59; for the general reception of the *Aufklärung*, see also Emanuel Turczynski, *Von der Aufklärung zum Frühliberalismus. Politische Tragergruppen und derren Förderungskatalog in Rumänien* (Munich, 1985).

45 Alexandru Duțu, 'La place de l'humanisme roumain dans l'histoire culturelle européenne', in *Cahiers roumains d'études littéraires 3* (1974), p. 8.

46 See his correspondence of 1794–5 in Judit Benda Kalman-Elek, *Vizsgálat Martinovits Ignác szászvári apát és társai ügyében* (*Investigation into the Case of Abbot Ignác Martinovits and His Associates*) (Budapest, 1983).

47 See especially his correspondence with József Hajnoczi, one of the leaders of Pest's Jacobin movement, in the Széchenyi National Library, Budapest, MS Quart. Germ. 810.

48 See the studies of G. Platon, E. Negruți and C. Papacostea-Danielopolu in *La Revolution Française et les Roumains*, ed. A. Zub (Iași, 1989).

49 François Furet and Ran Halévi, 'La Revolution Française. L'année 1789', *Annales*, no. 1 (1989), pp. 3–24.

50 Robert Darnton, *L'Aventure de l'Encyclopédie. Un best-seller au siècle des Lumières*, preface by Emmanuel Le Roy Ladurie (Paris, 1982), pp. 401–2.

Chapter VI

1 See 'Despre coridoarele culturale ale Europei de Sud-Est' ('On the Cultural Channels of Southeastern Europe'), in *Memoriile Secției de Științe Istorice* (*Memoirs of the Historical Science Section*), Romanian Academy, series IV, vol. VII (Bucharest, 1982), pp. 7–27.

2 Chaunu, p. 397.

3 For the contacts established by the scholars of Blaj with cultural centres across Europe and the Romanian lands see the map on pp. 98–9, 'East–West Contacts Associated with the Cultural Institutions of the 17th–18th Centuries'.

4 Iacob Mârza, *Școală și națiune* (*Școlile de la Blaj în epoca renașterii naționale*) (*School and Nation* (*Blaj Schools in the Era of National Rebirth*)) (Cluj, 1987), pp. 152–3.

5 Jakó.

6 The printing of this work in Samuil Micu's translation demonstrates the interest of Blaj intellectuals in medieval mysticism.

7 Mârza, p. 155.

8 On these influences and contacts, as well as on personal means of expression employed by writers in the region, see

especially Prodan, *Supplex*, pp. 331–54; an excellent study on similar lines is Iorga's *Etudes roumaines*.

9 See Franco Venturi, 'La première crise de l'ancien régime (1768–1776)', in *Etudes sur le XVIIIe siècle*, VII, ed. Roland Mortier and Hervé Hasquin (Brussels, 1980), p. 19; Chaunu, *op. cit.*, p. 265.

10 Prodan, *Supplex*, pp. 231–41.

11 See 'Praefatio' to *Bibliothecae Samuelis S. R. I. com. Teleki de Szék.* (1796), pp. i–vi.

12 Ibid., p. ix.

13 Ibid., p. xxii.

14 See the excellent chapter 'Reforma în Principatul transilvan și câteva ecouri de Renaștere' ('Reform in the Principality of Transylvania and Some Echoes of the Renaissance') in Theodorescu, *Civilizația românilor*, vol. I., pp. 48–84.

15 'Praefatio', pp. xxvi–xxvii.

16 I have consulted manuscript copies, written in German in Gothic characters specific to the period of the *Frühaufklärung*, that are full of information on the Austrian wars at the end of the seventeenth and the beginning of the eighteenth century, concerning the diplomatic history of European states, with reflections on religion, morality and politics.

17 'Praefatio', pp. xxxv–xxxvi.

18 Jakó, p. 387.

19 Ibid.

20 Prodan, *Supplex*.

21 The Brukenthal operated as a public library from 1817, while that of Teleki opened in a similar way in 1802.

22 The origins of the Kapellenbibliothek collection can be traced to the library of the town of Sibiu, which was founded around 1300, and to which was later added the library of the Dominican Order, abrogated in the sixteenth century by Luther's reforms. In 1592 the old books in Sibiu's collection came

into the possession of the German school, and were moved to the chapel of St Jakob.

23 Adolf Armbruster, *Dacoromano-Saxonica. Cronicari români despre sași. Românii în cronica sasească (Daco-Romano-Saxonica. Romanian Chroniclers on Saxons. Romanians in the Saxon Chronicle)* (Bucharest, 1980), p. 70.

24 See F. A. Eckstein, *Geschichte der Freimaurerloge im Orient von Halle* (Halle, 1844), pp. 2–3, reproduced in Adolf Armbruster, 'Opera culturală a lui Samuel von Brukenthal la Sibiu' ('The Cultural Work of Samuel von Brukenthal in Sibiu'), *Revista de Istorie* 4 (1978), p. 652.

25 Much was written about Brukenthal's character. Transylvanian historiography of the nineteenth and twentieth centuries discussed him repeatedly in a series of monographs. For an up-to-date bibliography and interpretation, see Armbruster, 'Opera culturală', *loc. cit.*

26 Ibid., p. 660.

27 Lucian Blaga, *Gândirea românească în Transilvania în secolul al XVIII-lea* ('Romanian Thinking in Transylvania in the 18th Century') (Bucharest, 1966), p. 208.

28 See Doina Nägler, *Biblioteca Muzeului Brukenthal. Catalogul Transilvanicelor (Brukenthal Museum Library. Catalogue of Transylvanian Books)*, vol. II (Sibiu, 1982), no. 385, p. 113.

29 Ibid., nos. 405–6, pp. 118–19.

30 Ibid., no. 209, p. 65.

31 Ibid., no. 257, p. 78.

32 Ibid., no. 211, p. 66.

33 Prodan, *Răscoala lui Horea (The Revolt of Horea)* (Bucharest, 1979), vol. I, p. 66.

34 Neumann, *Convergențe spirituale*, pp. 45 and 89.

35 See Ioan Budai-Deleanu, *Scrieri inedite (Unpublished Writings)*, ed. I. Pervain (Cluj, 1970), p. 181.

36 Wolf, 'Repere europene', p. 286. The author undertakes an analysis of Schlözer's writings, revealing the use he made of Romanian historiography of the Enlightenment. He also drew considerably on Transylvanian German and Hungarian historiography, and any correct assessment of the scope and perspective of his works at this point must take this into account.

37 See Johann Flistich, *Testamen Historiae Valachicae (Încercare de istorie românească)*, introduction, ed. and notes by Adolf Armbruster, trans. Radu Constantinescu (Bucharest, 1979).

38 The two paintings referred to here are in the Brukenthal Museum art collection.

39 Armbruster, 'Opera culturală', p. 670.

40 The citadel of Alba Iulia, rebuilt by Charles VI, is typical of the constructions erected by the Hapsburgs across Central and Eastern Europe: high red-brick walls, defended by ditches 4 to 5 metres deep, and massive wooden gates, closed by immense iron chains at night, evoking the triumphant entries of conquerors in centuries past.

41 See *Bibliotheca Batthyaneum din Alba-Iulia (The Batthyaneum Library in Alba Iulia)* (Bucharest, 1957).

42 Mârza, 'Un tezaur al culturii europene în biblioteca Batthyaneum din Alba-Iulia' ('A Treasure of European Culture in the Batthyaneum Library in Alba Iulia'), *Secolul XX* 272–4 / 8–10 (1983).

43 *Catalogus incunabulorum Bibliothecae Batthyanianae* (Szeged, 1965).

44 Jakó, p. 385.

45 József Szinnyei, *Magyar írók (Hungarian Writers)*, vol. II (Budapest, 1891), cols 695–7. For the first bibliographical references to the work and personality of Batthyány, see those included in Gábor Döbrentei's periodical *Erdelyi Muzeum (Transylvanian Museum)*, first series, vol. II (1815).

46 Batthyaneum, no. M4 VII-37.

47 Ibid., no. T VII 4.

48 Ibid., no. T VII 7.

49 Ibid., no. M IV 8.

50 Ibid., no. Q2 VII 39.

51 See Szinnyei, cols 1380–81.

52 Batthyaneum, no. N7 VII 5; the work in question is *Lamentationes obscurorum virorum. Epistola D. Erasmi Roterodami, quid de obscuris sentiat, cum caeteris quibusdam, non minus lectu iucundis, quam scitu necessariis* (London, 1688).

53 Ibid., no. G2 VI 17.

54 Chaunu, p. 285.

55 Werner Conze, 'Luthertum und Nationalismus. Deutsch-Protestantismus', in *Luther und Siebenbürgen. Ausstrahlungen von Reformation und Humanismus nach Südosteuropa*, ed. Georg and Renate Weber (Cologne and Vienna, 1985), pp. 145–6.

56 Batthyaneum, no. F II 1.

57 Ibid., no. G2V 9-2.

58 Ibid., no. G III 21.

59 Ibid., no. A2 IX 1.

60 Ibid., no. G III 20.

61 Ibid., no. E2 VI 18.

62 Ibid., no. X 17. The book is entitled *Kis-Katekizmusa (Small Catechism)* and was published in Braşov in 1748. It bears the notes *Ex libris Michaelis Buriani 1797* and, in Romanian, *Această cărticică e a lui Lutar Marton* [This book is by Martin Luther]. It is a Hungarian translation of the German edition, belonging to J. Honterus, *Der kleine Katechismus. Fur die Pfarrherr und Hausvater* (Braşov, 1548).

63 Ibid., no. C2 VII 4.

64 See Iorga, *Pagini alese (Selected Pages)*, ed. M. Berza (Bucharest, 1965), pp. 310–19.

65 Georges Blond, *Furioşii domnului (The Lord's Wrath)*, trans. Dumitru Almas (Bucharest, 1976).

66 See Bernard Fay, *La Franc-Maçonnerie et la révolution intellectuelle du XVIIIe siècle* (Paris, 1935), pp. 144–60.

67 Batthyaneum, no. XIII 33.

68 Ibid., no. X2 V13. The book arrived in Transylvania in the first decades of the nineteenth century and includes an *Ex libris Bibliothecae Fogarassyanae*, meaning that it joined the Batthyaneum collection fairly late.

69 Olahus, *Hungaria et Attila* (Vienna, 1762), pp. 60–70.

70 Batthyaneum, no. Q2 VII 36. *Rudimentorum cosmographicorum Ioan. Honteri Coronensis libri III. cum tabellis Geographicis elegantissimis. De variarum rerum nomenclaturis per classe*, book I (Zürich, 1548).

71 Nussbächer, 'Lucrările lui Johannes Honterus' ('The Works of Johannes Honterus') in Hans Barth (ed.), *Von Honterus zu Oberth. Beteutende siebenbürgisch-deutsche Naturwissenschaftler, Techniker und Mediziner* (Bucharest, 1984).

72 Batthyaneum, no. G3 VIII 10.

73 George Togan, *Manuscriptum*, no. 3 (1985), p. 107.

74 Batthyaneum, no. XIII-10. It is an edition from 1504 with no indication of where it was published; however, a note (probably from the seventeenth century) shows that it was bought in Košice by a certain Georgii Chohut.

75 Prodan, *Supplex*, p. 305.

76 See Mârza, 'La circulation de l'œuvre de Voltaire en Transylvanie au XVIIIe siècle', *Synthesis* V (1978), pp. 149–62.

77 His collection is documented in *Catalogus librorum variarum linguarum… qui venales iusto prostant pretio* (Sibiu, 1779).

78 Mârza, 'La circulation', p. 154.

79 Cassirer, *La Philosophie*, pp. 209–37.

80 Batthyaneum, nos. K 886 and H7 I 36.

81 Prodan, *Supplex*, note 15, p. 426.

82 J.-J. Rousseau, *Du contrat social ou principes du droit politique* (Rouen, 1792), p. 260.

83 Chaunu, p. 281.

84 Batthyaneum, no. U 2 VI 8.

85 Jakó, p. 393; for a useful history of the Bethlen School Aiud library during its first period (1622–58), see ibid., pp. 128–46.

86 Biblioteca documentară Bethlen-Aiud (now operating as a section of the Cluj Central University Library, which can only be accessed for historical and philological research), nos. 196, 550 and 33.

87 Ibid., no. 195, p. 60; he was born in Kőrös (Chiuruș), Harghita County, in 1784 and died in Darjeeling in 1842.

88 Sámuel Gyármáti (1751–1830), a doctor and linguist, prepared a doctoral thesis in Göttingen in 1796–8 entitled 'Principiul comparat al limbilor fino-ugrice' ('The Comparative Principle of the Finno-Ugric Languages').

89 This information was supplied by Cluj researcher Ioan-Viorel Bădică, for which I am greatly indebted to him.

90 N. Cartojan, *Istoria literaturii române vechi* (*The History of Old Romanian Literature*), afterword and bibliographies by Dan Simionescu, foreword by Dan Zamfirescu (Bucharest, 1980), p. 186.

91 Biblioteca documentară Bethlen-Aiud, no. 7269.

92 Ibid., no. 2968 C IV.

93 Ibid., no. 573 110.

94 Ibid., no. 822 1959.

95 Ibid., no. 53 (Hungarica collection). Michael Tsomós was a professor of law at the Reformed college of Cluj.

96 Ibid., no. 2968 C XIII. Its place of publication is not mentioned, but was probably Cluj, where the Reformed college possessed an excellent modern printing press which had been donated by the person in whose

memory the volume was written, Miklós Misztótfalusi Kis.

97 Ibid., no. 978.

98 See Andrei Brezianu, 'Excurs printr-o cetate a cărţii' ('Excursion through a Book City'), Secolul XX 272, 273, 274 (1983).

99 Jakó, pp. 394–5.

100 G. Henk van der Graaf, A Németalföldi akadémiák és az erdély protestantizmus a XVIII században 1690–1795 (The Dutch Academies and Transylvanian Protestantism in the 18th Century 1690–1795) (Cluj, 1979), pp. 223, 225–6.

101 Jakó, pp. 395–6.

102 Biblioteca Muzeului Judeţean din Deva (Library of the County Museum in Deva), no. 6153.

103 See Catalogum hunc Bibliothecae Conventus Maria Radnensis occasione Visitationes Generalis die 13 a Juii a. 1909 asservatae, revisum, subscripsit. Adm. Rev. P. Isidorus Ozonai-Commisarius Visitator Glis., kept in the archives of the Roman Catholic Church in Radna.

104 From Bibliotheca Conventus Radnensis.

105 See Iacob Radu, Manuscriptele bibliotecii episcopiei greco-catolice romîne din Oradea Mare. Studiu bibliografic (Manuscripts of the Greek Catholic Episcopal Library in Oradea Mare. Bibliographical Study) (Bucharest, 1923), p. 2.

106 See the Romanian publications of Buda in this period in 'Index Librorum Selectorum In Typographia Universitatis Hungaricae Budae 1777–1848 Impressorum', in Péter Király, Typographia Universitatis Hungaricae Budae 1777–1848 (Budapest, 1983), pp. 488–90.

107 See the next chapter.

108 Bocşan, p. 164.

109 Ion B. Mureşianu, Cartea veche bisericească din Banat (Old Religious Books in Banat) (Timişoara, 1985); E. R. Colta, 'Circulaţia tipăriturilor râmnicene pe teritoriul judeţului Arad' ('Circulation of Published

Romanian Works in Arad County'), in Valori bibliofile din patrimoniul cultural-naţional (Bibliophile Values in the National Cultural Heritage) (Râmnicu Vâlcea, 1980).

110 Constantin Diaconovici Loga, preface to Chiemare al tipărirea cărţilor româneşti (Call for the Printing of Romanian Books) (Buda, 1821).

111 I. D. Suciu and R. Constantinescu, Documente privitoare la istoria Mitropoliei Banatului (Documents regarding the History of the Orthodox Metropolis of Banat) (Timişoara, 1980), vol. I, doc. 303, pp. 605–7.

112 Ibid., doc. 302, pp. 605–6.

113 Bocşan, pp. 193–6.

114 Neumann, 'Principii iluministe şi diferenţialism etnocultural. Opera cărturarului Ştefan Stratimirović – mitropolit al ortodocşilor din Imperiul Habsburgic' ('Enlightenment Principles and Ethnocultural Differentialism. The Work of Scholar Stefan Stratimirović – Metropolitan of the Orthodox Church from the Hapsburg Empire'), in idem (ed.), Identitate şi Cultură. Studii privind istoria Banatului (Identity and Culture. Studies on the History of Banat) (Bucharest, 2009), pp. 38–48. See also idem, Convergenţe spirituale, pp. 33–4, notes 13 and 22, as well as the entire chapter dedicated to scholar and historian Stefan Stratimirović.

115 Suciu and Constantinescu, doc. 74, pp. 151–2; for factual information on the history of Serbian libraries during the Enlightenment, I have referred to the descriptions, based on sources, given by Bogoljub C. Cirković in Biblioteka Srpske pravoslavne crkve (Libraries of the Serbian Orthodox Church) (Belgrade, 1970).

116 Suciu and Constantinescu, doc. 79, p. 156. It is the Count Ladislau Nádasdy mentioned in Latin document no. 82, reproduced on pp. 161–3, and not Dimitrie Nádasdy, who appears in the first summary.

117 Neumann, 'Principii iluministe', pp. 41–2, 44–6.

118 Following the death of Stratimirović the collection grew slowly. This situation was exacerbated by the fact that the books of Patriarch Iosif Rajačić failed to reach the central collection, wandering between the many personal libraries of his nephews. See Cirković, p. 413.

119 See Dositej Obradović, *Soveti zdra voga razuma... (To Advise Common Sense...)* (1806), *Sobranije raznih vravoucitelnih vescej... (Meetings of Various Nature-Friendly Festivities...)* (1808), *Izbranne basne... (Selected Fables...)* (1810), *Mezimac (Minion)* (1818), *Hrestomatija (Chrestomathy)* (1826) and *Pisma (Letters)* (1829).

120 Andrija B. Stojković, *Filosofski pogledi Dositeja Obradović (Philosophical Views of Dositej Obradović)* (Belgrade, 1980), p. 314.

121 Chaunu, p. 281; see also Kosáry, pp. 37–8.

122 This sketch of the domain and the park can be found in Sándor Eckhardt, *Az Aradi közművelődesi palota francia könyvei (French Books in the Arad City Public Education House)* (Arad, 1917), p. 17.

123 Sándor Eckhardt (*op. cit.*) has reconstructed the fate of the collection, based on the Csáky family correspondence and documents in the Illésfalu Archives of the National Museum in Budapest.

124 Eckhardt, *op. cit.*, pp. 7–10.

125 Arad County Library, patrimony collection, no. 9990. The *ex libris* of Csáky is dated 1764 and is followed by the stamp of the Atzel family, indicating where Péter Atzel lived: Ineu.

126 Ibid., nos. 36.705, 36.835, 36.879, 10.442, 34.513, 36.609, 5.686, 34.351, 12.467, 34.387 (see also 132.218, 132.219) and 13.997

127 Ibid., no. 13997. A periodical that refers directly to the 1789 revolution (cited in the text with the title *Révolutions de Paris*) bears a note dated 1799, *Pestini a Kilian*, which indicates that there was rapid circulation of information in this time of great interest in political events, and proves that the intellectuals and bourgeoisie of Hungary accepted the new European ideas. This put the conservative nobility on high alert.

128 Prodan, *Supplex*, p. 307. See also the contributions of László Sziklay, Éva Balázs and Kálmán Benda in *Les Lumières en Hongrie, en Europe Centrale et en Europe Orientale* (Budapest, 1971).

129 See Éva Balázs' study in *Les Lumières en Europe Centrale...*, vol. II (Budapest, 1975), pp. 23–8.

130 See the copy of this letter, dated 25 August 1802, in the archives of the Serbian Academy of Sciences and Arts in Sremski Karlovci (ASANUK), Collection M.P. 'A', no. 169 1802; see also Neumann, *Convergențe spirituale*, pp. 78–82.

131 A copy of this *Index* came into the possession of Alexandru Papiu Ilarian: see the note on the title page of the copy now in the Romanian Academy Library, no. II 438620: *Ex libris A. Papiu Ilariani.*

132 Buda University Library initially acquired books and textbooks for theological and philosophical studies. Later, after the departments of Law and Medicine were founded and the monastic orders were abolished, scientific literature became its primary focus. Continually enriched by donations, in the eighteenth century the library received significant funds for the annual purchase of all the most important periodicals. After 1779 it became a legal deposit library, and during the years 1774–1821 its acquisitions reached the sum of 30,000 florins, of which more than half came from the publishing house. See András Toth, 'L'Université, son Imprimerie et sa Bibliothèque', in *Typographia Universitatis* (*ed. cit.*), pp. 69–71; see also idem, 'Geschichte der Universitäts Bibliothek Budapest 1561–1918', in *Bibliothek und Wissenschaft*, vol. VI (Heidelberg, 1969).

133 See 'Index Librorum Selectorum' in *Typographia Universitatis*, pp. 479–500.

134 Between 1777 and 1848 the publishing house produced 5,500 titles, of which 4,000 were in Latin, German and Hungarian. See ibid., and also Eva Ring, 'La Typographie Royale de Buda', in *Revue française d'histoire du livre*, Nouvelle Serie 106–9, *Les Trois Révolutions du Livre. Actes du Colloque International de Lyon-Villeurbanne* (1998), ed. Frédéric Barbier (Geneva, 2001), pp. 169–208.

135 This correspondence was published by János Váczy in the ninth volume of *Kazinczy Ferenc. Összes Müvei* (*Ferenc Kazinczy. Complete Works*).

136 See Sámuel Domokos, 'Activitatea lui Samuil Micu, Gheorghe Şincai şi Petru Maior…' ('The Activity of Samuil Micu, Gheorghe Şincai and Petru Maior…'), in *Typographia Universitatis*. For the correspondence of the Romanian scholars with the leaders of the publishing establishment in Buda, see *Magyar Országos Levéltár. Acta Typographia Illyrica*, Z 715, packet 295, pp. 13, 24–6, 32–4, 54, 64, 67–8, Z 715, packet 292, p. 254.

Chapter VII

1 Iorga, *Generalităţi*, pp. 91–2.

2 For further details concerning the history of this region see Neumann (ed.), *The Banat of Timişoara: A European Melting Pot* (London, 2019).

3 Iorga, 'Două concepţii istorice. Cuvântare la intrare în Academia Română, 1911' ('Two Historical Conceptions. Speech on Acceptance into the Romanian Academy, 1911'), in *Generalităţi cu privire la studiile istorice* (3rd edn, Bucharest, 1944), pp. 91–2.

4 Braudel, *La Méditerranée*, vol. I, p. 56.

5 *Călători străini despre ţările române* (*Foreign Travellers on the Romanian Principalities*), vol. VI, part II, 'Evlia Çelebi', ed. Mustafa Ali Mehmet (Bucharest, 1976), pp. 496–502.

6 Francesco Griselini, *Încercarea de istorie politică şi naturală a Banatului Timişoarei*, foreword, trans. from German and notes by Costin Feneşan (Timişoara, 1984), p. 22; original Italian edition, *Lettere odeporiche. Ove suoi viaggi e le di lui osservazioni spettanti all storia naturale ai costumi di vari popoli e sopra piu altri interessanti oggetti si descrivono* (*Travel Diary. Observations on Natural History, Customs of Different Communities and Description of Other Interesting Objects*) (Milan, 1780).

7 The first military governor, Claudius Florimund Mercy, divided Banat into twelve districts: Timişoara, Becicherecul Mare, Cenad or Sînjicolau, Ciacova, Lugoj, Vârşet, Mehadia, Panciova, Palanca Nouă, Lipova, Fóget, Caransebeş and Orşova; see Griselini (Romanian edn), p. 128.

8 See 'Temesvarer Nachrichten', 1771, no. IV of 9 May, in *Österreichischen Staatsdsarchiv, Finanz und Hofkammerarchiv* (Vienna), Banat Files no. 73, fasc. 1 (1770–8), f. 660; see also J. J. Ehrler, *Das Banat vom Erspurung bis jetzo*, Romanian trans. *Banatul de la origini pînă acum-1774*, ed. Costin Feneşan (Timişoara, 1982).

9 Neumann, *Convergenţe spirituale*, pp. 59–60.

10 Ehrler, p. 30.

11 Suciu and Constantinescu, vol. I, doc. 119, p. 223.

12 Ibid., doc. 93, pp. 178–80.

13 Ibid., doc. 96, pp. 185–7; see also doc. 107, p. 193, doc. 113, p. 200; doc. 115, p. 201; doc. 116, p. 202, etc.

14 Suciu, *Unitatea poporului român. Contribuţii istorice bănăţene* (*The Unity of the Romanian People. Contributions to Banat History*) (Timişoara, 1980), p. 60.

15 Jenő Szentkláray, *Száz év Dél-Magyarország ujabb történetéböl* (*One Hundred Years of the Recent History of Southern Hungary*) (Timişoara, 1879), p. 428; see also Lajos Kakucs, 'Unele aspecte privind înzestrarea

tehnică a agriculturii din Banat în secolele XVIII–XIX' ('Some Aspects of the Technical Endowment of Agriculture in Banat in the 18th–19th Centuries'), in *Analele Banatului* (*Annals of Banat*) (new series), vol. II (Timișoara, 1983), p. 30.

16 Griselini, p. 181.

17 Ibid., p. 183.

18 Ehrler (p. 30) notes that 1774 was an especially good year for wine production in Banat.

19 Emil Botiş, *Recherches sur la population française du Banat* (Timișoara, 1946).

20 Johann Wolf, 'Din istoria șvabilor din Banat (1717–1778)' ('On the History of the Swabian Community in the Banat Region (1717–1778)'), in *Studii de Istorie a naționalității germane și a înfrățirii ei cu națiunea română* (*Studies on the History of German Nationality and its Brotherhood with the Romanian Nation*), vol. II (Bucharest, 1981), p. 84.

21 Alexandru Rădulescu, 'Colecția de hartă veche a Muzeului Banatului sursă de informare multidisciplinară' ('The Antique Map Collection of the Banat Museum as a Source of Multidisciplinary Information'), in *Analele Banatului* (*Annals of Banat*), vol. II (Timișoara, 1983), pp. 324–5. The author shows that the old structure of Romanian villages – with a dispersed or concentrated arrangement of farms, and village houses at the edges – is different from the grid pattern of the villages of 'Swabian' occupation.

22 Neumann, *Convergențe spirituale*, pp. 59–60.

23 Ehrler, p. 81.

24 Neumann, *Convergențe spirituale*, pp. 84–103.

25 Neumann, *The End of a History. The Jews of Banat from the Beginning to Nowadays* (Bucharest, 2006), pp. 19–20, 42–4, 67–75. See also *Istoria evreilor din România. Studii*

documentare și teoretice (*History of the Jews in Romania. Documentary and Theoretical Studies*) (Bucharest, 2018), pp. 125–48, 149–69.

26 Ehrler, p. 30.

27 Ivan Bogdanov and Ildikó Szőke, 'The Bulgarian Catholics in the Banat Region', in *Euroregionalia. Journal of Interdisciplinary Studies*, no. 6/1 (Timișoara, 2019), pp. 45–92.

28 Prodan, *Supplex*, p. 331; for the sixteenth and seventeenth centuries, see my study 'Luminile Renașterii in Europa est-centrală. Tentația lui "Homo Europaeus". Sens și durată' ('Renaissance Lights in Central-Eastern Europe. The Temptation of "Homo Europaeus". Meaning and Duration'), in *Românii in istoria universală* (*Romanians in World History*), coordinated by I. Agrigoroaiei, G. Buzatu and V. Cristian (Iași, 1986), pp. 122–52.

29 Suciu and Constantinescu, vol. I, doc. 151, p. 378.

30 Ibid., doc. 228, pp. 510–11.

31 Neumann, *Convergențe spirituale*, pp. 38–43.

32 I. Grigorescu, 'Mișcări antihabsburgice româno-sârbe în granița militară bănățeană la începutul secolului al XIX-lea' ('Romanian-Serb Anti-Hapsburg Movements on the Banat Military Border at the Beginning of the Nineteenth Century'), in *Studii și articole de istorie* (*Historical Studies and Articles*), 15 (1970), pp. 97–106.

33 Bocșan, p. 400, note 53.

34 Alexandru Duțu, 'L'image de la France dans les Pays Roumains pendant les campagnes napoleoniénnes et le Congrès de Vienne', in *Nouvelles Etudes d'Histoire*, vol. III (1965), pp. 219–42.

35 Doina Bogdan-Dascălu and Crișu Dascălu, preface to Paul Iorgovici, *Observații de limbă românească* (*Notes on the Romanian Language*), foreword by Ștefan Munteanu (Timișoara, 1979), p. 13.

36 Iorga, *Istoria literaturii române în secolul al XVIII-lea (1688–1821)* (*The History of Romanian Literature in the Eighteenth Century (1688–1821)*), ed. Barbu Theodorescu, vol. II (Bucharest, 1969), p. 241.

37 For the Croatian movement, see Zvane Crnja, *Histoire de la culture croate* (Zagreb, 1966), pp. 261–2.

38 Biblioteca Academiei Române (Library of the Romanian Academy – BAR), MS 2441, f. 350 (1 January 1849). See C. Bodea, 'Independența și unitatea națională înainte de 1848' ('Romanian Independence and National Unity before 1848'), in *Independența României* (*Romania's Independence*), ed. Ștefan Pascu, C. C. Giurescu, I. Geyterchi, Ș. Ștefănescu and C. Olteanu (Bucharest, 1977), p. 71.

39 Ibid., pp. 71–2.

40 BAR, MS 2440, f. 122.

41 BAR, MS 2442, ff. 3–9, bearing the title 'Considerațiuni istorice asupra politicei de desbinare religioasă întreprinse de Hapsburgi între Romani și Sîrbi'. See Bodea, doc. CXXIV, p. 362.

42 Neumann, *Convergențe spirituale*, pp. 150–52.

43 Bocșan, pp. 187–9.

44 See 'Index Librorum Selectorum', in *Typographia Universitatis*, pp. 488–90.

45 Neumann, 'Rezeption und Einordnung der Geschehnisse in Banat des XVIII-ten Jahrhunderts', 'Temesvarer Nachrichten', in *Culture and Society*, ed. A. Zub (Iași, 1985), pp. 31–42; idem, 'Preliminarii la o sinteză a istoriografiei Banatului' ('Preliminaries to a Synthesis of Banat Historiography'), in *Convergențe spirituale* (*Spiritual Convergences*), pp. 1131–71; idem, 'Timișoara under the Sign of Prince Eugene of Savoy' and 'The German-Language Press and the Imperial Ideology', in *The Banat of Timișoara*, pp. 19–37, 201–16.

46 *Catalogum hunc Bibliothecae Conventus Maria Radnensis.*

47 Bodea, *1848 la români. O istorie în acte și mărturi* (*The Romanians of 1848. A History in Documents and Testimonies*) (Bucharest, 1982), pp. 93–6.

48 Ibid., p. 96.

49 Bocșan, p. 354.

Afterword

1 This Afterword, which includes the author's latest thoughts on the subjects covered by this book, is an edited version of work originally published in the collection *Conceptual History in the European Space*, ed. W. Steinmetz, M. Freeden and J. Fernández Sebastián (New York and Oxford, 2017), pp. 236–62.

2 Reinhart Koselleck, *Begriffsgeschichten: Studien zur Semantik und Pragmatik der politischen und sozialen Sprache* (Frankfurt, 2006), p. 108.

3 See Isaiah Berlin, *The Power of Ideas*, ed. Henry Hardy (Princeton, 2000), especially the chapter entitled 'One of the Boldest Innovators in the History of Human Thought', pp. 53–67.

4 On the false representation of the Balkans in the West, see Maria Todorova, *Imagining the Balkans* (New York, 1997); Vesna Goldsworthy, *Inventing Ruritania. The Imperialism of the Imagination* (London, 1998).

5 Goldsworthy, pp. 232–3.

6 Mario Scattola, 'Begriffsgeschichte und Geschichte der politischen Lehren', in Riccardo Pozzo and Marco Sgarbi (eds), *Typologie der Formen der Begriffsgeschichte* (Hamburg, 2010), pp. 75–6.

7 Berlin, *op. cit.*, especially the chapter entitled 'Russian Intellectual History', pp. 68–78.

8 Mihai Spăriosu defines the term as follows: 'The notion of liminality can be an important conceptual tool for choosing not

only the way in which cultural (and cognitive) transformations emerge or are produced, but also the way in which these changes can be molded into a peaceful model.' See Spăriosu, 'Studiile interetnice contemporane în Europa Centrală: Observații interetnice preliminare' ('Contemporary Interethnic Studies in Central Europe. Preliminary Interethnic Remarks'), in *Armonie și conflict intercultural în Banat și Transilvania* (*Harmony and Intercultural Conflict in the Regions of Banat and Transylvania*), ed. Vasile Boari and Mihai Spăriosu (Iași, 2013), pp. 66–7.

9 See Peter Niedermüller, 'Der Mythos des Unterschieds: vom Multikulturalismus zur Hybridität', in Johannes Feichtinger, Ursula Prutsch and Moritz Csáky (eds), *Habsburg Postcolonial* (Innsbruck, 2003), pp. 69–81.

10 Amy Gutmann, introduction to Charles Taylor et al., *Multiculturalism: Examining the Politics of Recognition* (Princeton, 1994), p. 5.

11 Ibid., p. 30.

12 Cf. Peter Gunst, 'Agrarian System of Central and Eastern Europe', in Daniel Chirot (ed.), *The Origins of Backwardness in Eastern Europe: Economics and Politics from the Middle Ages until the Early Twentieth Century* (Berkeley, 1989), pp. 53–92.

13 Moritz Csáky, *Ideologie der Operette und Wiener Moderne: Ein kulturhistorisches Essay* (Vienna, 1997); idem, *Das Gedächtnis der Städte: Kulturelle Verflechtungen – Wien und die urbanen Milieus in Zentraleuropa* (Vienna, 2010).

14 Idem, 'Ambivalenz des kulturellen Erbes: Zentraleuropa', in Moritz Csáky and Klaus Zeyringer, *Ambivalenz des kulturellen Erbes: Vielfachcodierung des historischen Gedächtnisses. Paradigma Österreich* (Innsbruck, 2000), pp. 27–49.

15 See Derek Beales' excellent book *Enlightenment and Reform in Eighteenth-Century Europe* (New York, 2011), p. 162.

16 See the list of necessary and useful measures to be introduced in Transylvania in Ileana Bozac and Teodor Pavel, *Călătoria împăratului Iosif al II-lea în Transilvania la 1773* (*Emperor Joseph II's 1773 Voyage to Transylvania*), vol. I (2nd edn, Cluj, 2007), pp. 204–15.

17 Csáky, 'Ambivalenz', p. 31.

18 Neumann, 'Multiculturality and interculturality: The Case of Timișoara', *Hungarian Studies* (Hungarian Academy of Sciences), 21(1) (2007), pp. 3–18; idem, 'Timișoara between "Fictive Ethnicity" and "Ideal Nation": The Identity Profile during the Interwar Period', in *Balcanica* (Serbian Academy of Sciences and Arts), XLIV (2013), pp. 391–412; idem (ed.), *Identitate și cultură*, pp. 25–38, 38–48, 77–89, 211–29, 325–47; idem, *Interculturalitatea Banatului/Die Interkulturalität des Banats* (*The Interculturality of Banat*) (Berlin, 2015).

19 See Chirot, *op. cit.*

20 Hans Erich Bödeker, 'Aufklärung über Aufklärung? Reinhart Kosellecks Interpretation der Aufklärung', in Carsten Dutt and Reinhard Laube (eds), *Zwischen Sprache und Geschichte: Zum Werk Reinhart Kosellecks* (Göttingen, 2013), pp. 128–74.

21 Răzvan Theodorescu, 'Despre coridoarele culturale', pp. 7–27; and see Chapter VI of the present volume.

22 The Hapsburgs reinstated the domination of the Catholic religion in Transylvania following their own interests. See Olga Lukács and Magyari András, 'Biserică și stat la maghiari' ('Church and State with the Hungarians'), in Ioan-Aurel Pop, Thomas Nägler and Magyari András (eds), *Istoria Transilvaniei: De la 1711 la 1918* (*The History of Transylvania, 1711–1918*), vol. III (Cluj, 2008), pp. 105–6.

23 Franz Szabo, *Kaunitz and Enlightened Absolutism, 1753–1780* (Cambridge, 1994).

24 Beales, *op. cit.*, chapters 'Joseph II and the Monasteries of Austria and Hungary', pp. 227–56, 'The Origins of the Pope's

Visit to Joseph II in 1782', pp. 256–72, and 'Was Joseph II an Enlightened Despot?', pp. 272–87.

25 Kosáry, *Ujjáépítes és polgárosodás 1711–1867* (*Reconstruction and Civilization 1711–1867*) (Budapest, 1990). See also Prodan, *Supplex*.

26 Cf. Chapter VI of the present volume.

27 Csáky, *Gedächtnis der Städte*.

28 See Martin Roos, *Die Alte Diözese Csanád*, vol. I, part 2b: 1800–1850 (Szeged, 2012), pp. 117–18.

29 Ibid., p. 171.

30 Neumann, *Identitate şi cultură*, pp. 38–48.

31 Idem, *Istoria evreilor din România*, p. 31.

32 Karl Popper, *The Open Society and Its Enemies*, vol. 2: *The High Tide of Prophecy: Hegel, Marx and the Aftermath* (London, 1996), p. 49. See detailed explanations, pp. 49–59. On Herder's contribution to oracular philosophy and the theory of nationalism, see pp. 52–3. For a more detailed presentation of Herder and Herderianism, see Neumann, 'Peculiarities of the Translation and Adaptation of the Concept of Nation in East-Central Europe: The Hungarian and Romanian Cases in the Nineteenth Century', *Contributions to the History of Concepts* 7(1) (2012), pp. 72–101.

33 Elias Palti, 'The Metaphor of Life: Herder's Philosophy of History and Uneven Developments in Late Eighteenth-Century Natural Sciences', *History and Theory* 38 (1999), pp. 322–3. See also Neumann, *Studia Politica: Romanian Political Science Review* 12(1) (2012), pp. 154–9.

34 See João Feres Jr, 'With an Eye on Future Research: The Theoretical Layers of Conceptual History', in Javier Fernández Sebastián (ed.), *Political Concepts and Time: New Approaches to Conceptual History* (Santander, 2011), pp. 223–39. See also Neumann, *Studia Politica*.

35 Cf. Stefan Jordan, 'Die Sattelzeit – Transformation des Denkens oder revolutionärer Paradigmenwechsel?', in Achim Landwehr (ed.), *Frühe Neue Zeiten: Zeitwissen zwischen Reformation und Revolution* (Bielefeld, 2012), pp. 373–88. I believe that irrespective of which concept we analyze, decoding its meanings or applicability to a certain time and space must take into account context, geography, society, and cultural and religious legacies.

36 Etienne Balibar, 'The Nation Form: History and Ideology', in Etienne Balibar and Immanuel Wallerstein (eds), *Race, Nation, Class: Ambiguous Identities* (London and New York, 2002), pp. 96–100.

37 Herder, *Über die Wirkung der Dichtkunst*, in *Werke*, vol. 2 (Weimar, 1963), p. 246.

38 Ibid., p. 253.

39 Palti, *op. cit.*

INDEX

Biblia Sacra (1730) 217
Biblioteca românească 255
Bloch, Marc 103
Blumenbach, Johann Friedrich 208
Bocșan, Nicolae 223, 255
Bod, Petru 84, 190, 209, 210, 211
Bodea, Cornelia 253–4
Bödeker, Hans Erich 269
Bodoki, József 211
Bojincă, Damaschin 219, 222, 251,
      254, 255
Bonfinius, Antonius 61
Borges, Jorge Luis 132
Bornemisza, Ignác 181
Borowsky, Samu 241
Bourbon, Nicolas 49
Bourel, Dominique 163–4
Brâncoveanu, Constantin 32, 126
Branković, George 95–6
Braudel, Fernand 17–18, 24–6, 70–71,
      75, 110, 131
Bretschneider, Gottfried von 245
Brukenthal, Samuel von 139, 158, 166,
      186, 187, 188–91, 192, 193
Brutus, Michael 60
Buczy, Emil 204
Budai-Deleanu, Ioan 158, 167, 180, 191, 204
Burckhardt, Jacob 26–7, 28
Burian, Paul 165
Byzantine orthodoxy 54

Caliani, Silvestru 180
Callimachi, Ioan Teodor 158
Calvin, John 54, 201
Calvinism 60
Campensis, Johannes 134
Cândea, Virgil 86
Canetti, Elias 123
Cantacuzino, Constantin 96, 212
Cantacuzino, Șerban 32, 95–6
Cantacuzino family 86
Cantemir, Dimitrie 32, 90–95, 154, 160,
      161, 166, 206–7
Cantemir family 86, 97
Carcalechi, Zaharia 255
Cardanus, Hieronymus 50
Caryofillis, Ioannis 89
Cassirer, Ernst 48, 157, 162, 204, 206
Castelano, Petro Ludovico Danes 217
Catalogus Alphabeticus Ilustris Collegii Alba
      N. Enyediensis... (inventory) 207–8
Catherine the Great 160, 249
Catholicae ac christianae religionis (Olahus) 201
Çelebi, Evliya 238
Cesarini, Giuliano 47

Charles VI, Emperor 137, 193, 243
Chaunu, Pierre 26, 152–3, 159, 177, 180,
      182, 197–8
Chorin, Rabbi Aaron 247
Chronicle (Nestor) 166, 225
Chronicles (Branković) 96
Cipariu, Timotei 171, 180, 186, 209
Civilizație românească și civilizație
      balcanică (Papacostea) 31–2
Climacus, John 77
Codex Aureus (Lorsch Gospels) 194, 207
Cohen, Aaron 128–9
Cohen, Isaiah 128
Colloquia familiaria (Erasmus) 196
Colloquia nunc emendatiora cum omnium
      notis (Erasmus) 196
Commentaria in octo libros politicorum
      Aristotelis (Aquinas) 212
Comments on Metaphysics (Corydalleus)
      87, 89
Compendiaria descriptio fundationis ac
      vicissitudinum episcopatus et capituli
      M. Varadiensis (Keresztúri) 211
Concionis Tergeminae rusticae, civicae,
      aulicae... (1709) 217
Condurachi, Emil 37
Congregation for the Propagation of the
      Faith (Propaganda Fide) 82
Considérations sur les causes de la grandeur
      des Romains et de leur décadence
      (Montesquieu) 162
Constantin 32
Contrat social, see Du contrat social ou principes
      du droit politique
Conze, Werner 198
Coresi, Deacon 62
Cornea, Paul 33, 170
Cornides, Daniel 232
Corvinus, Matthias 59, 60–61, 113, 184
Corydalleus, Theophilos 87–90, 93
Costin, Miron 96
Cotorea, Gherontie 158, 181
Craneveldius, Levinus Franciscus 67
Cremonini, Cesare 87
Cresci, Migliore 48
Cretensis, Elias ben Moses 95
Crise de la conscience européenne 1680–1715,
      La (Hazard) 23
Csáky, István 139, 186, 226–7
Csáky, Iulia 226
Csáky, Moritz 267
Csaplovics, Johann von 142
Curationum Medicinalium Centuriae Septem
      (Lusitanus) 128
Curtius, Ernst Robert 20–21, 58–9

Frederick II of Prussia 156, 187, 249
Friedman, M. V. 37
Frobenius, Leo 17, 21

Galileo 27–8, 197
Gavrilović, A. 33
Gavrilović, N. 33
Gaza, Theodor 50
Generalities Regarding Historical Studies (Iorga)
    30, 31
Gennadios, Patriarch of Constantinople 50
Gennady of Novgorod, Archbishop 63
Gerard Sagredo of Csanád 110
Goethe, Johann Wolfgang von 132, 164,
    198, 245
Goldsworthy, Vesna 261
Graaf, G. Henk van der 210–11
Grimm brothers 163
Griselini, Francesco 238–9, 242–3
Grotius, Hugo 56, 184
Gumplowitz, Ludwig 273
Gundulović, Traian 65
Gyármáti, Sámuel 208, 210

Hahnemann, Samuel 187, 188
Halakha (Angel) 129
Halici, Mihail 209, 210
Haliczky, András 232
Hamann, Johann Georg 162, 164
Hannover, Nathan 125, 143
Has, Jean Matthias 216
Haşdeu, B. P. 32
Haugwitz, Friedrich Wilhelm Graf von 156,
    268
Haupt Artikel des christlichen Glaubens wider
    den Papst und der Helen Pforten zu erhalten,
    Die 199
Hazard, Paul 23, 37, 75
Hegel, Georg Wilhelm Friedrich 160, 164,
    198, 275
Heimerl, Mathäus 217, 245
Heltai, Gáspár 58, 61–2
Helvétius, Claude Adrien 187
Heraclid, Iacob 85, 119
Herder, Johann Gottfried 160, 162, 163,
    166, 167–72, 192, 275–8, 279
Herfsttij der middeleeuwen (The Decline of the
    Middle Ages) (Huizinga) 21, 29–30, 57
Heydendorff, Michael Conrad von 189
Heyne, Christian Gottlob 208
Hiltebrandt, Conrad Jacob 125
Hirling, Georg 189
Histoire de la littérature néo-hellénique (History
    of Neo-Hellenic Literature) (Dimaras)
    34–5, 69

Histoire de l'idée européenne (Voyenne) 23–4
Historico-Phisica Topographica Valachicae
    Austriae Subterraneae Descriptio
    (Schendo) 192
Historisch-Geographisch und Politisch.
    Beschreibung der Moldau (Cantemir) 206
History of Charles XII, The (Voltaire) 160–61
History of Different Peoples, Especially of the
    Serbs, Bulgarians and Croatians (Raic) 158
History of the Beginnings of the Romanians in
    Dacia (Maior) 255
History of the Growth and Decay of the Ottoman
    Empire (Cantemir) 91–2, 94, 95, 166
History of Wallachia, The
    (C. Cantacuzino) 96
History of Yugoslav Jews, A (Eventov) 108
Hochmeister, Martin 204
Honter, Johannes 61, 201, 202
Horace (Q. Horatius Flaccus) 61
Horányi, Elek 206
Hornyánszky, Victor 273
Horváth, Michael 167
How Should We Then Live? The Rise and Decline
    of Western Thought and Culture
    (Schaeffer) 22
Huet, Albert 60
Huizinga, Johan 21, 26, 29–30, 42, 49, 57
Humboldt, Alexander 187
Humboldt, Wilhelm von 166, 187, 198
Hungaria et Attila (Olahus) 67, 201–2
Hutten, Ulrich von 56
'Hymns' (Ephrem the Syrian) 77

Ideen zur Philosophie der Geschichte der
    Menschheit (Herder) 171, 198
Ignacio de Loyola 21
Ignatie Darabant, Bishop Ignatie 218
Ilarian, Alexandru Papiu 171, 229
Index alter libros Bibliotechae Hungaricae
    Széchenyiano regnicolaris in scientiarum
    ordines (1807–8) 229
Institutiones doctrinae christianae sive
    compendium theologiae dogmaticae et moralis
    (Castelano) 217
Întâmplările războiului franţozilor şi
    întoarcerea lor de la Moscova
    (Ţichindeal) 255
Introduction to Logic (Corydalleus) 87, 89
Inventing Ruritania (Goldsworthy) 261
Iorga, Nicolae 30, 37, 63, 157, 235–6
Iorgovici, Paul 158, 219, 221, 251, 251–2
Isaac, Aaron 138
Istoria Slaveanobalgarsko (Paisius of
    Hilandar) 158
Istvánffy, Miklós 211

Tentația lui Homo Europaeus: Geneza idelior moderne în Europa Centrală și de Sud-Est was originally published by Editura Științifică și Enciclopedică, Bucharest, in 1991. The translation on which the text of this edition is based was originally published in 1993 as volume 384 in the series East European Monographs, Boulder, and distributed by Columbia University Press, New York. The translation has been extensively revised for this edition.

© 1993 by Victor Neumann
Preface and Afterword © 2020 by Victor Neumann

This edition © 2020 by
Scala Arts & Heritage Publishers Ltd
27 Old Gloucester Street
London WC1N 3AX, UK
www.scalapublishers.com

ISBN 978-1-78551-241-4

Translation edited and revised by Neil Titman

Dust jacket and binding design, maps and image retouching by Dieter Penteliuc-Cotoșman

Interior book design by Linda Lundin

Printed in Turkey

10 9 8 7 6 5 4 3 2 1

Plates 1–30 between pages 192 and 193 are reproductions of postcards from the collections of Dr Thomas Mochnács, Timișoara, Romania.